OXFORD MEDIEVAL TEXTS

General Editors
D. E. GREENWAY   B. F. HARVEY
M. LAPIDGE

HISTORIA VIE HIEROSOLIMITANE

THE *HISTORIA*
VIE HIEROSOLIMITANE
OF
GILO OF PARIS
AND A SECOND,
ANONYMOUS AUTHOR

EDITED AND TRANSLATED BY

C. W. GROCOCK AND J. E. SIBERRY

CLARENDON PRESS · OXFORD
1997

Oxford University Press, Gt. Clarendon Street, Oxford OX2 6DP

Oxford New York

Athens Auckland Bangkok Bogota Bombay
Buenos Aires Calcutta Cape Town Dar es Salaam
Delhi Florence Hong Kong Istanbul Karachi
Kuala Lumpur Madras Madrid Melbourne
Mexico City Nairobi Paris Singapore
Taipei Tokyo Toronto

and associated companies in
Berlin Ibadan

Oxford is a trade mark of Oxford University Press

Published in the United States
by Oxford University Press Inc., New York

British Library Cataloguing in Publication Data
Data available

Library of Congress Cataloging in Publication Data
Gilo, of Paris, d. ca. 1142.
[De via Hierosolymitana. English]
The Historia vie [sic] Hierosolimitane / of Gilo of Paris, and a
second, anonymous author; introduction and notes by C. W. Grocock
and J. E. Siberry. — Critical ed. and English translation / by C. W.
Grocock.
p. cm. — (Oxford medieval texts)
1. Christian poetry, Latin (Medieval and modern) — Translations
into English. 2. Epic poetry, Latin (Medieval and modern) —
Translations into English. 3. Jerusalem—History—Latin Kingdom, —
1099–1244—Poetry. 4. Bohemond I, Prince of Antioch, 1058?–1111—
Poetry. 5. Christian poetry, Latin (Medieval and modern)
6. Godfrey, of Bouillon, ca. 1060–1100—Poetry. 7. Epic poetry,
Latin (Medieval and modern) 8. Crusades—First, 1096–1099—Poetry.
I. Crocock, C. W. II. Siberry, Elizabeth. III. Title. IV. Series.
PA8330.G53D4313 1996
873'.03—dc20 96–2390
ISBN 0–19–822274–2

1 3 5 7 9 10 8 6 4 2

Typeset by Joshua Associates Limited, Oxford
Printed in Great Britain on acid-free paper by
Bookcraft Ltd., Midsomer-Norton
Nr. Bath, Somerset

PREFACE

THIS volume of Oxford Medieval Texts began its life as a Ph.D. thesis by Dr C. W. Grocock at Bedford College, University of London. The work as it stands is a collaborative venture by Drs Grocock and Elizabeth Siberry. The Latin text, translation, and apparatus are by Dr Grocock, as are the sections of the introduction and notes related to textual, metrical, and literary matters; the historical notes and historical sections of the introduction are the work of Dr Siberry. Our thanks are due to our respective mentors, Professors Barrie Hall and Jonathan Riley-Smith, for their ongoing help, guidance, and encouragement in the preparation of this work. The authors are also indebted to the general editors of OMT for their patience, careful guidance, and generous assistance while the typescript was being prepared for the press.

C.W.G.
J.E.S.

March 1995

CONTENTS

ABBREVIATIONS

Note: unless otherwise stated below, all references to primary sources are made by page.

Albert of Aachen	Albert of Aachen, *Historia Hierosolimitana*, in *RHC, Hist. occ.* iv. 265–713.
Anonymus Littorensis	in *RHC, Hist. occ.* v. 253–92.
Archives de l'Orient latin	ed. P. Riant, 2 vols. (Paris, 1881–4).
Baldric of Dol	*Historia Ierosolimitana*, in *RHC, Hist. occ.* iv. 1–111.
Balduini III Historia Nicaena uel Antiochena	in *RHC, Hist. occ.* v. 133–85.
Bernold of St Blasien	*Chronicon*, in *MGH, Scriptores in Folio et Quarto*, v. 385–467.
Caffaro	Caffaro de Caschifelone, *De Liberatione Ciuitatum Orientis*, ed. L. T. Belgrano, in *Fonti per la Storia d'Italia*, 5 vols. (Rome, 1890–1929), i.
Chanson d'Antioche	*La Chanson d'Antioche*, ed. S. Duparc-Quioc, 2 vols. (Paris, 1976–8), cited by line.
Crusade and Settlement	*Crusade and Settlement: Papers Read at the First Conference of the Society for the Study of the Crusades and the Latin East and Presented to R. C. Smail*, ed. P. W. Edbury (Cardiff, 1985).
Curtius, *European Literature*	E. R. Curtius, *European Literature and the Latin Middle Ages*, trans. W. R. Trask (London, 1953).
David, *Robert Curthose*	C. W. David, *Robert Curthose, Duke of Normandy* (Cambridge, 1920).
Decreta Claromontensia	R. Somerville, *The Councils of Urban II*, i: *Decreta Claromontensia* (Amsterdam, 1972).

Duparc-Quioc, 'Poème latin'
: S. Duparc-Quioc, 'Un poème latin du XIIᵉ siècle sur la première Croisade par Gilon de Toucy, augmenté par Fulco', *Zeitschrift für französische Sprache und Literatur*, NF ii (1987), 35–49.

Ekkehard of Aura, *Hierosolymita*
: in *RHC, Hist. occ.* v. 1–40.

Faral, *Arts poétiques*
: E. Faral, *Les Arts poétiques du XIIᵉ et du XIIIᵉ siècle: recherches et documents sur la technique littéraire du Moyen Âge* (Paris, 1924).

Fulcher of Chartres
: *Fulcher von Chartres, Historia Hierosolimitana*, ed. H. Hagenmeyer (Heidelberg, 1913).

Gesta Francorum
: *The Deeds of the Franks and the Other Pilgrims to Jerusalem*, ed. R. Hill (NMT, 1962).

Gesta Triumphalia per Pisanos Facta
: ed. L. A. Muratori, *Rerum Italicarum Scriptores*, vi. 99–106.

Grocock, 'Ovid the Crusader'
: C. W. Grocock, 'Ovid the Crusader', *Ovid Renewed*, ed. C. Martindale (Cambridge, 1988), pp. 55–69.

Guibert of Nogent
: Guibert of Nogent, *Gesta Dei per Francos*, in *RHC, Hist. occ.* iv. 113–263.

Hagenmeyer, 'Zimmern'
: H. Hagenmeyer, 'Étude sur la Chronique de Zimmern: renseignements qu'elle fournit sur la Première Croisade', *Archives de l'Orient latin*, ii (1884), 17–88.

HGL
: *Histoire générale de Languedoc*, ed. C. Devic and J. Vaissette, rev. A. Molinier *et al.* (Toulouse, 1879–1904).

Historia Gotfridi
: *Anonymi Rhenani Historia et Gesta Ducis Gotfridi*, in *RHC, Hist. occ.* v. 439–524.

Ibn al-ʾAthīr
: *Kāmil al-tawārīkh* ('Sum of the Histories'), in *RHC, Hist. or.* i. 189–744, ii/1. 1–180.

Klopsch, *Einführung*
: P. Klopsch, *Einführung in die mittellateinische Verslehre* (Darmstadt, 1972).

Die Kreuzzugsbriefe H. Hagenmeyer, *Die Kreuzzugsbriefe aus den Jahren 1088–1100* (Innsbruck, 1901).

Matthew of Edessa *Chronicle*, in *RHC, Doc. arm.* i. 1–150.

Meeting of Two Worlds *Meeting of Two Worlds: Cultural Exchange between East and West during the Period of the Crusades*, ed. V. P. Goss (Kalamazoo, 1986).

Norberg, *Introduction* D. Norberg, *Introduction à l'étude de la versification latine médiévale* (Stockholm, 1958).

Orderic Vitalis *The Ecclesiastical History of Orderic Vitalis*, ed. M. Chibnall, 6 vols. (OMT, 1969–80).

Outremer *Outremer: Studies in the Crusading Kingdom of Jerusalem, presented to J. Prawer*, ed. B. Z. Kedar, H. E. Mayer, and R. C. Smail (Jerusalem, 1982).

Peter the Venerable *The Letters of Peter the Venerable*, ed. G. Constable, 2 vols. (Cambridge, Mass., 1967), cited by letter.

Peter Tudebode Petrus Tudebodus, *Historia de Hierosolymitano Itinere*, ed. J. H. and L. L. Hill (Paris, 1977).

PL J. P. Migne, *Patrologia Latina* (Paris, 1844–64).

Ralph of Caen Ralph of Caen, *Gesta Tancredi*, in *RHC, Hist. occ.* iii. 587–716.

Raymond of Aguilers *Le Liber de Raymond d'Aguilers*, ed. J. H. et L. L. Hill (Paris, 1969).

RHC *Recueil des historiens des Croisades* (Paris, Académie des Inscriptions et Belles-Lettres, 1841–1906).

Doc. arm. *Documents arméniens*
Hist. occ. *Historiens occidentaux*
Hist. or. *Historiens orientaux*

Riley-Smith, 'The motives' J. S. C. Riley-Smith, 'The motives of the earliest Crusaders and the settlement of Latin Palestine', *English Historical Review*, xcviii (1983), 721–36.

Riley-Smith, 'Death on the First Crusade'	J. S. C. Riley-Smith, 'Death on the First Crusade', in *The End of Strife*, ed. D. M. Loades (Edinburgh, 1984), pp. 14–32.
Riley-Smith, *Idea of Crusading*	J. S. C. Riley-Smith, *The First Crusade and the Idea of Crusading* (London, 1986).
Riley-Smith, 'The First Crusade and St Peter'	in *Outremer*, q.v. above, pp. 41–64.
Robert of Rheims	Robertus Monachus, *Historia Hierosolimitana*, in *RHC, Hist. occ.* iii. 717–893.
Runciman, *Hist. Crus.*	S. Runciman, *A History of the Crusades*, 3 vols. (Cambridge, 1951–4).
SCH	*Studies in Church History*.
Setton, *History of the Crusades*	K. M. Setton (ed.), *A History of the Crusades*, 6 vols. (Madison and Milwaukee, 1969–90).
Siberry, *Criticism of Crusading*	J. E. Siberry, *Criticism of Crusading, 1095–1274* (Oxford, 1985).
Smail, *Crusading Warfare*	R. C. Smail, *Crusading Warfare, 1097–1193* (Cambridge, 1956).
Tudebodus Imitatus et Continuatus	in *RHC, Hist. occ.* iii. 165–229.
William of Tyre	*Willelmi Tyrensis Archiepiscopi Chronicon*, ed. R. H. B. C. Huygens, 2 vols. (*Corpus Christianorum. Continuatio Medievalis*, 63, 63A; Turnhout, 1986).

INTRODUCTION

I. THE POEM

THE text of the medieval Latin epic poem *Historia uie Hierosolimitane*
which is presented in this volume of Oxford Medieval Texts is
unusual in that it is the work of not one but two authors, whose
perspectives and interests in the First Crusade were as different as
were their respective poetic styles. The first author, Gilo of Paris,
narrates a tale which resembles very closely in its contents the
anonymous *Gesta Francorum*, and displays a command of Latin
hexameters which (by twelfth-century standards) is both competent
and fairly classicizing, though the earlier part of his work does make
extensive use of leonine rhyme.

The text of Gilo's poem survives in two very similar recensions, in
five manuscripts.[1] A sixth manuscript alone, manuscript G, contains
both the poem by Gilo and additional work of a second, anonymous,
poet, whose approach to the First Crusade and whose source mater-
ial reveal him to be an ardent supporter of Godfrey of Bouillon
(whereas for Gilo, the hero of the crusade was Bohemond), and
whose poetic style is at variance with that of Gilo, employing as it
does consistent end-rhyme and linear constructions which are quite
clumsy compared to Gilo's altogether neater verses. This second
poet is referred to in this edition as the Charleville Poet, from the
present location of the manuscript which contains his work at
Charleville-Mézières. He has in previous editions been referred to
as 'Fulco', though the attribution of this name to him appears to be
unfounded (see the discussion below, Section II). Gilo's part of the
poem presented here is complete as it stands, as the anonymous
continuator makes clear; the second poet does not attempt to rewrite
it, but rather adopts an extremely deferential attitude to it (cf. iii.
445–8). In fact his work is far from being a later reworking of Gilo's
poem, which begins with the siege of Nicaea and ends with the elec-
tion of Godfrey as ruler. The text preserved in the Charleville-
Mézières manuscript contains Gilo's poem with further passages

[1] See below, Sect. V.

(four whole books and two substantial additional sections added on to the end of Gilo's books) written by the second poet to incorporate episodes such as the council of Clermont, the journeys of the various groups of crusaders across Europe, including the disastrous 'Peasants' Crusade', and the expeditions to Edessa and Egypt, in order to complete the story as he knew it from the sources available to him. The present volume went to press before reference could be made to John France's new study *Victory in the East: A Military History of the First Crusade* (Cambridge, 1994).

The authorship of the poem as set out in this edition (and indeed in MS G, the sole repository of the Charleville Poet's work) can therefore be attributed as follows:

BOOK AUTHOR AND SUBJECT

i Charleville Poet: the Council of Clermont

ii Charleville Poet: the Peasants' Crusade

iii Charleville Poet: the arrival of the armies at Constantinople

iv (vv. i–59, 120–355) Gilo of Paris: the siege of Nicaea (vv. 60–119, 356–435) Charleville Poet: supplementary episodes involving Godfrey

v (vv. 1–460) Gilo of Paris: the first siege of Antioch (vv. 461–76) Charleville Poet: brief conclusion

vi Charleville Poet: the expeditions to Edessa and to Babylon (Cairo)

vii Gilo of Paris: the second siege of Antioch

viii Gilo of Paris: the capture of Albara, Maʿarrat an-Nuʿman, and Tortosa

ix Gilo of Paris: the siege and capture of Jerusalem

In style, content, and emphasis, there are noticeable differences between the two authors. For example, like the lay author of the *Gesta Francorum*,[2] Gilo chose Bohemond as the hero of his tale, whereas the Charleville Poet favoured Godfrey of Bouillon. Indeed he only mentioned Bohemond by name twice.[3] Both also included some unique details, and this suggests that they were drawing upon local traditions, or had access to eyewitness accounts.

In order to underline the key role played by Godfrey of Bouillon, the Charleville Poet was quite capable of manipulating the facts and

---

[2] *Gesta Francorum*, pp. xi–xvi.   [3] i. 243; iii. 419.

accepted chronology of the expedition. For example, in his account, Godfrey heads the list of Western nobles who took part in the First Crusade,[4] and becomes the first leader to arrive in Constantinople;[5] after a victorious skirmish with Byzantine forces he and his men cross over into Asia Minor,[6] and he thereby becomes the only leader not to swear an oath to the Byzantine emperor, Alexius Comnenus.[7] In fact Raymond of Toulouse was the first of the leaders to take the cross and may even have been consulted about the expedition before Urban II's sermon at Clermont.[8] Hugh of Vermandois was already in the Byzantine capital when Godfrey arrived on the outskirts of the city in December 1096, and it was Raymond rather than Godfrey who refused to take the oath to Alexius. Finally Godfrey was forced to sail to Asia Minor after his troops had been defeated in a skirmish with the Byzantine army.[9] In addition, in his description of the march across Hungary, the Charleville Poet uses an exhortatory speech to his forces as a vehicle to underline Godfrey's devotion both to God and to the Crusade,[10] and the route which he describes takes little account of the journeys of the other crusading leaders.[11]

The chronology of book ii is also rather confused, because the Charleville Poet chose to treat the Peasants' Crusade as one large and united expedition, rather than as a series of separate armies. This was to underline the main theme of the book, namely, the contrast between the unruly Germans who accompanied Peter the Hermit and the more disciplined body led by Godfrey, whose devotion to God is consistently underscored by the Charleville Poet. In the additional material added to book iv, the Charleville Poet also made Godfrey, as well as his brother Baldwin, journey through Cilicia[12] and he attributed the embassy from Edessa in book vi to the

---

[4] i. 174. As the hero of the Charleville Poet's work, Godfrey of Bouillon naturally heads this list of prominent crusaders.

[5] iii. 218–31.

[6] iii. 408–12. In fact after some initial successes in skirmishes outside the walls of Constantinople, Godfrey's men were defeated by the seasoned Byzantine troops.

[7] iii. 427–40.

[8] See J. H. and L. L. Hill, *Raymond IV de Saint-Gilles, 1041 (ou 1042)–1105* (Toulouse, 1959), pp. 23–6.

[9] Again the Charleville Poet emphasizes Godfrey's role as hero of the crusade, making him the first leader both to arrive in Constantinople and to cross over into Asia Minor. This emphasis is not simply due to his origins in Lorraine, as Duparc-Quioc points out ('Poème latin', p. 38): Albert of Aachen makes it clear that the passage of time altered the emphasis placed on the different leaders of the crusade when he writes *Bohemondi semper fama claruit . . . nunc Godefridi primum nomen scintillabat* (Albert of Aachen, pp. 344–5).

[10] iii. 75–108.   [11] i. 270–304.   [12] iv. 356–97 and nn.

fame of Godfrey, whereas both Fulcher of Chartres and Albert of Aachen wrote that the people of Edessa asked specifically for Baldwin.[13] In book vi, which is partly devoted to Baldwin's exploits, the Charleville Poet took care to distance the brother of his hero from any involvement in the deposition and subsequent murder of the Armenian ruler of Edessa, Thoros.[14]

There are other indications that the poet's own interests were centred on Lorraine. For example, he refers to Henry IV as the ruler of Lorraine, rather than as Emperor of Germany[15] and alludes to the dispute over the county of Flanders, which involved two of the leading figures of the First Crusade, Robert of Flanders and Baldwin of Hainault.[16]

The Charleville Poet, however, did not slavishly follow local tradition. Recent research has shown that the story that Peter the Hermit had been on a pilgrimage to Jerusalem, and there received an appeal for aid from the Patriarch which he subsequently delivered to the Pope, was a Lotharingian tradition.[17] It was repeated by Albert of Aachen,[18] but not by the Charleville Poet. The latter's graphic account of the defeat of the Germans at Xerigordon is also unique,[19] and he is the only source to describe in such detail the disheartening effect upon morale which their encounter with the survivors of the Peasants' Crusade had upon Godfrey's forces.[20] Of particular interest, however, is the implication in book i that Godfrey's participation in the First Crusade owed much to a personal appeal for aid from Patriarch Euthymius of Jerusalem. No other source mentions this detail, but a mission from the Patriarch, led by Abbot Sergius of Jerusalem, did travel to France in 1088 on business matters concerning the abbey's European properties.[21] Thus far no reference has been traced to any appeal for military aid made at this time, but it is conceivable that the opportunity was taken to discuss the plight of the Holy City with prominent lay figures.

It is quite likely that the Charleville Poet was the recipient of oral tradition about Godfrey of Bouillon, the existence and nature of which has been examined in relation to the vernacular *Chansons*

---

[13] vi. 68–75, 90–5, and n. [14] vi. 150–5, 288–91.
[15] i. 86. [16] i. 208–12.
[17] E. O. Blake and C. Morris, 'A hermit goes to war: Peter and the origins of the First Crusade', *SCH* xxii (1985), 79–107.
[18] Albert of Aachen, pp. 272–3. [19] ii. 117–20.
[20] iii. 15–64. [21] i. 72, and nn. 5, 6.

de Croisade, but without any real reference to the quasi-legendary material found both in the Charleville Poet and in Albert of Aachen.[22] Bouillon is only 20 km. to the east of Charleville, and assuming (as seems likely) that the poet was a member of one of the religious foundations whose libraries eventually found their way to the municipal library at Charleville, he would have been ideally situated to know about and to draw upon such a tradition. The use of orally transmitted material would also explain the divergences between the Charleville Poet's account and that of Albert of Aachen.

There remains one problem: is all the additional work found in the Charleville manuscript the work of one poet, or was a multiplicity of writers involved? Mas-Latrie[23] lays great store on the conclusion to book iii, where 'Fulco' (as he names the Charleville Poet) professes to leave all the rest of the telling of the story to Gilo. Mas-Latrie claims that although the additions to books iv and v (as well as the complete book vi) are clearly not Gilo's work, they ought not to be attributed to 'Fulco' either: 'ces morceaux intercalaires seraient donc d'un troisième auteur, écrivant postérieurement à Albert d'Aix et, très probablement aussi, postérieurement à Foulques'.[24] Mas-Latrie also notes that some typographical means ought to be employed to differentiate the work of Gilo and the additional material. Riant made no attempt to do so, whereas in the present edition the additional work is clearly distinguished by printing text and translation in italic.

The problem concerning the authorship of the additional material pivots on the veracity of the Charleville Poet's statement at the end of book iii that he is leaving all the remainder of the storytelling to Gilo. On stylistic grounds it is clear that the additions found in MS G after this are not by Gilo, but are very similar in both style and content to books i–iii. These similarities include: lists, an interest in matters geographical, digressions, a characteristic use of the Bible,[25] and above all a concentration on Godfrey of Bouillon as *the* central figure of the crusade. The situation is perhaps best explained by the contents of Gilo's poem itself; not only does it omit the subject-matter of books i–iii, it also fails to include

---

[22] See e.g. P. Knoch, *Studien zu Albert von Aachen* (Stuttgart, 1966), p. 67, who maintains that his primary source was a 'Lotharingian Crusade chronicle'.

[23] *RHC* (*Hist. occ.*), v, pp. cxl–cxliii.

[24] Ibid., p. cxliii; Duparc-Quioc, 'Poème latin', pp. 36–7.

[25] See Grocock, 'Ovid the Crusader', pp. 55–7.

any mention of other episodes (such as Godfrey's fight with a bear) that the Charleville Poet knew and felt ought to be included. Above all, we need to remember that the twelfth century had little regard for the notions of ownership of a text, plagiarism, or literary falsehood that are commonplace in our own day. The metrical practices evidenced in the additions to books iv and v and in book vi also point to their being the work of the same author as books i–iii.[26] In conclusion, it seems likely that, despite the statement we read at the end of book iii, all the additional material contained in the Charleville manuscript is the work of a single author.

II. THE AUTHORS

At the end of book ix, Gilo of Paris identifies himself as

> Gilo nomine, Parisiensis
> incola, Tutiaci non inficiandus alumnus.

> (ix. 374–5)

Gilo, a resident of Paris and a native of Toucy, which by no means disowns me.

And in the Prologue to book iv (which is found in only three of the six MSS which preserve Gilo's work), he refers to himself as someone of advancing age, who had already attempted to write an epic poem and who had composed 'light verse' in his youth. More details are found in the *explicit* to MSS B and C, which reads:

explicit libellus Gilonis, Parisiensis clerici, postea Cluniacensis monachi, inde cardinalis episcopi, de via Iherosolimitana, quando expulsis et occisis paganis devicte sunt Nicea, Antiochia et Iherusalem a Christianis.

Here ends the little book of Gilo, a cleric of Paris, afterwards monk at Cluny, thereafter cardinal-bishop, about the journey to Jerusalem, when Nicaea, Antioch, and Jerusalem were conquered by the Christians, and the pagans driven out and killed.

Finally, the Charleville poet refers to him as 'domnus Gilo Parisiensis', 'my lord Gilo of Paris', in the *explicit* of book iii.[27]

From these scattered references it is possible to identify the author as Gilo, a Cluniac monk from Toucy in the county of Auxerre, who subsequently became cardinal-bishop of Tusculum

---

[26] See below, Section IV.   [27] iii. 447.

(Frascati). Unfortunately nothing is known about the early part of his life, but he appears to have spent some time as a clerk in Paris before he became a monk at Cluny. He subsequently went to Rome, where he was elected cardinal-bishop of Tusculum. Gilo first appears as such in papal documents on 28 December 1121;[28] it is possible that he was drawn into the papal entourage when Calixtus II visited Cluny early in January 1120.[29] This was also the occasion when the pope canonized a former abbot of that house, St Hugh.[30] While he was resident in Rome, Gilo composed a life of St Hugh.[31] There has been some controversy about the dating of this work,[32] but in the dedicatory letter to Abbot Pons of Melgueil, which prefaces the work, Gilo makes it clear that it was written after his arrival in this city:

Dignum profecto fuit ut uita illius Romae particulatim scriberetur, qui, dum uiuit, Romanorum principum, Petri dico et Pauli, maximus cultor exstitisse cognoscitur.

Truly it was fitting that his *Life* should be written at Rome above all places, for while he lived he is known to have stood out as a very great devotee of the princes of Rome, that is, of Peter and Paul.

Gilo also laments that he exchanged the peace of the cloister for the corruption of Rome.[33] The writing of this letter (and of the poem) must therefore be dated after St Hugh's canonization in 1120 and before the resignation of Abbot Pons in the spring of 1122. Gilo's life of St Hugh seems to have been widely read and was the principal source used by a later and more famous biographer, Hildebert of Lavardin.[34] In the 1120s, Gilo undertook two embassies on behalf of Popes Calixtus II and Honorius II. The first of these was to Hungary and Poland. A few brief references to this legation have survived in medieval Polish cartularies. Gilo is

[28] *Regesta Pontificum Romanorum*, ed. P. Jaffé *et al.*, 2 vols. (Leipzig, 1881–8), i. 802, citation no. 6940 (5073); *PL* clxiii. 1227. Gilo is the third signatory, using the formula *ego Aegidius Tusculanus Episcopus*, to the bull *Ad uniuersos fideles*.

[29] See Calixtus II, *Bullaire*, ed. U. Robert (Paris, 1891), nos. 120–4.

[30] The *Chronica Cluniacensis* (Bibliothèque Nationale, MS lat. 9875), quoted by U. Robert, *Histoire du Pape Calixte II* (Paris and Besançon, 1891), p. 99 n. 3.

[31] For the text of this, see *Vie de saint Hugues, abbé de Cluny, 1024–1109*, ed. A. L'Huillier (Solesmes, 1888), pp. 574–618.

[32] Ibid., pp. 569–72; T. Schieffer, 'Notice sur les vies de saint Hugues, abbé de Cluny', *Le Moyen Âge*, 3rd ser., vii (1936), 85–7.

[33] Gilo of Paris, *Epistolae*, in *PL* clxxiii. 1389–90.

[34] Schieffer, 'Notice', pp. 88–9; Hildebert of Le Mans, *Vita Sancti Hugonis*, in *PL* clix. 857–94.

known to have authenticated a list of donations which had been made to the Benedictine house of Tyniec in 1105,[35] and he also reached an agreement with King Bolesław III Krzywousty ('Wrymouth') of Poland about the boundaries of the new diocese of Włocławek. These were later confirmed by Pope Eugenius III in April 1148.[36] Gilo also issued a document from the Carinthian monastery of Arnoldstein, in the diocese of Aquileia, dated 1126.[37] This prompted the German historian Bachmann to place Gilo's mission some time between 1125 and 1128,[38] but it should also be noted that the Arnoldstein charter has only survived in a fifteenth-century copy and its date of 1126 may therefore be considered unreliable. In fact Gilo's legation is more likely to have taken place between 6 April 1123 and 7 March 1125, when his name is missing from papal documents[39] and probably before the death of Calixtus II in December 1124.[40] In April 1125 Gilo was certainly in Rome, for he appeared as one of the signatories of a series of privileges given to Cluny by Calixtus' successor Honorius II.[41]

Gilo's second mission was to the Latin kingdom of Jerusalem. Its purpose was to settle a long-standing dispute about the ecclesiastical province of Tyre, which was claimed as a suffragan see by the patriarchs of both Antioch and Jerusalem. When the new archbishop of Tyre, the historian William, was consecrated in 1127, Honorius II confirmed that his see should be subject to the patriarch of Jerusalem, but Bernard of Valence, the patriarch of Antioch, refused to accept this. In the spring of 1128, William of Tyre and Roger, bishop of Ramleh, arrived in Rome to plead their case and as a result of their visit the pope restated his previous ruling. It was still not accepted, however, by the other party, Bernard, and Gilo was therefore sent to the Latin kingdom in 1129 to enforce the papal decree.[42] Not surprisingly there is a reference

---

[35] *Codex Diplomaticus Monasterii Tynecensis*, ed. W. Kętrzyński and S. Smolka (Lwów, 1875), pp. 1–3. These privileges were subsequently confirmed by Popes Gregory IX and X in 1229 and 1275. See ibid., pp. 19–28, 54–6.

[36] Eugenius III, *Opera*, in *PL* clxxx. 1328–9.

[37] *Germania Pontificia*, ed. A. Brackmann, 3 vols. (Göttingen, 1911–35), i. 134.

[38] See J. Bachmann, *Die päpstlichen Legaten in Deutschland und Skandinavien (1125–59)* (Berlin, 1913), pp. 15–16.

[39] *Regesta Pontificum Romanorum*, ed. Jaffé, i. 780.

[40] See P. David, 'Le monachisme bénédictin et l'Ordre de Cluny dans la Pologne médiévale', *Revue Mabillon*, xxvii (1937), 43–54, 125–38, 157–87, at p. 161.

[41] Honorius II, *Epistolae*, in *PL* clxvi. 1225–7.

[42] See J. G. Rowe, 'The papacy and the ecclesiastical province of Tyre (1110–1187)', *Bulletin of the John Rylands Library*, xliii (1960–1), 174–8.

to this legation in William of Tyre's *Historia rerum in partibus trans-marinis gestarum*. In fact William quotes a letter of warning sent by Pope Honorius to the patriarch of Antioch.[43] One of Gilo's letters to Bernard has also survived, in which he urges the patriarch to settle his quarrel and be reconciled with Rome.[44] His pleas, however, do not seem to have been heeded, and the affiliation of Tyre remained a matter of controversy until Bernard's death in 1135.[45]

Soon after his return to the West in 1130, Gilo became involved in the schism between the two rival popes, Innocent II and Anacletus II.[46] He chose to side with the latter, although Innocent had the support of powerful figures within the church such as Bernard of Clairvaux and Peter the Venerable, abbot of Gilo's former house, Cluny, as well as the support of King Henry I of England and the Emperor Lothar of Germany. Gilo became Anacletus' representative in France and took up residence in Poitiers, shortly after another of the antipope's supporters, Gérard of Angoulême, was elected archbishop of Bordeaux in 1131.[47] Indeed he acted as witness to one of the archbishop's first acts, the grant of the church of Saint-Pierre-de-Bensac to the monks of Sainte-Croix at Bordeaux.[48] Peter the Venerable was among those who sought to persuade Gilo to abandon Anacletus and in a letter dated some time between 1130 and 1134, he appealed to him to be reconciled to Innocent. Peter and Gilo may even have met in Poitiers in 1133.[49] But even in 1135, when Gérard was excommunicated by the papal legate Geoffrey of Chartres, Gilo refused to change his allegiance. In the same year, Gilo witnessed two further charters for Saint-Hilaire and Montierneuf as a supporter of Anacletus.[50] In 1136 the

---

[43] William of Tyre, i. 617–18. William refers to Gilo as *uirum eloquentem et litteratum admodum*. The same letter is found in *PL* clxvi. 1281.

[44] Gilo of Paris, *Epistolae*, in *PL* clxxiii. 1389–94.

[45] See B. Hamilton, *The Latin Church in the Crusader States* (London, 1980), pp. 27–9.

[46] See F. J. Schmale, *Studien zum Schisma des Jahres 1130* (Cologne, 1961), pp. 33, 77–9.

[47] Ernaldus, *Vita Sancti Bernardi*, in *PL* clxxxv. 286. See also H. Bloch, 'The schism of Anacletus II and the Glanfeuil forgeries of Peter the Deacon', *Traditio*, viii (1952), 159–264, at pp. 169, 171.

[48] A. Maratu, *Girard, évêque d'Angoulême, légat du Saint-Siège, 1060–1136* (Angoulême, 1866), pp. 306–7, 370–1.

[49] Peter the Venerable, *epp.* 40 and 66 (i. 134–6, ii. 126), and appendix J.

[50] W. Janssen, 'Die päpstlichen Legaten in Frankreich vom Schisma Anaklets II. bis zum Tode Coelestins III. (1130–98)', *Kölner historische Abhandlungen*, v (1961), 5–15, at p. 14 and n. 48; *Gallia Christiana in prouincias ecclesiasticas distributa*, ed. Congregation of Saint-Maur, 16 vols. (Paris, 1715–1865; repr. Farnborough, 1970), ii, Instrumenta, 355.

schismatics lost the support of Duke William of Aquitaine and in March Gérard died.[51]

Little is known about the next period of Gilo's life, but it is possible that he met Peter the Venerable again in Grenoble in 1137 and after Anacletus' death, in January 1138, Peter wrote a second letter urging Gilo to return to the fold.[52] Gilo seems to have heeded this advice and his name appears again on papal documents between 21 June 1138 and 1 March 1139.[53] However, at the Second Lateran Council in 1139, Innocent II denounced all the followers of Anacletus, including Gérard of Angoulême and Gilo.[54] Gilo seems to have died shortly afterwards and certainly he was dead before April 1142, when Imarus is mentioned in papal letters as cardinal-bishop of Tusculum.[55]

When one comes to consider the author of the additional material found only in the Charleville manuscript, a problem immediately rears its head. Sirmond stated that the author of books i–iii was a certain Fulk (Fulco),[56] and all subsequent editions of this poem have attributed this part of the work to a writer of that name.[57] Indeed, it has even been suggested that he may have been the same person as the *Magister Fulco* who taught at the schools in Rheims and was dean there from 1165 to 1175.[58] However, a question-mark was placed against the attribution to 'Fulco' by Berthereau,[59] who makes the pertinent remark *quis et unde fuerit Fulco nusquam apparet* ('There is no mention of who this Fulco was or where he came from'). In the manuscript itself (and the contents of their various editions make it clear that all the previous editors

[51] Maratu, *Girard*, p. 323.

[52] Peter the Venerable, i. 195–7; ii. 141, 293.

[53] *Regesta Pontificum Romanorum*, ed. Jaffé, i. 840.

[54] *Conciliorum Oecumenicorum Decreta*, ed. G. Alberigo *et al.* (Bologna, 1973), p. 203; *Chronique de Morigny*, ed. L. Mirot (Paris, 1909), pp. 72–3.

[55] *Regesta Pontificum Romanorum*, ed. Jaffé, i. 840; Peter the Venerable, App. J.

[56] In *Historia Francorum Scriptores*, ed. A. Du Chesne (Paris, 1639–48), iv. 890.

[57] See below, Sect. VIII. The error was repeated as recently as 1987 by Suzanne Duparc-Quioc, who accepts Du Chesne's identification of the anonymous poet as 'Fulco' without question ('Poème latin', p. 35 and n. 4).

[58] J. R. Williams, 'The cathedral school of Rheims in the time of Master Alberic, 1118–1136', *Traditio*, xx (1964), 93–114, at p. 112 and n. 123. See also J. W. Baldwin, *Masters, Princes and Merchants: The Social Views of Peter the Chanter and his Circle*, 2 vols. (Princeton, 1970), i. 154–5, ii. 107.

[59] 'Recueil sur les Croisades, X': Berthereau's original notes are contained in Paris, BN Fr. 9080, fo. 127ʳ. They are calendared in *Archives de l'Orient latin*, ii (1884), 105–30, 'Inventaire sommaire des manuscrits relatifs à l'histoire et à la géographie de l'Orient latin, I. Inventaire des recueils Berthereau', at p. 130.

who have attributed the work to 'Fulco' have known only the Charleville manuscript, and no other sources), the writer nowhere gives his own name, and the name 'Fulco' does not appear. Sirmond himself gives no source for the name; the text he presents demonstrates that no leaves have been lost from the MS, and that the text was in as poor a state in his day as it is now.

In the absence of any positive identification of authorship, the poem contained in this manuscript must be regarded as anonymous, and its author is referred to in this edition as the 'Charleville Poet'. A study of the Charleville Poet's contribution to the work shows that he was an accomplished writer, and the form of the Charleville manuscript itself suggests that it was the personal possession of an individual, rather than part of a library. It is very small, is coarsely bound (the binding is almost certainly original)[60] in wooden boards, and is written on poorly palimpsested parchment entirely in a single hand. The presence in the same manuscript of the works of Avitus and the *Ecloga Theoduli*, which were texts commonly used in the schools, may imply that the Charleville Poet was a teacher. Other evidence for this supposition is the poet's knowledge of the classics, which is by no means as evident as is the case with Gilo, or better-known twelfth-century poets such as Walter of Châtillon, but which is evident none the less. The poet also has a vivid interest in geography and ethnography, which is illustrated by the copious lists which he includes in his work. The decorations in the text imply a provenance from the Champagne area, which would accord with its presence in Charleville, though its exact origin is unknown.[61] As Williams has pointed out, most of the Charleville manuscripts came from religious houses which had close links with Rheims, such as Signy and Mont-Dieu.[62] However, it may also be significant that Charleville is only 20 km. due east of Lower Lorraine and Bouillon. From the evidence of the poem and the manuscript, it would therefore seem that the Charleville Poet came from the Champagne area or the vicinity of Bouillon. He chose as his hero a notable local figure,

[60] P. Gasnault, *Le Manuscrit médiéval* (Paris, 1976), p. 20; L. Gilissen, *La Reliure occidentale antérieure à 1400* (Turnhout, 1983), pp. 37–9, and pl. X.

[61] The decoration of the initial capital to book i is very similar in execution to, though less ornate than, those found in Rheims MS 372, a manuscript of St Hilary and Boethius: see the illustration in *Trésors de la bibliothèque municipale de Reims*, ed. M. de Lemps and R. Laslier (Rheims, 1978), ex. 25.

[62] Williams, 'Cathedral school', p. 112.

Godfrey of Bouillon and, apart from his desire to add important details to what he had considered an incomplete account of the First Crusade, his work clearly has another, specific, purpose: to glorify Godfrey, the duke of Lorraine, who became the first ruler of the Latin Kingdom of Jerusalem.

III. DATE

At one point (ix. 374–5) Gilo states that he was resident in Paris at the time of the poem's completion, but apart from this passing observation we have no real indication of its date.[63] Several previous editors of the work have suggested 1119 as the date of its composition, presumably on the grounds of a brief reference to King Baldwin I implying that at the time of writing he was no longer ruler of the Latin kingdom:

> iste minor natu fuit eius denique frater,
> qui post se rexit Solimorum sceptra decenter.

> (vi. 94–5)

This was his younger brother, and he ruled Jerusalem worthily after him.

This was obviously taken as a clear *terminus post quem* for the work; Baldwin died in 1118. However, book vi is now identified as the work of the Charleville Poet, and not of Gilo, and can therefore provide a *terminus post quem* only for the Charleville Poet's work.[64] We can therefore only speculate that Gilo's part of the poem was written whilst he was a clerk in Paris, and before he became a monk at Cluny, in other words before 1120 at the very latest, and probably in the first decade of the century. Gilo's part of the poem should therefore be classed with the other histories of the First Crusade written by ecclesiastics in the West such as Guibert of Nogent, in the first two decades of the twelfth century.[65]

IV. STYLISTIC FEATURES

1. *General*

The two poets whose combined work makes up the *Historia uie Hierosolimitane* are noticeably different with regard to their general

---

[63] See above, Sect. I.   [64] Ibid.
[65] See below, Section IX, pp. lvii–lxi, lxiii–lxiv.

style. Gilo writes in a restrained, careful manner for the most part, using periodically structured sentences. He occasionally employs a pithy, epigrammatic style, as for example at v. 130–6, 230–1, 369, and vii. 151–2. This may be encouraged to some extent by the use in the early part of his work of the leonine rhyme-scheme, which tends to militate against the more linear sentences found in the Charleville Poet. Other features of Gilo's writing include the frequent use of zeugma (cf. viii. 35), and of the ablative absolute.

The Charleville Poet, on the other hand, writes in a paratactic style, utilizing series of main verbs strung together by *et* and other conjunctions, and has a tendency not to employ subordination. In this his style recalls some of the linear features found in vernacular epic of the time (cf. i. 35–41). He also resorts to redundancy, adding words simply to make up the line where required (e.g. vi. 262).

2. *Speeches*

The two poets are very different in the way they represent speeches. Gilo follows classical models in the inclusion of sometimes lengthy speeches in *oratio recta*. These recall the speeches found in Vergil and Lucan, except for the elegiac lament of Humberga (v. 437–58), which, as is demonstrated elsewhere, belongs firmly in the Ovidian tradition.[66] Especially noteworthy are the lengthy pre-battle speeches attributed to Bohemond in vii. 45–59, and to Adhémar of Le Puy in vii. 378–99. Another long speech is put in the mouth of Peter the Hermit in vii. 343–56, and shorter speeches are to be found at vii. 85–6, 358–60, 405–9, 437–9, and ix. 202–4.

The Charleville Poet, on the other hand, consistently uses *oratio obliqua* for his speeches, despite the fact that many of them are as lengthy as those penned by Gilo (cf. iii. 75–108, 115–22, 295–308, vi. 448–69). It is a very unusual feature of the Charleville Poet's work that he only resorts to *oratio recta* in two places, iii. 95–100 and vi. 448–53, reverting to *oratio obliqua* on both occasions.

3. *Other features*

Another notable feature of the Charleville Poet is his frequent use of lists, which is a commonplace both in late Latin epic and in

---

[66] Grocock, 'Ovid the Crusader', pp. 66–7.

vernacular epic too. Lengthy lists are included in his poem of the peoples and rivers of the Middle East (i. 59–64), of rivers (i. 159–64), nations (i. 165–8), peoples (i. 184–6), participants in the crusade (i. 195–244), ports in Italy (i. 261–4), areas of Greece (iii. 181–4), and biblical writers on Antioch (iv. 404–15). The nearest Gilo comes to this practice is on the solitary occasion found at v. 221–2.

Repetition of words is found in the Charleville Poet at i. 27–8 (*in proprias . . ./in proprios*), and at iii. 335–6, an example of polyptoton which seems to owe a good deal to Statius *Theb.* viii. 398–9. Gilo also employs repetition, though to a much lesser extent (cf. *alterutrum . . ./alterutrumque* at v. 284–5). Stock phrases do occur in both poets, though, as with other features noted, they are more common in the Charleville Poet than in Gilo, who shows a much greater ability to vary his phrases and vocabulary. Thus *milia densa mouet* is found at i. 197 and i. 230; *sancti sub honore sepulchri* at i. 230, ii. 139, iii. 126, and (with minor variations) at iii. 271; *peditumque equitumque* at ii. 4 and iv. 368; and, finally, *concursus ad aulam* at vi. 129 and 258. There is just one instance of this in Gilo, *uenerat illa dies* being found at both ix. 119 and ix. 271.

Interiectio ex persona poetae is a major feature of both Latin and vernacular medieval poetry, and it is to be found in both poets, in the Charleville Poet at i. 249 and iii. 1–8, where he carefully signposts his intentions, and in Gilo at v. 80–2, v. 190, vii. 203–6, vii. 389, viii. 121, viii. 173, viii. 265, and ix. 56. A variant of this occurs in the concluding verses to the Charleville Poet's books (i. 307–8, ii. 303–4, iii. 445–9, vi. 482–3).

There are marked differences between the two poets in the names they use to denote certain places and groups of people. For example, in referring to the Franks, the Charleville Poet uses both *Galli* and *Franci*, whereas Gilo uses only *Franci* or *Francigenae*. Similarly, the Charleville Poet refers to the English as *Brytanni* (i. 168), Gilo as *Angli* (v. 129, 130, 229). *Turci*, denoting the Saracens, is found only in Gilo. The people of Venice are called *Veneti* by the Charleville Poet (i. 167, 261, 264) but *Venetici* by Gilo (vii. 91).

Another difference is seen in the way the Charleville Poet uses abstract terms to refer to God, as at i. 7, i. 75, and iii. 153, and to refer to other entities at i. 35 and vi. 150. Gilo restricts himself to the more common terms, such as *Deus*, which the Charleville Poet also uses.

4. *Imagery and mythology*

Differences can also be detected in the way the two poets use imagery. The Charleville Poet tends to employ single-line images, which recall the imagery found in the *Chanson de Roland* and other vernacular epics: e.g. i. 52, *confixam segetem potuisses cernere ferri*, and i. 190, *ac si concuterent elisa tonitrua fulmen*. Other examples occur at ii. 214 (which owes much to Vergil), 217, 275, iii. 376, and iv. 79. Another similarity to the *Roland* is found at iii. 387.

Images occupying more than one single line in the Charleville Poet are found at ii. 156–7 and iii. 41–2, and a lengthier series of biblical images occurs at iii. 97–100. Gilo also makes use of one-line images, such as *Hugo comes magnus, leo seuis, mitibus agnus* at iv. 29, and this also demonstrates the pithiness of his style. Other instances are to be seen at iv. 55, iv. 340, v. 277, v. 303, vii. 473, and viii. 99. Gilo differs from the Charleville Poet, however, in his inclusion of some very fine similes, varying in length between three and six lines. These owe a great deal in their style to Vergil, but do not follow that author slavishly. They are to be found at iv. 234–6, iv. 262–4, v. 156–9, v. 341–4, and ix. 324–9. The last of these in particular is crafted very carefully, the first two lines setting the scene of a storm in the mountains (*in plano uelut a summis cum montibus ingens | grando cadit mixtisque simul tonat imbribus ether*), the next two describing the effects of the swollen rivers, each more devastating than the one before (*tunc collecta petunt demissas flumina ualles | saxa trahunt siluasque ferunt totaque uagantur | agri planitie*), and culminating finally with the despairing groan of the rustic observing the scene (*gemitus dat rusticus imo | pectore*).

Both poets display a knowledge of classical mythology, though the Charleville Poet seems on the whole to be freer in his use of classical stories and images. His opening rejection of the pagan Muses (i. 15–32) is a commonplace in medieval literature, and is discussed in the notes on these verses; but this rejection is belied by the references to *Phlegrae certamina* at i. 64, the reminiscence from Caesar's *De bello Gallico* at i. 106, and the mentions of Acheron (ii. 186), Hercules (iii. 170), Hero and Leander (iii. 191), the 'horn of plenty' (iii. 325), *brevibus Gyaris* (iii. 380), and Semiramis (vi. 18). Gilo tends to be less adventurous in his use of classical epithets, but still makes reference to *Homerus*, using stock phraseology (v. 23), *Bellona* (v. 295), *Tideus* and other heroes of classical epic

(v. 353–4), *Tempe* (v. 426), to the recherché *Matuta* (vii. 83), and to *Erebus* (viii. 270). He also claims that not even the talented poets of ancient times could fittingly tell what deeds were done by the heroes of his own work (*non Maro non Macer*, v. 374). In so far as classical poets may be seen to have contributed to the style of these authors, the influence of Vergil, Lucan, Statius, and Ovid's *Metamorphoses* is apparent in both, as is only to be expected. The Charleville Poet also has some unusual reminiscences of Juvenal, and Gilo has some of Claudian and, quite strikingly, of Ovid's elegiac poetry, especially in his Prologue.[67]

These differences in the styles of the two poets are mirrored in the differences they show in their metrical technique. Gilo emerges as being more polished while the Charleville Poet seems less learned, but wears what learning he has on his sleeve. They are also mirrored in the differing interests each has in the events of the crusade. Gilo is straightforward and precise in both his language and in the story he has to tell, whereas the Charleville Poet leans much more towards folk-tale and vernacular epic in the manner of telling his story, and in the source material on which he draws. Together, they provide a particularly varied and fascinating source for the history of, and attitudes towards, the First Crusade.

V. METRE AND RHYME

The two poets vary in their poetic style and practice as much as in any other matter, although both appear to conform to the norms of classicizing verse which saw a resurgence in twelfth-century France.[68] Their poetry illustrates in differing degrees the way in which the root stock of metrical, classicizing verse had had grafted into it developments such as rhyme, resulting in the various types of rhymed hexameters found in eleventh- and twelfth-century poetry. Different influences are evident in the manner in which each of the poets writes; Gilo is conservative, reflecting his monastic background, and is old-fashioned in his extensive use of leonines in the earlier part of the poem, as is illustrated below. The Charleville Poet perhaps had more exposure to secular schools, and his style is in general looser, and more 'modern'. He is, for example, extremely fluid in his use of elision, something which

---

[67] Grocock, 'Ovid the Crusader', pp. 66–7. [68] Klopsch, *Einführung*, p. 72.

Gilo avoids completely, but on the other hand the caesura patterns in his verses are much more fixed, and the differing styles evinced in his prologue show that Gilo was a conscious master of his poetic art, and was fully able to shape the style of his verse according to the subject-matter and also to the mode in which he wished to relate his tale. The Charleville Poet refers (i. 6) to his work with the phrase *uersibus et numeris*. This is a hendiadys for 'metrical verse', as in Ovid, *Amores*, i. i. 27, *Remedia Amoris*, 381. Gilo also uses the word *numeris* in his Prologue, v. 14, and refers to the epic poem he is about to embark on as a *carmen*.

In matters of general style and content, the Charleville Poet can be extremely precise, and evidently had access to extremely detailed source material on occasion (cf. i. 103–50, his account of the council of Clermont, and i. 204, where he specifies the relationship of Philip and Hugh in exact detail). He speaks in i. 248 of a *pagina* or written source which he has used in assembling a list of participants in the crusade, and this is almost certainly a reference to written source material on which he was able to draw. At the same time, he frequently makes use of 'padding' (e.g. at i. 240). His style also tends on occasion to mirror that of vernacular poetry, particularly when he makes use of non-periodic, linear sentence constructions, with strings of phrases connected by *et*, and a heavy emphasis on double-rhymed couplets.

1. *Caesura*

Caesura patterns are closely related to the rhyme-schemes which a poet chose to use. In the case of the leonine rhyme, the pattern of the rhyme itself leads almost invariably to a strong third-foot caesura.[69]

Gilo's work in particular shows how the adoption of a given rhyme-scheme (notably the leonines, in the earlier books) fixes the caesura rigidly in a predetermined position. In book iv, all the lines have a strong third-foot caesura, except for 19, 230, and 347, which have second- and fourth-foot caesuras, as in addition do 57–8, 153–7, 305, and 313–14, which are all rhymed as *trinini salientes*, a scheme which fixes the caesura rigidly in the same way that leonines do.[70] iv. 204 has a fourth-foot caesura, and is in *caudati*, the second half of a couplet which rhymes with the preceding leonine.

---

[69] Norberg, *Introduction*, p. 65; Klopsch, *Einführung*, pp. 47–8.
[70] Norberg, *Introduction*, p. 66; Klopsch, *Einführung*, pp. 65, 77–8.

Book v is a hotchpotch of leonines, *caudati*, and *trinini salientes* (couplets, or strings of verses, with internal rhyme at the end of the second and fourth feet and end-rhyme; see below for full analysis). As a result the strong third-foot caesura is prevalent in the leonines and *caudati*, with second- and fourth-foot positions obligatory in *trinini salientes* and verses with which they form couplets (314–15, 343–4, 355–6, 367–8). Book vii shows more variation, with 58 verses having their caesuras in second- and fourth-foot positions, and a further 19 in the fourth-foot position; vii. 436, with the Vergilian ending *tunc ita fatur*, has a diaeresis after the fourth foot, as may vii. 60 (though this might be second- and fourth-foot). The 'battle scene', vii. 331–459, shows a remarkable variety of caesura positions, and in many ways is a much more fluid and vivid piece of writing than is found elsewhere. Twenty-eight of the verses with second- and fourth-foot caesura are found in this section, written entirely in *caudati*.

Book viii continues in similar vein, with 73 verses in this book having caesuras at the second and fourth foot, and a further six with fourth-foot caesura only. viii. 129 has a weak third-foot break, and viii. 269—a rarity, consisting of four dactyls—has both a bucolic and a weak third-foot caesura; Gilo begins the line with a tag from Lucan (*De bello ciuili*, i. 509), where in the original it comes at the end of the verse. Book ix continues with this same manner of variety of caesura positions, 86 of its 376 verses having a caesura at the second and fourth feet, and 10 with fourth-foot caesura only. One unusual verse is ix. 11, a type of leonine rhyme with a weak third-foot caesura, supported by second- and fourth-foot caesura.

The Charleville Poet is much more rigid than Gilo in using 'set position' for the caesura. Books i, ii, and iii are all written in *caudati*, which in theory should allow more flexibility, but his verses show none of the variety that is found in Gilo's *caudati* verses in books vii–ix. A strong third-foot caesura is found in all the verses of book i save two, 57 and 194; 57 has (at most) a second-foot caesura, and 194 has elision after the strong third-foot position. In book ii, only lines 126, with a weak third-foot caesura supported by breaks in the second and fourth feet, and 8, with a caesura in the fourth foot, deviate from the standard pattern employed by the poet. Book iii maintains the same pattern, with only two verses varying from the strong third-foot pattern: in line 30, elision is employed at the usual caesura position. The other exception in this book is line 274 (second- and fourth-foot—again attributable to elision at the strong third-foot position). Line 169 appears to be an accidental leonine.

The additions to book iv by the Charleville Poet contain five of the few leonines he writes (iv. 86, 357, 360, 407, and 417; the others are v. 461, vi. 15, 28). At iv. 357 the leonine is employed to help the additions blend in with the earlier material, and then lead on to become the first of two *caudati*. One verse in the additional material to book iv has its caesura at second- and fourth-foot positions, and iv. 81 has fourth-foot alone—again, due to elision before the strong third-foot position. Much of this section of the work is unfortunately in too poor a condition for hard and fast conclusions to be drawn.

The additional material to book v continues the pattern of strong third-foot caesuras, except v. 476, which has elision in the third foot, and a diaeresis after the fourth foot. Book vi follows the same pattern, with only vi. 236, 287, and 356 having second- and fourth-foot caesura, and two verses (221 and 284) having fourth-foot caesura only. Line 153 has a 'weak' fourth-foot caesura where, like the examples described above, there is elision before the third foot.

Two verses in the Charleville Poet's work have no caesura at all (iii. 30, vi. 81, though the latter is corrupt).

2. *Elision and hiatus*

Gilo is very careful to avoid both elision and hiatus; occasional slips in the metre in the first recension of his work, preserved in MSS ADG, are corrected in the 'refined' version contained in BCF, as is illustrated below.[71] Gilo shares this desire to avoid hiatus as far as possible with the author of the medieval poem *Ruodlieb*, among many others (including 'Marcus Valerius'),[72] and there is only one example of hiatus at the caesura, at ix. 94. The only exceptions to Gilo's strict practice with regard to elision are six Vergilian enclitic monosyllable endings with *est* (e.g. *tanta est*, vii. 320), a feature found also at ix. 1, 14, 147, 305, and 307.

[71] Klopsch, *Einführung*, pp. 79–85; Norberg, *Introduction*, pp. 32–3.

[72] F. Munari, *Marci Valerii Bucolica* (Florence, 1955), pp. 47–8. However, F. Dolbeau, 'Les bucoliques de Marcus Valerius sont-elles une œuvre médiévale', *Mittellateinisches Jahrbuch*, xxii (1987), 166–70, at pp. 166–8, assembles some cogent arguments which cast doubt on the commonly accepted 12th-c. date for 'Marcis Valerius', and prefers a date in late antiquity for the poems.

The Charleville Poet, on the other hand, employs elision on occasions far too numerous to mention, making use of both synaloepha and ecthlipsis[73] (i.e. the running-together of vowels, and the absorption of final -*m* and initial -*h*). Most medieval poets used elision sparingly, though two exceptions were Joseph of Exeter and Walter of Châtillon, whom Klopsch calls 'Vertreter des antikisierenden Epos',[74] a classical poet by proxy, a not particularly suitable description for the Charleville Poet. The number of occasions in which elision is employed in each book is as shown in Table 1.

TABLE 1. *The Charleville Poet's use of elision*

Book	Elisions	Verses	%
i	47	308	15.26
ii	59	304	19.41
iii	78	448	17.41
iv addns.	18	60	30.00
v addns.	4	16	25.00
vi	79	483	16.36
TOTAL	285	1619	18.60

At i. 37, i. 115, and vi. 354, *urbem Hierusalem* is allowed to stand, because the beginning of *Hierusalem* was to be treated as a consonant. Similarly, *ualli Hierusalem* is found at ii. 198. There are two examples of hiatus at the caesura in the Charleville Poet, both in book ii, at ll. 150 and 239.[75]

3. *Metrical analysis*

Statistical analysis of the different parts of the poem reveals both similarities and differences between the styles of the two poets. Some of the figures are distorted because of the small number of lines to be considered, especially in the case of the additions to

[73] Klopsch, *Einführung*, pp. 80–2, and Munari, *Marci Valerii Bucolica*, pp. 47–8, give comparative statistics for other medieval poets.
[74] Klopsch, *Einführung*, p. 82.
[75] Ibid., p. 87.

book v. The method used follows that laid down by Duckworth's[76] *Vergil and Classical Hexameter Poetry: A Study in Metrical Variety*, which uses statistical analysis of the possible patterns in the hexameter to draw distinctions between the preferences and habits of different Latin poets.

As Table 2 shows, both Gilo and the Charleville Poet are fond of DDSS and DSSS, and this preference is paralleled by the two major twelfth-century hexameter poets, Joseph of Exeter and Walter of Châtillon; sample examination of their works gives percentages of 13.5 and 12.5 for DDSS, and 8.5 and 10 for DSSS respectively. On the whole the Charleville Poet's writing is more spondaic than Gilo's, especially in the additions to books iv and v, and he also has a greater liking for the unusual pattern SSSD, particularly in books i and iii. The rhyme-schemes adopted by the poets are also a significant factor in the metrical patterns which are used in their work: the Charleville Poet sticks closely to the use of *caudati* end-rhymes, as will be seen in the discussion below, whereas Gilo uses a variety of schemes; such patterns as DSDS or DDDS are virtually dictated by rhyme-patterns like *trinini salientes*.

4. *Productio ob caesuram and short* -o *in final position*

In common with the practice of the majority of medieval Latin poets, both Gilo and the Charleville Poet admit a short syllable before the caesura on numerous occasions (e.g. Gilo at iv. 16; v. 93, 94; vii. 9, Charleville Poet at i. 151, 250, 297; ii. 128, 237, 254, 260; iii. 28, 43, 44, 58; iv. 85; vi. 187, 416);[77] and both permit the ablative gerund to stand where the final -o must be scanned short. In one instance, vii. 9, *miserendo* in ADG is replaced by the more correct *miserata* in BCF, though *uigilando* is found in this position in the verse with the final -o scanned short (though in one instance only) in Juvenal, *Sat.* iii. 232. Mayor notes similarities to this in Nemesianus and Maximianus,[78] and the phenomenon is also found in Sidonius Apollinaris, who was a popular poet in the eleventh and twelfth centuries. Norberg[79] notes that Walter of Châtillon only permits *productio* with a penthemimeral caesura.

In fact, in the case of the gerund, final -o is almost always short

---

[76] G. E. Duckworth, *Vergil and Classical Hexameter Poetry: A Study In Metrical Variety* (Ann Arbor, 1969).

[77] Klopsch, *Einführung*, pp. 74–6; Norberg, *Introduction*, p. 68.

[78] Juvenal, *Thirteen Satires*, ed. J. E. B. Mayor (2nd edn., London, 1886), ad loc.

[79] Norberg, *Introduction*, p. 68.

TABLE 2. *Distribution of dactyls and spondees* (%)

Type	Charleville Poet										Gilo					
	i	ii	iii	Total i-iii	iv. 60-119	iv. 356-435	v. 461-76	Total iv-v addns.	vi	Total overall	iv	v	vii	viii	ix	Total
DDDD	4.81	2.99	3.56	3.87	3.39	0.00	1.70	1.47	1.67	3.04	2.09	2.99	3.54	6.67	3.73	3.89
DDDS	6.73	5.32	3.56	4.43	0.00	3.70	1.85	2.21	5.45	4.47	3.83	2.99	9.25	5.29	9.33	6.77
DDSD	12.50	6.65	9.26	9.53	1.69	4.56	6.25	5.15	5.03	7.74	4.18	5.29	7.87	9.66	6.13	6.82
DSDD	5.76	4.98	5.22	5.28	5.09	4.40	0.00	3.68	4.61	4.76	5.23	5.52	4.13	5.60	6.68	5.74
SDDD	6.25	2.99	6.18	5.47	3.39	1.70	0.00	1.47	4.19	4.76	1.74	1.38	2.17	1.61	2.67	1.90
DDSS	10.10	7.79	5.70	7.74	8.48	8.87	18.75	10.29	6.29	7.50	3.83	5.98	7.87	9.66	12.27	7.55
DSDS	9.16	9.30	8.79	9.06	10.17	10.64	12.50	11.76	10.48	9.71	12.54	12.64	11.62	10.81	12.53	11.93
DSSD	15.87	9.64	10.93	11.98	5.09	9.95	6.25	11.02	8.81	11.02	11.50	12.87	8.86	7.13	5.34	9.06
SDSD	10.10	2.66	7.36	6.89	3.39	6.33	0.00	5.88	5.45	6.61	1.05	2.76	4.13	7.17	5.07	4.19
SSDD	6.73	2.66	2.85	4.05	6.78	5.24	0.00	4.41	4.19	4.05	5.23	5.29	2.36	2.07	1.07	3.07
SDDS	5.77	5.69	5.23	5.19	3.39	1.70	0.00	1.47	5.87	4.88	1.74	3.68	5.51	5.29	5.33	5.21
DSSS	18.75	12.63	9.98	13.30	10.17	13.42	0.00	11.76	11.31	12.63	19.86	11.26	11.02	11.95	8.53	12.07
SDSS	12.10	8.97	6.41	8.68	15.26	13.19	18.75	14.70	9.64	9.47	3.83	3.91	7.48	7.13	8.80	6.28
SSDS	6.73	7.31	5.94	6.60	5.09	2.54	0.00	2.21	5.66	5.95	7.67	7.36	6.30	5.29	6.67	6.57
SSSD	10.10	3.99	5.70	6.32	3.39	2.62	6.25	2.94	5.24	5.12	8.71	6.68	3.35	3.45	2.67	4.72
SSSS	6.25	6.31	3.32	5.09	15.25	11.33	25.00	13.24	5.87	6.02	6.62	9.20	4.53	2.23	2.92	5.06

in twelfth-century verse, although this was not the case for other words ending in -o.[80] The gerund functions as a present participle in such constructions as are found at vii. 9 in ADG, and also at vii. 42–3. The Charleville Poet also permits *impie* (adverbial) to stand with a short final -e at iii. 262.

Another instance of the metre being corrected as Gilo revised his poem is to be found at iv. 252. Here *rupibus*, the first reading (found in AD), will not scan; Gilo himself corrects it to *caueis*, found in BCF. The Charleville Poet (assuming G is an autograph, or incorporates no further corrections) independently corrects the false reading to *saxis*. Here, the metre is used as an aid to critical correction and emendation, and demonstrates an intelligent reading of the text by the anonymous continuator.

5. *Spondaic fifth foot*

An unusual feature of the Charleville Poet's metrical practice is the use of the spondaic fifth foot (e.g. at ii. 73, 111, 113, 261; iii. 199, 237, 287). As is the case with Heiric of Auxerre,[81] it is usually the inclusion of four-syllable words which leads to its use.

6. *Other points of prosody*

At iii. 183, the Charleville Poet permits elision after the fifth foot, something which, in strictly classicizing verse, should not occur. Synezesis may occur at ii. 240 and definitely at 293, and diastole at i. 186.

There are additionally some instances of unusual prosody: *deesset* is (correctly) scanned as a disyllable at i. 145, as are *deinde* at v. 165, and *deinceps* at vi. 78.[82] *noceret* is scanned with the second syllable short at iii. 132, and *acerrima* with the first syllable short at v. 80. *experimenta* is scanned with the third syllable short instead of long at iv. 88, and at vi. 43, 213, there is a very rare correption of the adverb *hic* (confined, according to the *Thesaurus Linguae Latinae*, s.v. to Old Latin). At iii. 339, the true reading of the manuscript seems to be *calpes*, even though this is clearly unmetrical.

Other instances of unusual prosody worthy of note in the Charleville Poet are i. 57 *impētrarent*; i. 192–3 *ipsĭus*; iii. 20 *retrŏgradis*, iii. 50 *genētricis*.

[80] Strecker, *Introduction to Medieval Latin*, trans. and rev. R. B. Palmer (Dublin and Zürich, 1968), p. 72.

[81] Norberg, *Introduction*, p. 64.　　　[82] Cf. Norberg, *Introduction*, pp. 17, 29.

7. *Monosyllable at end of verse*

A monosyllable is found at the end of the verse in Gilo at ix. 14, 306, and 308, noted above, plus v. 349 and ix. 215—in each case the elided word *est*. In the Charleville Poet's work, monosyllables are used at the ends of lines i. 124, 125; iii. 59, 119; vi. 199, 439, 442, and 450. Norberg draws attention to a poem by Marbod of Rennes which is composed entirely of verses ending in monosyllables;[83] by contrast, Munari notes that there are only two examples to be found in the *Bucolici* of 'Marcus Valerius' (not certainly a twelfth-century poet).[84]

8. *Elegiacs*

Other than the Prologue there is only one section of elegiacs, used to describe Humberga's lament in book vii. The use of elegiacs for such a purpose went back as far as Ovid, in his *Heroides*, and was also recommended by Isidore of Seville and, at a later date than our poets, by Matthew of Vendôme.[85]

9. *Rhyme*

Both poets use rhyme to embellish their verses, as well as holding (as fast as they were able) to the canons of classical metre, or at least what they understood correct metrical practice to be. They show considerable differences in their practice, and this may well reflect the schooling and exposure to literature each had received and to their differing origins, as they were writing some twenty to thirty years apart.

By comparison with many Latin poets of the Middle Ages, Gilo's practice is very complex, and shows considerable development within the work itself. He begins his work by writing almost entirely in leonine rhyme (so book iv); book v is a mixture of *leonini* and *caudati*, together with some *trinini salientes* at iv. 153–8 (also found at vii. 55–9). By the end of book v, *caudati* are in the ascendant. For the period in which Gilo was writing, the use of leonines is unusual; for they were becoming very unfashionable in the twelfth century, and were condemned utterly by Matthew of Vendôme in his *Ars uersificatoria*.[86] The move away from leonines

[83] Norberg, *Introduction*, p. 59. [84] F. Munari, *Marci Valerii Bucolica*, p. 53.
[85] Cf. Klopsch, *Einführung*, pp. 88–9, where he cites Matthew of Vendôme (*Ars uersificatoria*, ii. 40) and also Isidore of Seville (*Etym.* i. 39. 14).
[86] Klopsch, *Einführung*, pp. 44–5; cf. Matthew, *Ars uersificatoria*, ii. 43.

employed at the start of the work perhaps illustrates a tension felt by Gilo as he worked on the books between a style of poetry he had learnt in school (and his leonine writing is very competent) and the newer types of rhyme which he knew to be more fashionable. Eventually he gives up the task of writing in rhyme altogether, as we shall see when we examine his address to his audience at the beginning of book ix.

There are also instances of *Tiradenreim* (more than two verses end-rhymed) at v. 355–8, 367–9, as well as *caudati* (and some leonines) which in their rhythm are similar to *Tiradenreim* at v. 10–11, 23–4, 46–7, 203–4, 205–6, 339–40, 343–4, 349–50, and 355–6. At one point in book v, at line 95, the rhyme causes irregular syntax, and we find *in* with the accusative in place of the expected ablative. In fact from line 284 onwards, book v flits back and forth from leonines to *caudati* in short bursts of each: six lines of *caudati* break up the flow of leonines at v. 389–94, and other *caudati* occur at v. 404–7 and 409–10.

Book vii begins, like book v, with a mixture of leonines and *caudati*, but from vii. 118 onwards, *caudati* are used with only minor exceptions. *Caudati* and *catenati* (i.e. *chains* of end-rhymed verses) only are used in book viii, and finally, in book ix, the poet abandons any attempt at maintaining a rhyme-scheme, warning his readership that he intends to do this in an example of *interiectio ex persona poetae* in ix. 5–10:

> quod tamen incepi, sed non quo tramite cepi
> aggrediar, sensumque sequar, non uerba sonora,
> nec patiar caudas sibi respondere uicissim,
> pruriet et nulli modulatio carminis auri,
> quodque coartabant humilis stilus et rude metrum,
> latius effundet prolixa relatio rerum.

I shall attempt what I began, but not along the path that I first took, and shall pursue the sense of the story, not fine-sounding words; I shall not allow the verse-endings to respond to one another by turns, and the charm of the poetry shall tickle no one's ears: the story which my humble pen and my unpolished verse hampered shall now flow more broadly in a relaxed narrative of events.

The thought here appears to be that the use of poetic devices has hindered or hampered the full expression of the narrative; perhaps

Gilo is responding to criticism that such a holy topic as the Cru-
sade ought not to have been handled in verse.[87]

That the development of Gilo's poetic style is not entirely due to
chance is demonstrated by Gilo's command of metrical and
rhyming techniques elsewhere, and particularly in his Prologue, at
the start of book iv. Gilo is here at pains to stress his change in
direction from writing about worldly things to writing about
spiritual matters, and does so not merely by the *sense* of his words,
but by the rhyme and metre in which he expresses them.[88] The first
half of the Prologue is full of Ovidian reminiscences, is light,
sprightly and dactylic in metre, and contains no rhyme; in the first
four feet of the hexameters there are 16 dactyls out of 32, a high
proportion for Latin, and in the first two feet of the pentameters 13
out of 16. The second half, in a contrast that could hardly be more
marked, is spondaic (10 dactyls out of 32 in the hexameters and 6
out of 16 in the pentameters), contains only Christian reminis-
cences, is weighty in tone, and is rhymed. The Prologue reveals
Gilo to have been a poet of some talent, and, moreover, conscious
talent, so that one must assume that, when there are changes in his
technique elsewhere, he was aware of what he was doing.

The Charleville Poet's clear intent was to maintain a regular
poetic style as is shown by his use of the term *uersibus et numeris* at
i. 6. He uses rhyming couplets (*caudati*) consistently in books i, ii,
iii and vi. At iv. 39–40, 54–5, 60–3, 89–90, 134–9, and 188–9 he uses
leonines, to blend in with Gilo's work. The sole leonine in i, ii, iii,
or vi is to be found at vi. 28. Two verses in the Charleville Poet, iv.
64 and iv. 150, are completely unrhymed. The rhyme is imperfect
elsewhere, as at i. 211–12 and 225, where double and single rhymes
are mingled,[89] and at iii. 119–20.

VI. THE MANUSCRIPTS

The poem survives in seven manuscripts which are described
below. Manitius makes reference to various other manuscripts
which do not in fact contain the text of Gilo;[90] these are discussed
in the Appendix. The genuine MSS containing Gilo are as follows:

[87] Grocock, 'Ovid the Crusader', p. 62.
[88] Klopsch, *Einführung*, pp. 44; Norberg, *Introduction*, p. 48.
[89] Klopsch, *Einführung*, pp. 43–4.
[90] M. Manitius, *Geschichte der lateinischen Literatur des Mittelalters*, 3 vols. (Munich,
1911–31), iii. 667–70.

A = Paris, Bibliothèque Nationale de France, MS lat. 12945 (ancien fonds Saint-Germain 1080). Probably mid-thirteenth century. Written in double columns, with 36 or 37 lines to a column. This contains Gilo's poem on fos. 113–36, under the metrical title *Textus gestorum memorandus Christicolarum*. It also contains the histories of the First Crusade by Guibert of Nogent (fos. 1–64) and by Fulcher of Chartres (fos. 65–112); the *Apologeticus* of St Bernard; a document relating the divisions of parishes at Corbie; extracts from St Jerome; and William Brito's metrical glossary of biblical words. This was the manuscript used by Dom Martène in his edition of the poem (see below, Section VIII).

B = Douai, Bibliothèque Municipale, MS 882 (formerly 838 and G. 629). Parchment, late twelfth century. This manuscript originally belonged to the abbey of Marchiennes, where it carried the number 10. It is written in various hands in double columns with 40 or 41 lines to a column. As well as the poem by Gilo, which is found on fos. 113–25, this contains poems by Marbod of Rennes and Hildebert of Lavardin, together with a collection of proverbs and *uersus de contemptu mundi*; the *History of the crusade* by Bartolf of Nangis; a rhythmical poem on the crusade and various historical documents relating to it; Jerome's *De uiris illustribus*; the *History of the Crusade* by Fulcher of Chartres; excerpts from Quintus Curtius; poems by Hildebert on the Virgin Mary and on Muhammad; pseudo-Dares' *Historia Troianorum*; more documents on the crusade; and Geoffrey of Monmouth's *Historia regum Britanniae*. This manuscript was known to Martène (*Amplissima collectio*, v. 507), but he did not discover it before his own edition had gone to press.

C = Paris, Bibliothèque Nationale de France, MS lat. 5129 (formerly Tellier 274 and Regius 3855A). Parchment. According to Samaran and Marichal,[91] this manuscript was written during the papacy of Eugenius III (1145–53). It is written in double columns, with 35 lines to a column. It contains Gilo's poem on fos. 71–86, under the title *Historia Gilonis cardinalis episcopi de uia Hierosolimitana*. It also contains the *Historia Hierosolimitana* of Robert of Rheims, an elegiac poem on the capture of Jerusalem, and a work

---

[91] C. Samaran and R. Marichal, *Catalogue des manuscrits en écriture latine portant des indications de date, de lieu ou de capiste* (Paris, 1959–), ii. 261.

on the topography of the Holy City; poems of Hildebert of Lavar-
din, the *Carmen de opere sex dierum* and the *Carmen elegiacum de
nummo*; a list of the names of popes and cardinals of Rome; poems
on St Victor and St Maurice; the *Expositio in Symbolum* of Goscelin
of Soissons; a poem on famous places in the world; lamentations
on the fate of Troy; and Hildebert's poem *De Mahumete*. As P. T.
Eden has pointed out, this manuscript and B, even on a superficial
examination, show 'unmistakeable signs of the closest relation-
ship', and the text they contain of the *Physiologus* descends from a
common exemplar, 'which represents what is virtually a new
recension of the poem made during the great revival of interest in
learning and letters in the twelfth century in northern France'.[92]

D = Brussels, Bibliothèque Royale Albert Ier, MS 10615–10729.
Twelfth century, written in double columns with 68–71 lines per
column. This manuscript contains Gilo's poem on fos. 165^r–172^v,
under the metrical title *Textus gestorum memorandus Christicolarum*
(the same as A). According to the Brussels Library card catalogue,
this manuscript was written *c.*1150, and came originally from St
Nicholas at Cues, passing thence to the Bollandists, who were
then at Antwerp, and made its way to the Bibliothèque Nationale
in Paris before reaching Brussels. As well as Gilo's poem, it also
contains a number of sermons, works on law and grammar, and
many classical and late Christian works. Other notable medieval
works it contains are the *Ecbasis captiui* and Guy of Amiens' *Carmen
de Hastingae proelio*.

E = Brussels, Bibliothèque Royale Albert Ier, MS 7442 (formerly
7575–7585). Paper, late seventeenth century, written in a single
hand in single columns with 41–4 lines to a column. This contains
Gilo's poem, bibliographical notes, the *Historia Hierosolimitana* of
Robert the Monk, and anonymous letters to the King of Egypt and
the Egyptians. Its text shows that it is a copy of D, and is of no
independent value as a witness, hence its treatment as a *codex
eliminandus*

F = Rome, Biblioteca Vallicelliana, MS B. 33. Twelfth century,
written in double columns with 39 lines per column. Gilo's poem is
found on fos. 44^r–54^v. It is introduced by the words *Incipit historia*

[92] *Theobaldi Physiologus*, ed. P. T. Eden (Leiden, 1972), p. 10.

Gilonis Parisiensis. It also contains the *Historia Hierosolimitana* of Baldric of Dol (fos. 1–43ᵛ), and the *Legenda et passio sancti Matthaei apostoli*.

G = Charleville-Mézières, Bibliothèque Municipale, MS 97. A palimpsested parchment of the mid-twelfth century, written in single columns with 30 lines to a column. This manuscript, only 18 cm. × 12 cm. in size, is the sole source of the additions to Gilo's poem by the Charleville Poet, and was the manuscript used by Sirmond in the *editio princeps* which appeared in Du Chesne's *Historiae Francorum Scriptores*. Some of the sheets in the manuscript were originally at least twice their present size, as can be seen from the original ruling on them which shows through in many places; after being palimpsested, these leaves were cut in half and rebound, so that the original text now shows through as vertical lines. The first text seems to have been a lectionary, probably dating from the tenth century; on fo. 109ᵛ, for example, the following words can be read: *Dominum nostrum . . . ficate in cordibus uestris* (cf. 1 Pet. 3: 15), and on fo. 111ᵛ, *In natalem S. Pauli. Lectio Actuum Apostolorum. Saulus autem spirans minarum . . .* (Acts 9: 1).

The text superimposed above this is itself in a very poor state, having apparently suffered water-damage at some time. Much of the writing is smudged, and the parchment itself is swollen and cracked, rendering the manuscript illegible in many places where the ink has flaked off or disintegrated. There are as a result several lacunae in the text of the Charleville Poet, and even after examination under ultraviolet light at the Bibliothèque Nationale in Paris, parts of the text remain illegible. Sample trial photographs using both ultraviolet and infrared processes did little to make these passages any clearer.

In addition to the work of the Charleville Poet and of Gilo, this manuscript contains the following poems and texts: Alcimus Ecdicius Avitus, bishop of Vienne, books ii (incomplete), iii, iv, v, vi (fos. 1–40ᵛ); an excerpt from the *De uiris illustribus* of Isidore of Seville; Proba Falconia, *Cento Vergilianus* (fos. 42ʳ–52ᵛ); *Ecloga Theoduli* (fos. 53–60). The text written by the Charleville Poet begins on fo. 60ʳ with the rubricated title *Historia gestorum uiae nostri temporis Hierosolimitanae*, and book iii of his work ends on fo. 78ʳ, with the rubric *incipit quartus* (sc. *liber*) *a domno Giloni Parisiensi cum ceteris sequentibus eleganter editus*. As is made clear in the discussion on the authors, there is good reason to question the precise accuracy of this last assertion. Gilo's poem, together with additions to books iv and v, and the intercalated book vi, follow on directly until fo. 109^v, where the text breaks off at the verse [.]*t rapido cursu belli robur petiere* (vii. 471). Only six lines of this page have been written, and the initial letters to each line, elsewhere written in red, are missing. The rest of the manuscript is already palimpsested and lined to receive the text, but blank; why the text should break off so suddenly must remain a mystery.

The manuscript is written in a single hand in brown (or possibly faded black), with decorated capitals in red to mark the beginning of each new book. The initial letter of each line is also in red ink. A member of the staff of the Bibliothèque Nationale kindly identified the decoration in the manuscript as being typical of the late eleventh or early twelfth centuries in the Champagne region, which fits in very well with its present location to the east of that area. The hand itself is somewhat irregular, and many of the letters are poorly formed. In view of the date and provenance of the manuscript, as well as its contents, it may possibly be regarded as the autograph of the Charleville Poet himself.

VII. RELATIONSHIP OF THE MANUSCRIPTS

The most important divergence to be noted between the manuscripts is in their contents: ABCDF contain the five books of the poem by Gilo, which is complete in itself. G, on the other hand, is the sole manuscript to preserve the work of the Charleville Poet: the arrangement of its contents demonstrates that the additional material written by this second author was not intended to constitute a separate work; it is to be regarded rather as a revision and expansion of Gilo's earlier composition. In G, three additional books precede Gilo's work, the first two books of which follow with lengthy sections added. A further entire book is then intercalated between Gilo's second and third books. This intercalated book is, like the first three, found uniquely in G, whose contents resemble that of the other manuscripts from this point on, until at vii. 471 the text breaks off abruptly. Gilo's poem stands complete in the rest of the manuscripts.

G has been deserving of especial discussion at this stage, because a crucial piece of evidence in the establishment of the stemma must be inferred from its divergences from ABCDF, namely that the text which it preserves is the work both of Gilo and of a second author, a reviser. This produces at the very outset the division set out in Fig. 1.

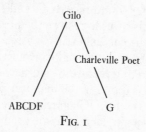

FIG. 1

As well as the added four books and the insertions to books iv and v, G also interpolates variant readings and shorter insertions in the text reported by ABCDF, which seem to be of the nature of deliberate alterations and 'improvements' to the version contained in the other manuscripts, as follows:

iv. 24 *plaustro* ABCDF: *?aratro* G   iv. 40–1 added by G only   iv. 57 *utrinque* ABCDF: *ubique* G   iv. 122–3 *en sexaginta Turcorum milia structa | ensibus et clipeis ad opem uenere Niceis* ABCDF: *ecce repentino clamore ululante Nycea | milibus auditis montana uidentur operta | que dum desiliunt hinc per decliuia montis | altera contigue properant per concaua uallis* G   iv. 124 *nimis metuens* ABCDF: *satis nemens* G   iv. 128 *fecerunt* ABCDF: *struxerunt* G   iv. 133 *multo* ABCDF: *cuneos* G   iv. 150 added by G only   iv. 160 *transiuere* ABCDF: *transiliere* G   iv. 170 *depellat* ABCDF: *depellati* G   iv. 182 *fugiebant* ABCDF: *fugitabant* G   iv. 188–9 added by G only   iv. 252 *rupibus* AD: *caueis* BCF: *saxis* G   iv. 267 *pugnantibus* ABCDF: *pugnabant* G   iv. 269 *riuum* ABCDF: *murum* G   iv. 315 *gladiis* AD: *iaculis* BCFG   iv. 345 added by G only   v. 110 *admirati* ABCDF: *ammiraldi* G   v. 143 *putantes* ABCDF: *timentes* G   v. 164 *horret* ABCDF: *audet* G   v. 237 *prius* ABCDF: *post* G   v. 239 *confractos* ABCDF: *fugientes* G   v. 294 *hostes* ABCDF: *Perse* G   v. 391 *postquam* ABCDF: *post ubi* G   v. 441 *languet morte graui bello non languida dextra* ABCF, omitted by D: *eheu quis mihi det misera decedere uita* G   vii. 128 *sponte cadunt quibus exciderant cum corpore mentes* ABCDF: *hos non sponte cadunt quibus et cum corpore mentes* G   vii. 206 *uestigia* ABCDF: *fastigia* G   vii. 224 *lustrat* ABCF: *uastat* D: *uisit* G   vii. 330 *tertio ieiunant omnes* ABCDF: *ieiunant omnes triduo* G   vii. 387 added by G only   vii. 413 *rara* ABCDF: *parua* G

These variants show that the Charleville Poet felt quite free to make minor amendments or improvements to the text he had before him when the need arose. At iv. 252, for example, he replaces the unmetrical *rupibus* found in AD with *saxis*, where BCF have the correct *caueis*. Again, at v. 441, the common source of DG omitted the hexameter found in ABCF, and the Charleville Poet composes a line of his own, to restore the hexameter–pentameter sequence. On an earlier occasion, he was not above replacing two of Gilo's original lines with four of his own (iv. 122–3).

The next most striking feature which may be observed among the divergent readings found in the manuscripts is the great number of occasions on which ADG agree together against BCF. This class represents by far the largest single group of variants, occurring a total of 163 times, as follows:

Prologue 1–32 only contained in BCF   iv. 34 *assultus* ADG: *assaltus* BCF   iv. 42 placed after iv. 34 by ADG   iv. 47 *uerba* ADG: *dicta* BCF   iv. 54 *telo proprio* ADG: *proprio telo* BCF   iv. 130 *preberet* ADG: *prestaret* BCF   iv. 214 *nimioque timore* ADG: *nimio terrore* BCF   iv. 215 *et* ADG: *sed* BCF   iv. 221 *spe ducti* ADG; *ducti spe* BCF   iv. 222 *circum* ADG: *circa* BCF   iv. 231 *raptum capit* ADG: *captum rapit* BCF   iv. 237 *nostros Turci* ADG: *Turci nostros* BCF   iv. 241 placed after 242 by ADG   iv. 252 *rupibus* AD: *saxis* G: *caueis* BCF   iv. 271 *comiti fecit* ADG: *fecit comiti* BC: *cofecit comiti* F   iv. 282 placed after 283 by ADG   iv. 283 *iactu…in uno* ADG: *aliquis sapiens* BCF   v. 31 *inimice* ADG: *iactum.. in unum* BCF   iv. 293 *furtis* ADG: *furtim* BCF   iv. 297 *montes* ADG: *montem* BCF   iv. 315 *gladiis aut ense* AD: *iaculis aut ense* BCFG   iv. 334 *colligit* ADG: *collocat* BCF

v. 22 *tam multis* ADG: *non paucis* BCF   v. 23 *sapiens aliquis* ADG: *aliquis sapiens* BCF   v. 31 *inimice* ADG: *munite* BCF   v. 39 *mortem pauci* ADG: *pauci mortem* BCF   v. 56 *multos* ADG: *plures* BCF   v. 72 *penas nimias* ADG: *nimias penas* BCF   v. 76 *tela* ADG: *arma* BCF   v. 85 *dederant sua membra* ADG: *sua membra dedere* BCF   v. 111 *Calapi* ADG: *Scalapi* BCF   v. 152 *hoc* ADG: *hec* BCF   v. 163 not found in ADG   v. 195 *castellum quoddam* ADG: *quoddam castellum* BCF   v. 196 *ilico* ADG: *illi* BCF   v. 205 *non* ADG: *nec* BCF   v. 211 *iuxta* ADG: *preter* BCF   v. 213 *ne* ADG: *non* BCF   v. 216 *uergentibus* ADG: *surgentibus* BCF   v. 241 *exhaustas* ADG: *exactas* BCF   v. 246 *necdum* ADG: *nondum* BCF   v. 255 *pedites tria milia* ADG: *peditum tria milia* BCF   v. 270 *summi signat* ADG: *signat summi* BCF   v. 286 *Persas* ADG: *Perses* BCF   v. 293 *bellatur* ADG: *pugnatur* BCF   v. 310 *rimam* ADG: *ripam* BCF   v. 318 *immodice* ADG: *non modice* BCF   v. 335 *exhaustas* ADG: *exactas* BCF   *uires uoluit* ADG: *uoluit uires* BCF   v. 350 *animos firmat* ADG: *subigit uires* BCF   v. 360 *altius erigit* ADG: *erigit altius* BCF   v. 364 *rumpit* ADG: *rupit* BCF   v. 365 *truncatus* ADG: *prostratus* BCF   v. 386 *fitque pauimentum de corporibus morientum* ADG: *dextraque cedentum deforme facit pauimentum* BC: *de iugulis flentum miserabile fit pauimentum* F   v. 401 *ad* ADG: *in* BCF   v. 406 *hic* ADG: *huc* BCF   v. 447–8 not found in ADG   v. 453 *quid faciam procul a patria procul a patre degens* A: verse not found in DG: *an sine te uiuam patris a patria procul absens* BCF   v. 454 *quid faciet fragilis femina castra sequens* A: not found in DG: *absque uiro uiuet femina castra sequens* BCF

vii. 6 *gentis* ADG: *turbe* BCF   viii. 9 *miserendo* ADG: *miserata* BCF   vii. 27 *obscuros* ADG: *occultos* BCF   vii. 35 *tecti* ADG: *tuti* BCF   vii. 67 *perculsa* ADG: *percussa* BCF   vii. 69 *turrim* A: *turres* DG: *turrem* BCF   vii. 79 *referunt* AD: *redeunt* G: *repetunt* BCF   vii. 147 *paruo* ADG: *modico* BCF   vii. 167 *turrim* ADG: *turrem* BCF   vii. 273 *subito* ADG: *tandem* BCF   vii. 291 *modicum* ADG: *minimum* BCF   vii. 300 *luctantur* ADG: *franguntur* BCF   vii. 316 *caro* ADG: *care* BC: *quare* F   vii. 351 *at* ADG: *aut* BC: *aud* F   vii. 355 *triginta siue uiginti* ADG: *ter deni seu duodeni* BC: *ter deni uel duodeni* F   vii. 357 *dixit* ADG: *inquit* BCF   vii. 363 *patres* ADG: *duces* BCF   vii. 368 *quos medios* ADG: *quas medium* BCF   vii. 395 *pugiles* ADG: *equites* BCF   vii. 400 *dux Persarum* ADG: *Persarum dux* BCF   vii. 401 *dici* ADG: *duci* BCF   vii. 412 *gessit* ADG: *fecit* BCF   vii. 414 *muris* ADG: *muro* BCF   vii. 428 *Pusiaco* ADG: *Puteolo* BCF   vii. 443 *sunt* ADG: *stant* BCF   vii. 446 *mouenti* ADG: *monenti* BCF   vii. 459 *iuuenique uiam fecit* ADG: *fecitque uiam iuueni* BCF   vii. 482 *uoluere* AD: *uoluerunt* BCF   vii. 483 *petiere* AD: *petierunt* BCF   vii. 505 *inherme* AD: *in urbe* BCF   vii. 509 *induperatori* A: *imperio domini* D: *imperii domino* BCF

viii. 23 *breue regnum* AD: *regnum breue* BCF   viii. 26 *contempta* AD: *detenta* BCF   viii. 30 *in* AD: *ad* BCF   viii. 43 *agitata* AD: *agiturque* BCF   viii. 44 *clipei reddunt* AD: *reddunt clipei* BCF   viii. 63 *latrantis* A: *latrantes* D: *latratu* BCF   viii. 75 *doluisse* AD: *gemuisse* BCF   viii. 77 *presul moritur* AD: *moritur presul* BCF   vii. 91 *homines* A: *necem* D: *uiri* BCF   viii. 96 *hinc sanctis* AD: *ergo bonis* BCF   viii. 103 *coniugia* AD: *conubia* BCF   viii. 134 *martem* AD: *muros* BCF   viii. 145 *ac* AD: *et* BCF   viii. 151 *crepitum* A: *strepitum* D: *sonitum* BCF   viii. 182 *metuatque* AD: *fugiatque* BCF   viii. 183 *Chrisi nomen* AD: *nomen Christi* BCF *conantur* AD: *conatur* BCF   viii. 184–5 not found in AD   viii. 212 *turba* AD: *turma* BCF   viii. 217 *contentus* AD: *intentus* F: *intensus* BC   viii. 242 *et* AD: *at* BCF   viii. 255 *uires modicas* AD: *modicas uires* BCF   viii. 268 *seruare ducis quos cura* AD: *quos cura ducis seruare* BCF   viii. 289 *sed* AD: *at* BCF   viii. 291 *si* AD: *sit* BCF   viii. 324 *occurrerunt* AD: *occurrentes* BCF   viii. 333 *muroque* AD: *ualloque* BCF   viii. 339 *non* AD: *nec* BCF   viii. 350 *quod* AD: *que* BCF   viii. 405 *haud impar erat* A: *erat haud impar* D: *non impar erat* BCF   viii. 432 *nostri* AD: *proceres* BCF

ix. 7 *fines* AD: *caudas* BCF   ix. 12 *primus* AD: *primum* BCF   ix. 33 *cuius*
A: *cuius* D: *huius* BCF   ix. 44 *tegunt* AD: *tegit* BCF   ix. 56 *cur* AD:
quid   ix. 67 *de Sem* AD: *Desem* BCF   ix. 80 *urbs* AD: *opus* BCF   ix.
81 *grata* AD: *cara* BCF   ix. 95 *se* AD: *sua* BCF   ix. 97 *et* AD: *dant*
BCF   ix. 98 not found in BCF   ix. 108 *solitos labores* AD: *solitum laborem*
BCF   ix. 109 *mensis erat maius* AD: *mensis erat maii* BCF   ix. 119 *ille dies*
AD: *illa dies* BCF   ix. 199 *quo* AD: *qua* BCF   ix. 137 *tempore* AD: *frigore*
BCF   ix. 143 *adheret* AD: *adhesit* BCF   ix. 146 *a* AD: *e* BCF   ix. 152 *at*
AD: *aut* BCF   ix. 166 *et* AD: *at* BCF   ix. 172 *fortis miles* AD: *nostra*
iuuentus BCF   ix. 195 *cum paucis ante cucurrit* AD: *cum triginta prior iuit*
BCF   ix. 200 *subcubit* A: *succumbit* D: *succubuit* BCF   ix. 204 *sociis pro-*
ceres AD: *proceres sociis* BCF   ix. 220 *dubitans* AD: *dubius* BCF   ix.
224 *afflictus* AD: *afflicti* BCF   ix. 241 *crederet umquam* AD: *credere posset* F:
scribere posset BC   ix. 244 *undam* AD: *undas* BCF   ix. 269 *quibusue* AD:
quibusque BCF   ix. 299 *inerti* AD: *inertis* BCF   ix. 305 *est* added in
BCF   ix. 308 *gladiumque* AD: *gladiosque* BCF   ix. 309 *desudet* AD: *desu-*
dent BCF   ix. 317 *reuulsa* AD: *reuulsum* BCF   ix. 318 *niueo* AD: *rubeo*
BCF   ix. 320 *etiam* AD: *gemino* F: *geminos* BC   ix. 324 *planum* AD:
plano BCF   ix. 327 *uagatur* AD: *uagantur* BCF   ix. 333 *Guastonque* AD:
Gastonque BCF   ix. 363 *digna* AD: *digne* BCF   ix. 368 *regimen* AD: *reg-*
num BCF

The epilogue is contained only in AD.

The deep division between these two groupings is made yet
starker by the presence of the author's own prologue, written in
elegiac couplets in the first person, in BCF only. Likewise, the
divide is well illustrated by the presence in AD only of a verse
epilogue written by another writer about Gilo. G, being an incom-
plete witness to the text, plays no part in this latter section of the
argument, though it may be considered fair to assume that in view
of its close affinities with AD, it would also have contained this
verse epilogue. At any event the epilogue is certainly not Gilo's
own work, being very clumsy by comparison, and is probably the
work of a copyist. It contains no historical information which
might enable a precise date to be assigned to it. The stage at which
it was introduced into the tradition is represented in Fig. 2 by α.
This stemma presumes that the variant readings were introduced
at the α stage, where the verse prologue would have been lost, and
the epilogue added. However, a closer inspection of the variations
between ADG and BCF shows that it is not always possible to say
that either side contains 'right' or 'wrong' readings. On most occa-
sions there is little to choose between the two. They suggest rather

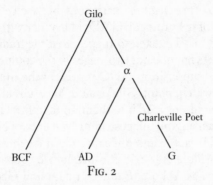

Fig. 2

that in many cases (e.g. v. 22, v. 85) one reading has been sub-
stituted for another on aesthetic grounds. These include changes
in word order, notably from noun–verb in ADG to verb–noun in
BCF. More telling are the variants at v. 453 and v. 454. A's reading
in v. 453 may recall Vergil, *Ecl.* x. 46, but in this line and the one fol-
lowing, the inherent innuendo has been replaced by a less infelici-
tous turn of phrase. A more complex situation is to be found at v.
386, where there are two divergences from ADG. One of these
might be a gloss, incorporated by F in error (the verse is markedly
inferior to the reading of BC, and F contains a large number of
fairly inane glosses on the text).

On the whole, the readings from BCF are preferable aesthetic-
ally to those in ADG. There are also some unmetrical readings in
AD which are corrected in BCF and (independently) in G. On the
other hand, there are a few instances (e.g. at iv. 283, vii. 67) where
ADG's readings seem preferable. It seems odd for a scribe to have
interpolated so often, deliberately altering the text, when all he
achieves is depravation of it: the version supplied by BCF is
preferable, with only a few exceptions. The presence of unmetrical
readings in AD also points toward the conclusion that the BCF
version is later than the other. To assume that the alterations took
place in α would also then entail the assumption that the prologue
was either deliberately omitted at this stage, or that the exemplar
from which ADG descend had lost the leaves or leaf containing
just the prologue.

The presence of the author's prologue on the one side only of
the tradition, as well as the corrections to errors of metre, suggests
an alternative explanation, and a more illuminating one, for the

existence of so many minor variations between ADG and BCF.
The absence of the prologue in ADG, together with its slightly less
polished text, may be taken to suggest that the tradition as we now
have it presents not one but two stages in the composition of Gilo's
work. On this supposition, ADG represent the first stage of com-
position, at which point Gilo would have circulated the poem
among his friends, or read it to them, so that they could make con-
structive criticism and suggest improvements. This practice was
enjoined by Horace,[93] and appears to have been a common prac-
tice in the Middle Ages; it is illustrated by remarks from such
varied authors as Abbo of Saint-Germain and Geoffrey of Mon-
mouth.[94] Geoffrey in particular addresses his dedicatees as though
they were to sit in judgement on his work, and John of Salisbury
would appear to have been asked by Peter of Celle to act in a simi-
lar way and to comment on Peter's *De panibus*.[95] Walter of Châtil-
lon speaks of his own fear for the reception of his work in the
Preface to his *Alexandreis*.[96] No doubt there is some hyperbole, or
mere convention, in these statements, but they point to great inter-
est being shown in new works, so that an author would be well

---

[93] Cf. especially *Ars Poetica* 386–90, 438–41.

[94] Cf. Abbo's comments in the preface to his work, *Bella Parisiacae Vrbis*, ed.
H. Waquet (Paris 1964), p. 2: 'numquam enim otio reficiendi ob scolarum pluralitatem,
cuius commoditati ubique locorum vacaverim; verum qui primum fuerit prolata, con-
stat adhuc sequens pagina, membranis semel tantum mutatis, post quoque, ceu quo-
piam Foebo, tuo sagaci lustretur arbitrio.' Geoffrey refers to Robert, duke of
Gloucester, as his *doctor* and *monitor*, and to Galeran of Mellent as having *moderatio*
which will enable his work to shine with a greater brilliance. Later in the 12th c., Ralph
Niger urged the archbishop of Rheims, William of the White Hands, to have his book
De re militari examined to see if it contained any error. See L. Schmugge's edition (Ber-
lin, 1977), and G. B. Flahiff, 'Ralph Niger—an introduction to his life and works',
Mediaeval Studies ii (1940), 104–26, at p. 111 and n. 43; and for the way in which this form
of criticism could be used as censorship, see G. B. Flahiff, 'The censorship of books in
the 12th century', *Mediaeval Studies* iv (1942), pp. 1–23.

[95] John's comments in *Ep.* xxxiii are particularly apposite: 'manum correctionis eis
apponere non praesumo, quia nichil invenio in eis corrigendum, qui eos tanta aviditate
vorasse voluerim, ut nec de substantia sensuum. . .'. (*The Letters of John of Salisbury.
Volume One. The Early Letters (1153–1161)*, ed. W. J. Miller, S.J. and H. E. Butler, rev.
C. N. L. Brooke (OMT: Oxford, 1986), p. 56).

[96] Walter of Châtillon, *Alexandreis*, ed. M. L. Colker (Padua, 1978), prologue: 'et mirum
est, humanum genus a prima sui natura, secundum quam cuncta que fecit Deus valde
bona creata sunt, ita esse depravatum ut pronius sit ad condempnandum quam ad indul-
gendum et facilius sit ei ambigua depravare quam in partem interpretari meliorem. Hoc
ego reveritus diu te, o mea Alexandrei, in mente habui semper supprimere et opus quin-
quennio laboratum aut penitus delere aut certe quoad viverem in occulto sepelire.'

advised to seek critical opinion of his own efforts before laying them before the judgement of the world.

On this hypothesis, the text preserved by ADG would be the 'first draft', and BCF the 'post-revision' stage of composition, at which point the prologue would have been appended. The text of α, descending from the earlier draft, would never have contained the prologue, and the work would (save for the brief notice in ix. 374–5) have been anonymous, which would explain the necessity for a third party to add the verse epilogue, crediting Gilo with the work and supplying a suitably laudatory *explicit*.

After receiving criticism and suggestions for improving the text, Gilo would then have prepared the final version, incorporating more polished and more felicitous expressions, and correcting the few metrical faults still to be detected in AD. He may even have left alternative readings as marginalia, as the complex tradition at v. 386 seems to show. To this final draft Gilo would have prefixed his own verse prologue, so typical of medieval literature, and the work would have been ready to publish. This is the version preserved in BCF. This explanation seems to fit the evidence best of all. It accounts for the superiority of the variants in BCF, and also explains why ADG's readings, while for the most part inferior, still make sense. It also gives a reason for the presence of the prologue on one side of the tradition only.[97] In addition, BCF also contain after the text of the poem itself some brief prose notes, giving a few details of the author's life in the form of an *explicit* to the work. From their content, it would appear that they were composed between 1121 and 1133; they are obviously not by Gilo himself, and as they appear in all three manuscripts on this side of the tradition, they must have entered it at the point shown as β below.[98] The two stages of Gilo's own recension are shown as 'Gilo I' and 'Gilo II'. This may be represented as in Fig. 3.

·

---

[97] T. A. P. Klein, 'Editing the Chronicle of Gui de Bazoches', *Journal of Medieval Latin*, iii (1993), 27–33, at pp. 30–1, interprets the manuscript tradition of Gui's work as providing evidence of another example of this practice of revision, though with far less evidence than is apparent from Gilo.

[98] See above, 'The Authors', pp. xxi–xxii.

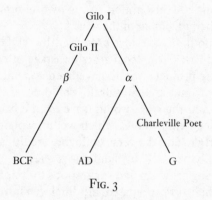

Fɪɢ. 3

Having dealt with the two major divergences in the tradition of the work, we turn to other instances of divergence among the manuscripts. The second most numerous group occurs where BC agree together against the rest, as follows:

Prologue 4 *multa*: *plura* BC   16 *littore ex humili* : *ex humili littore* BC   iv. 35 *multaque*: *multa* BC   *uligine* A: *putredine* FDG: *hirundine* B: *hirudine* C   iv. 156 *siti*: *sitis* BC   iv. 205 *hoc*: *hec* BC   iv. 212 *illic*: *illinc* BC   iv. 294 *annisque*: *animusque* B: *animisque* C

v. 66 *Armeniique*: *Ermeniique* BC   v. 128 *Normanno*: *Hermanno* BC   v. 132 *oratum*: *ornatum* BC   v. 144 *inscia*: *nescia* BC   v. 153 *redeuntes*: *redientes* BC   v. 155 *ubique*: *utrinque* BC   v. 119 *fulti*: *freti* BC   v. 213 *sed*: *si* BC   v. 216 *conuocat* ADG: *euocat* F: *euolat* BC   *aliquos*: *aliquot* BC   v. 219 *suffragia*: *uires sibi* BC   v. 242 *defunctis*: *defunctus* BC   v. 261 *Statinus*: *Catinus* BC   v. 280 *emersit*: *emisit* BC   v. 289 *tela*: *pila* BC   v. 322 *sola*: *soli* BC   v. 338 *noua*: *fera* BC   v. 353 *Capaneo*: *Canapeo* BC   v. 354 *non Diomedes*: *siue Titides* BC   v. 366 *super scutum*: *scutum gladio* BC   v. 373 *essem*: *ensem* BC   v. 386 *fitque pauimentum de corporibus morientum* ADG: *de iugulis flentum miserabile fit pauimentum* F: *dextraque cedentum deforme facit pauimentum* BC   v. 388 *leti* not found in BC   *dant*: *sua reddunt* BC   v. 451 *quam* ADG: *quod* F: *quia* BC   v. 457 *Galoni*: *Galonis* BC

vii. 1 *nec*: *neque* BC   vii. 10 *urbem tradat*: *tradat urbem* BC   vii. 27 *lucebat*: *lucebant* BC   vii. 32 *hactenus*: *iam satis* BC   vii. 33 *utque locum uotis multoque labore petitum*: *utque locum spectant uotis multoque petitum* BC   vii. 44 *uerbis*: *hortans* BC   vii. 63 *tenebras*: *latebras* BC   vii. 154 *Arminio*: *Erminio* BC   vii. 212 *celebris*: *salubris* BC   vii. 221 *soporem*: *saporem* BC   vii. 288 *tecta*: *tela* BC   vii. 314 *corpore*: *pectore* BC   vii. 334 *portum*:

portam BC   vii. 362 *proceres: hostes* BC   vii. 364 *turba: turma* BC   vii.
409 *proueniunt: prouenient* BC   vii. 418 *inuadit: iuvasit* BC   vii.
419 *recessu: recursu* BC   vii. 423 not found in BC   vii. 461 *urgebat: ange-*
bat BC   vii. 468 *Rainaldus: Tainaldus* BC   vii. 471 *rapido: rabido*
BC   vii. 493 *pedites miseri: miseri pedites* BC   vii. 499 *subducere: submittere*
BC

viii. 31 *Aleph: Alep* BC   viii. 34 *passim* ADG, F m. sec.: *spassim* F m. pr.
sparsim BC   viii. 37 *receptant: retentant* BC   vii. 41 *uertitur: utitur*
BC   viii. 57 *minutos: munitos* BC   viii. 98 *tam: tunc* BC   viii. 114 *hunc:*
huic BC   viii. 137 *uolunt: uolent* BC   viii. 151 *equites sub eis: sub eis equites*
BC   viii. 157 *delecta: dilecta* BC   viii. 172 *tedis: telis* BC   viii. 192 *ipse:*
ille BC   viii. 193 *inertis: inermis* BC   viii. 217 *contentus* ADG: *intentus* F:
intensus BC   viii. 226 *eques: equus* BC   viii. 237 *mors una modis hos: hos*
una modis mors BC   viii. 263 *fedabat: fedabant* BC   viii. 275 *gens: plebs*
BC   viii. 279 *ueribus: uerubus* BC   viii. 283 *recipi: recipit* BC   viii.
287 *amata: amena* BC   viii. 292 *summetur res: summe turres* BC   viii.
293 *Rugiosam: Ruginosam* BC   viii. 312 *terra: turba* BC   viii. 313 *corpori-*
bus: corporis BC   viii. 316 *et: at* BC   viii. 329 *predam: predia* BC   viii.
360 *et: at* BC   viii. 370 *hosti: isti* BC   viii. 377 *Publicanique: gentes*
Medique BC   viii. 393 *primus: magnus* BC

ix. 49 *lacessere: lacescere* BC   ix. 57 *iam Partus ope: Parthus ope iam* BC   ix.
88 *castris: castro* BC   ix. 162 *dura: dira* BC   ix. 203 *clamans: clamat*
BC   ix. 205 *mortem: mortes* BC   ix. 211 *inde* AD: *unde* F: *inque* BC   ix.
220 *hos non homines: non hos homines* BC   ix. 241 *quis crederet umquam* AD:
quis credere posset F: *quis scribere posset* BC   ix. 256 *ingentis: ingenti*
BC   ix. 264 not found in BC   ix. 308 *nitentem* AD: *nitente* F: *nitentes*
BC   ix. 312 *tegantur: teguntur* BC   ix. 320 *gemino: geminos* BC

These many variants clearly indicate that B and C share a common
parentage, which will be designated γ. On these occasions B and C
are almost always in error, though it is possible that some of their
shared variants are glosses, erroneously taken to be corrections
and interpolated into the text. This is almost certainly the cause for
the variants at v. 386. Their common parentage is also shown by
their common *explicit*.

   In the same way D and G agree together, though with much less
frequency than is the case with BC, against ABCF. On these occa-
sions DG are almost invariably in error. Again, this points to a lost
parent for DG, which is designated δ. DG's common variants are
as follows:

iv. 121 *constricti* BCF: *cum stricti* A: *cum strati* D: *constrati* G iv. 247 *nichil*: *nil* DG iv. 250 *factos*: *facti* DG *stupefactos*: *stupefacti* DG iv. 287 *cessissent*: *pressissent* DG iv. 292 *necopino* BCF: *nec primo* A: *inopino* DG

v. 34 *nostros*: *muros* DG v. 37 *dum* ABC: *cum* DFG v. 124 *nati*: *fidi* DG v. 165 *inde* ABC: *deinde* DFG v. 277 *summa*: *signa* DG v. 441 not found in D: G adds a verse of its own v. 453–4 not found in DG

vii. 9 *laborum*: *suorum* DG v. 29 *mentem*: *mens et* DG v. 69 *turrem* BCF: *turrim* A: *turres* DG vii. 104 *arce*: *urbe* DG vii. 224 *lustrat*: *uastat* D: *uisit* G vii. 413 *turres*: *muros* DG vii. 418 *emittunt*: *inuadunt* DG vii. 451 *iaculis*: *telis* DG

Finally, a few occasions where G agrees with BCF against AD should be noted:

iv. 41 *sontes*: *fontes* AD iv. 59 *trepidantis*: *trepidantes* AD iv. 207 *hosque*: *hos* AD iv. 315 *iaculis*: *gladiis* AD vii. 204 *poterit*: *poterat* AD

This difference of G from AD might possibly be the result of contamination on G's part from the BCF side of the tradition, though how and when it occurred, if it did occur (since it is not a common phenomenon) is difficult to explain. However, since G is an inveterate interpolator, and on one occasion corrects AD independently of BCF (iv. 252, noted above), as well as introducing many new readings of its own, these occasions where G agrees against AD with BCF are best viewed as the result of independent, fortuitous corrections by G of faults in 'Gilo I'.

There are two instances where BF or AB agree against the rest. At v. 77, BF read *extruxe* against *extruxere* in the others. Here C may have corrected a fault which may derive from 'Gilo II', or (more likely) the scribes of both B and F have omitted the mark indicating the *-er* of the *-ere* ending. At vii. 389, AB read *superet* against *superat* in the rest. Again, this is best explained as a simple error made independently by two scribes.

The text as found in each manuscript also contains errors of its own; these are detailed in the *apparatus criticus* to the text. For this reason, although it is possible (as has been stated above) that G is the autograph of the Charleville Poet, an intermediate stage in the transmission may be suspected. The final stemma may be drawn up as shown in Fig. 4:

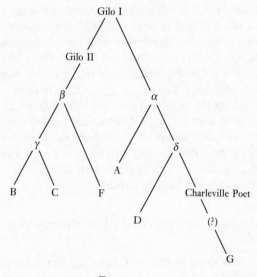

FIG. 4

VIII. PREVIOUS EDITIONS

There have been several editions of Gilo's poem prior to the present one, as follows:

1. F. Du Chesne, A. Du Chesne, *Historiae Francorum Scriptores*. 4 vols. (Paris, 1636–49), iv. 890–912.

The *editio princeps* of the *Historiae uiae Hierosolimitanae* was printed in the *Historiae Francorum Scriptores* series, which appeared over several years in the early seventeenth century, the first volume appearing in 1636 and the fourth and last (which contains the text of the poem) being published in 1649. The Du Chesnes, André (the father) and François (the son), were well-known antiquaries, and were aided in their endeavours by many acquaintances of like mind, in particular Jesuits. It is to one such, Jacques Sirmond, that François Du Chesne owed the text of the *Historia uiae Hierosolimitanae*. Sirmond appears to be the source of the name 'Fulco' given to the author of the additions to Gilo's work; the text he sent to Du Chesne is a transcription of the damaged Charleville manuscript (designated G in this edition), although it is not identified as such by Sirmond, who refers to it simply as his *exemplar*. There is no doubt that it was the Charleville manuscript, however; Sirmond's text contains numerous lacunae at precisely those places where the text of the Charleville manuscript is illegible, contains all G's additions, and stops short at vii. 471, where G does.

Sirmond seems to have found the task of transcribing a manuscript of such poor quality a difficult one, and the text he presents is fragmented and disjointed to such an extent that Martène, who next edited the poem, judged it to be *tot lacunis foedatum, ut Gilonem in ipso Gilone quaeras*: 'it is spoiled with so many lacunae that you may search for Gilo in Gilo himself'.[99]

2. E. Martène, *Thesaurus Novus Anecdotorum*, 5 vols. (Paris, 1717), iii. 211–66.

The text contained in the Du Chesne collection remained all that was known of the poem until another collection of recondite works and memorabilia, the *Thesaurus Novus Anecdotorum*, appeared in 1717 under the editorship of Edmond Martène. In his text of the *Historia uiae Hierosolimitanae*, Martène admitted that he had one major advantage over his predecessor, in that while he had been leafing through some manuscript books of the Bibliothèque Saint-Germain, he had come across 'idem Gilonis Parisiensis opus' with a note on it written by Luc d'Achéry, another worthy *savant* of the period: 'sequens historia edita est in fine tom. iv Hist. Franc. SS. Andreae du Chesne at maxima parte differt. Praeterea edita est plena lacunis: ea de causa haec MS digna prelo submitti' ('moreover, the edition was full of gaps: for this reason this manuscript is worthy of publication').[100] It is clear from the information that Martène gives about the location of the manuscript he had found that this is the Paris Saint-Germain manuscript designated in the

[99] E. Martène, *Thesaurus Novus Anecdotorum*, 5 vols. (Paris, 1717), iii. 211, pref.; *PL* clv. 943–4.

[100] Ibid.: 'cum vero nostras Parisiensis S. Germ. bibliothecae codices manuscriptos evolverem, incidit in manus meas idem Gilonis Parisiensis opus cum hac epigraphe Acherii nostri manu exarata: "sequens historia edita est in fine tom. iv Hist. Franc. SS. Andreae du Chesne at maxima parte differt. Praeterea edita est plena lacunis: ea de causa haec MS digna prelo submitti." Hanc cum legissem, statim rapuit me desiderium editum cum MS conferendi, ex cuius collatione reperi non solum ducentas circa lacunas sarciri posse, pluresque locos vitiatos emendari, sed partem libri quarti cum quinto et sexto integro in editis desiderari.'

present edition as A (now Paris, BN, lat. 12945); this is also corroborated by the readings found in Martène's edition, and, as he himself says, he was able by judicious use of the new manuscript to fill in all the lacunae in the text of Gilo. The text Martène printed, however, is irrationally eclectic; he ignored the first three books printed by Du Chesne and attributed to 'Fulco', printing six books only (Gilo's five books and the intercalated book vi) which he assumes are all Gilo's work. He makes no mention of 'Fulco' anywhere, and neither does he discuss the issue raised by the differing contents of the sources, how one contains material not found in the other, and which ought to be given priority. More than this, the addition he supplied about the actual contents of the Sirmond–Du Chesne edition and the Saint-Germain manuscript is incomplete, and does not include all the additions supplied by the first edition. In his book i (book iv of the present edition) he includes ll. 40–1 and 60–119, drawing on the earlier edition for the purpose, and also notes that the *editio* has four verses after v. 120, whereas his manuscript only has two, but on the other hand he totally ignores the addition at the end of this book (357–435), not even mentioning its existence in Sirmond's edition. Elsewhere he is scrupulous in noting in his footnotes variant readings found in Sirmond's work, and verses missing in it but found in his manuscript. However, what is really misleading about Martène's edition is his printing of the intercalated book without any suggestion that it is not found in the Saint-Germain manuscript. In this he follows Du Chesne, who printed only the first three books under the name 'Fulco', and attributed all the rest to Gilo.

This error is even more widespread since Martène's text is the one reprinted in Migne, *Patrologia Latina*, clv. 943–94, which was published in 1854. It also accounts for the erroneous date so long ascribed to the poem.[101] The error is further compounded by Manitius, who writes of 'Der Französe Fulco, der wohl noch ins erste Drittel des 12. Jahrhunderts gehört'.[102] The authorship of the intercalated books is rightly questioned by Louis de Mas-Latrie in the preface to Riant's edition. The Latin paragraph headings which further subdivide the six books in both Martène and Migne are not found in any of the extant MSS, and are presumably the work of Martène himself.

---

[101] See above, Sect. III, p. xxiv. [102] Manitius, *Geschichte*, iii. 667.

3. Dom Berthereau

The work of Dom Berthereau is worthy of mention in this section, since he planned to produce an edition of the poem by Gilo and the Charleville Poet, although he died before the project could be completed. His papers were, however, collected together, and those concerning the First Crusade are now bound together in Paris, BN fr. 9080 (ancien supp. fr. 2503. 16. 10), under the heading 'Recueil des Croisades X'. Those parts which have a direct bearing on the crusade were collected by Riant, and published for the Société de l'Orient Latin of Paris in vol. ii of the *Archives de l'Orient latin* in 1884. In his 'Observatio praevia',[103] Berthereau summarized the earlier work of Du Chesne and Martène, noting in addition that the latter had stated[104] that he had also discovered the poem by Gilo in a 'codex Marchianensis' (now Douai 882, which was once the property of the abbey of Marchiennes; MS B of the current edition). He makes it clear that he took the Charleville Poet (whom he unquestioningly names Fulco, following Sirmond, while he admits that the name does not appear anywhere) at his word, since he comments that the final four lines of book iii show not only that the work is the result of two authors, but serve clearly to distinguish the one from the other,[105] thus assuming that the intercalated book vi and the other additions to the poem came from the pen of Gilo. This becomes clearer still when he states later that he felt that the Du Chesne manuscript was Gilo's first attempt at the poem, while the Martène edition represented the same poet's work, but with corrections and alterations.[106] In view of the contents of the Charleville manuscript and its similarity to the legendary stories found in Albert of Aachen, the priority of the five books by Gilo over the rest is quite certain. Berthereau left among his papers printed texts of the *Historia uiae Hierosolimitanae* by Sirmond–Du Chesne and by Martène, with summaries, notes, and corrections, and a list of variants of Gilo from the Paris manuscript BN lat. 5129 (MS C in the present edition). He also left a

---

[103] Printed in *Archives de l'Orient latin*, ii. 130, and in *RHC (Hist. occ.)* v. 695–6.

[104] *Amplissima Collectio*, ed. E. Martène (Paris, 1724–33), v. 507.

[105] *RHC (Hist. occ.)*, v. 695–6: 'quibus verbis non solum huius historiae duplex auctor, sed etiam ab alterutro planius innotescit.'

[106] Ibid.: 'ducor ad suspicandum Chesnianum exemplar primigenium opus esse Gilonis; Martenianum vero opus idem esse ab ipso Gilone correctum et emendatum.'

further copy of Martène's text with other collations and philo-
logical notes.[107]

4. P. Riant, *Recueil des historiens des croisades: Historiens Occidentaux*, v
(Paris, 1895).

This edition, the latest prior to the present one, was the first to take
account of all the known manuscripts of the text, and the sigla used
by Riant are therefore followed in the present edition. However,
Riant's use of the manuscripts was far from methodical or scien-
tific; he made no attempt to discover their relationships, and
adopted readings in a haphazard fashion. In addition his reporting
of the readings is not always accurate or complete; the agreement
of BCF against ADG, and especially of DE, is far more frequent
than his footnotes indicate. Riant also perpetuates the error of
attributing the intercalated book vi to Gilo, as Mas-Latrie, writing
in the preface to the poem in the introduction to the volume,
makes clear.[108]   Riant's reporting of the more difficult readings in
the Charleville manuscript is not always trustworthy; this manu-
script was already in a very poor state when Sirmond read it in the
seventeenth century. Riant frequently relies on Sirmond in the Du
Chesne edition for his text of the Charleville Poet's work; the use
of an ultraviolet lamp for the preparation of the present edition
shows that some of what Sirmond printed was (educated) guess-
work, especially in places where the text can only just be picked
out, even under artificial light. On other occasions, where ultra-
violet or infrared has revealed the true reading, Riant shows by his
lacunae that he found the manuscript impossible to read. Where
his readings differ from the truth, they are noted in the *apparatus
criticus* of the current edition. The prologue to Riant's text, by
Louis de Mas-Latrie, is discussed at length above.[109]

IX. RELATIONSHIPS WITH OTHER SOURCES

The interrelationship between the various sources on the First
Crusade is complex and often far from clear. The earliest accounts
of the expedition are eyewitness narratives written by four par-
ticipants: the priests Fulcher of Chartres, Peter Tudebod, and

---

[107] *Archives de l'Orient latin*, ii. 130.   [108] *RHC* (*Hist. occ.*), v. cxl–cxlvii.
[109] See above, Sect. I, p. xvii.

Raymond of Aguilers, and the anonymous lay author of the *Gesta Francorum*, who seems to have been a member of Bohemond's contingent. Fulcher served as chaplain to Baldwin of Boulogne, and accompanied his lord to Edessa, while Raymond was the chaplain of Raymond of Toulouse. Further histories were written by Bartolf of Nangis, Ekkehard of Aura, and Ralph of Caen, who visited the East soon after the crusade. Most valuable, however, for the development of the *idea* of the crusade were the chronicles of the expedition written by four learned clerics in the West: Robert of Rheims, a former abbot of Saint-Remi; Guibert, abbot of Nogent; Baldric of Bourgueil, archbishop of Dol, all three writing in the first decade of the twelfth century; and Albert of Aachen, writing in its first quarter.[110]

Although von Sybel, the first scholar to treat the problem, supposed that both Gilo and the Charleville Poet drew on the anonymous *Gesta Francorum* and 'quite useless oral narratives',[111] the closest parallel to Gilo's work is Robert of Rheims' *Historia Hierosolimitana*. This was pointed out by Theodor Wolff, though his inability correctly to distinguish between Gilo and the Charleville Poet confused the analysis he made. Although there is only one phrase common to both sources,[112] their description of events is often very similar.[113] They also agree on details such as numbers and dates,[114] both refer to the use of poisoned arrows during the siege of Nicaea,[115] and they are the only sources to mention the wounding of Bohemond[116] and the truce after the first siege of

[110] There are 'strong reasons for supposing that [Robert of Rheims's *Historia Iherosolimitana*] was completed by 1107': Riley-Smith, *Idea of Crusading*, p. 136, who also gives dates of 'between 1104 and 1108' for Guibert of Nogent's *Gesta Dei per Francos* and 1108 for Baldric of Dol's *Historia Iherosolimitana*. Albert of Aachen's work was probably completed before 1119 and possibly much earlier. For the importance of the development of the *idea* of the crusade, see Riley-Smith, *Idea of Crusading*, pp. 135–6.

[111] 'Sehr unbrauchbare mündliche Mitteilungen'. Quoted by B. von Kugler, *Albert von Aachen* (Stuttgart, 1889), p. 421.

[112] Gilo, v. 38 and Robert of Rheims, p. 776.

[113] There are close similarities between the descriptions of the siege of Nicaea (Gilo, iv. 45–59, Robert of Rheims, p. 756) and certain aspects of the capture of Jerusalem (Gilo, ix. 242–76; Robert of Rheims, pp. 866–7).

[114] For example, the size of the force which accompanied Bohemond and Robert of Flanders on their foraging expedition from Antioch. Gilo and Robert stated that it numbered 30,000 (Gilo, v. 104; Robert of Rheims, p. 778) whereas the *Gesta*, p. 30, maintained that it was 20,000. Similarly they estimated that Kerbogha's army was 300,000 strong (Gilo, iv. 166–7, Robert of Rheims, p. 759), whereas Raymond of Aguilers, p. 45, estimated 150,000. Both also stated that the siege of Antioch lasted ten months.

[115] Book iv, n. 24.   [116] Book vii, n. 37.

Antioch.[117] They also single out for particular mention crusaders such as Gérard of Melion and Guarin of Petramora, who do not figure highly in the other primary accounts.[118]

There are also, however, significant differences. Whereas Robert provided an eyewitness account of the council of Clermont, Gilo's history of the First Crusade commences with the siege of Nicaea. In this respect, it is possible that Gilo's source was similar to if not identical with the one to which Robert refers in his Prologue. Robert wrote his history at the express command of Abbot Bernard, who had access to a written account of the Crusade, but disliked it for a number of reasons, as Robert describes:

for a certain abbot named Bernard of Marmoutier, a man well known for his knowledge of literature and his upright conduct, showed me a history which followed this subject-matter, but which displeased him somewhat, partly because it did not have its beginning, which concerned the council of Clermont, and because its composition was weak and its style coarse. He therefore instructed me, since I was present at Clermont, to place a head upon this decapitated subject-matter and set it out for its readers with a more accurate pen.[119]

From this it is clear that Robert's source lacked any discussion of the council of Clermont, though it is not clear whether this was because the copy was damaged, or whether it simply omitted any mention of the event. As well as using the word *historia*, a 'history' or 'account', Robert also speaks of the *leuitas carminis*, the 'slightness of verse', which made it so displeasing to Bernard and made his task of rewriting it more onerous. From this it appears that the source was at least partly in verse; this could be the origin of the hexameter lines found in Robert's work. Robert probably began his work before 1107, as this was the year in which Abbot Bernard died, though its composition may have continued in succeeding years.[120]

It is most unlikely that Robert was drawing on Gilo himself for his history of the crusade. He calls his source *inculta*, 'unpolished' or 'rough', on two counts, firstly because what he calls its *series...materiei* or 'ordering of the subject-matter' was disjointed, and

[117] Book v, n. 88.   [118] Book vii, n. 91, ix, n. 22.
[119] Robert of Rheims, *prologue*.
[120] A. C. Krey, 'A neglected passage in the *Gesta*', *The Crusades and Other Historical Essays Presented to D. C. Munro by his Students*, ed. L. J. Paetow (New York, 1928), pp. 57–78, at 74–5.

secondly because its *litteralium compositio dictionum*, its 'manner of literary expression', was offensive to Abbot Bernard. Gilo may not be uniformly brilliant as a stylist, but he does demonstrate an excellent command of the Latin hexameter, and his expression can be very well developed and attractive, particularly in some of his similes. He is certainly not coarse or crude in his writing. However, many of the hexameters which Robert inserted into his work very closely resemble lines of Gilo, and one verse is absolutely identical,[121] which (along with other factors) points to a close affinity between their source material.

It is equally unlikely that Gilo used Robert as a source; Robert's history contains a host of episodes which Gilo does not include, and if he did draw on Robert, then he was peculiarly eclectic in his handling of the material. The evidence suggests rather that both Robert and Gilo had access to a common source which lacked any detail on the early part of the crusade, and especially the council of Clermont. Robert seems also to have used the *Gesta Francorum* and a number of other written sources in writing his account, and also had access to oral traditions.[122]

Gilo also provides additional details not found in Robert's account: for example, the death of the French royal constable, Gualo of Chaumont-en-Vexin, is mentioned by several sources, though he is not always precisely identified. Gilo and Robert go further and describe his wife's inconsolable grief, but only Gilo names her as Humberga.[123] Gilo also refers to individuals such as Lethold of Tournai and William of Sabran, who are not named by Robert,[124] and sometimes differs from Robert on points of detail.[125] In addition in his imagery and use of particular words Gilo was influenced by the four eyewitness accounts of the expedition. There are parallels with Fulcher of Chartres's description of the battle of Dorylaeum[126] and with the *Gesta Francorum*'s account of the suffering experienced by the crusaders during the siege of Jerusalem.[127]

---

[121] Book v. 39, *partim predati partimque fuere necati*, is also found in Robert of Rheims, p. 776, and (presumably copied from Robert) in the *Historia Gotfridi*, ii. 2, and *Balduini III Historia Nicaena uel Antiochena*, p. 22.

[122] H. Glaesner, 'La prise d'Antioche en 1098', *Revue belge de philologie et d'histoire*, xix (1940), 65–88, at p. 66.

[123] Book v, n. 91.   [124] Book ix, nn. 58, 78.

[125] For example, Gilo states that the Emir of Tripoli sent Raymond of Toulouse a gift of seven horses (viii. 370), whereas Robert and the *Gesta* both assert that there were ten.

[126] Book iv, nn. 45, 46, 59.   [127] Book ix, n. 53.

In his studies on Albert of Aachen, Knoch notes evidence that there was a quite widespread diffusion of traditions about the crusade in the early twelfth century.[128] One strand of this survives in the form of the vernacular *Chanson d'Antioche*; there is a number of close similarities to passages in this poem in Gilo's work, especially at vii. 400–97, where Kerbogha's troops are vanquished by the Christians in a 'do-or-die' battle. The similarities are as follows (*CA* = *Chanson d'Antioche*; *RM* = Robert of Rheims; *GF* = *Gesta Francorum*; *AA* = Albert of Aachen; *CAP* = *Chanson d'Antioche en Provençal*):

1. Kerbogha offers to decide the battle by ordeal by combat (*CA* 8396–419, 8420–33 *CAP* 245–7)
2. Bohemond refuses (*CA* 8440–62 says Robert of Normandy does so)
3. Hugh leads the attack (*CA* 8625–37; *RM* vii. 11)
4. Mention of Everard of Le Puiset (*CA* 9150)
5. Bohemond recalls Hugh (*CA* 8625–37)
6. Godfrey fights alongside them (*GF* iv. 39; *CA* 8689)
7. 'Lucas' of Damascus and other kings fight against the Franks (*CA* 9015–26 lists many other kings besides)
8. Odo de Beaugency the standard-bearer dies (*RM* viii. 12, *CA* 8650, 8670)
9. William of Benium takes over from him (*CA* 8661–7, *RM* viii. 12)
10. The Turks set the grass on fire (*CA* 9107–21, *RM* vii. 14, *GF* ix. 39, *AA* iv. 49)
11. Rainald of Beauvais (*CA* 8978, *RM* vii. 15)
12. Pagan (*CA* 9153, 9163)
13. Thomas (*CA* 9152, 9163, *RM* vii. 15)
14. Drogo (*CA* 9152, 9163)
15. Clarebaldus (*CA* 9152, 9163)
16. The Turks attack again (*CA* 9143–9, *RM* vii. 15)
17. Gérard of Melion, an old man, dies (*CA* 9145, *RM* vii. 15)

Other similarities with the *Chanson d'Antioche* may be noted. First, there is the emphasis in Gilo on the campaign at Antioch itself: in Gilo's poem this occupies two whole books (a similar emphasis is to be found in the *Gesta Francorum*; the siege of Antioch was a far more costly and arduous undertaking than the siege of Jerusalem).

[128] *Studien zu Albert von Aachen*, p. 48.

Second, there is the fact, already noted above, that Gilo's poem omits all events prior to the siege of Nicaea; like the *Chanson d'Antioche*, it begins its account with the crusade already under way. In addition is the small but very significant point that Gilo regards the Byzantine general Statinus exactly as the *Chanson d'Antioche* does, namely as friendly to the Franks, whereas all the other accounts regard him as a hostile figure. Both Gilo and the vernacular poet also stress his facial disfigurement (*Estatins l'Esnasé*). This link with the *Chanson d'Antioche* finds support from Tiedau,[129] who sees a primitive *Chanson d'Antioche* as the source for many details in Albert of Aachen, Gilo, Robert, and other versions.

Gilo's continuator, the Charleville Poet, makes use of the word *pagina*,[130] which may imply that for his part of the poem, he was working from a written source. Indeed, Mas-Latrie pointed out that the contributions he made to the poem bore similarities to Albert of Aachen's *Historia Hierosolimitana*.[131] Duparc-Quioc follows Cahen in asserting that Albert was indeed Gilo's principal source.[132] Albert also makes Godfrey of Bouillon the hero of his tale, and both authors describe the Peasants' Crusade in detail. *Pagina* is, however, used a little later on simply as a reference to another part of the poem,[133] and its significance should not be exaggerated. Moreover, many of the parallels are often scanty, and suggest that the poet was drawing on a mutual source rather than directly on Albert's own work, and there are also some significant differences: the Charleville Poet does not show the same sympathy for Peter the Hermit that Albert of Aachen does, and introduces him baldly as *eremita Petrus quidam*.[134] He is also, by contrast with Albert, sceptical about Stephen of Blois's illness.[135]

The location and probable origin of the manuscript itself so close to Bouillon might indicate that the poet would have been ideally situated to draw on the oral tradition of 'crusade stories from Lorraine' as Knoch calls it. Koehler pointed out in his introduction to Riant's edition that the use of the word *Transrhenani* at i. 184 shows that the poet meant the right bank of the river.[136] Duparc-Quioc[137] adds that the poet's method of dating the council

---

[129] Quoted by L. A. Sumberg, *La Chanson d'Antioche, étude et analyse* (Paris, 1968), p. 15.
[130] Book i. 248.   [131] *RHC* (*Hist. occ.*) v. cxlii.
[132] Duparc-Quioc, 'Poème latin', p. 38; C. Cahen, *La Syrie du nord à l'époque des croisades et la principauté franque d'Antioche*, 2 vols. (Paris, 1940), i. 15 n. 1.
[133] i. 257.   [134] ii. 6.   [135] i. 213–26; Albert of Aachen, p. 398.
[136] *RHC* (*Hist. occ.*) v. cxliii.   [137] Duparc-Quioc, 'Poème latin', p. 38.

of Clermont at i. 86, saying that it was held in the reigns of Philip I of France and Henry IV of Lorraine, adds additional weight to this argument. However, the divergences listed above show that the Charleville Poet was not dependent on Albert for his primary source, and there are some verses in the Charleville Poet's work that point to an oral report for the origin of his material.[138] Wolff[139] suggested that the work of both Gilo and the Charleville Poet was related to Albert of Aachen, but Knoch dismisses this theory and expresses a preference for the opinion of Manitius that the Charleville Poet shares a common source with Albert, and this on the whole seems to be the best way of explaining the presence of such episodes as are found in the Charleville Poet's work. Each author appears to be drawing on a different strand of related material, which would account for the similarities in subject-matter and also for the sharp divergences in the detail of their stories.

Neither Gilo nor the Charleville Poet were participants in the First Crusade, and their contribution to the telling of the heroic tale of the achievements of the *milites Christi* cannot be described as a primary or indispensable source for the events of the expedition like Fulcher of Chartres or the *Gesta Francorum*. That said, both poets make distinct contributions to the corpus of First Crusade historiography, incorporating material from what appear to be eyewitness accounts, and drawing from both the vernacular (the *Chanson d'Antioche*) and the Latin traditions.

Their work is therefore of value, and deserves its place in what might be described as the second stage of First Crusade historiography represented by Baldric of Dol, Robert of Rheims, and Guibert of Nogent. Like them, Gilo was a monk in the Benedictine tradition, and his purpose seems to have been like theirs, namely to 'rework in better language a popular eyewitness account of the crusade . . . because they felt the subject merited proper literary treatment'.[140] The importance of the poem thus lies not in its being an immediate witness to the event which it describes, but rather in the way it witnesses to the development of the *idea* of the crusade.

Professor Riley-Smith has noted of Robert, Baldric, and Guibert that 'intelligent minds were working in the decade after

---

[138] iv. 418: *quod nunc accipimus a nostra gente.*

[139] T. Wolff, *Die Bauernkreuzzüge des Jahres 1096* (Tübingen, 1891), p. 1. Cf. also B. von Kugler, *Analekten zur Kritik Alberts von Aachen* (Stuttgart, 1888), p. 4; Knoch, *Studien zu Albert von Aachen*, pp. 89–90; cf. Manitius, *Geschichte*, iii. 667–70.

[140] Riley-Smith, *Idea of Crusading*, p. 138.

the fall of Jerusalem . . . in them we find an intellectual expression of the semi-popular ideology forged in the traumas of the expedition'.[141] The same might be said of Gilo, whose work is clearly associated with that of Robert of Rheims. The difference between Gilo and his three fellow Benedictine authors is that whereas the other writers stayed within the genre of prose history, Gilo chose the epic form, to restate the heroic enterprise that the Christian knights had undertaken in a style which did justice to the glory of their achievement. Moreover, the composite nature of the work as it was revised by the Charleville Poet brings in a further strand of the development of the *idea* of the crusade, bringing in episodes like those found in Albert of Aachen which have more in common with the background of the *Chansons de Geste* and of folk-tale than the considered, theological writings of the Benedictine scholars. They also stand as witnesses to the development of the *concept* of the crusade and to the different possibilities for emphasis that lay in the narrative, Gilo's work giving pride of place to Bohemond, Baldwin and Tancred, while the Charleville Poet redresses the balance, as it were, and places his hero, Godfrey of Bouillon, firmly in the centre of the stage.

X. EDITORIAL CONVENTIONS

To distinguish the work of Gilo from that of the Charleville Poet, the former is printed in Roman type and the latter in italic. Cross-references to the work in the footnotes are by book and line.

[141] Ibid., p. 139.

HISTORIA VIE HIEROSOLIMITANE

SIGLA

A   Paris, BN lat. 12945
B   Douai, Bibliothèque Municipale 882
C   Paris, BN lat. 5129
D   Brussels, Bibliothèque Royale Albert 1ᵉʳ, 10615–10729
F   Rome, Biblioteca Vallicelliana B. 33
G   Charleville-Mézières, Bibliothèque Municipale 97

The following abbreviations are also used in the apparatus:

m. pr.   first hand
m. alt.   second hand (of two)
m. sec.   second hand (of more than two)
m. tert.   third hand
cod.   codex (i.e. the reading of the MS itself where the text is reported only by one MS)

LIBER I

Incipit libellus uiae nostri temporis Hierosolimitanae

Inclyta gesta ducum perscribere magnanimorum
Fert animus,[1] patrum qui fortia facta suorum
Non solum magnis successibus aequiperare
Sed maiore fide certarunt exsuperare.
Ardor inest, inquam, sententia fixaque menti,[2]   5
Versibus et numeris transmittere posteritati
Qualiter instinctu deitatis et auspice nutu[a]
Est aggressa uia memorando nobilis actu,
Qua sacrosancti uiolantes iura sepulchri
Digna receperunt meriti commercia praui,[3]   10
Inque suis Francis antiqua resurgere Troia[4]
Coepit et edomuit Christo contraria regna.
Ista nihil fictum, nil tegmine fraudis amictum,
Sed puri ueri referet narratio fructum.
Non hic Pegasei gestimus pocula fontis,   15
Nec Parnasiaci spelea loquacia montis,[5]
Nec libet Aonio deducere uertice Musas,
Quas sibi ter ternas finxit mendosa uetustas,[6]
Sed petimus trina uirtus deitatis et una

Rore suae lucis nostra arida colluat ora,   20
Clarificet pingues tersa caligine uisus,
Exacuatque hebetes subtili indagine sensus
Materie ut tanta ualeamus promere[b] digna,
Dictaque cum factis sint uel uicina uel aequa;

This book is found only in G   [a] nutu *cod.;* cultu *Sirmond, Riant*   [b] promere
m. alt.; dicere *m. pr.*

---

[1] Ovid, *Met.* i. 1–2, xii. 575; Persius, *Sat.* iv. 7; Maximianus, *Elegiae,* v. 36; Sidonius Apollinaris, *Carm.* vii. 197.

[2] Cf. Claudian, *In Ruf.* i. 1.

[3] Rom. 6: 23. This theme of the violation of the Holy Places, in particular the Holy Sepulchre, and the suffering endured by Christians in the East, is brought out in the

BOOK I

Here begins the little book of the journey to Jerusalem which took place in our time

My mind moves me[1] *to describe the celebrated actions of the great-hearted leaders who strove not only to equal the brave deeds of their fathers by their great achievement, but to outdo them in deeper faith.* [5] *I am fired, I say, and my mind is firmly set,*[2] *to pass on to posterity in verse how, by the impulse and auspicious favour of God, in a memorable fashion the noble journey was undertaken by which those who were violating the rights of the Holy Sepulchre* [10] *deservedly received fitting wages*[3] *for their evil deeds; how Troy of old*[4] *began in her own Franks to rise again, and crushed the kingdoms hostile to Christ. This account shall set forth no fiction, nor anything shrouded in the cloak of deceit, but rather the fruit of pure truth.* [15] *Here we do not wish for the cups of Pegasus' fountain, nor the chattering caves of Mount Parnassus,*[5] *nor are we pleased to bring down the Muses from the Aonian summit, those nine whom mendacious antiquity*[6] *invented for itself, but we beseech the glory of God the three-in-one to moisten our parched lips with the dew of his light,* [20] *to sweep away the fog and enlighten our bleary eyes, and to sharpen our slothful senses with his searching subtlety, so that we may prove capable of writing things worthy of such great subject-matter, and our words may come near to or equal the deeds they describe;* [25] *and that*

four eyewitness accounts of Urban II's sermon at Clermont (Robert of Rheims, pp. 727–30; Fulcher of Chartres, pp. 132–8; Baldric of Dol, pp. 12–16; Guibert of Nogent, pp. 137–41); and Urban's letter to the people of Flanders, *Die Kreuzzugsbriefe*, pp. 136–7. See also J. S. C. Riley-Smith, 'Crusading as an act of love', *History*, lxv (1980), 177–92, at pp. 190–1.

[4] Vergil, *Aen.* i. 206, *illic fas regna resurgere Troiae*. The legend that the Franks were descended from the Trojan race can be traced back to the Chronicle of Fredegar, especially ii. 2. 5–6, dating from the mid-7th c. See *The Fourth Book of the Chronicle of Fredegar with its Continuations*, ed. J. M. Wallace-Hadrill (NMT, 1960), pp. xi–xii. Cf. also E. Faral, *La Légende arthurienne: Études et documents*, 3 vols. (Paris, 1929), i. 262–93. Some French historians of the First Crusade regarded the Franks as God's chosen people (e.g. Robert of Rheims, pp. 723, 727; Raymond of Aguilers, pp. 79–80), and Guibert of Nogent entitled his history of the expedition *Gesta Dei per Francos*. See Riley-Smith, 'The First Crusade and St. Peter', pp. 45–7.

[5] Persius, *Sat.*, *Prol.* 1–2. The rejection of the pagan Muses and consequent turning to Christ itself became a poetic topos in both early and late Christian poetry. See Curtius, *European Literature*, pp. 233, 235.

[6] Proba, *Cent. Verg.* 17 (= Vergil, *Georg.* iii. 11).

Quique uel infantum linguas facit esse disertas,[1]   25
Mutisque et brutis uoces[2] *dedit articulatas,*[a]
Auferat a nobis puerilia brutaque sensa,
Conferat et nobis matura et congrua pensa,
Queque dedit ducibus magnis euincere posse,
Concedat nobis gratanter dicere nosse,   30
Vt bene gesta patrum reminiscens emula virtus
Euolet ad similes per flammam pectoris actus.[3]
Sed prelibati quoniam satis[b] *esse uidetur,*
Propositam seriem iam nunc stilus aggrediatur.

Multorum spatio feritas pagana dierum,   35
Nisibus omnimodis Domino contraria rerum,
Vrbem Hierusalem seua ditione tenebat,
Christicolasque inibi nimia asperitate premebat,
Hinc Domini uiolans polluta per idola templum,[4]
Illinc catholicis claudens uitale sepulchrum.   40
Nulli namque aditus uel ad hec uel ad illa patebat
Si non preueniens merces iter expediebat;[5]
Et cum Paschali[c] *festo resonantibus ymnis*
Expectabatur super affore celicus ignis,[6]
Tum uice flammicome ferrata lucerna papyri   45
Aptabatur, auens diuino obstare nitori.
Cum tamen omnipotens sua per miracula numen
Ferro ceu stuppe clarum daret edere lumen,
fo. 61ʳ   *Hostis deuictus, sed non compunctus in istis,*
Temptabat stolidis celestia dona sagittis,   50
Vt circum sacri laquearia fulgida tecti[7]

---

[a] arsitulatas *m. pr.*   [b] satis *Sirmond;* sates *cod.*   [c] Paschale *m. pr.*

---

[1] Ps. 8: 3, Matt. 21: 16.

[2] Matt. 15: 31, Mark 7: 37.

[3] The Franks were urged to follow the example of their ancestors, in particular Charlemagne, from whom several of the leaders of the First Crusade, including Godfrey of Bouillon, were descended. See Riley-Smith, 'The First Crusade and St. Peter', pp. 47–8; Robert of Rheims, p. 728. By the end of the 11th c., the legend had developed that after his victory over the Muslims in Spain, Charlemagne had travelled to Jerusalem and established a Frankish protectorate there. See R. Folz, *Le Souvenir et la légende de Charlemagne dans l'Empire germanique médiéval* (Paris, 1905), pp. 337–44, and *Le Voyage de Charlemagne*, ed. P. Aebischer (Geneva, 1965); E. Delaruelle, 'Essai sur la formation de l'idée de croisade', *Bulletin de littérature ecclésiastique*, iv (1954), 50–63, at p. 59; Riley-Smith, 'The First Crusade and St. Peter', pp. 48–9.

[4] Ovid, *Met.* vii. 17. The Seljuk Turks had captured Jerusalem from the Fatimids in

he who makes eloquent the tongues even of infants[1] *and gave rational speech to the mute and dumb*[2] *may remove from us childish and stupid understanding, and endow us with adult and fitting thought,* [30] *and that he may bestow on us knowledge to speak pleasingly of those things which he granted the mighty leaders the power to accomplish, so that mindful of the good deeds of our fathers, and seeking to rival them, our vigour shall spring up to similar achievements through the desire burning in our hearts.*[3] *But since that seems to be enough of a foretaste, let our pen now set about the proposed order of events.*

[35] *Over a period of many days, the heathen, in their barbarity, striving to oppose the Lord of the Universe in every way they could, held the city of Jerusalem under their savage rule, and oppressed the followers of Christ there with savage harshness. They outraged the temple of the Lord God with foul idols,*[4] [40] *and closed off the living sepulchre to Catholic people; for access to the one or the other place lay open to no man unless payment in advance opened the road up to him;*[5] *and when at the Easter festival with hymns resounding the heavenly fire was expected to come down,*[6] [45] *then an iron wick was put in the place of the flame-bearing papyrus, with the intention of hindering the divine ardour. But when the almighty Spirit, working his miracles, made the iron give a bright light like that of tow, the thwarted enemy still did not repent of these deeds, and stubbornly assailed the heavenly gifts with uncomprehending arrows, so that around the glittering panelled roof*[7] *you could see a whole*

1071. The worship of idols is also mentioned by Robert of Rheims, p. 727 and Baldric of Dol, p. 12. See below, ii. 186 and n. The crusaders may have mistaken an ancient statue of Jupiter for an idol. See X. Muratova, 'Western chronicles of the First Crusade as sources for the history of art in the Holy Land', *Crusader Art in the Twelfth Century*, ed. J. Folda, British School of Archaeology in Jerusalem–BAR International Series, clii (1982), 47–71. Similar accounts of the Muslims' idolatry were reportedly given by Urban II in his sermon at Clermont.

[5] Guibert of Nogent, p. 140. For the difficulties experienced by pilgrims in the 11th c., see S. Runciman, 'The pilgrimages to Palestine before 1095', in id., *History of the Crusades*, 3 vols. (Cambridge, 1951), i. 77–8.

[6] The earliest account of the miracle of the Holy Fire was given by a Breton pilgrim, Bernard the Wise, in about 870: *The Itinerary of Bernard the Wise*, trans. J. H. Bernard, Palestine Pilgrim Texts Society, iii (London, 1893), p. 71. See also P. Riant, 'Lettre du clerc Nicetas à Constantin VII Porphyrogénète sur le feu sacré (avril 942)', *Archives de l'Orient latin*, i (1881), 375–83. For Arab references to this miracle, see A. S. Tritton, 'The Easter Fire at Jerusalem', *Journal of the Royal Asiatic Society*, 1963/2, 249–50. The Charleville Poet's description is particularly detailed, but early 12th-c. references to this miracle are also to be found in Ekkehard of Aura, *Hierosolymita*, p. 49; Baldric of Dol, p. 13; and a very full account is given by *Tudebodus Imitatus et Continuatus*, p. 102. See also B. McGinn, 'Iter Sancti Sepulchri: the piety of the first crusaders', in *Essays in Medieval Civilisation*, ed. B. K. Lackner and K. R. Philips (Arlington, Tex, 1978), pp. 33–5; J. Prawer, *The Latin Kingdom of Jerusalem* (London, 1972), pp. 172–80.

[7] Vergil, *Aen.* viii. 25, Silius Italicus, *Punica*, vii. 142.

Confixam segetem potuisses cernere ferri.
Sin uero hec tarde miracula proueniebant,
Tempore nec solito sacra lumina se referebant,
Tum gladii circum sacra limina triste micabant,   55
Atque pios capitum discrimine terrificabant
Ni precibus celerem impetrarent affore lucem.
Nec cita nec tarda sedabant[a] signa furorem.

Sic Arabes, Persae, Moedi simul atque Elamite,[1]
Assyrii, Allophyli, Parthi quoque Caspiadaeque   60
Et que mille colunt gentes Babylonia regna,
Quas Nilus, Eufrates, quas Tigridis alluit unda,
Aduersus celum coniurata arma[2] ferebant,
Et ueluti Phlegrae certamina[3] restituebant,
Sic ut et omne sacrum penitus ne[b] dirueretur   65
Multa Dei seruis auraria praeciperetur,
Presulis Euthymii[4] quod epistola significauit
Dum sua per Gallos legatio peruolitauit,
Nec columen sperans armorum exercituumque
Quesiuit potius auri solamen opemque.   70
Cuius ad egregium querimonia tunc Godefridum[5]
Nomine scripta tenus lacrimarum mouit abyssum,
Dum gentile nefas, dum blasphemantia uerba
Replicat, inque pios minitantia dicta uel acta.[6]

Talibus et tantis Deitas permota procellis,   75
Sanctorumque etiam grauibus pulsata querelis
Mouit belligeras per plurima regna cateruas,
Vt super his iustas inflammarentur in iras,
Et pro uindicta pietatis suscipienda
Corpora cum uita ferrent in aperta pericla.   80
Qualiter hoc autem uel quo sit tempore gestum,
Ordo sequens operis non differet inreseratum.

Anno milleno sexto deciesque noueno
A Patris Verbo uelamine carnis amicto,[7]
Cum rex eximius Francorum sceptra Phylippus   85

fo. 61ᵛ

---

[a] sedabant m. pr.   [b] ne cod.; tunc Sirmond, Riant

---

[1] Acts 2: 9, Ps. 55(56), Vulgate heading. *Allophyli* strictly means 'foreigners'; the Charleville Poet here uses it as a proper name, following the usage found in the Fathers.
[2] Ovid, *Met.* xv. 763.
[3] Ovid, *Met.* x. 151, Statius, *Achilleid*, i. 484, *Thebaid*, ii. 595–601.

harvest of iron fixed there. But if ever these miracles were late in occurring, and the holy light did not appear at the usual time, [55] *swords gleamed harshly around the holy shrine, striking the devout Christians with the fear of being beheaded if by their prayers they did not succeed in making the light appear. Whether early or late, these signs did nothing to abate their fury. And so the Arabs, the Persians, the Medes and the Elamites,*[1] [60] *the Assyrians, the Philistines, the Parthians and Caspiadeans, and the thousand races that dwell in the kingdom of Babylon, those whom the waters of the Nile, the Euphrates, and the Tigris flow by, swore an oath and took up arms against heaven,*[2] *as though renewing the struggles of Phlegra.*[3] [65] *And, lest every holy place be utterly destroyed, a great quantity of gold was to be levied on the servants of God, a fact which the letter of Bishop Euthymius*[4] *made known when his legation hastened on its way among the Gauls, and, not hoping for the support of an army of fighting men,* [70] *sought rather the assistance and aid of gold. The bishop's protest, addressed by name to noble Godfrey,*[5] *moved him to a flood of tears, as he reflected on the wickedness of the heathen and their blasphemous words,*[6] *their threatening speech and behaviour towards the godly.* [75] *Provoked by so many great outbursts of violence of this kind, and disturbed by the anguished cries of his holy people, God stirred up companies of warriors throughout many realms to burn with righteous anger over all these things,* [80] *and to expose their bodies — their lives, even — to overt dangers as they sought to avenge true religion. The plan of the following work will not leave unmentioned how or at what time this happened.*

In the one-thousand-and-ninety-sixth year since the Word of the Father took on a covering of flesh,[7] [85] *when the noble King Philip bore the sceptre of the*

[4] No other history of the First Crusade mentions this legation, but the Charleville Poet is probably referring to an embassy sent by Patriarch Euthymius of Jerusalem in 1088 and headed by Abbot Sergius of Jerusalem. A. Gieysztor, 'The genesis of the crusades: the encyclical of Sergius IV (1009–1092)', *Medievalia et Humanistica*, vi (1948), 3–34, at p. 25 n. 102, published the text of an agreement dated 8 May 1088 between Sergius and the Cluniac abbot of Moissac, whereby the latter was given lands belonging to Jerusalem at La Salvetat de Montcorbeil, in return for an annual rent to be paid to collectors sent by the patriarch. See also H. E. J. Cowdrey, 'Cluny and the First Crusade', *Revue Bénédictine*, lxxxiii (1973), 285–311, at pp. 296–7. The patriarch of Jerusalem is shown in discussions with Peter the Hermit in the *Chanson d'Antioche*, ll. 266 ff.

[5] There is no other evidence that the patriarch of Jerusalem addressed a specific appeal for aid to Godfrey, but the latter was of course the hero of the Charleville Poet's work.

[6] Caffaro, pp. 99–100, links Godfrey's decision to take the Cross with a visit to Raymond of Toulouse, and a vision at the shrine of the Virgin Mary at Le Puy; the Chronicler of Zimmern associates it with a vow made during the siege of Rome in 1081: Hagenmeyer, pp. 22–3. The portrayal of Godfrey's character here accords well with what other sources reveal about him; see J. C. Anderessohn, *The Ancestry and Life of Godfrey de Bouillon* (Bloomington, Ind., 1947).

[7] Prudentius, *Apoth.* 333–4.

Ferret, et Heinricus[a] *regeret Lotharingica quartus,*[1]
Contigit Vrbanum Romanis pontificantem
Gallorum fines inuisere iura dicantem
Ecclesiis Christi, sua commoda prospicientem,
Pro meritis poenas et premia constituentem.   90
Hic postquam primum gelidas pertransiit Alpes
Famaque precessit discurrens per regiones,
Vndique conueniunt[b] *diuersis agmina uotis,*
Diuersi cultus, diuerse conditionis,
Multa super multis passim rogitantia[2] *causis,*   95
Plurimaque ex uariis responsa petentia curis,[3]
Pars[c] *auscultandi studio noua siue uidendi,*
Pars quoque discendi nihilo minus atque docendi.
Qui, quia non cunctis[d] *per singula sufficiebat,*
Sepius atque eadem repeti non suppeditabat,   100
Concilium statuit generale indicere cunctis,
Atque ibi proposita simul et semel edere multis.
Vrbs Aruernorum Clarmontis nomine dicta
Huius concilii locus extitit; huc reuocata
Agmina concurrunt que misit Gallia tota   105
(Nam tres in partes ea noscitur esse dirempta,[4]
Hinc Belgis Celtisque colentibus, hinc Aquitanis,
Legibus et studiis distantibus atque loquelis).

fo. 62[r]   *Quo postquam uentum et de pluribus est agitatum,*
Et uice concordi finita negotia centum,[5]   110
Inspirante Deo se questio maxima iecit
Et memorata satis querimonia pectora mouit
De domibus Christo carnem gestante sacratis
Et modo paganis male ritibus obtenebratis.
Vrbem Hierusalem, primum caput ecclesiarum,   115
Matrem ac nutricem sanctorum discipulorum
Atque inspectricem signorum uiuificorum,
Sanguine sacratam primorum martyriorum,
Nunc fore[e] *speluncam*[f] *protectricemque latronum,*
Perque eius caueam lacerari membra piorum   120

[a] Henricus *Sirmond, Riant*   [b] conueniunt *cod.;* concurrunt *Sirmond, Riant*
[c] parrs *cod.*   [d] cunctis *cod., Sirmond;* cunctos *Riant*   [e] foret *m. pr.*
[f] speluncam *m. pr.*

[1] Philip I of France (1060–1108) had been excommunicated at the time by Urban II for his adultery with the wife of Count Fulk of Anjou. It is interesting that the domain

Franks, and Henry the Fourth[1] *ruled over Lorraine, it happened that Urban the bishop of Rome visited the Gallic regions, giving decrees and granting his blessings to the churches of Christ,* [90] *and deciding rewards and punishments as each deserved. After he had first crossed the frozen Alps, report preceded him swiftly through all areas, and men of differing customs and different status gathered from all parts, with differing requests, everywhere asking questions on many cases,*[2] [95] *seeking numerous replies on different matters.*[3] *Some came eager to hear or to see something new, some came to learn as well, and no less to give instruction. Because he was not able to attend to the individual needs of all,* [100] *and it was not possible to repeat the same thing so often, Urban decided to proclaim a general council for them all, to issue his proposals there to many once and for all. The city called Clermont, in the Auvergne, was the venue for this council;* [105] *bands of men summoned there hastened on their way, sent by the whole region of Gaul (for as is known, it is divided into three parts,*[4] *the Belgians and Celts living on one side, and the Aquitanians on the other; they are quite different in their laws, pursuits, and language). When they had assembled there, many matters were debated,* [110] *and a hundred items of business*[5] *were settled harmoniously. Then the aforementioned protest stirred the hearts of men as, at the prompting of God, the paramount question was raised about the churches which had been consecrated in Christ's own lifetime, how they were now foully darkened by pagan rites,* [115] *and how the city of Jerusalem, the first head of the churches, mother and nurse of the holy disciples and witness of life-bringing miracles, hallowed by the blood of the first martyrs, was now a hideout and refuge for bandits,* [120] *and how*

of the German Emperor Henry IV (1056–1106) should be localized in Lorraine. This detail provides further evidence that the Charleville Poet came from this area. Godfrey was granted the Duchy of Lower Lorraine by Henry IV in 1089. The reference to Lorraine alone here supports Knoch's thesis, in *Studien zu Albert von Aachen* (Stuttgart, 1966) that such stories about Godfrey as are found in the Charleville Poet trace their source to oral traditions emanating from the region.

[2] Vergil, *Aen.* i. 750.

[3] Pope Urban II (1088–99), formerly Odo of Lagery or Châtillon, monk and prior of Cluny. See A. Becker, *Papst Urban II. (1088–1099)* (Stuttgart, 1964), pp. 27–30. For the details of Urban II's itinerary, see R. Crozet, 'Le Voyage d'Urbain II et ses négotiations avec le clergé de France (1095–1096)', *Revue Historique*, clxxix (1937), 271–310, and 'Le voyage d'Urbain II en France (1095–1096) et son importance au point de vue archéologique', *Annales du Midi*, xlix (1937), 42–69.

[4] Caesar, *De bello Gallico*, i. 1. 1–2.

[5] The Council of Clermont was held in late Nov. 1095. The texts of only two decrees of the council have survived, and a description of a third. See R. Somerville, *The Councils of Urban II*, i: *Decreta Claromontensia* (Amsterdam, 1972), and 'The council of Clermont (1095) and Latin Christian Society', *Archivum Historiae Pontificiae*, xii (1974), 55–90.

Et blasphemari nomen super omnia sanctum[1]
Calcarique Dei templum sperni que sepulchrum;
Ergo laborandum quo conuertatur et ad se
Iam tandem rediens ipsam se queritet in se,[2]
Ac nihilum[a] *spernens ad uerum se trahat esse;*   125
Amodo namque sui miserendi tempus adesse.

Prospiceret domnus sapienti pectore Papa
Quid facto sit opus, quo sint loca sacra recepta,
Agmina namque sua concorditer esse parata[b]
Ad subeunda Dei pro laude pericula cuncta;[3]   130
Non ignes uel aquas, sibi non obsistere ferrum
Quin paribus uotis agmen uolet inreuocatum,
Si tutela Dei sibi propitiabilis assit,
Si non pontificum fauor et benedictio desit.

Talibus atque aliis conuentio pertonat omnis,   135
Vt sic uelle Deum bene posset credere quiuis.

Tum uir apostolicus peruoluens singula queque[4]
Cum uidet in cunctis unum fore foedus idemque,

fo. 62ᵛ   *Vsus consilio primatum pontificumque*
Cumque ipsis fundens Domino pia uota precesque,   140
Tunc super orando cunctos a crimine soluit.[5]

Inde uoluntati deuote frena remisit
Et pro culparum uenia tolerare labores[6]
Iussit, et illatos patienter ferre dolores,

Atque illis presens ne consolatio deesset,   145
Immo prompta satis benedictio semper adesset,
Pontificem Podii quem dicimus Aniciensem[7]
Militie sacre stabiliuit precipientem,

---

[a] nihilam *Sirmond*   [b] *this verse seems to have been erased or obliterated by the scribe*

---

[1] Phil. 2: 9. Jerusalem was clearly regarded as the goal of the crusade. See H. J. Cowdrey, 'Pope Urban II's preaching of the First Crusade', *History*, lv (1970), 177–88; Riley-Smith, *Idea of Crusading*, pp. 21–2.

[2] The Latin phrasing is awkward, and may owe something to John 7: 34, *quaeritis me et non inuenitis*. The idea seems to be that Jerusalem should seek her true identity in herself, the presence of the Holy Sepulchre.

[3] Urban II had stated that laymen should seek permission from their priest or bishop before they embarked upon the crusade. See *Die Kreuzzugsbriefe*, p. 138; Robert of Rheims, p. 729. For an analysis of the various accounts of Urban's sermon, see P. J. Cole, *The Preaching of the Crusades to the Holy Land, 1095–1290* (Cambridge, Mass., 1991), pp. 1–33.

[4] See Robert of Rheims, p. 729; *Gesta Francorum*, p. 7. Unlike the author of the *Gesta*, Robert was actually present at the council of Clermont. The phrase *velle Deum* is an

in its depths the limbs of the godly were torn apart and the name holy above
every name¹ was blasphemed, how the temple of God was trampled over and
the sepulchre despised; therefore they needed to strive to make the city turn, so
that, coming to her senses at last, she should seek herself within herself,² [125]
and turning away from empty falsehood should return to the true being; now
indeed the time had come to show pity on her. Let the Lord Pope, with wisdom
in his heart, look to what needed to be done, so that the holy places might be
regained, for their forces with one mind were ready [130] to undergo every
danger for the praise of God; not fire nor flood nor weapon could keep that
unstoppable host from sallying forth, all with the same prayer, if the protec-
tion and favour of God was with them, and if the will and blessing of the
bishops was not lacking.³ [135] The whole assembly thundered with these
and other words, so that anyone could well believe that this was indeed God's
will.⁴ Then the heir to the apostles reflected on each separate aspect, and when
he saw that one and the same resolution united them all, he took counsel with
the primates and bishops, [140] pouring out holy prayers and petitions to the
Lord God with them, and then praying in addition he absolved them from all
sin.⁵ Then he relaxed the constraints on their devout desire, and ordered
them, for mercy for their sins, to endure hardship⁶ and to bear with patience
the suffering which bore upon them. [145] And so that an ever-present
comfort might not be lacking to them, but rather that his blessing might
always be sufficiently at hand, he established the bishop of Le Puy (or, as we
say, Anician)⁷ as the leader of the holy expedition, and, for fear that he might

obvious reference to the reaction 'Deus le volt' reportedly provoked by Urban's speech.
See Cole, loc. cit.

⁵ *Decreta Claromontensia*, p. 74. There has been much discussion of the meaning of the indulgence given by Urban II. In fact it appears to have been simply a statement that the crusade was a severe and therefore satisfactory penance for all previous sins. He did not offer total absolution, but rather remission of the penance imposed by the Church for all sins properly confessed. See Riley-Smith, *Idea of Crusading*, pp. 27–9; R. Somerville, 'The council of Clermont and the First Crusade', *Studia Gratiana*, xx (1976), 325–37, at p. 329; M. Villey, *La Croisade: Essai sur la formation d'une théorie juridique* (Paris, 1942), pp. 142–5.

⁶ Ovid, *Met.* ix. 289, Claudian, *Prob. Olybr.* 131.

⁷ i.e., Adhémar of Monteuil, bishop of Le Puy. According to one account (*Chronicon Sancti Theoffred* in *Cartulaire de Saint-Chaffre du Monastier* (Paris, 1881), pp. 13–14), Adhémar had already been to the Holy Land as a pilgrim. Coming from the line of the counts of Valentinois, he was an ideal choice as spiritual leader of the expedition. On his appointment, see Urban II's letter to the people of Flanders, *Die Kreuzzugsbriefe*, pp. 136–7. A discussion on Adhémar's role in the First Crusade is found in J. A. Brundage, 'Adhémar of Le Puy: the bishop and his critics', *Speculum*, xxxiv (1959), 201–13; cf. also J. H. and L. L. Hill, 'Contemporary accounts and later reputation of Adhémar, bishop of Le Puy', *Medievalia et Humanistica*, ix (1955), 30–9; H. E. Mayer, 'Zur Beurteilung Adhemars von Le Puy', *Deutsches Archiv für Erforschung des Mittelalters*, xvi (1960), 547–53; J. Richard, 'La papauté et la direction de la première croisade', *Journal des savants*, 1960, 45–59.

Ac, ne ferre minus solus sua pondera possit,
Collegam posuit quem clara Aurengia misit.[1]   150

His ducibus[2] *freta diuinitus agmina sacra*
Insumunt contra cuncta aspera pectora digna.
Non urbes, castra retinent, non praedia larga,
Non thalami, nati, non sollicitudo paterna,[3]
Quin pro laude Dei concorditer arma capescant   155
Iuratisque animis in cuncta pericula currant.
Ergo parant sese fidei, ferrique nitore
Stipantur passim pedites equitumque caterue,
Quos[a] *Liger atque Elaber, Matrona et Sequana*[4] *mittit,*
Quos[a] *Arar et Rhodanus,*[b5] *Durentia et Isara promit,*   160
Exona et Esia quos agitat magnusque Garumna,
Quos Scaldes, Mosa, Rhenus[c] *pariterque Mosella,*
Quos Athesis pulcher preterfluit Heridanusque,
Quos Tyberis, Macra, Vulturnus Crustumiumque.
Concurrunt Itali, Galli, pariterque Alemanni,[6]   165
Noricii,[7] *Sueui, tum Saxones atque Boemii.*
Pisani[8] *ac Veneti propulsant equora remis,*
Oceanus flauis distendit uela Brytannis.[9]

fo. 63[r]   *Procedunt*[d] *alacres diuersis partibus, atque*
Condicunt ubi se socient terraque marique.[10]   170

Nunc libet ex parte populos memorare ducesque[11]
Quorum uirtute uiguit uia sacra fidesque.
Inclitus ille ducum Godefridus[12] *culmen honosque*
Omnibus exemplum bonitatis militieque.

---

[a] quos *Grocock;* quas *cod.*   [b] Rodanus *m. pr.*   [c] Renus *m. pr.*
[d] pprocedunt *m. pr.*

---

[1] William, bishop of Orange. He was present at the council of Clermont (William of Tyre, i. 137) and in September 1097 was sent on an embassy to Genoa (Caffaro, p. 101). He died on 2 Dec. 1098 at Ma'arrat-an-Nu'man (see below, at viii. 272).

[2] The only other sources remotely similar to this narrative here are Fulcher of Chartres, pp. 138–43, Ekkehard of Aura, *Hierosolymita*, p. 5, and Peter Tudebode, p. 32.

[3] See below, iii. 23–4. The theme of sacrifice when parting from families, lands, and possessions is found in most other crusading narratives, and was intended to underline the crusader's devotion. See Fulcher of Chartres, pp. 153–63, and lines 23–4 of Gilo's Prologue, below; see also Riley-Smith, 'Crusading as an act of love', pp. 178–80.

[4] Sidonius Apollinaris, *Carmina*, v. 27–9; Caesar, *De bello Gallico*, i. 1. 2. A similar list of rivers, which may well have been the Charleville Poet's inspiration, occurs in Lucan, *Bellum ciuile*, i. 419–40, and one of peoples in Sidonius Apollinaris, *Carm.*, v. 474–9.

not manage his onerous duties so well alone, [150] *he gave him a colleague sent from renowned Orange.*[1]

Relying by God's will on these leaders,[2] *the holy armies strengthened their hearts worthily against every hardship. Neither their cities and castles, nor their immense wealth, nor their wives and children, nor the anxious care of their parents*[3] [155] *held them back from taking up arms with one heart for the praise of God, and with souls sworn to the task they sped off to face every danger. Therefore they made themselves ready for this act of faith, and everywhere bands of infantry and knights crowded together, glittering with shining metal. They came from the Loire and the Allier, the Marne and the Seine,*[4] [160] *the Saône, the Rhône,*[5] *the Durance and the Isère, the Aisne and the Oise, the mighty Garonne, the Schelde, the Meuse, the Rhine, and the Moselle too, from beside the lovely Adige and the Po, the Tiber, the Magra, the Volturno, and the Corica.* [165] *There hastened there Italians, Gauls and Alemannians,*[6] *Noricians,*[7] *Swabians, Saxons, and Bohemians. Pisans*[8] *and Venetians struck the seas with their oars, and the ocean swelled the sails of the fair-haired British.*[9] *They set out eagerly from their various regions,* [170] *and decided together where they should join forces by land and sea.*[10]

Now is a suitable point to recall in part those peoples and leaders[11] *by whose excellence the holy journey of faith flourished. That renowned Godfrey,*[12] *foremost glory of the dukes, was the example of goodness and soldiery to*

---

[5] Tibullus, *Carm.* i. 7. 11.

[6] For the German participnts on the First Crusade, see R. Röhricht, *Die Deutschen im Heiligen Lande 650–1291* (Innsbruck, 1894; repr. Aalen, 1968); Hagenmeyer, 'Zimmern', ii. 22–3.

[7] Noricum, a Roman province lying between the Danube and the Alps, corresponding roughly to modern Austria.

[8] See 'Gesta triumphalia per Pisanos facta', *RIS* vi (2), 89; Giovanni Villani, *Cronica*, ed. F. Gherardi Dragomanni (Florence, 1844), i. 171–2; Orderic Vitalis, v. 30; F. Cardini, 'L'inizio del movimento crociato in Toscana', *Studi di storia medievale e moderna per Ernesto Sestan*, i (Florence, 1980), pp. 147–57. The Pisan expedition was headed by Archbishop Daimbert of Pisa, who later became patriarch of Jerusalem.

[9] Lucan, *Bellum ciuile*, iii. 78. On the English, see A. Grabois, 'Anglo-Norman England and the Holy Land', *Anglo-Norman Studies*, vii (1984), 132–41, at pp. 135–6.

[10] Lucan, *Bellum ciuile*, i. 201. For similar lists of the nationalities which took part in the First Crusade, see Sigebert of Gembloux, *Chronica*, *MGH, Scriptores in Folio*, vi. 367; Ekkehard of Aura, *Hierosolymita*, p. 16.

[11] Lists of the leaders of the crusade are also given by Guibert of Nogent, p. 148; Peter Tudebode, pp. 33, 37; Albert of Aachen, pp. 313–14.

[12] As the hero of the Charleville Poet's work, Godfrey of Bouillon naturally heads this list of prominent crusaders; in later myth he became associated with the swan-knight legend (cf. the epic cycle *Le Chevalier au Cygne*; see below, Gilo, v. 352 n.)

Siue hastam iaculans equaret Parthica tela,   175
Comminus aut feriens terebraret ferrea suta,[a]
Seu gladio pugnans carnes resecaret et ossa,
Siue eques atque pedes propelleret agmina densa,
Hic, inimicitiis cunctis sibi conciliatis,
Cunctis possessis pro Christi pace relictis   180
Arripuit callem Christum sectando uocantem.
Quem iuxta gemini fratres comitantur euntem,[1]
Stipantur circum proceres[2] equites peditesque,
Vtraque Belgica quos Transrhenanique dedere,
Namque Alemannorum quicquid uel Vindelicorum   185
Siue Sueuorum petiit uitale sepulchrum,[3]
Illis elegit sua iungere coetibus arma,
Nosse minus nihilo uocalia mutaque signa.
Eius enim resonans turbat gentilia nomen
Ac si concuterent elisa tonitrua fulmen,   190
Eius uexillis uolitantibus intremit hostis,
Ipsius gladio socius defenditur omnis,
Ipsius populos currentes undique ad arma
Conperimus creuisse ad milia septuaginta.[4]

Ex hinc Rotbertus,[5] Morinorum uiuida uirtus,[6]   195
Quos nunc Flandrenses appellat temporis usus,
Milia densa mouet, cuius memorabile dextra
Promeruit nomen Parthorum cede probata.

fo. 63ᵛ   Post hunc magnifice Rotbertus[7] claruit alter,
Qui Normannorum ductor praesignis et acer   200
Propulit egregias in Christi bella cohortes
Cum quibus anthideas alacer uolat in legiones.

[a] scuta Riant

---

[1] Eustace III was the elder brother and succeeded his father Eustace II as count of Boulogne. He returned to the West after the crusade, but the younger brother, Baldwin, later became Baldwin I of the Latin Kingdom of Jerusalem. After his death in 1118, Eustace was offered the throne, but it ultimately passed to his cousin Baldwin of Le Bourg. See William of Tyre, i. 549–50.
[2] The members of Godfrey of Bouillon's household or domus are listed by Riley-Smith, 'The motives', pp. 724–6. Those from Bouillon itself who took the cross are

all, [175] *whether in throwing the spear as far as a Parthian shoots his arrow, or piercing chain mail in close-quarters combat, or cutting into flesh and bone, fighting with the sword, or urging on the close-packed ranks on horseback or on foot. He made peace with all those at enmity with him,* [180] *left all his possessions for the peace of Christ, and struck out on his way, following Christ who called him on. His two brothers rode along beside him,*[1] *and his nobles,*[2] *knights and infantry, issuing forth from both Belgiums and the lands beyond the Rhine, crowded around him,* [185] *for whichever of the Alemannians or the Vindelicians or the Swabians sought the living sepulchre,*[3] *they chose to join their arms with his company, and no less to recognize his summons and standards. His resounding name shook the pagans* [190] *as if unleashed thunderbolts and lightning struck them. The foe shuddered at his fluttering banners, every ally was defended by his sword, and we understand that the peoples flocking to his forces from all sides grew to seventy thousand.*[4]

[195] *Then there was Robert,*[5] *the vigour and glory of the Morini*[6] *(who have now come to be called 'men of Flanders'); he brought thousands in serried ranks, and his memorable right hand well deserved the renown it won, as the slaughter of the Parthians well shows.*

After him shone forth in splendour the other Robert,[7] [200] *the foremost and ardent leader of the Normans; he urged his outstanding forces on into Christ's battles, and flew with them energetically against the legions hostile to God.*

mentioned by a local chronicler in the *Chronicon Sancti Huberti Andaginensis, MGH, Scriptores in Folio,* viii. 615.

[3] Cf. above, i. 40.

[4] This figure is clearly an exaggeration, but Raymond of Aguilers noted that when the march to Jerusalem began, Godfrey's army was larger than either Tancred's or Robert of Flanders', and equal to that of Robert of Normandy.

[5] Robert II, count of Flanders, the son of Robert I 'the Frisian', who went on pilgrimage to the Holy Land between 1087 and 1088, and subsequently sent 500 Flemish knights to assist Alexius Comnenus. Robert I was also the alleged recipient of the letter from the Byzantine Emperor. See E. Joranson, 'The problem of the spurious letter of Emperor Alexius to the count of Flanders', *American Historical Review,* lv (1950), 811–33; M. de Waha, 'La lettre d'Alexis Comnène à Robert I le Frison: une revision', *Byzantion,* xlvii (1977), 113–25. On the career of Robert II, see M. M. Knappen, 'Robert of Flanders in the First Crusade', in *The Crusades and Other Historical Essays Presented to Dana C. Munro* (New York, 1928), pp. 79–100.

[6] Proba, *Cent. Verg.* 664 = Vergil, *Aen.* v. 754.

[7] Robert, duke of Normandy, son of William the Conqueror. He was also the cousin of Robert II of Flanders, and his sister Adela was married to Stephen of Blois. See below, p. 17, n. 6. For a list of his companions, see C. W. David, *Robert Curthose* (Cambridge, Mass., 1920), app. D.

At comes eximius Hugo[1] *cognomine Magnus,*
Phylippi regis uterinus frater et unus,
Agmina nobilium comitantia Francigenarum   205
Duxit in exitium memorabile Nilicolarum.[2]

Rector Montensis,[3] *populus quem nomine prisco*
Neruius assequitur, Heidonariusque[a] *moderno,*
Cui patrui tulerat Morinos dampnabile crimen,[4]
Arnulfum perimens dominum pariterque nepotem,   210
Proruit, instructis in Christi prelia turmis,
Coniuge cum natis, domibus, castrisque relictis.

Hinc Stephanus[5] *comitis Tetbaldi clara propago*
Calcat iter sacrum, circumdatus agmine denso,
Sed spe siue metu media inter prelia uictus   215
Effectu gemino sociis fit inutile pignus,
Cum primo regis Constantinopolitani[6]
Diuitiis captus ceruicem flecteret ipsi,
Ac post desperans Dominum fore cunctipotentem
Exiit Antiochi foedis egressibus urbem,   220
Atque fuga turpi retrogradus absque pudore,
Consimiles secum traxit, stimulante pauore;
Quin et subsidio conclusis aduenientem
Armorum et uictus stipendia multa ferentem
Predictum regem retro celerare coegit   225
Dum socios omnes falso periisse retexit.[7]
Ista tamen longo post tempore gesta fuere,
Que nunc hic breuiter suffecerit inseruisse.

---

[a] Heinodatius *Riant*

---

[1] Hugh, brother of King Philip I, was the second son of Henry I of France, hence *le Maisné*, 'younger', which was consistently corrupted by Latin writers into *Magnus*; see L. Bréhier, *Histoire anonyme de la Première Croisade* (Paris, 1924), p. 5. He had obtained the small county of Vermandois through marriage.

[2] This reference is puzzling if taken literally to mean the Fatimid rulers of Egypt. They were the crusaders' opponents at Jerusalem and at the battle of Ascalon, but Hugh was not present on either occasion; he had returned to the West after the capture of Ascalon. The word *Nilicolae* is probably used for the sake of the rhyme.

[3] Baldwin II of Hainault, count of Mons, and first cousin of Robert II of Flanders. He may have been at the council of Clermont (*PL* cl. 1388–9), and was afterwards a member of Godfrey of Bouillon's contingent. After the capture of Antioch, he accom-

The famous Count Hugh,[1] *known as the Great, was also there; he was the one and only brother of King Philip,* [205] *and he led the assembled companies of noble Franks to the notable destruction of the Nile-dwelling peoples.*[2]

The ruler of Mons[3] *was followed by the people named in ancient times Nervii and in modern days 'of Hainault'. He lost the county of Flanders through the dastardly crime of his uncle,*[4] [210] *who killed Arnulf, at the same time his liege-lord and his nephew. Leaving behind wife and children, home and castle, he blazed forth with his troops drawn up to do battle for Christ.*

Next to tread the holy journey was Stephen,[5] *the famous offspring of Count Theobald. He was accompanied by a close-packed throng,* [215] *but whether through hope or through fear, he was overcome twice over in the midst of the fighting, and became a worthless pledge to his companions; first, he succumbed to the riches of the king of Constantinople,*[6] *and bowed his neck to him; and afterwards, despairing that the Lord God really was all-powerful,* [220] *he left the city of Antioch, disgracefully slipping away, and, having embarked without shame on this evil flight, he took those like him along with him, spurred on by terror,* [225] *and even forced the aforementioned king to hurry in retreat (though he was coming to help those who were besieged, bringing great supplies of weapons and provisions) when he falsely related that all his allies had perished.*[7] *However, these things were done much later on; it is enough to have included a brief note of them here.*

panied Hugh of Vermandois on an embassy to the Byzantine emperor, but disappeared after a skirmish in Asia Minor. See Albert of Aachen, pp. 434–5.

[4] The Charleville Poet here makes another 'local' allusion. When Baldwin VI of Flanders died in 1070, he left the county of Hainault, which he had acquired through his wife Richilde, to his youngest son Baldwin, and Flanders to his nephew Arnulf, under the guardianship of his brother Robert 'the Frisian'. In the ensuing squabbles, influenced by racial rivalries between Flemings and Walloons and by Richilde's own plotting, Arnulf was killed (in the battle of Brinkhove, 21 Feb. 1071) and Robert became ruler of Flanders. Baldwin retained only Hainault.

[5] Stephen, son of Theobald III, count of Blois and Chartres. For further details on his career, see Brundage, 'An errant crusader: Stephen of Blois', *Traditio*, xvi (1960), 380–95; P. Rousset, 'Étienne de Blois, croisé, fuyard et martyr', *Genava*, NS xi (1963), 183–95. For Gilo of Paris's own account of Stephen's treachery, see vii. 498–503.

[6] Stephen wrote to his wife Adela of the reception and gifts which he had received at Constantinople: see *Die Kreuzzugsbriefe*, pp. 138–40.

[7] See the *Gesta Francorum*, pp. 63–5; Raymond of Aguilers, p. 77. Stephen met the Byzantine Emperor, who was marching to relieve the crusaders at Antioch, at Philomelium.

fo. 64ʳ

Hinc comes Egidii[1] *discernens iura beati*
Milia densa mouet sancti sub honore sepulchri,[2]   230
*Que sibi dat magnis opibus Prouintia*ᵃ *florens,*
Queque ministrauit populose Gothia[3] *pollens.*

At trans aerias diuersis tractibus Alpes,[4]
*Quas*ᵇ *diuersi uoce compellant circa habitantes—*
Nam Gothias, Graias, Penninas Iuliadasque[5]   235
Appellare solent positi propiusque proculque—
*Qui Rutuli, Marsi, Samnites atque Peligni,*ᶜ
Qui Ligures, Itali, Tusci pariterque Sabini,
Vmbri, Lucani, Calabri simul atque Sabelli,
Aurunci, Volsci uel qui memorantur Etrusci,   240
Queque etiam gentes sparguntur in Apula rura,
Quis conferre manus uisum est in prelia dura,[6]
Sub iuga Tancradi[7] *et Boimundi*[8] *corripuere*
Et contra fidei refugas patria arma tulere.

Multi praeterea comites proceresque minores   245
Inter primores quos enumerauimus omnes
Adiunxere suas collato robore uires,
Galli siue Itali, uel quos dat pagina plures,
Quos ne lecturis (siqui tamen esse ualebunt
Quos positis curis hec uilia nostra tenebunt)   250
Rusticitas calami[9] *pariat fastidia longa,*
Non est consilium per nomina promere cuncta.

Omnibus his pastor bene prouidus ac moderator
Presul Haimarus Podii fuit atque sacrator,
Cumque sodale suo quem clara Aurengia misit[10]   255
Vt pater in natos curam conferre sategit,

ᵃ Prouincia *Sirmond, Riant*   ᵇ quas *Riant, correctly in my opinion;* quos *cod., Sirmond*   ᶜ *this whole verse was omitted by Sirmond and Riant*

---

[1] Raymond IV, count of Toulouse, was the principal lord of southern France. According to Baldric of Dol, p. 16, his envoys arrived at Clermont shortly after Urban II had made his appeal; this speedy response has been taken to imply that he had been consulted by the pope about the project during the latter's journey through France. Raymond's progress on the crusade was chronicled by his chaplain Raymond of Aguilers. See J. H. and L. L. Hill, *Raymond IV de Saint-Gilles, 1041 (ou 1042)–1105* (Toulouse, 1959).   [2] Cf. i. 197, iii. 126.

[3] The marquisate of Gothia stretched from Narbonne in the south to the banks of the Rhône at Orange. For its involvement in the crusade, see Raymond of Aguilers, p. 52.

Next was the count of Saint-Gilles,[1] *a man who knew what was right;* [230]
he brought thousands in serried ranks for the honour of the Holy Sepulchre,[2]
men given by wealthy Provence, with her vast riches, and supplied in great
numbers by the flourishing marquisate of Gothia.[3]

In various lands over the lofty Alps,[4] *to which those dwelling round about*
give divers names [235] *(for those who dwell near to them and far off are*
accustomed to call them the Gothic, Graian, the Pennine, and Julian Alps),[5]
there gathered Rutulians, Marsians, Samnites and Paelignians, Ligurians,
Italians, Tuscans and Sabines, Umbrians, Lucanians, Calabrians and
Sabellians, [240] *Auruncians, Volscians, and those called Etruscans; the*
people also who are scattered in the country districts of Apulia, to whom it
seemed right to contribute their contingents in the hardships of battle,[6] *swiftly*
gathered their native arms under the yoke of Tancred[7] *and Bohemond,*[8] *and*
took them up against the renegades of the faith.

[245] *Moreover, many lesser counts and nobles mustered their strength and*
joined forces with the more important leaders, whom we have listed fully.
There were Gauls, Italians, and many others attested in the written sources.
We do not propose to mention them all by name, lest our uncultured style[9]
should give birth to aversion and boredom in our readers (if there will be any
[250] *who will lay aside their anxious cares and take up these paltry offerings*
of ours).

Bishop Adhémar of Le Puy acted with good foresight as shepherd, governor,
and priest for all these, [255] *and with his comrade,*[10] *whom renowned*
Orange sent, he strove to bring them comfort as a father to his sons, which (as

---

[4] Vergil, *Georg.* iii. 474; Ovid, *Met.* ii. 226.

[5] Pliny, *Hist. Nat.* iii. 38. The Charleville Poet is here referring to the three ranges of
Alps, the Western, consisting of the Maritime, Cottian, and Graian Alps; the Central,
made up of the Pennine or Wallisian, Lepontine and Rhaetian or Tyrolese Alps, and
the Eastern, comprising the Noric or Salzburg, Carnic, and Julian Alps.

[6] Vergil, *Aen.* xii. 345.

[7] Tancred, probably the eldest son of Bohemond's sister Emma, subsequently
became prince of Galilee. His brother William joined Hugh of Vermandois' army;
other south Italian knights who took the cross are listed in the *Gesta Francorum*, pp. 7–8.

[8] Bohemond of Taranto, eldest son of Robert Guiscard. The circumstances in
which Bohemond took the cross are described by the author of the *Gesta Francorum* (p.
7), who was a member of his contingent. See also R. B. Yewdale, *Bohemond I, Prince of
Antioch* (Princeton, 1924).

[9] The poet's apology for his rustic style or 'affected modesty' is a common feature of
both classical and medieval literature. See Curtius, *European Literature*, pp. 83–5; see
also below, iv. 1–2, and Corippus, *Iohannidos*, praef. 37.

[10] Cf. i. 150.

Quod uelut anterior iam pagina commemorauit
Domnus Papa sibi diuinitus imperitauit.

Impensis igitur cum strenuitate paratis[1]
Diuersos portus[2] *adeunt exercitus omnis.* 260
Quidam per Venetos trans Adriacosque Liburnos,
Quidam Brundisium, nonnulli molle Tarentum,[3]
Quidam piscosi tenuerunt moenia Bari,
Qua Veneti fortes, felici merce beati,
Torpentes Lycios furto populante fideli, 265
Deportauerunt Nicholai pignora Sancti,[4]
Atque per hos omnes portus feliciter acti
Iuxta condictum sunt agmina in una redacti,
Per maria et fluctus optata ad litora uecti.
At uero insignis Godefridus iam memoratus, 270
Ordinibus densis armato milite septus,[5]
Castellis, terris, uillis,[a] *domibus spoliatus,*
Argenti atque auri summa multiplice fartus,[6]
Omnibus impensis plene atque decenter onustus,
Expetiit Rhenum, qua se Maguntia[7] *pollens* 275
Iuxtaque Vuormatia reserat, naualia praebens;
Quo preteruectus tentoria candida figit
Et memoratorum uenientia milia iungit.
Agmine multiplici tunc metans[b] *ulteriora*
Atque in processu socium crescente chorea 280
Hinc Reganeiburgi[c] *formosum permeat Hystrum,*
Hunc quoque Danubium, uerax est fama,[8] *uocatum.*
Amnibus hic[d] *multis magnisque et nauibus aptis,*
Nam deties senis spatioso uentre receptis,[9]
In mare prorumpit Scythicum quod Thracia censet, 285

[a] uillis *Grocock;* uallis *cod.*   [b] maetans *cod.*   [c] Reganetburgi *Sirmond;* Reganiciburgi *Riant*   [d] hic *om. m. pr.*

---

[1] See above, i. 147–50 and nn. For the role of the clergy in this expedition, see W. Porges, 'The clergy, the poor and the non-combatants on the First Crusade', *Speculum*, xxi (1946), 1–23.

[2] A similar list of ports is to be found in Robert of Rheims, p. 742, and Peter Tudebode, p. 38. The armies used three main routes: Raymond of Toulouse marched along the Dalmatian coast; Godfrey of Bouillon went via the Danube and Maritsa valleys; and the French, Flemish, and Norman contingents crossed by sea from Southern Italy.

[3] Horace, *Sat.* ii. 4. 34.

[4] The relics and tomb of St Nicholas had a chequered history, some of which is

a previous page has already noted) the Lord Pope ordered him to do, at the prompting of God.[1]

Therefore, when preparations had been made with great energy, [260] the whole army made its way to different ports;[2] *some crossed the Adriatic from Venice to Croatia, some went to Brindisi, several to gentle Taranto;*[3] *some made for the stronghold of Bari, famous for its fish, from where the brave Venetians, blessed by their happy commerce, [265] despoiled the sluggish Lycians (an act of theft, and yet of faith) and carried off the relics of St Nicholas.*[4] *Having journeyed through all these ports without mishap, they assembled again in a single column, as had been decided, and were conveyed over the waves of the sea to the shore they longed for. [270] However, the above-mentioned noble Godfrey, surrounded by close-packed ranks of armed knights,*[5] *despoiled of his castle, lands, villages and houses, but laden with a copious supply of silver and gold,*[6] *fully equipped with everything proper and necessary, [275] set out for the Rhine, where the flourishing city of Mainz*[7] *spreads out its flourishing dockyards, next to Worms. Journeying along it he pitched his white tents, and joined the thousands of those arriving there whom we have mentioned. As his company increased greatly, he crossed to the other side, [280] and with his band growing in strength at each step of the journey, he crossed the well-known river Hister (also called the Danube, according to true report)*[8] *at Regensburg. The Hister is formed by many tributaries which are suitable for large ships, for, taking the waters of sixty streams in its broad bed,*[9] *[285] it bursts forth into the sea called by Thrace the Scythian sea in*

described here by the Charleville Poet. Nicholas de Porta, *Documenta Lipsanographica* (*RHC Hist. occ.* v. 243), and another anonymous author (ibid. 293–4) record that the people of Bari transferred the relics of St Nicholas to Bari from Myra in 1087. Some of the relics were subsequently given by Roger Borsa, Duke of Apulia, to his brother-in-law, Robert of Flanders. See Fulcher of Chartres, p. 167; *Die Kreuzzugsbriefe*, pp. 142–3. The *Anonymus Littorensis* (*RHC Hist. occ.* v. 261) adds that the Saint's tomb was found by the Venetians in 1100, who then moved the relics to the monastery of S. Nicola del Lido in Venice.

[5] *Ilias Latina*, 173.
[6] Anna Comnena, *Alexiad*, ed. B. Leib, 2 vols. (Paris, 1937–45), ii. 209, also stated that Godfrey had considerable wealth. In fact he had to sell or mortgage much of his land in order to finance the expedition. See Riley-Smith, *Idea of Crusading*, pp. 37, 44; F. Duncalf, 'The First Crusade: from Clermont to Constantinople', in Setton, *History of the Crusades*, i. 267; A. M. Stahl, 'The circulation of European coinage in the crusader states', *Meeting of Two Worlds*, pp. 86–8.
[7] Mainz, Worms, and Regensburg witnessed Jewish massacres between Dec. 1095 and July 1096 by members of the Peasants' Crusade. See J. Riley-Smith, 'The First Crusade and the persecution of the Jews', *SCH* xxi (1984), 51–72, at pp. 51, 54.
[8] Horace, *Sat.* ii. 1. 36.
[9] Ovid, *Fasti*, iii. 163. The grammar here, as at other points in the Charleville Poet, is convoluted.

Tanta mole fluens ut amara in dulcia mutet,
Quod prope Cholcorum fines septemfluus[1] intrat,
Obuius ac undis aurati Phasidos extat.[2]

Huic etiam ripa uicina est[a] silua[3] sinistra
Quam uocat Herquinam scriptorum pagina multa.   290
Ista uia septem memoratur lata dierum,
Porro tricenorum bis tenditur agmine longum,[4]
Nutrit et alarum uolucres fulgore suarum
Noctibus obscuris pandentes strata uiarum;[5]
Nutrit et externis animalia plura figuris: 295
Unis nomen inest alces, comitantibus uris.
Alcibus haud ulla sunt internodia cruris,
Vris cornua sunt immensae concauitatis
Ex quibus ampla satis et leuia pocula fiunt,
Ditibus et mensis et honora et commoda prosunt,   300
Seu docti artifices ea quadrificata rotundent,
Integra siue sinant et fissa caloribus aptent.
Digrediens ergo generosus ductor ab Hystro[6]
Versus Pannonias iter arripit agmine toto.
Quod quali fuerit ratione uel ordine gestum,[7]   305
Que causa excitum potuit sedare tumultum,
Ad praesens refugit mens dicere, lassaque multum
Palpitat, inque alium gestit referre libellum.

Explicit liber primus. Incipit secundus.

[a] et silua *Riant*

---

[1] Ovid, *Met.* xv. 753.
[2] Cf. the similar detail in Pomponius Mela, *Chorog.* i. 108: *hic sunt Colchi, huc Phasis erumpit*.

such a torrent that it turns the bitter waters sweet. It flows into the sea through seven channels[1] *near the borders of the Colchians, opposite the waves of the golden Phasis.*[2] *Neighbouring the left bank of the river is the forest*[3] [290] *which the pages of many an author call the Hercynian forest. This is said to be seven days' journey across, and actually stretches for sixty days' march in length.*[4] *It is host to birds that lighten up its twisting paths*[5] *in the darkness of night with the brilliance of their wings,* [295] *and is also the home of many animals of exotic appearance. One type bears the name elk, and there is another, too, called the aurochs. The elk has no joints at all in its legs, and the aurochs has massive, hollow horns, from which polished cups of a good size are made* [300] *which serve as splendid ornaments for wealthy tables, whether skilled craftsmen cut them into blocks and round them off, or leave them whole and shape them when they have been split in the fire. And so the great-hearted leader left the Hister behind*[6] *and set out with his whole force towards Hungary.* [305] *For what purpose and in what order this was done,*[7] *and in what circumstances he was able to quell an outbreak of violent disorder, we shall for the time being leave unsaid, for our mind is most weary and breathless, and chooses to put this off till another book.*

The first book ends, the second begins.

[3] i.e. the Black Forest. In his account the Charleville Poet uses details garnered from a variety of classical sources, as the notes below indicate. Cf. also Pliny, *Hist. Nat.* viii. 15, 16; C. Iulius Solinus, *Collectanea rerum memorabilium*, xx. 3, ed. T. Mommsen (Berlin, 1895), p. 96; Priscian, *Periegesis*, 275–8.

[4] Caesar, *De bello Gallico*, vi. 25–8.

[5] Cf. ii. 205; Vergil, *Aen.* i. 241.

[6] Godfrey's army set out in mid-Aug. 1096 and reached the Hungarian border in September, shortly after the disastrous defeats suffered by the Peasants' Crusade. Before Godfrey entered the kingdom he sent an embassy to negotiate with King Coloman.

[7] The poet 'signposts' the next stage of his story with a stock excuse (cf. Curtius, *European Literature*, p. 90); in fact the narrative continues in Book iii. Book ii deals with the adventures of Peter the Hermit and the Peasants' Crusade.

LIBER II

Ante uiam ceptam ducis[1] in Domini famulatum,
Cum primum proceres niti coepere paratum,
Pars quaedam stolide reliquos processerat ante,
Agmen agens magnum pariter peditumque equitumque.
Hos heremita Petrus quidam, sic nomine dictus,   5
Ducere ceptarat, sed numquam ad talia doctus,[2]
Cuius in hoc socius quidam Vualtarius ibat,
Qui 'Sine Merce'[a][3] superpositum cognomen habebat,
His ducibus dicti gestantes arma manipli
Ibant securi, nullo moderamine cauti,   10
Credentes proprii gratisque existere iuris
Omnia que cupidis demonstrarentur ocellis,
Nec per iter ceptum quicquam sibi iure negandum
Quin potius ferro quouis prohibente petendum.[4]
Nam neque curarant stipendia multa parare   15
Que sibi sperarent stipendia ubique patere,
Seque, euangelii precones discipulosque,
Ex euangelio capere indumenta cibosque.[5]
Talia dum sperant, sperataque mente recursant,
Et iam deficere sibi parce parta retractant,   20
Pannonias ueniunt, crucis ante insignia monstrant
Vestibus insuta, nullisque[b] instantibus intrant.[6]
Ingressi gratis queque[c] sibi uisa requirunt;
Non data diripiunt, hostiliter ostia frangunt,

This book is found only in G.

This book is found only in G.
[a] Sine Merce *cod.*; Sine Habere *Sirmond*; Sine Auere *Riant*   [b] nullis (*om.* -que)
m. pr.   [c] queque *Grocock*; que*** *cod., written over an erasure*

[1] Godfrey of Bouillon.
[2] Hagenmeyer, *Le vrai et le faux sur Pierre l'Hermite*, trans. F. Reynaud (Paris, 1883) is still
the standard work on Peter the Hermit. More recently, however, E. Blake and C. Morris,
'A hermit goes to war: Peter and the origins of the First Crusade', *SCH* xxi (1985), 79–107,
have re-examined certain aspects of his career, in particular the story of his pilgrimage to
Jerusalem and the appeal for aid from the patriarch that he subsequently delivered to the
pope, who was then prompted to summon the council of Clermont. Since this tradition
appears to have flourished in the region of Lorraine and Flanders, it is interesting that the
Charleville Poet should present such a different picture of Peter's role in the First Cru-
sade. For his later involvement in it, see below, vii. 331–64.

BOOK II

Before the duke[1] began his journey for the service of the Lord God, while the nobles had first begun to labour at their preparations, a certain group had stupidly gone on ahead before all the rest, forming a great throng of infantry and knights alike. [5] A certain hermit, called by name Peter, had undertaken to lead these people, although he had no experience in such tasks.[2] A certain Walter went along as his comrade in this enterprise; this man was nicknamed 'the Penniless'.[3] Brandishing their weapons, these forces proceeded without a care under the leadership of these men, [10] undisciplined and incautious, in the belief that everything that presented itself to their greedy eyes was their own, free and by right, and that on the journey they had undertaken, nothing should be denied them—but rather, that it was to be sought after by force of arms, no matter who tried to stop them.[4] [15] In fact, they had given no thought to making ready a good supply of provisions, as they hoped such provisions would be readily available everywhere, and that as heralds and disciples of the Gospel, they would gain their food and clothing in accordance with the Gospel.[5] Such hopes were in their minds; as they were thinking on what they had hoped for, [20] and realized that their meagre supplies were already running out, they came to Hungary. They displayed the sign of the cross sewn on to the front of their garments, met with no one in their way, and crossed into that land.[6] Having entered the country they asked for things that seemed necessary to them, free of charge; when these things were not given them, they plundered them, breaking down doors in a hostile

[3] Walter of Poissy was better known by name in French, Sans Avoir. The Gesta Francorum, p. 4, translates this as sine habere (see also app. crit.). He was accompanied by his two brothers, Simon and William. After Walter's death at Civetot, they seem to have returned to the West, but both joined the 1101 Crusade. Orderic Vitalis, v. 29, 39, 346; Fulcher of Chartres, p. 159.

[4] The fullest account of the so-called 'Peasants' Crusade' remains F. Duncalf, 'The Peasants' Crusade', AHR xxvi (1921), 400–53. References to this expedition are also to be found in Gesta Francorum, pp. 2–5; Guibert of Nogent, pp. 142–6; Fulcher of Chartres, pp. 158–9; Albert of Aachen, pp. 272–95.

[5] Matt. 10: 9–10. The Peasants' Crusade set out before the good harvest of 1096, from which the succeeding armies benefited.

[6] In the following account, the Charleville Poet treats the various contingents on the Peasants' Crusade as one. In fact Walter the Penniless reached Hungary in late May; Peter the Hermit arrived shortly afterwards, and the three remaining contingents, led by the German priests Folkmar and Gottschalk, and Count Emicho of Leiningen, arrived in Hungary in July or August.

Horrea frumentis, uino cellaria fraudant. 25
Siqui uestis egent, indutos tegmine nudant.
In proprias escas aliena animalia mactant,
In proprios usus aliena negotia captant,
Instituunt festas alieno ex iure tabernas,
Dant mercaturas alieno ex foenore largas. 30
Qui ueluti ciues intrarant hospita tecta
Ipsis in tectis peragunt hostilia cuncta.
Quid moror in multis?[1] *non ulla exempla malorum*
Disconuenerunt plus genti Christicolarum.

fo. 66ʳ *His irritantur uesanis motibus Huni.* 35
Fama uolans patrio facit omnia cognita regi;[2]
Vndique conueniunt, conclusos undique mactant,
Hic fugit, hic pugnat, cuncti moriendo laborant;
Maxima pars gladiis, pars fluminibus periere,
Pauci cum ducibus se morti subripuere. 40
Cumque fuga medium regionis iam tenuissent
Et solitos iterum raptus agere instituissent,
Rex iterum accitus fama uolitante recurrit
Et circumducta medios indagine claudit.[3]

Conseritur bellum, uirtus fortunaque certat, 45
Comminus obtruncant se quos[a] *strictura coartat.*
Anceps pugna diu[4] *populi morientis utrimque,*
Dum desperanter[b] *pugnant audensque pauensque,*
Donec externi concursibus indigenarum
Turbati fugiunt metuentes tela sequentum. 50
Forte fuit iuxta Christi uenerabile templum[5]
Pignoribus multis sanctorum nobilitatum:
Huc bello pulsi, gens inconsulta, manipli
Intendere fugam, spe morti se eripiendi.

Sed gens barbaricis assueta furoribus uti 55
Nil reuerens sanctae seruarunt relligioni,[6]
Namque locum sacrum uallantes obsidione
Allexere aliquos male fida deditione;
Quos tamen egressos contra fas decapitantes
Expauefecerunt reliquos, ne progredientes 60
More trucidati pecorum sine laude perirent,
Ast ibi quidquid eis ferret fortuna subirent.
Quapropter, rursus furiis immanibus acti,

ᵃ si quos *Sirmond, Riant*   ᵇ desperantes *Sirmond, Riant*

manner, [25] and emptying the stores of grain and the cellars of wine. If any lacked clothing, they stripped those who were dressed of their garments. They slaughtered the animals of others for their own food; they took over the property of others for their own use, made merry in the taverns where others had the right, [30] and generously gave goods away at others' expense. They had entered friendly houses as though they were citizens, but everything they did in those houses, they did as enemies. But why dwell on all these things?[1] No instances of evil were ever less worthy of Christian people. [35] The Hungarians were vexed by this wild behaviour. News spread quickly, and all became known to the king of that land.[2] His people gathered together from all sides, hemmed the invaders in and slaughtered them everywhere; some fled, some fought, all were overwhelmed by death; most died in combat, some drowned in rivers, [40] and only a few with their leaders escaped death. When in their flight they already commanded the central region of the country, they began once again to carry out their habitual raids. The king was alerted by the swiftly spreading news, and made haste to cut them off, trapping them in an encircling manœuvre.[3] [45] Battle was joined, courage and fortune entered the fray, and hemmed in and crammed together they hacked at each other in close combat. The battle wavered for a long time[4] with casualties on both sides, but the brave man and the coward fought despairingly, until the invaders were put to flight by the charges of the natives, [50] and fled in terror of their pursuers' weapons. There happened to be nearby a venerable temple of Christ,[5] graced with many relics of the saints; driven by the fighting, the bands of infantry (reckless men!) fled to this place in the hope of snatching themselves from death. [55] But this people was accustomed to indulging in savage frenzy, and showed no respect at all for religion:[6] for they blocked off the holy place and laid siege to it, and enticed some to surrender, though they did not keep faith; for against all right they cut their heads off when they came out, [60] and terrified the rest into resolving not to come out to die ingloriously, butchered like cattle, but rather to endure whatever fortune brought them where they stood. The Hungarians were once again

[1] Terence, *Andria*, 114, cf. Vergil, *Aen.* ii. 102. Walter in fact negotiated market privileges with the Hungarian king and his orderly band passed through Hungary almost without incident. Peter made similar arrangements, although his force was less well disciplined. See Albert of Aachen, pp. 274, 276. Once again the Charleville Poet draws no distinctions between the behaviour of the various groups and ascribes to the earlier armies the violence and pillaging carried out by the later bands.

[2] Coloman, king of Hungary 1095–1114.

[3] Lucan, *Bellum ciuile*, vi. 42.   [4] Vergil, *Aen.* x. 359.

[5] The narrative here is without close parallels in any other sources of the First Crusade.

[6] The Hungarians' conversion to Christianity was only recent, having taken place under King Stephen I (997–1038); Hungary had been handed over to the Papacy as a fiefdom under Géza I (1074–7).

Igne superiecto circum fastigia templi,

Non dubitauerunt ipsosque domumque cremare   65
Atque Deo non suaue fragrantiaᵃ thura adolere:
Sed, quia non fuerat penes omnes culpa malorum,
Cumque malis pariter fuit obruta uita bonorum,
Ac simul almifici periit reuerentia templi,
Nec cuiquam menti insedit miseratio Christi,   70
Ostendit Dominus sibi talia non placuisse,
Dum per signa locum sacra contulit enituisse;
Namque ibi per triduum fons sanguinis emanauit,
*Atque locum cedis condigno horrore notauit.*¹
Preterea dignis loca percrebrescere signis   75
Ex tunc affirmat discurrens fama celebris,
*Dum cecis, claudis uarioque dolore grauatis*²
Omnipotens Virtus ibi prestat dona salutis.

His ita transactis, quoniam ille exercitus omnis
Agmine non uno nec eisdem incedere castris   80
Ob numerum poterat, non parua sede capacem
Atque ideo inter se non magna parte sequacem,
*Quedam pars istas*ᵇ *precesserat hic*³ *residentes,*
Iamque uidebatur regionis tangere fines,
Sed sibi preclusum castello et flumine magno   85
*Inuenit egressum, nec posse excedere claustro.*⁴
*Egressu uetito*ᶜ *castellum prendere ceptant,*
*Donec [iam trepi]di*ᵈ *castrenses coepta remittant:*
*Dantque*ᵉ *locum, claustris reseratis, egrediendi,*
Sic ex Pannoniis laceri excessere manipli.   90
Hinc iter aggressi per fines Vulgariorum,
Quos uocitant Thracas, ut habent monimenta priorum,
*Deuenere Gnidon, urbem sic nomine dictam,*⁵

ᵃ fragrantia *Sirmond:* flagrantia *cod.*   ᵇ istos *Sirmond, Riant*   ᶜ uetito *is written over an erasure*   ᵈ iam trepi]di *Holford-Strevens; in the lacuna Professor Hall suggested* ad extremum; *Riant put* exigui   ᵉ dentque *Riant, perhaps correctly*

---

¹ Albert of Aachen, pp. 274–5, places this incident at Semlin. His account is much less detailed than the one given here. There is no mention of any miraculous sign. F. Duncalf, 'The First Crusade: Clermont to Constantinople', in Setton, *A History of the Crusades*, i. 253–79, at p. 259, argues that the burning of the church took place at Belgrade.
² Matt. 11: 5.
³ Either Semlin or Belgrade.

roused to terrible anger because of this, and threw fire on to the roof of the temple all around, [65] not hesitating to burn both men and building, offering up to God an incense that did not smell sweet. Not all of those inside were guilty of evil deeds, however, and the lives of good men had been swept along with the wicked; moreover the devotion due to that temple, the source of blessing, also perished, [70] and the mercy of Christ was fixed in the mind of no man. On this account the Lord God demonstrated that such deeds had not pleased him, and made the spot shine forth in glory through holy signs: for a spring of blood flowed out there for three days, and marked the site of the slaughter with horror that was deserved and fitting.[1] [75] Moreover the place became even better known by its worthy signs from that time on, as the famous news about it made clear as it spread abroad, for the glory of the Almighty bestowed gifts of healing there on the blind, the lame, and those burdened with different kinds of pain.[2]

After all this had taken place, since that whole army [80] could not march in a single column, nor camp in a single spot, because their weight of numbers made them unable to fit into a small place, and they were consequently following on behind one another in groups a short distance apart, some of the force left the rest behind in this place,[3] and went on ahead. When they seemed almost to have come right to the borders of that region, [85] they found the way out blocked by a castle and a broad river, and were unable to pass by that obstacle.[4] With their way out blocked, they began to assail the castle, until the terrified occupants abandoned the action they had begun, unlocked their barricades and gave them space to withdraw. [90] And so those mangled squads of men got away from the Hungarians. From here they made their way through Bulgarian territory, which (as the chronicles of old have it) men call Thrace, and came down to a city called by the name of Nish,[5] where the way is

---

[4] The only other account of this episode is in Guibert of Nogent, p. 143. The passage here is extremely obscure, and the lacunae only make matters worse. The reference may be (albeit obliquely) to the arrival not of the 'front-line' of the Peasants' Crusade, but to the final wave, led by Count Emicho of Leiningen. They arrived at the gates of Wieselberg, at the confluence of the Mosoni-Duna (a branch of the Danube) and Letha rivers, to find their way blocked by command of King Coloman of Hungary. As the town was surrounded by swamps they could find no way round, and after an abortive attempt to force their way through they spent six weeks constructing a bridge in order to launch a final assault. However they panicked after forcing an entrance and were cut down between town and river. The Charleville Poet has the incident quite out of context, which may account for his obscurity.

[5] *Gnidon* is a common medieval corruption of Cnidos, though here Nish is the seat of Nicetas, the Byzantine governor of Nicaea. The city was located in the valley of the river Morava, hence the Charleville Poet's description. For similarities in the Latin, cf. Gilo, vii. 508; Sidonius Apollinaris, *Carm.* v. 376.

Calle perangusto ceu carceris ore patentem,
Cuius pacificam poscentes transitionem　　　　　95
Vnus post unum quasi transiuere fenestram.
Postquam progressi campo potiuntur aperto,
Clamauere forum, famis instimulante magistro;ᵃ
Agmine uendentum sollempniter adueniente
Monstrantur species, sed censu deficiente　　　　　100
Ceperunt rapere quod mercari cupiebant,
Et mandante fame cupide raptis inhiabant.[1]
Protinus excita concurrunt agmina ad arma.
Propulsant, abigunt iaciendo hastilia densa.
Corpora et arma simul consternunt strata uiarum,[2]　　105
Nec fuga cessauit ternorum fine dierum.[3]
His depulsa locis acies male consiliata,
Imperio nullo, nullo moderamine ducta,[4]
Dum sibi cuncta forent contraria, prospera nulla,
Duratis animis tendebat ad ulteriora:　　　　　110
Ergo male expertam fugere exoptans Europam,
Finibus inque Asiae fortunam querere blandam,
Qua breuis est iuxta Byzantion Hellespontus,[5]
Cuius ab hocᵇ artus dirimit Chalcedona cursus,
Transiit atque urbem Nichomedis nomine dictam[6]　　115
Inter et egregiam stabiliuit castra Niceam.[7]

Hos fuerant inter modica non parte Alemanni,
Ante ducem dictum proprio sub nomine moti,[8]
Qui naturali nimium feritate tumentes
Indignabantur reliquis fore consociales.　　　　　120
At postquam fines quos diximus applicuerunt,
Cuncta suis per se titulis agere instituerunt.[9]
Ergo Bythinorum castellum[10] *repperientes*
Incustoditum, moxque illud preripientes
Muniuere satis muris, custodibus, armis;　　　　125

ᵃ magitro *m. pr.*　　　　ᵇ ab hoc *Grocock;* ab hac *cod.*

---

[1] Albert of Aachen, pp. 278–80, also refers to some form of altercation in the market, which led to fighting between Peter's forces and the local Byzantine troops.

[2] Cf. i. 293; Vergil, *Aen.* i. 421.

[3] The army was reunited at Bela Palanka. See Albert of Aachen, p. 281, who states that they spent three days gathering the harvest there.

[4] At this point the army was in fact under the command of Peter the Hermit.

[5] The Charleville Poet, like most historians of the crusade, fails to differentiate

very narrow, opening up like the mouth of a cave. [95] They asked to cross through there in peace, and crossed through one after another, as though going through a window. Passing on, they reached open country and, mastered by the pain of hunger, they cried out for a market. An assortment of wares was displayed by a crowd of merchants in the usual way, [100] but being short of money they took to stealing what they desired to buy, and spurred on by hunger they greedily swallowed up what they stole.[1] Straightaway the crowd was roused to hurry and take up arms. They drove them off and assailed them, throwing showers of spears. [105] Bodies and weapons alike were strewn over the roadway,[2] and their flight did not end until three days had passed.[3] That ill-advised force, driven off from this region, was under no authority and led under no direction;[4] although they felt everything would be against them, with no prospect of success, [110] they stiffened their resolve and headed further on. And so, in the desire to flee from Europe, where their experience was bad, and to seek a kinder fate in the regions of Asia, they crossed over the Hellespont[5] where it is narrow, next to Byzantium; its narrows divide Chalcedon from this place. [115] They pitched their camp between the city called Nicomedia[6] and famed Nicaea.[7]

Some Germans had been stirred to come there before their leader, mentioned above, on their own account;[8] they formed a substantial part of these men. They were swollen overmuch with their native fierceness, [120] and found it insufferable to be comrades of the rest. But after they came to the regions of which we have spoken, they decided to act entirely for themselves, on their own authority.[9] So, when they came across an unguarded Bithynian castle,[10] they at once seized hold of it [125] and fortified it strongly with walls and

between the Hellespont and the Bosporus; the latter is clearly what is intended here. See also iii. 195–6.

[6] Cf. ii. 93. Nicomedia had been deserted since it was sacked by the Seljuks in 1081.

[7] Albert of Aachen, p. 263, states that the army encamped at Civetot, which lies on the coast between these two cities and was originally built to house the Byzantine emperor's English mercenaries. See J. Shepard, 'The English and Byzantium: a study of their role in the Byzantine army in the later eleventh century', *Traditio*, xxix (1973), 53–92.

[8] The contrast is drawn here between the unruly Germans, who accompanied Peter the Hermit, and the more disciplined body which was led by Godfrey of Bouillon. Orderic Vitalis (v. 28) claims that 15,000 Germans joined the Peasants' Crusade after hearing Peter preach. A list of the southern German nobles on this expedition is also given by the Chronicler of Zimmern.

[9] This breakaway group was stirred up by jealousy of a party of Franks which had carried out a successful raid near Nicaea. It was led by an Italian noble named Rainald. For their exploits, see *Gesta Francorum*, p. 3; Robert of Rheims, pp. 732–3; Guibert of Nogent, pp. 144–5; Albert of Aachen, pp. 284–5.

[10] The castle was named Xerigordon, but its exact location has not been identified. Albert of Aachen, p. 284, places it three miles from Nicaea, but *Gesta Francorum*, p. 3, describes it as being three days' journey from there.

Saxa, sudes, tormenta locant in turribus altis,[1]
Ordine disposito statuunt qui menia seruent,
Qui uero utilia residentibus omnia curent.
Inde per extente fines regionis oberrant,
Comportant predas et rapto uiuere certant,[2]   130
Et, licet in patria sint omnimodis aliena,
Sic agitant ueluti sua sit prouintia tota.
Hoc ubi fama tulit[a] *per compita tot regionum,*
Quo iam nullus erat manifestus Christicolarum,
Vndique barbarice properant concurrere gentes,   135
Vndique multiplices protendunt obsidiones:
Nam quia compererant ductores Francigenarum
(Quorum nomen erat per totum nobile mundum)
Coniurasse uiam sancti sub honore sepulchri,[3]
Et uiolatorum animatos cedibus uti,   140
Si precursores habuissent mortificatos,
A reliquis sese sperabant iam fore tutos.
Hoc igitur uoto se totis uiribus aptant,
Artibus, ingeniis que ducunt commoda curant:
Aggeribus, pluteis, onagris quoque, fustibalisque   145
Assultus ineunt cunctis utensilibusque.[4]
Nube sagittarum tenebrosus redditur aer,
Vocibus atque tubis ululantibus obstrepit ether;[5]
Succedunt aliis alii, uel uulnere tardis
Vel diuturnarum operarum pondere lassis.   150
Obsessi porro feritate et robore freti
Et, si deficiant, nusquam[b] *se uiuere certi,*
Omni telorum genere oppugnantibus instant,
Ossaque corporaque et uitalia tota terebrant.

fo. 68[r]   *Nec solum pereunt quos duro uulnere quassant,*   155
Quos sude quos ferro quos igne uel assere mactant,
Quos uelut hylla[6] *terunt muralis pondera saxi,*
Quos quasi transiliunt uelamen acumina[c] *teli,*
Sed rabidos oculos uultusque uidendo minaces
Exanimante metu fugiunt in terga furentes,[d]   160
Sepius hoc igitur temptantes, sepe repulsi,

---

[a] tulit *Grocock;* telit *cod.*   [b] nunquam *Sirmond, Riant*   [c] uelamen acumina
cod.: ...la..acumina *Sirmond:* letalia acumina *Riant*   [d] furentes *Grocock:* ruentes
Riant: ...entes *cod.*

---

[1] Vergil, *Aen.* xi. 473.   [2] Vergil, *Aen.* vii. 749.   [3] Cf. i. 230.

*armed guards; they put war-engines with rocks and spikes in the high tow-
ers,*[1] *and decided a rota for who should go on sentry-duty and who should
busy themselves in everything needful for the occupants. From there they
wandered over the far-flung lands of that region,* [130] *bringing back plun-
der and booty on which they strove to live,*[2] *and, although they were in a com-
pletely foreign land, they behaved just as though the whole province was
theirs. When news of this spread along every highway and byway round
about, where there was as yet no sign of the Christians,* [135] *the heathen
peoples made haste to join together from every place, and in every place they
marshalled their numerous forces for a blockade. They had found out that the
leaders of the Franks (whose name was renowned throughout the whole
world) had sworn to undertake their journey for the honour of the Holy
Sepulchre,*[3] [140] *and were impassioned to slaughter those who had
desecrated it. Because of this they hoped that by bringing about the death of the
advance-guard, they would then be safe from the rest. With this wish in mind
they therefore made themselves ready with all their strength, and prepared
with skill and thought the things they considered useful:* [145] *siege-engines,
protective covers, ballistas, and slingshots too. They went into the attack with
all the weapons of war.*[4] *The sky was darkened by a cloud of arrows, and the
air rang loud*[5] *with shouting and hornblasts; men took one another's places as
they were crippled with wounds* [150] *or grew tired from the weight of their
daily labours. Those besieged relied even more on their savage strength:
certain that if they grew weak they stood no chance of survival, they fought
back at their assailants with every kind of weapon, cutting into flesh and bone
and the very seat of life.* [155] *It was not just those whom they smote with
serious wounds who died, or those they cut down with spike and sword or with
burning stakes, those on whom the weight of rocks from the wall beat down
like hail,*[6] *those whom weapon-points pierced like cloth, but also those who
saw the wild look in their eyes and their threatening faces,* [160] *who were
driven out of their minds with fear and turned and fled like madmen. And so
they tried this course of action several times, but each time they were driven*

---

[4] The different types of siege-weapons used in medieval warfare are described by
P. Contamine, *War in the Middle Ages*, trans. M. Jones (Oxford, 1984), pp. 102–6.

[5] Statius, *Thebaid*, xi. 247.

[6] The word *hylla* is the clear reading of the MS, but it does not seem that any of the
Latin forms *hilla, illa, ylla, hyle,* or *yle* are intended. Neither Ducange or *TLL* gives any
senses that fit the meaning here. Riant capitalizes the word, presumably taking it to be a
proper noun. However, an explanation of the word that does fit the sense is to take it as
a transcription of an OHG or OF variant meaning 'hail'; cf. *SOED*, which traces 'hail'
from OE *hagalian* and O. Teut. *hag(a)lojan*. Cf. Tobler–Lommatzsch, *Altfranz. Wört.*,
s.v. gresler; = '*intr. hageln*: il grele, *Gl.* haylet = hails'.

Nullo conatu castro ualuere potiri.
Postquam nulla uiam uirtus ad talia confert,
Protinus ad fraudem se contio barbara transfert.[1]
Mittitur extemplo legatio non bene cautis,   165
Alliciens stolidos affatibus insidiosis:
Cur maneant illic ubi uexet inedia lassos,[a]
Et mors, sera licet, rerum consumat egenos?
Si uellent sanctum properanter adire sepulchrum,
Cuius proposito uacuassent tecta parentum,   170
Ex facili posse uotis gaudere peractis
Si cum pace uelint castris exire relictis;
Denique se uotis concordibus esse paratos
Vsque in Hierusalem cunctos deducere sanos,[b]
Hoc quoque iurando sibi se promittere ferre.   175
Si non credendi, teneantur perditione.[c]
Talibus atque aliis rationibus amplificatis
Inflexe mentes populi non certa pauentis;
Nam, si fortune presens ostensio blanda,
Ignorabatur quid haberet ferre futura.   180
Vestigatur[d] ab his que sit fiducia coepti:[2]
Iurant legati penitus nihil esse pericli;
Ductores etenim iam dudum stare paratos
Ducere qui ualeant iterumque reducere tutos.

fo. 68ᵛ   Hoc se per legem cupide firmare paternam,   185
Per superos et si qua fides apud est Acherontem,[3]
Sic tamen ut positis se pacifica agmina telis
Credere non dubitent sibi iungi foedere certis.
Sic offirmatis[e] mediante interprete dictis
Et male percussis sub pacis[f] imagine pactis,   190
Credita res miseris, legatio quam male suada
Pertulit, et pepigit iuratio plus male fida.[4]
Excedunt castris et tradunt hostibus arma
Agmina capta dolis[g] et proditione subacta.
Excipiunt[h] ipsos ductores assimulati,   195
Deducunt aliquot[i] spatiis sub nomine pacti,
Donec in exesam uenientes undique uallem,[5]
Valli Hierusalem studuerunt ponere nomen:

---

[a] clausos *Sirmond, Riant*   [b] uiuos *Sirmond, Riant*   [c] perditione *sugg. Prof.*
Hall; conditione *Sirmond, Riant; the cod. has a lacuna*   [d] uestigiatur *cod.*
[e] confirmatis *Sirmond;* affirmatis *Riant*   [f] sub pacis *sugg. Riant in the lacuna*
[g] captan dolis *cod.*   [h] decipiunt *Sirmond, Riant*   [i] aliquoti *m. pr.*

off; they were not strong enough to gain the castle by any endeavour. When courage supplied no way of attaining their goal, the heathen horde at once turned to treachery.[1] *[165] A delegation was swiftly sent to those reckless men, enticing their stubborn hearts with words of deceit: why should they stay there, where in their exhaustion they would be ravaged by starvation, and death would eat them up, even if it were delayed, since they had nothing? If they wished to arrive quickly at the Holy Sepulchre, [170] for whose sake they had emptied the houses of their ancestors, they could easily enjoy the fulfilment of their prayers, if only they would come out in peace and leave the castle; in short, they were ready with one heart and mind to lead all of them right to Jerusalem in safety, [175] and to promise on oath that they would do it; if they were not to be believed then let them be damned. By means of this and other arguments which they piled up, they swayed the minds of the people, fearful of their uncertain fate, for even if their fortune's appearance seemed kindly at present, [180] what guise it might assume in future was unknown. They probed what faith they could put in the proposal of these men;*[2] *the envoys swore that there was absolutely no danger; their leaders had been standing by for some time, ready and able to take them and to bring them back again safely. [185] They swore this eagerly by their ancestral law, by the gods above and by whatever faith exists below,*[3] *in such a way that those fighting men at last laid their weapons aside in peace, not doubting that they could trust them, nor that they were joined with honest men in this treaty. And so their words were confirmed through the mediation of an interpreter, [190] and their agreements were sealed under the appearance of peace. The wretched troops believed the bargain that the ill-advised legation had brought, and their even more faithless oath had sworn.*[4] *They left the castle and gave their weapons over to the enemy, a force captured by trickery and overwhelmed by betrayal. [195] The so-called leaders took charge of them and led them some way in a pretence of an agreement, until they reached a steep-sided valley,*[5] *and tried to fasten to this valley the name 'Jerusalem'.*

[1] The Charleville Poet's graphic account of the Germans' defeat is unique. According to Albert of Aachen, p. 285, they suffered greatly during the siege and Rainald finally agreed to surrender. Those who renounced Christianity were sent into captivity in the East and those who remained true to their faith were slaughtered. For other brief accounts, cf. *Gesta Francorum*, pp. 3–4, and Robert of Rheims, p. 733.

[2] Vergil, *Aen.* ii. 75.

[3] Vergil, *Aen.* vi. 459.

[4] Albert of Aachen, pp. 290–1, relates a similar act of treachery when a group led by Gottschalk handed over their weapons to the Hungarians, who either killed or captured them.

[5] This may be a reference to the narrow wooded valley near Dracon, where the Seljuks ambushed the remaining members of both armies as they marched to avenge the massacre at Xerigordon. See S. Runciman, 'The First Crusade: Constantinople to Antioch', in Setton, *A History of the Crusades*, i. 280–307, at p. 283.

Quo facto medios densa statione coronant,
Hos in Hierusalem iam se statuisse perorant;   200
Quicquid promissum fuerit complesse recursant,
Nil illis post hac iam se debere recensent.
Vndique conclamant; gladiorum[a] spicula nudant,
Armati nudos cedunt feriuntque, trucidant,
Nil prohibente metu, circumque infraque uagantur;   205
Hinc etenim iugulis, hinc ferro bella geruntur.
Nuda perit uirtus nec quo se ostendere possit
Inuenit, et quid agat nulla ratione capescit.
Ceduntur pauci media inter milia pressi,
Et quod erat grauius, armis ac tegmine nudi   210
Sic detruncantur, media sic cede rotantur,
Sic illi faciunt, sic isti perpetiuntur,
Vt morti addicti medios clauduntur in enses,
Vt dibachantur pecora inter inertia tygres.[1]

fo. 69ʳ   Tali fine ruit uirtus temeraria frustra,   215
Dum sine consilio[2] sperat sibi cedere cuncta,
Et uelut in messe succisi disperiere,
Dum se non ualuit uirtus compressa mouere.
Ex hac clade ferunt non euasisse uel unum
Alterius partis qui detinuere recessum.   220

Nam meminisse decet, si qui sunt ista legentes,
Nos dixisse supra diuisas tunc legiones
Quando Alemanni isti per se caput instituerunt
Ac sese a reliquis secernere non timuerunt.
Qui postquam per se statuerunt castra mouere[b]   225
Et male conducti ceu diximus interiere,
Illi quos dictum est moetatos pone Niceam
Non minus aggressi stolida leuitate rapinam,[3]
Lance pari timidum pariterque lacessere fortem,
Pene paris dampni meruere incurrere sortem: 230
Namque acie sparsa mox discurrendo per arua
Oppida predari primum cepere minora;
Ex hinc paulatim longe lateque uagari,
Insignes uillas castellaque depopulari,
Donec asspirans primo fortuna labori[4]   235
Suasit eos ausum ceco prebere furori.

---

[a] gladios & (sic) Sirmond; gladios et Riant   [b] mouer. cod.

This done, they encircled them all round with a close guard. [200] They
persisted in saying that they had now brought them to Jerusalem, stated that
whatever they had promised was now fulfilled, and that in their opinion they
owed them nothing from now on. Then they raised a shout on every side, and
bared the points of their swords; armed men slew defenceless men, slashed at
them, cut them down; [205] no fear stood in their way as they rampaged all
round among them; one side waged war with the sword, the other could only
offer up their throats to be cut. Their courage died naked, and found no place
where it could display itself; it could find no course of action to seize upon. In
the midst of thousands the few were slain, hemmed in; [210] and what was
worse, they were cut down stripped of weapons and armour, whirled about in
the midst of slaughter. Thus did the one side fight, thus did the other side
suffer. Like men delivered up to death they were shut in the midst of the
swords; the other side ran wild like tigers[1] among harmless cattle. [215]
Heedless courage perished in vain by such an end, while without proper
counsel[2] they hoped that all would give way before them, and they perished as
though cut down in the harvest, and their bravery, hemmed in, could not
display itself. [220] Those of the second group who stayed behind say that not
a single man escaped this disaster.

For it should be remembered by any who chance to be reading this account
that we said above that the forces divided when the Germans took it upon
themselves to form the advance-guard, and were not afraid to cut them-
selves off from the rest. [225] After they had decided of their own accord
to break camp, and were led foully to destruction, as we have said, those
who as I said encamped behind Nicaea set out to plunder[3] just like the
others, stupid and reckless as they were; they attacked the timorous and the
brave without distinction, [230] and almost deserved to meet as disastrous
a fate; for, racing swiftly over the fields in a straggling formation, they
began at first to plunder the lesser towns; then little by little they wandered
further afield and laid waste substantial villages and fortified towns,
[235] until the wind of fortune, having blown favourably on their first
endeavour,[4] persuaded them in their blind frenzy to attempt a deed

---

[1] Cf. Vergil, *Aen.* iv. 158–9.

[2] The Charleville Poet is anxious to emphasize the importance of acting with *con-*
silium, and stresses the disasters that befall those who do not. There are obvious
parallels with, for example, the *Chanson de Roland*, ll. 1724–7.

[3] The chronology here is rather muddled. The French sortie and sack of the area
surrounding Nicaea in fact predated the German capture of Xerigordon. See Albert of
Aachen, p. 284.

[4] Vergil, *Aen.* ii. 385.

Vrbs etenim clara bis iam memorata Nycea[1]
Olim ter centum patribus ter sexque sacrata,
Dum per concilium,[2] omni memorabile terra,[a]
Dogmata sunt Arii penes ipsam[b] mortificata,   240
Haec erat et pollens opibus, tum robore firma
Natura atque manu, populisque immane referta;
Qua dominabatur uenerans tamen idola turba
Et famulabatur diuino fonte renata;[3]

fo. 69ᵛ

Hanc primum predis temptatam necne rapinis,   245
Post etiam uexant discursibus anteforanis,[4]
Creuit inexplicitus processu temporis ausus:
Iam quatitur murus, nisi qua lacus imminet altus:
Iam quasi capturi crebris assultibus urbem
Comminus incursant plus quam sit causa timentem: 250
Nam quis mirari populum male desipientem,
Quis queat indocilem digne incusare cohortem?
Vrbanos etenim, quos Christi fonte nitentes
Diximus, inque urbe non primos sed famulantes,
Viderunt calamos sine ferro conicientes,   255
Et manuum gestu se significando cientes,
Vt prope congressi muris portisque recepti
Vrbe potirentur, socio conamine freti;
Sed neque id obtunsus ualuit perpendere sensus
Aut intercipere uoluit male credulus ausus.   260
Sic igitur ceptum medio tenus intermissum,
Sic opere infecto est iter ad tentoria uersum.

Tunc gemini proceres fuerant hec regna tenentes,
Incertum nobis an fratres siue nepotes,
Vni Sultannus, alii nomen Solimannus,[5]   265
Diues uterque satis et opimo milite cinctus;
Fama relatarum ueniens his nuntia rerum
Ammonuit tantum non dissimulare tumultum.
Cogunt militiam, ueniunt properando Nyceam,
Inueniunt predis compluribus exspoliatam;   270

[a] memorabile terra *sugg.* Sirmond; memo…t terra *cod.*   [b] ipsam *Grocock;* ipsa
cod.

---

[1] Note that this sentence, rambling as it is, never finishes in the Latin, lacking as it
does a main verb.

[2] The council of Nicaea, summoned by Constantine in 325 to deal with the Arian

of daring. For the famous city of Nicaea,[1] *already twice referred to, was once hallowed by three hundred and eighteen fathers of the church, when in a council*[2] *which all the earth should know of,* [240] *the teachings of Arius were condemned within its walls. It was wealthy and flourishing, made strong by nature and man, and filled to capacity with people. But in it the host that worshipped idols ruled, and the host born again by baptism served.*[3] [245] *At first they tested it with raids and plundering, and later they harried it with attacks beneath its very gates.*[4] *As time passed, their daring reached hitherto unseen heights, the city wall was soon being shaken, except where the deep lake bordered it, and soon they were racing in frequent attacks right up to the city,* [250] *which feared them unjustifiably as though they were about to take it; for who could be surprised at such a stupid people? Who could find fault with this headstrong troop as much as they deserved? Those citizens aglow with Christian baptism, as we have said, and not leaders but servants in the city,* [255] *they actually saw them throwing shafts without iron tips, and calling out loud, showing who they were by waving their hands, so that they should gather near the walls, be let in at the gates, and take possession of the city, aided by the effort of their allies; but their dulled minds were not capable of grasping this action,* [260] *and their unbelieving boldness was not willing to take up the opportunity. And so they broke off their enterprise halfway through, and with the task unfinished they made their way to their tents.*

At that time there were two nobles ruling these kingdoms. It is not clear to us whether they were brothers or cousins: [265] *one was called Sultan, the other Suleiman;*[5] *both were very wealthy, and were attended by a sumptuous escort. A report reached them telling of what had been happening, and advising them not to leave so massive an uprising unattended. They gathered their troops and came with haste to Nicaea,* [270] *which they found ravaged*

heresy, is reputed to have been attended by 318 bishops, but contemporary accounts give a variety of figures for those present. See G. Alberigo *et al.*, *Conciliorum Oecumenicorum Decreta* (Bologna, 1973), i; J. Rivière, '"Trois cent dix-huit": un cas de symbolisme arithmétique chez saint Ambroise', *Recherches de théologie ancienne et médiévale*, vi (1934), 361–7; E. Honigmann, 'La liste originale des Pères de Nicée: à propos de l'évêché de "Sodoma" en Arabie', *Byzantion*, xiv (1939), 17–76.

[3] Cf. Arator, *Hist. apost.* ii. 600. The Byzantines lost Nicaea, which became the capital of the Seljuk sultan Suleiman ibn Kutulmish, in 1078.

[4] Albert of Aachen, pp. 287–8, states that the fighting took place in a wood and on the plain, but not near Nicaea. The Charleville Poet, however, gives an accurate description of the city surrounded by walls and fortifications dating from the period of Byzantine rule. The city lies at the eastern end of Lake Ascanius, its western wall rising directly from the water.

[5] Other Latin chroniclers also confused the title and patronymic of the Seljuk sultan, Kilij Arslan ibn Suleiman (the son of Suleiman ibn Kutulmish). See William of Tyre, i. 59, Albert of Aachen, p. 284.

Que gesta inquirunt. multi conspecta renarrant,
Multi comperta, cuncti ulciscenda perorant.
Procedunt contra, sed non opus est uia longa:
Inueniunt prope se quibus est penuria amara,
Namque lupos matrem solita extra pellere siluam[1]   275
Non sinit hos placidam membris dare cura quietem.[2]
Ad primos uisus acies statuuntur utrimque,
Sed non consimilis constantia perstat utrisque:
Primo congressu metuens fugit aduena turma,
Solaque pugna fuit fugientum cedere terga.   280
Nulli spes cordi, nulli constantia menti
Pectora uel facies hosti obiectare sequenti;
Nudatis manibus, proiectis turpiter armis
In pedibus tota fiducia mansit inermis.
Nec prius absistit[a] *patientia commoriendi*   285
Quam saties tenuit uictores interimendi:
Namque retro pulsos atque in sua terga regressos[b]
Fines usque suos proculcauere supremos.
Hac in clade ruit Vualterius, unus eorum
Diximus istorum quos assumpsisse ducatum.[3]   290
Alter, id est Petrus, retro fugiendo relatus,
Cum reliquis uiuis torrente Propontidis actus
Circa Byzantii latebras confinia fouit,[4]
Donec se ducibus uenientibus associauit.
Talia diuersis stolidus comitatus in oris   295
Aspera sustinuit, qui laxis fusus habenis[5]
Quicquid sperauit se posse explere putauit,
Nec ducis imperio moderarier[c] *utile*[d] *duxit.*
Has de se poenas gentilibus exhibuerunt
Ac fidei nostre spernendae exempla dederunt,   300
Quamuis non longum fuerint hac laude hylarati
Aut impune diu tulerint hac cede potiri.[e][6]
Sed quia iam rauca uult respirare camena,
Tertius ista thomus referet uirtute resumpta.[7]

fo. 70ᵛ   *Explicit liber secundus. Incipit tertius.*

fo. 70ʳ (line 275)

[a] absistit *Grocock:* abstitit *cod.*   [b] repressos *Sirmond, Riant*   [c] moderantis *Sirmond, Riant*   [d] uiuere *Sirmond, Riant*   [e] potiti *Riant*

---

[1] This was a popular medieval proverb. See *Proverbes français antérieurs au XVᵉ siècle,*

by numerous raids. They asked what had happened. Many told them what they had seen, and many what they had found; all begged them for vengeance. They set out against the enemy, and did not have to go far: they found those to whom hunger was bitter nearby; [275] *for anxiety, which commonly drives wolves from their mother the forest,*[1] *did not allow these men to grant rest to their limbs.*[2] *As soon as they saw one another, both sides drew up their battle-lines, but a similar firm resolve did not possess both: at the first clash the foreign troops fled in terror,* [280] *and the only fighting involved stabbing the backs of men running away. They had no hope in their hearts, no firm resolve in their minds to expose their chests and faces to the pursuing enemy, but with empty hands, their weapons disgracefully thrown away, they put all their helpless trust in running.* [285] *Nor did their suffering and dying cease until the victors had had their fill of slaughter, for they drove back those who turned on their heels and trampled them down until they came right up to the borders of that land. In this disaster perished Walter, one of those who,* [290] *as we said, had taken on the leadership of the group.*[3] *The other, that is, Peter, fled right back in retreat, and driven on by the fast-flowing Propontis he found a hiding-place in the neighbourhood of Byzantium with the rest of the surviv-ors,*[4] *until he joined up with the approaching leaders.* [295] *Such were the hardships endured in various places by this stubborn company, which ran unchecked and unbridled,*[5] *with the thought that they could achieve what-ever they hoped for, and did not consider it useful to be governed by the authority of a proper leader. Through their own doing they paid this penalty to the heathen* [300] *and gave them precedents for despising our faith, though they were not cheered by this praiseworthy exploit for long, nor were they for long allowed to possess the victory won by slaughter without retribution.*[6] *But now because my Muse is hoarse and wishes to regain her breath, the third volume will tell of these things, with strength renewed.*[7]

The second book ends. The third begins.

---

ed. J. Morawski (Paris, 1925), no. 1000, 'la fains eschache le louf du bois', and also Fran-çois Villon, *Testament*, 168.   [2] Vergil, *Aen.* iv. 5.

[3] The massacre of the crusaders took place on 21 Oct. 1096. Walter was among several minor leaders who perished.

[4] Other sources state that Peter the Hermit had already returned to Constantinople before the fighting began. See *Gesta Francorum*, p. 4; Albert of Aachen, p. 286; Raymond of Aguilers, p. 44.

[5] Vergil, *Georg.* ii. 364. Once again there is a contrast between the undisciplined behaviour of these crusaders and the *consilium* displayed by Godfrey's force.

[6] This looks ahead to the surrender of Nicaea in June 1097, which is described by the Charleville Poet in the interpolated section of book iv, ll. 60–119.

[7] The book closes with a stock excuse and a promise of what is to come.

LIBER III

Post ea que primo sunt enumerata libello
A diuerticulo repetendum est ordine terno.
Quo diuerticulo docuit liber iste secundus
Qualiter excitus fuerit malus iste tumultus,
Quo fuerat sancti uia pene relicta sepulchri,   5
Ni uirtute foret procerum reparata potenti.
Premisso satis est iam dicta uolumine plaga.
Nunc isto[a] superest dicenda sequente medela.[1]

Postquam dux rapidum Godefridus transiit Hystrum[b]
Disposuitque suas turmas, per aperta uiarum   10
Norycios fines iam preteruectus abibat.[2]
Pannonias uersus iter indefessus agebat,
Cum subito rumor nil tale timentibus asper[c]
Aduenit,[d] inque animos leuium pauor obruit acer;
Agmina perculsi[e] bellum fugientia uulgi   15
Quod sibi in introitu terre sua culpa mereri
Fecerat in predis grassantibus atque rapinis[3]
(Quod memorasse sat est libri sermone prioris)
Occurrunt stupidis et acerbant funera dictis.[4]
Orant retrogradis celerent uestigia plantis,[5]   20
Vulnera demonstrant putri insiccata cruore,
Quicquid perpessi digno deflente dolore
Deplorant structos capitum miseranter aceruos,
Congeminant multos fluuiorum uortice mersos,
Deflent innumeros cinerem tenus igne perustos   25
Sanguinis errantes sacra circa altaria riuos,

fo. 71ʳ

This book is found only in G   [a] ista *Sirmond, Riant*   [b] Hystrum *is written at the end of l. 10, where there is space*   [c] asper *and* acer *are written beside* Hystrum *at the end of l. 10; each word is marked to show its correct position in the text*   [d] aduenit *Sirmond*   [e] perculsi *Holford-Strevens;* per*** *cod.*

[1] The Charleville Poet again contrasts the Peasants' Crusade, described as *malus tumultus* and *plaga*, with the main expedition and the good deeds of the *proceres* or *uirtute potentes*.

[2] See above, i. 166 and n. Godfrey set out in mid-August and arrived at the Hungarian border in early October.

BOOK III

To what happened after those events which are set out in the first book we must now return in the third, from the digression by which our second book stated how that fateful commotion was stirred up [5] *which almost caused the journey to the Holy Sepulchre to be abandoned, had it not been renewed again by the vigorous courage of its leaders. This sore wound has already been sufficiently spoken of in the preceding volume. Now in the following one it remains to tell how its healing took place.*[1]

[10] *After Duke Godfrey had crossed the fast-flowing Danube and arranged his squadrons, he made his way along open roads and was soon leaving behind the borders of Noricum.*[2] *Unwearying he was making his way towards Hungary* [when suddenly] *idle talk sprang up, bitter to those who feared no such thing, and dreadful terror assailed the minds of men who were easily swayed;* [15] *the bands of common people, fleeing in terror, related what their own fault had made them suffer on their entering the land, through their going about pillaging*[3] *and plundering (which is recalled quite enough in the previous book's account). They ran to meet the shocked troops and made the slaughter worse as they told of it.*[4] [20] *They pleaded with them to retrace their steps*[5] *and make haste about it, they showed off their wounds, still wet with putrid gore, and with merited grief lamenting over what they had suffered, they wept for the heaps of heads wretchedly piled up, and bewailed the many drowned in the currents of the rivers,* [25] *and wept over the countless men burned to a cinder in the fire, over the streams of blood*

---

[3] A divine judgement upon human sinfulness became the standard explanation for a crusading defeat. See Siberry, *Criticism of Crusading*, pp. 69–100. For a similar interpretation of the failure of the Peasants' Crusade, see Ekkehard of Aura, *Hierosolimita*, p. 19; Albert of Aachen, p. 295; Bernold of St Blasien, p. 466.

[4] Godfrey of Bouillon's army must undoubtedly have encountered some survivors of the Peasants' Crusade, but the Charleville Poet is the only source to describe the disheartening effect which this had upon its morale. Albert of Aachen, pp. 299–306, is otherwise the main source for information about Godfrey's journey to Constantinople. Here again the chronology may be muddled. These could not have been the survivors of Civetot, since that massacre did not take place until 21 Oct. They may have been the remnants of the later German bands led by Gottschalk, Folkmar, and Emicho of Leiningen, which were massacred in Hungary. For example, Hartmann of Dillingen-Kyburg appears to have been in Godfrey's camp at Nicaea. See Albert of Aachen, pp. 299, 332, 427.

[5] Vergil, *Aen.* vi. 159, Alcimus Avitus, *Carm.* i. 130.

Omnigenum mota populorum comminus arma,
Nullum sufficere numerum ad gentilia monstra:
Quin potius dum spes fugiendi percelerarent
Ne consectati insatiata clade perirent. 　　　　30
Talia cuncta phalanx grauioraque comperientes,
Non solum timidi, turbantur denique fortes.
Exoptantur equi multis, [tot milia]ᵃ longi
Quot processissent ultra confinia Rheni,ᵇ
Seque super frontes illorum [.......]plorare 　　　　35
Ne nece cogantur grau[iora pericula adire]ᶜ
Consilium fractis angusto pectore [rebus]ᵈ
Electum multis agitant cumᵉ singula [sensus]ᶠ
Circumstare ducem durosque re[uoluere casus]:ᵍ
Implorare fidem summe Deitatis [..........] 　　　　40
Ne quasi se uiles animas [concedere morti],ʰ
Neu uelit ut pecudes addicere perditioni.¹
Sat sibi sufficere debere exempla priorum:
Nec positos facile fines transcendere patrum;
Non sapere optandum plus quam sit copia nosse, 　　　　45
Nec facere audendum plus quam foret utile posse:
Multa per extentos pollere sacraria Gallos,
Multos esse locos orandi iure dicatos,
Siue Coloniaci² subeant oracula Petri
Siue genetricis ueneranda palatia Christi³ 　　　　50
Si loca sanctorum per plurima regna piorum
Quorum sit precibus moles subiecta malorum.

fo. 71ᵛ 　　　*Posse ubicumque pias Diue Bonitatis ad aures*
Illacrimando preces transmittere spirituales,
Ipsum namque Deum nullatenus esse localem 　　　　55
Sed totum totis in partibus esse potentem,
Nec pretiosarum gazarum querere templa
Sed pia, sed pura, sed amare innoxia corda.⁴
Desinerent igitur temptare impossibiles res
Frustraque incertasⁱ adamare superfluitates, 　　　　60

ᵃ tot milia *Grocock;* miliaria longe *Sirmond;* miliaria longis *Riant*　　　ᵇ Rhenis *Sir-*
mond, Riant　　　ᶜ *Sirmond sugg.* grauiora pericula adire *in the lacuna*　　　ᵈ *Sirmond*
sugg. in tempore rebus *in the lacuna he saw:* pectore *is the MS reading*　　　ᵉ dum *Sir-*
mond, Riant　　　ᶠ *Riant sugg.* sensus *in the lacuna*　　　ᵍ reuoluere casus *Sirmond in*
the lacuna　　　ʰ immittere morti *Sirmond*　　　ⁱ incoeptas *Sirmond, Riant*

---

¹ Ekkehard of Aura (*Hierosolymita*, p. 21) commented that after the defeat of Emicho

flowing round the holy altars, over the weapons of all kinds people raised to
meet them, over the fact that no number was great enough to face the heathen
horror; rather, while hope of fleeing remained, they ought to make haste [30]
lest they perished, cut to pieces in an insatiable slaughter. As the whole force
found out about these acts and worse, not only the fearful but even the stout-
hearted were shaken. Horses were sought by many, as many thousands had
gone across the borders of the Rhine far away, [35] *and [throwing] them-*
selves upon the horses' heads, they begged not to be forced on pain of death to
undergo worse torments. In these dire straits they lighted on a narrow-minded
plan, while individual troubles stirred up their feelings: they stood round the
duke and called their hard labour to witness, [40] *they invoked and prayed*
for the protection of the most high God not to wish that they should [pour out
their souls to death] like worthless men, nor to give them over to destruction
like cattle.[1] *The examples of those who had gone before must surely be enough*
for them, and it was not easy to cross over the frontiers established by their
fathers; [45] *it was unwise to want to know too much, or to dare to do more*
than could possibly be of use. Many holy places were to be found spread
through Gaul, and there were many places of prayer consecrated by law; they
could go to the mercy-seat of Peter at Cologne,[2] [50] *or to the hallowed palace*
of the Mother of Christ,[3] *or in many a kingdom to the shrines of the holy*
saints, by whose prayers the mass of evil is held in check. In every place they
could send up spiritual prayers with tears for the Holy God of goodness to
hear, [55] *for God himself was in no way fixed in one place, but was wholly*
powerful throughout the whole world, and did not seek temples of precious
treasures, but rather loved holy, pure, and blameless hearts.[4] *Therefore, they*
ought to refrain from trying to do such impossible things, [60] *and vainly*

of Leiningen at the siege of Wieselberg in Aug. 1096, some of the 'more simple brethren'
dismissed the whole expedition as 'vain and frivolous'.

[2] Cologne is normally associated with the relics of the three Magi; by the end of the
12th c. it had become one of the main pilgrimage sites in Europe, the others being
Santiago, Rome, and Canterbury. This, however, may be a reference to an earlier
legend that St Peter had been the first bishop of Cologne. See *Catholic Encyclopaedia*, art.
'Cologne', 1013, 1017. Cologne's Gothic cathedral, begun in the late 13th c., is dedicated
to St Peter and the Virgin Mary. Other accounts of the First Crusade by contrast focus
on St Peter as the first bishop of Antioch.

[3] The exact meaning of 'the palace of the Mother of Christ' is not clear. It could be a
reference to Le Puy, which was already a centre of Marian devotion and the setting for a
vision described by Caffaro, p. 100; alternatively, it could refer to Rocamadour, which
was another place of Marian pilgrimage in late 11th-c. France. See E. Mason, 'Rocama-
dour in Quercy above all other churches: the healing of Henry II', *SCH* xix (1982), 39–
54, at 40, 42.

[4] Matt. 5: 8. For the importance of 'right intention', see Siberry, *Criticism of Crusading*,
pp. 95–6; E. O. Blake, 'The formation of the "crusade idea"', *Journal of Ecclesiastical His-
tory*, xxi (1970), 11–32.

Et si non possent euincere quod uoluissent,
Id demum uellent insumere[a] quod potuissent.[1]

Talibus atque aliis grauioribus ingeminatis
Pene retro uersis inflectebantur habenis:
At ductor ualidis angoribus intima pressus   65
Atque hamo duplici circum precordia fixus,
Ex uno profugos cernens graue passa gementes,
Ex alio timidos bello grauiora pauentes—
Nam fortes animo timidis agitantibus ista
Nutabant inter [Thers]itis[b] et Herculis arma,[2]   70
Spemque metumque inter,[3] *non belli munia poscunt,*
Non indigna fugae [quer]enda[c] latibula promunt—
His, inquam, grauibus uir maximus undique septus[4]
Nunc prece nuncque minis[5] *nunc uero hortatibus usus*
Increpitat quenam sit eis mutatio tanta   75
Qui deuouissent Domino sese et sua cuncta,[6]
Qui se martyrio pro Christi nomine promptos
Vsque uel in mortem iurassent subiciendos?
Cur necdum positos in belli limine primo[7]
Cogat eos retro fugiendi dira cupido?[8]   80
Cur quos terrifici necdum canor increpet eris,
Nec moueant pulsis uexilla uolantia uentis,
Rumor iners agitet generosa relinquere coepta
Et nondum uisa dare terga fugacia pugna?
Quid mirum si pacifica statione recepti   85
In predam uersi fuerint bellando repulsi?
Hoc se facturos siquid sibi tale ueniret,
Et mala quisquam illis propter benefacta referret;
Non debere uiam rapto feruere beatam,
Sed dare quam rapere plebem pia uota professam.[9]   90
Qui uenit ut ciuis et mox grassatur ut hostis,
Non mirum sua si patiatur seua tyrannis.
Nequid forte sibi possit contingere tale,
Se curaturum non sanguine sed ratione,
Namque manus meritis que dat sua iura superbis   95
Mitibus hec eadem dat munera prosperitatis.[10]
Denique splendiferum que fornax comprobat aurum,
Hec eadem reprobat uelut ad nihil utile plumbum.[11]

fo. 72[r]

---

[a] adsumere *Sirmond, Riant*   [b] Thersitis *Sirmond*   [c] querenda *Sirmond*

*desiring uncertain and empty excesses, and if they were unable to prevail in
what they wished for, then they should desire what they were able to do.*[1]

*When they had poured out such complaints as these, and other more serious ones
too, they were quite prepared to wheel their horses round and to head for home,*
[65] *but their leader was pained with a terrible anguish within, and his heart
pierced by a double-barbed hook, first by the sight of the runaways weeping
over their sufferings, and second by the fainthearted, fearful of worse to come in
the fighting, for as the fainthearted continued to talk of those things, so those
who were strong at heart* [70] *were wavering between the weapons of Thersites
and Hercules,*[2] *between hope and fear,*[3] *and neither asked for the duties of war,
nor suggested hiding-places to be sought out disgracefully in flight—hemmed
in on all sides by these pressures, as I say,*[4] *the great man upbraided them now
with prayers, now with threats, now with exhortation:*[5] [75] *what great
change had come over them, they who had dedicated themselves and all they
had to the Lord God,*[6] *who had sworn themselves ready to be martyred for the
name of Christ and to put themselves in peril even of death? Why, when they
were not even on the threshold of war,*[7] [80] *did this terrible desire*[8] *to flee in
retreat compel them? Why, when the blare of the fearful bugle had not yet
reproached them, and the banners that flutter in the wind had not yet moved
them, did an idle rumour stir them to abandon their noble undertaking and
turn tail, running away from a fight they had not yet seen?* [85] *Was it any
wonder that men who had been welcomed at a peaceful staging-place had been
driven off in a hostile manner when they had turned to pillaging? They them-
selves would do this if such a thing happened to them: would anyone repay them
with evil if they had done good deeds? Their holy journey ought not to be
inflamed with pillaging,* [90] *but a people who professed holy aims*[9] *ought to
give rather than take. If a man arrived as a citizen and then laid about him as
an enemy, it was no surprise if his tyranny suffered savage treatment. So that
nothing like this could happen to him, he was going to conduct himself with
reason, not bloodshed,* [95] *for the same hand that metes out just retribution to
proud deeds also gives the gifts of prosperity to the humble;*[10] *the same furnace
which proves shining gold also proves the lead to be good for nothing;*[11] *the*

---

[1] See also Ekkehard of Aura, *Hierosolymita*, pp. 17–18.
[2] Thersites was the type of a coward; see Juvenal *Sat.* viii. 269–71, xi. 31.
[3] Proba, *Cent. Verg.* 542 = *Aen.* i. 218; Avitus, *Carm.* vi. 72.
[4] Prudentius, *Apoth.* 708.   [5] Lucan, *Bellum ciuile*, v. 480–1.
[6] Gilo, vii. 197.   [7] Statius, *Achilleid*, ii. 34.
[8] Vergil, *Georg.* i. 37.   [9] Acts. 2: 35.   [10] Jas. 4: 6; 1 Pet. 5: 5.
[11] Prov. 17: 3, 27: 21. The same image is found in Fulcher of Chartres, p. 226. See
Siberry, *Criticism of Crusading*, pp. 69–70.

Que moto paleas exterminat area uento,
Hec eadem puro seruat loca congrua grano.[1]   100
Nosse decere omnes, constantes mentis in actu,
Non sine diuino hec suscepta pericula nutu,[2]
Que sic per cuncti placuissent clymata mundi
In quibus accipitur nomen uenerabile Christi.
Et siquos fidei modice ferus atterat hostis,[3]   105
Nil hoc officere fidei integritate probatis,[4]
Que montes etiam Deitate fauente moueret,[5]
Talia si poscens[a] nullatenus addubitaret.[6]

Talibus ammoniti redeunt in fortia cuncti,
Et timidos etiam piguit uoluisse reuerti,   110
Vt reuocantur apes post tedia mellificandi,[7]
Dum recreant animos eris commenta sonori.
fo. 72[v]   Tunc ad rumigeros uersus profugosque maniplos
Increpat atque minis prope territat exanimatos;
Quid turbare rudes ipsis conuenerit aures   115
Atque eneruandas animi conquirere uires?
Cetera si pergant, non hos sibi perpetiendos,
Stigmatibus sedenim candentibus inficiendos;
Discedant potius melioribus atque locum dent
Ne sibi coniunctos ueluti contagia ledant;   120
Vnumquemque suis satis est fore inutile membrum,
Nedum sepositis morbum inculcare nociuum.

Mittitur interea rectori[b] Pannoniarum
Dicta ferens legum legatio pacificarum:[8]
Ductorem regni stipatum milite Christi   125
Deuouisse uiam sancti sub honore sepulchri,[9]
Velle iter impauidum sua per confinia ferre,
Exorare sibi blande sua claustra patere;
Mercaturarum precio [communia][c] iusto
Commutare uelit, pacis prebente ministro;   130
Velle etiam stabili se conditione pacisci
Ne sibi quis noceret[d] Pannon neque quis suus ulli;
Quod commisissent male qui commissa luissent,

[a] noscens *Sirmond, Riant*   [b] praetori *Riant*   [c] communia *Grocock;* sibi
munia *Riant;* commercia *sugg. Holford-Strevens*   [d] noceat *Sirmond, Riant*

[1] Matt. 3: 12; Hos. 13: 3.   [2] Charleville Poet, i. 7.

same threshing-floor sifts out the chaff in the breeze that blows, [100] *and provides a fitting place for the pure grain.*[1] *It behoved all who were constant in purpose of mind to know that this dangerous enterprise had not been undertaken without divine prompting,*[2] *since it was thus approved of throughout every land where the venerable name of Christ was acknowledged.* [105] *And if a wild foe had destroyed those whose faith was feeble,*[3] *this posed no threat to those who were tried and tested by the firmness of their faith,*[4] *which would with God's favour move even mountains*[5] *if he who asked such things did not doubt at all.*[6]

Chastened by these words they all strengthened their hearts once again, [110] *and even the fainthearted were ashamed to have wanted to turn back: just as bees are called back after the tiring work of making honey when the deceiving sound of ringing brass revives their spirits.*[7] *Then turning to the tellers of tales and the bands who had run away, he upbraided them and well-nigh scared them out of their wits with his threats:* [115] *what business was it of theirs to unsettle the ears of the simple and to try to weaken their strength of mind? If they persisted in future, he would not put up with them, but would brand them with red-hot irons; so they had better take their leave and make way for their betters,* [120] *lest like a plague they infected those joined with them; it was quite enough that each and every one of them was a useless appendage to his associates, without their spreading their harmful disease to those kept apart from them.*

Meanwhile there was sent to the ruler of Hungary an embassy bearing a message setting out peaceful terms.[8] [125] *They said that the duke of their land, with a host of Christ's knights, had vowed to journey for the honour of the Holy Sepulchre,*[9] *and wished to pursue his journey without fear through the ruler's territory; that the duke asked him kindly to open his gates to him, and to be so good as to enter into the exchange of merchandise* [130] *at a fair price, his servant organizing it peacefully; that he also wished to fix binding terms of agreement, so that no Hungarian should harm his men, and no man of his harm anyone of theirs. Those who had behaved badly had paid the*

---

[3] Sidonius Apollinaris, *Carm.* vii. 285.

[4] Again a sharp contrast is intended between the members of the Peasants' Crusade and Godfrey's contingent. See above, iii. 8 and n. 1.   [5] Matt. 17: 20.

[6] Matt. 17: 22; Mark 11: 23. This speech is used by the Charleville Poet as a vehicle to underline Godfrey's devotion both to God and to the crusade.

[7] Vergil, *Georg.* iv. 71–2.

[8] Albert of Aachen, p. 300, notes that Godfrey sent an embassy headed by Geoffrey of Esch to King Coloman of Hungary to ask for permission to cross his territory.

[9] Charleville Poet, i. 230.

Ne quis speraret, firma ratione cauerent,
Obsidibus namque firmaret protinus ipse, [1]   135
Et non externis, sed germano obside fratre, [2]
Quod nihil aduersi per se accideret regioni,
Hoc et idemque sibi per eos debere rependi,
Hoc et ab ingressu regionis continuari
Donec in egressu contingeret exspatiari.   140
Talia dum passim legatio docta perorat,
Rex cum consilio seriatim singula tractat.

fo. 73ʳ

Omnia rimantes dum disceptando trahuntur,
Nil fore quod possit reprehendi iure fatentur.
Censent mandatis responsa decentia reddi: 145
Vt bene sit ueniens ductori notificari,
Officiis onerant legatos muneribusque.
Aduentus statuunt signando diemque locumque.
Gaudent non modice regiones Pannoniarum
Quod digne exceptae legiones Francigenarum   150
Sufficerent sese purgare a crimine cedis,
Vnde supra cesae est descripta tragoedia gentis.
Dicta dies uenit, locus alma Sabaria[3] *fulsit,* [a]
Qua, Martine, tuus sacer ortus in orbe reluxit.
Huc rex deuotus cum coetu pontificali,   155
Cum ducibus, populo, sacri sed et agmine cleri,
Cumque faris,[b] *crucibus, librisque euangeliorum,*
Relliquiis sacris et honoribus ecclesiarum,
Obuius accurrit, uenientibus [oscula][c] *figit;*
Cum iubilo ac ymnis intra sacraria ducit,   160
Hospitio celebri regaliter amplificauit,
Obsidibus pactum sumptisque datisque sacrauit.
Per totum regnum uenalia multiplicari
Ac per iter totum gradientibus associari
Iussit et emensis proprie regionibus orae   165
Munera cum uadibus regalia contulit, atque
Auxilio tutos, opibusque et honoribus auctos,
Iussit abire Dei cum pace beatificandos.

---

[a] cessit *Sirmond, Riant*   [b] facis *Riant*   [c] oscula *Riant*

---

[1] The writing is very awkward here. The two phrases in l. 134 are appositional, but a

penalty for their evil behaviour, and, so that no man should have hopes of doing the same, they should take good care with firm resolve, [135] because he himself would forthwith confirm the agreement with hostages,[1] and not with outsiders, but with his own blood brother as a hostage,[2] so that nothing untoward should happen to the country through his doing, and that the same treatment should be repaid to him by them. This agreement should be maintained from his entering the country [140] until he came to leave it. While the learned embassy went through all these requests, the king pondered each point in turn with his council. They spent some time in weighing and examining everything, and admitted that in law there was nothing with which they could justly find fault. [145] They thought that a fitting reply should be given to the proposals; and so that the announcement might come pleasantly to the leader, they bestowed gifts and courtesies on the envoys. They fixed the day and place of his arrival, marking it with a seal. The Hungarian dominions rejoiced with no little enthusiasm [150] that the Frankish forces, worthily welcomed, were able to clear themselves of the charge of slaughter which led to people being tragically cut down, as is described above. The appointed day came, and the place shone clear, bountiful Sabaria,[3] where your holy birth, Martin, blazed forth in the world. [155] To this place the godly king came, with the gathering of bishops, with his nobles, the common people, and the holy clergy all assembled too, with candlesticks, crosses, and books of the gospels, holy relics, and precious items from the churches, to meet them. He kissed them as they came, [160] and with a shout of joy, and hymns resounding, he led them into the holy place, extended a great and hospitable welcome to them in a royal manner, and confirmed their treaty with the giving and receiving of hostages. [165] He ordered that throughout the whole kingdom, all manner of items be offered for sale to them, and that they be welcomed all along their journey, and when they had crossed through the locality of his own area, he gave them gifts along with his pledges of good faith. He gave them safe passage, enriched them with wealth and honours, and ordered them to depart with the blessing of God's peace.

---

great deal needs to be supplied to complete the sense, and in addition, an object must be understood for *firmaret* in l. 135.

[2] Godfrey's brother Baldwin and his family remained at the Hungarian court as hostages for the army's good behaviour. See Albert of Aachen, pp. 301–2.

[3] Sabaria (Szombat-Hély) was the birthplace of St Martin of Tours in 316; Albert of Aachen, however, states that Godfrey's meeting with King Coloman took place at Oedenberg, which is some 30 miles further north.

Hinc pretergressi uestigia longaque mensi,
Per que pertulerant memorata pericula primi,   170
Discunt quid ualeat moderatio consiliumque,
Contra quid noceat temeraria causa furorque,

fo. 73ᵛ   Cum modo seruitio sibi sint et subditioni
Qui fuerant illis inhonestae perditioni.

Inde per extentas regiones multimodasque   175
Ire uiam Domini properans exercitus ille,[1]
Leua dexter habet Mytridatis Pontica regna,[2]
Dextra conspiciens Danaos et Achaica rura,
Nomina que tellus generali Grecia dicta
Scinditur in multa specialia[a] nomina ducta:[3]   180
Namque est Epyrus, Pelopis tunc insula et Hellas,[4]
Archadia atque Argi, tunc que tenet ora Laconas,
Attica, Boeti,[b] Locrisque et Thessalia acris;
Hinc Macedum regio, Dodona, Etholia, Phocis,
Qua quondam rabie Persarum mortificata   185
Massylia est profugis a ciuibus edificata.
Ex hinc longarum post interiecta uiarum
Ad solis rutilum semper tendentibus[c] ortum,
Est regio gemini sortita uocabula mundi,
Seston uicini dirimens a litore Abydi,[5]   190
Qua iuuenis [ual]idis[d] strictum mare dum secat ulnis
Pertulit iratis miserabile funus ab undis,
Qua fugiens socia Phryxus patria arma sorore
Perpetuum ponto dat ab ipsa nomen habere,[6]
Qua Constantini Chalcedone diuidit urbem   195
Stringens se fluctus stadia in uelocia septem,
Sic a se dirimens simul Europen Asiamque,
Vt Zephryro atque Euro sit terminus unus utrisque.[7]

Vltra non magnis distantibus interuallis
Arua iacent Frygie maioris itemque minoris,   200
In quibus effulsit preclaro nomine Troia,
Inclyta per bella[8] longe per saecula nota,

---

[a] specialia *Hall;* specialiter *cod.*   [b] Boetis *Sirmond, Riant*   [c] semper tendentibus *Grocock;* se pertendentibus *cod., Sirmond;* pertendentibus *Riant* [d] ualidis *Grocock;* calidis *Sirmond, Riant*

---

[1] Godfrey's army travelled through Manđelos, Belgrade, Nish, and Plovdiv. See Albert of Aachen, pp. 303–4.

They went on from here and progressed on a long march [170] *through the areas where the first to go had endured the aforementioned dangers. They learned the value of moderation and good counsel, and the harm caused by rashness and wild frenzy, for those who had been hostile to their predecessors, bringing about their tragic downfall, were now their humble and obedient servants.*

[175] *Then that army hastened through far-flung lands of many different types on the way of the Lord;*[1] *on their left those righteous men had Pontus, the realms of Mithridates,*[2] *and on their right their gaze met the Danai and the lands of Achaia; this latter is the general name of the land of Greece,* [180] *which is split into many parts, each with its own particular name:*[3] *for there is Epirus, the island of Pelops, and Hellas,*[4] *Arcadia and Argos, the shore which is the home of the Lacedaemonians, Attica, Boeotia, Locris, and rugged Thessaly; then there is the land of the Macedonians, Dodona, Aetolia, Phocis,* [185] *which was once sacked by the Persian hordes, and whose fleeing citizens built Marseilles; beyond this, after many long roads which lie between, always heading towards the rosy rising of the sun, is an area which has received the names of two worlds,* [190] *dividing Sestos from the shore of neighbouring Abydos,*[5] *where the young Leander met a wretched end because of the angry waves, as he cut through the narrow sea with his powerful arms, and where Phrixus, fleeing along with his sister from his father's armies, gave the sea her name to keep for ever.*[6] [195] *Here the waves divide the city of Constantine from Chalcedon, squeezing themselves tightly into seven rapid furlongs, so separating Europe and Asia from one another that there is a single boundary to both East and West.*[7]

Beyond there, and at no great distance away, [200] *lie the fields of both Greater and Lesser Phrygia, where there flourished Troy, of far-famed renown, long known through the centuries for the famous war;*[8] *it would*

---

[2] Mithridates was the king of Pontus who was defeated by Pompey. The Sultanate of Rūm in fact lay ahead of the crusaders at this point.

[3] Pliny, *Hist. Nat.* iv. 1.

[4] Servius, *Scol. Verg.*, on *Georg.* iii. 7; Hyginus, *Fab.* viii. 3–4.

[5] Lucan, *Bellum ciuile*, ii. 674, Ovid, *Heroides*, xvii(xviii). 2; Sidonius Apollinaris, *Carm.* v. 451.

[6] i.e. Helle. Ovid, *Met.* iv. 450–1, Hyginus, *Fab.* ii. 4; Pliny, *Hist. Nat.* iv. 11; Solinus, *Collectanea rerum memorabilium*, 10.

[7] Pliny, and Solinus, loc. cit. Constantinople was inaugurated as Constantine's capital in 330.

[8] Vergil, *Aen.* ii. 241–2.

Que, quia non umquam nisi prodita uicta fuisset;
Prodita uero etiam capta atque excisa flagrasset,
Eius dispersi per mundi clymata ciues   205
Multas struxerunt uariis regionibus urbes,
Vt Bataui sedes,[1] ut menia iuncta Timauo,
Vt Salamina potens in opima condita Cypro,
Vt Capua atque Alba, necnon pulcherrima Roma,
Ostia quin etiam Tyberina uel Apula Troia,   210
Vt fera uicino constructa Sycambria[a] Rheno,[2]
Que post deuicto circum Meotida[3] Halano
Francorum nomen meruit uirtute fidei,
Mixtaque cum Gallis sumpsit sibi culmina regni.
Sed quia ab incepto disgressio facta remorit,   215
Propositum calamus repetat[b] qua forte reliquit.

Progrediens ductor memoratus in ulteriora
Constantinopolis tendebat ad anteriora;
Quo dum metatur, dum sollicitus spaciatur,
Dum de non certis euentibus immeditatur,[c]   220
Venit ei rumor quoniam proceres memorati[d]
Portus Brundisii, Bari, uel adisse Tarenti,[e4]
Transgressi maria, residentes Dalmatie aruis,
Epyro et mediis posuissent castra Lyburnis.
Complacuit fines non urbis adire superbae,   225
Non, quoniam[f] tumido, cum Cesare participare,
Sed socios[5] inibi communiter opperiendos,
Ipsos[g] consilio concorditer associandos,
Et quicquid fieri bello uel pace sederet
Cunctorum concors consensus conciliaret: 230
Et quoniam magna peditum se turba secuta
Longius hinc aberat, retro sua terga relicta,

Nec breuis horror erat precedere longius illos,
Hostiles manus inter se linquere et ipsos,
Hos sibi mandauit celeri succedere passu.   235
Ipse autem tardo mouit tentoria gressu,
Castrorumque usus breuioribus interuallis,
Prebebat tempus legionibus opperiendis,

---

[a] Sycambri *cod.*   [b] repetat calamus *Sirmond, Riant*   [c] immeditatur *Gro-*
cock: immediatur *cod.*   [d] memoratis *m. pr.*   [e] uel...... *Sirmond;* uel
(?Hydrunti) (*sic*) *Riant*   [f] quicquam *Sirmond, Riant*   [g] ipsis *Sirmond, Riant*

*never have been conquered had it not been betrayed, but betrayed it was, and
taken, and fell in flames;* [205] *its citizens, scattered throughout the different
parts of the world, built many cities in various lands, such as the citadel of
Padua,*[1] *the fortress which lies by the Timavus, like mighty Salamis, founded
in fertile Cyprus, such as Capua and Alba, and of course the most beautiful,
Rome,* [210] *Ostia on the Tiber and Troy in Apulia, wild Sycambria,*[2] *built
beside the Rhine, a city which after the defeat of the Alans around Lake Mae-
otis*[3] *earned through its faith and courage the name of the Franks, and took
for itself the highest position in the kingdom, mingled with the Gauls.* [215]
*But because the digression we have made is keeping us from the tale we began,
let our pen now return to the place where it left off.*

*The aforementioned leader, journeying ever onward, was heading towards
the regions lying before Constantinople; as he made his way there, proceeding
in a state of anxiety* [220] *and pondering on the uncertain outcome of their
venture, news came to him that the nobles we have mentioned had reached the
ports of Brindisi, Bari, and Taranto,*[4] *crossed the seas, and halting in the
plains of Dalmatia had pitched their camp at Epirus and in the middle of
Liburnia.* [225] *He resolved not to enter the limits of the haughty city, and
not to enter into talks with the emperor, since that man was swollen with
pride, but rather that he ought to wait in a friendly manner for his allies*[5] *who
were in the city, and to join forces with them with good counsel and a harmony
of wills; and* [230] *then they would all decide together on a common policy in
peace or war; and since the great host of infantry following him was a long
way from here, having been left behind, and he had no little fear of going too
far ahead of them and of leaving hostile bands between them and himself,*
[235] *he ordered them to come to him at the double. He himself, however,
moved his tents at a slow pace, making camp at quite short intervals, and
made time to wait for these forces, so that he could join together the allied*

---

[1] *Patavi* is also found spelled with initial B- in the so-called *Florilegium Angelicum*.

[2] In classical times the Sycambri were a tribe living on the banks of the Rhine. The
town referred to here may be Buda; Dr L. Holford-Strevens has suggested that the
words here recall Bishop Remigius' words to Clovis on his baptism, 'mitis depone colla,
Sycamber', and that logically Aachen should be meant, though there is no attestation
for its being called Sygambria.

[3] The sea of Azov, the northern part of the Black Sea. The reference here is obscure,
but see Gregory of Tours, *Hist. Franc.* ii. 7 'Thorismodus . . . Alanos bello edomuit' and
the *Add. ad Prosp. Havn.*, s.a. 452 (*MGH, Auctores Antiquissimi*, ix. 302), 'Thorismotus rex
Gothorum post mortem patris Alanos bello perdomuit'.

[4] See above, i. 262–3. This was the route taken by Raymond of Toulouse's army.

[5] Presumably a reference to Hugh of Vermandois, who had already arrived in Con-
stantinople and had been well received by the Byzantine emperor.

Quatinus et socias posset coniungere uires
Et tardos faceret comprendere preuenientes.   240
Perueniens igitur citra quam diximus urbem
Castellum Karoli[1] *quod dicitur in stationem*
Deligit, interea ut socii fierent propiores
Atque urbanorum posset perdiscere mores.
Sic aliquantorum functis statione dierum,   245
Dum sollemne forum sibi plurima[a] *fert specierum,*
Monstra palatina dominoque simillima prauo
Rumores uarios confingunt more profano
Quid sibi tanta uelit mora, quid portendere possit
Maxima que uulgo pretiorum copia prosit,   250
Quidnam concursus hic spondeat atque recursus,
Quidnam sollicitans popularia corda tumultus;
Talia credendum celebrari non sine causa,
Quod sic alliceret manus extera patria regna;
Non uerisimilem speciem debere uideri   255
Hos in seruitium Domini potuisse moueri
Et nunc inceptis cessantibus hic remorari
Ac uelut expletis affectibus inspatiari.
Tales regia mens, solita est quae cuncta pauere,
Rumores captans, monita est sua facta cauere,   260
Vtpote qui Dominum famulus diademate cassum
Fecerat et super hunc peruaserat impie sceptrum.[2]

fo. 75[r]   *Inde sibi merito male conscius atque pauescens*
Verbaque adulantum cum sollicitudine uersans
Ductori mandat que sese intentio ducat,   265
Quid struat aut quidnam sua prestolatio nectat:
Non sibi uel tutum uel honestum posse uideri
Hos alienigenas intra sua tecta morari
Nec uelut hospitium mutandaque claustra tueri,
Sed quasi mansores inter possessa foueri.   270
Ille refert sancti sese sub honore sepulchri[3]
Has agitare uias et spe loca sacra[b] *uidendi,*
Sed, ne gentili succumberet impietati,
Nolle minus caute externe se credere genti,[4]
Ne, uelut infaustis accesserat ante maniplis,[5]   275

---

[a] plurim *m. pr.*   [b] loca sacra *Grocock;* sacra loca *cod.*

---

[1] Only the Charleville Poet refers to 'Charlemagne's Castle', and its site has not

strength [240] *and could cause the slow-moving troops to catch up with those*
who were going on ahead. And so, drawing up in front of the city we have spo-
ken of, he chose 'Charlemagne's Castle',[1] *as it is called, as a place to rest, so*
that in the meantime his allies could come closer to him and he could become
fully acquainted with the character of the citizens. [245] *They passed several*
days waiting in this way, while the usual trading offered them a large variety
of commodities; and the monstrous minions in the palace, so very like their
evil master, put together different stories in their godless way, speculating as to
what he could possibly want with such a long delay, what benefit [250] *the*
vast quantities of wealth could be to the common people, what on earth the
hurrying to and fro could promise, or the excitement stirring the people's
hearts; it was incredible that such things were happening so regularly without
cause; rather, the band of foreigners was drawing over the kingdom of their
fathers in this way; [255] *it did not seem a likely notion that they could have*
been stirred to serve God and now were waiting here, delaying the venture
they had started and walking about as though their desires had been achieved.
The imperial mind, which fears everything as a matter of course, [260] *took*
hold of such stories as these, and was warned to look out for its own deeds,
especially in view of the fact that as a servant he had robbed his lord of his
crown and had misappropriated his own ungodly sceptre over him.[2] *Rightly*
troubled in mind and fearing for himself, he turned over the words of the
fawning courtiers with apprehension, [265] *and sent word to the leader*
asking what he had in mind to do, what he was plotting, what on earth the
purpose was of his waiting; it could not seem safe or proper to him to have
these foreigners staying within these walls, or to have them looking on his city
not as a hospice or a temporary shelter, [270] *but cherishing their property*
in it as though they were permanent residents. The duke replied that he
himself had undertaken these journeys for the honour of the Holy
Sepulchre,[3] *and in the hope of seeing the holy places, but that so that he*
should not fall prey to the godless heathen, he did not want to show too little
caution and trust himself to a strange people,[4] [275] *lest (as had happened*
before to those ill-starred squadrons)[5] *calamity and contempt of a holy*

been identified. The reference here, however, is also symbolic, and is used to underline
Godfrey of Bouillon's descent from Charlemagne, and perhaps also to suggest parallels
between the latter's legendary crusade (as recounted in the *Voyage de Charlemagne*) and
Godfrey's own expedition. See above, i. 31.

[2] Alexius Comnenus had overthrown the then Byzantine emperor, Nicephorus
Botaneiates, in 1081.

[3] See above, iii. 126, and i. 230.

[4] The hostile feeling of the Latins towards the Byzantines is underlined here.

[5] i.e. the Peasants' Crusade.

Acciderent sanctae lues et despectio plebis;
Iccirco istorum spatio cessare dierum
Quo sibi iungatur sociorum turma sequentum;
Hoc ut pace sua fiat deposcere, namque
Cuncta sui iuris a se fore tuta suisque.   280
Talia maiores acuerunt dicta timores
Atque ex consiliis exortae suspiciones
Non alia mente tota agmina iungere uelle
Quam peruadendi bello sua regna locosque.
Dirigitur maior numerus mandata ferentum: 285
Accipiat gazas, geminorum pondus equorum;
Transeat abductis legionibus Hellespontum[1]
Inque Asie expectet parte explementa suorum:[2]
Ni faciat non iam patienter se tolerare
Quin prohibere forum studeat uictumque negare,[3]   290
Et prius adductis quam crescant agmina turmis
Pellere collectis extra sua castra maniplis.

Haec audita duci dum sunt, nil flectitur heros,
Sed responsa refert fastus spernentia uanos:
Fallere, ait, cunctos se talia uelle putantes   295
Nec famulos Domini tales dare suspiciones;
Se famulum Domini, peregrinum exsistere Christi,
Nec nisi paganis debere[a] *piacula belli;*
Siquis Christicolum sibi tale quid inferat ultro,
Se pre se posito debere resistere Christo;   300
Si sponderet opes geminorum pondus equorum,[4]
Se spondere trium, liceat modo currere ceptum;[b]
Esse sibi fixum socios adiungere cunctos,
Viribus ut iunctis pulsarent Christi inimicos;
Ni pretio oblato ueniant uenalia digno,   305
Se quesituros sua commoda fine coacto,
Namque ideo ceptum pro consuetudine tolli,[5]
Poscenti quoniam sunt cepta petita negari.[6]

His irritatur furiosi Cesaris ira.
Infremit ac primo prohibet uenalia cuncta;   310

---

[a] deferre *Sirmond, Riant*   [b] *ll. 301–2 are written vertically in the right-hand margin, and marked to show their location in the text*

[1] Ovid, *Met.* xiii. 407, Avienus, *Descriptio orbis terrae*, 34, 466, 717, *et al.*

people might overtake them; for that reason he was delaying for as many days as it would take for the host of his allies, following on behind, to join up with him, and asked that this might happen with his consent, for [280] *everything under the emperor's jurisdiction would be safe from him and his men. Such words as these gave rise to even greater fears, and suspicions arose from the plans he outlined that he wished to join together all his forces for no other design than to invade his kingdoms and lands in an act of war.* [285] *A greater number of men was sent, carrying the emperor's commands that he should receive treasures, to the weight of two horses; that he should lead his forces away across the Hellespont,*[1] *and await the remaining complement of his men in the region of Asia:*[2] *unless he did this, the emperor would no longer patiently put up with him,* [290] *but would endeavour to close the market to him and deny him provisions,*[3] *and before his forces grew larger with the arrival of the rest of his bands, he would gather his troops and drive them out of the city.*

When these messages were reported to the duke, that hero was unabashed, but gave replies that disdained empty pride: [295] *he said that all who thought he wished such a thing were deluded, and that servants of the Lord should not give rise to suspicions of this kind; he was a servant of the Lord God, was Christ's pilgrim, and owed the punishments of war to none save the heathen; if any Christian moreover were to bring such a charge against him,* [300] *he was in duty bound to set Christ before him and to fight back for himself; if the emperor had promised wealth to the weight of two horses,*[4] *he would promise to the weight of three, provided only that his undertaking might run its course: he was determined to join up all his allies, so that they might rout the enemies of Christ with united strength;* [305] *and if goods were not offered for sale with a reasonable price attached, his men would seek what they needed where they were forced to: this was the reason they had begun to take things, as habitually took place,*[5] *since things a man wanted began to be denied him when he asked for them.*[6]

The wrath of the hot-tempered emperor was aroused by these words. [310] *He went into a rage, and first forbade the sale of all goods; next he ordered the*

---

[2] The Sultanate of Rūm, in enemy territory.

[3] Albert of Aachen, p. 306.   [4] See also iii. 286.

[5] The Latin here is very abrupt; and the sense must be expanded in translation. For the impersonal construction cf. Cicero, *Dom.* 10 (I am indebted to Dr Holford-Strevens for reminding me of this reference).

[6] Albert of Aachen, p. 309, states that Godfrey sent word to Bohemond, who offered to join forces with him and attack Constantinople.

Hinc iubet extrudi [*perg*]*entibus*[a] *omnia claustra.*
Post, apices mittens, bello parat agmina tota.[1]
Dux quid ad hec faceret?[b] *uictum perquirere primo*
Censuit et post hoc uenienti occurrere bello.
Discurrunt celeres per pascua plena manipli,   315
Abduquntque pecus uarium, numerabile nulli.
Et quia tempus erat referens pia gaudia festi
Quo fuit eterni facta incarnatio Verbi,[2]
Venit ei rumor proponens munera magna:[3]
Bis binos proceres, socia comitante caterua,   320
Affore ducentes porcorum milia plura,
Vnde pararentur suicidia Cesariana.
Oblatum credit diuinitus emolumentum,
Occurrensque capit proceresque pecusque coactum.

Sic exercitibus data pleno copia cornu[4]   325
Diuino cunctos animauit fidere nutu.[5]

His gestis bellum fert nuntius esse paratum
Atque sequente[c] *die dubio sine conficiendum.*
Exoritur multus per Gallica castra tumultus,
Feruor adhortantum magno clamore relatus   330
Territat hostiles socias acuitque cohortes,
Monstrans quam leue sit pigris[d] *concurrere fortes.*[e]
Procedunt castris, uolitant uexilla iubeque.[f]
Itur in aduersos, resonant lituique tubeque.
Non clipei clipeis,[6] *non telis tela repulsa,*   335
Non gladii gladiis, non ossibus ossa relisa,
Sed ferit hec acies, sed corruit ictibus illa,
Bella sed ista gerit, patitur sed comminus illa.
Non retinent ictus nostrorum[g] *scuta calpesque,*[7]
Totum transadigit quod percutit hasta sudesque,   340
Per galeas, gladii cerebrorum aspergine manant,
Plura superque humeros capita huc illucque supinant.[h]
Non arcus, iaculum, non hic ualuere sagittae,
Lancea sed totum socio diiudicat ense.
Armis corporibus campus consternitur omnis.   345

---

[a] pergentibus *Grocock;* excedentibus *Sirmond, Riant*   [b] faciat *Sirmond, Riant*
[c] sequentes *m. pr.*   [d] pigris *Grocock;* pigr s *cod.;* pigras *Sirmond, Riant*
[e] gentes *Sirmond, Riant*   [f] iubeque *cod.;* (?trahuntque) (*sic*) *Riant;* tr......*Sirmond*
[g] quorum *Riant; Sirmond has a lacuna here*   [h] recursant *Sirmond, Riant*

new arrivals to be driven out of the gates. After this, he sent letters and prepared all his forces for war. How could the duke respond to this? He decided first of all to seek out provisions, and after this to go to meet the approaching battle-lines.[1] [315] *The swift-moving squadrons ran off through the meadows, which were well stocked, and led away a variety of animals which no man could number. It was that time, bringing the holy joys of the feast, when the incarnation of the eternal Word took place,*[2] *and news fittingly came to him telling of great gifts:*[3] [320] *four nobles, accompanied by a band of men, were approaching, leading many thousand swine, intended for the imperial pork supplies. He believed that this was a blessing divinely supplied, and hurrying there he caught and captured both nobles and animals.* [325] *In this way supplies were furnished to the armies in full measure,*[4] *which encouraged them all to have faith in the favour of God.*[5]

After this took place, a messenger brought news that preparations had been made for fighting, which would without doubt take place on the following day. A mighty clamour rose up through the Gallic camp, [330] *and their zealous exhortations were conveyed through loud shouts, which terrified the enemy forces and encouraged the allies, making plain how trifling it is for the brave to attack the slothful. They made their way out of the camp with banners and plumes fluttering. They went towards the enemy line with horns and bugles blaring.* [335] *Shield did not crash against shield,*[6] *nor spear on spear, sword was not struck by sword, nor bone by bone, but one battle-line struck hard, and the other was felled by their blows, one side waged war, and the other side endured it. Their shields and helms*[7] *did not withstand the blows of our men:* [340] *spear and spike pierced right through what they hit, and swords that cut through helmets dripped with the spattering of brains; all around, heads flopped down on shoulders. Bow and spear and arrow were of no value here: the lance and its ally the sword decided it all.* [345] *The entire plain was strewn with bodies and weapons. They fled with screams, and were*

[1] Robert of Rheims, p. 744.
[2] Godfrey reached Constantinople on 23 Dec. 1096. His forces crossed the Bosporus the following February.
[3] Matt. 2: 11.
[4] Horace, *Carmen saeculare*, 59–60; Boethius, *Cons. Phil.* ii. met. 2. 6.
[5] See above, i. 6, iii. 102.
[6] Statius, *Thebaid*, viii. 398–9; Walter of Châtillon, *Alexandreis*, i. 141–2.
[7] *Calpes*, despite the difficulties it presents in scansion, appears to be the reading of the MS under ultra-violet light. Ducange, under 2 *calpes*, gives 'galeae militum apud Isid. in glossis', and Goetz, *Gloss. Latin*, iv. 27 (Vaticanus 3321) and iv. 315 (Glossae Abavius), reads 'calpes galeae militum'. Its forced use here may be due to the poet's efforts to find a rhyme for *sudesque*.

Fit fuga cum gemitu, portis mactantur in ipsis.
Vsque palatinas arces fugientia nostri
Agmina sectantur dextra feriente minaci.
Sic ope diuina[1] nostris uictoria plena
Claruit, ast illis patuit miseranda ruina.[2]   350

Qui tamen infausto potuere euadere bello
Occurrunt populo redeuntes in sua nostro:
Nam supra dictum peditum superesse cateruam
Et post terga ducis longa statione relictam,
  Ipse quibus Cesar claustrum precluserat omne,   355
Iusserat et pulsos retro in sua terga redire.
Sed Phylipopolleosᵃ Andronopolisque receptu
Iam pulsi fuerant spoliatique undique censu.
Cum male sic habiti peterent tamen ulteriora,
Occurrere sibi que diximus agmina uicta.   360
His se conspectis, magno quatiente pauore
(Nam male dispersi fuerant uix milia quinque)
Hortantes alios fuerantᵇ qui pectore forti,
Vt non sic facile cuncti morerentur inulti,
Conspiciunt iuxta saxosi culmina montis,   365
Quo pertendentes onerant sua pallia saxis.
Hoc uiso, facti timidi nihilominus hostes,
Non presumentes peruadere sic agitantes,
Sollicitant placidis sub pacis nomine dictis
Vt resident secum transcense menia ad urbis   370
Et fore mercatum pretii solamen habenti,
Panem uero dari nil quod mutaret habenti.
Credunt [promissis]ᶜ nil suspicionis habentes
Atque iterᵈ ad pontem retro petiere ruentes.
Mox circumfusi media inter milia pauci   375
Vndique uallantur uelut uno carcere clausi.
Diuiditur rumor per multas suspiciones
Et uarios fingunt sibi credula corda timores:
Quidam namque omnes dicebant decapitandos,
Exilio quidam breuibus Gyaris[3] religandos,   380
Quidam diuersis dampnandos quaque metallis,
Et quidam grauibus luituros prelia poenis.
Quid miseri facerent?[4] tanto quatiente pauore
Optabant citius quam prestolando perire.

slain even in the gateways. Our men chased the fleeing forces right up to the heights of the palace, striking at them with a menacing hand. And so with divine aid,[1] *total victory shone out for our side,* [350] *whereas wretched ruin lay before the enemy.*[2]

Those who were able to escape the ill-starred fight, however, made their way back to their own lands, only to run into our people; for it was said above that there was another company of infantry left behind in a place far to the rear of the duke; [355] *the emperor himself had closed every town against them, and had ordered them to be driven back and made to retreat. They had been welcomed at Philippopolis and Adrianople, but then driven out, and stripped of all their possessions.* [360] *While in this woeful state they were heading inland, the defeated forces we have spoken of came across them. At the sight of them they [the Crusaders] shook with terrible fear (for there were scarcely five thousand of them, and they were scattered at that). Those who were courageous at heart urged the others not to die so easily without vengeance.* [365] *They saw nearby the summit of a rocky hill, and making their way there, they loaded their cloaks with rocks. The enemy were made no less afraid by this sight, and thinking it unwise to rush in to the attack against men who behaved in this way, they entreated them with soothing words in the name of peace* [370] *to come with them to the fortifications of the city they had passed by; the man comforted by having money would have a market, and bread would be given to the man who had nothing to give in exchange. They believed their promises, with no suspicions in their minds, and hurried back to regain the road to the bridge.* [375] *Suddenly the few were surrounded in the midst of thousands, hemmed in on every side as though shut up in a solitary cell. Rumour spread many suspicions abroad, and credulous hearts invented differing fears for themselves:* [380] *some said that they were all to be beheaded, some that they were to be locked away in exile in the confines of Gyara,*[3] *some that they were to be condemned to various mines, and some that they would pay grievous penalties for their fighting. What could the wretches do?*[4] *Shaking with such terrible fear, they chose to die quickly rather than wait for it to*

---

[a] Phylipopoleos *Grocock;* Phylippoleos *cod.* sugg. *Hall*   [c] promissis *Grocock;* auditis *Raint* iter *cod.*

[b] sociant *Sirmond, Riant;* aderant   [d] atque iter *Grocock;* et qua

---

[1] See below, Gilo, iv. 1, for a parallel expression.
[2] In fact, after some success in small skirmishes outside the walls of Constantinople, Godfrey's men were defeated by the Byzantine troops.
[3] Juvenal, *Sat.* i. 73.
[4] Charleville Poet, iii. 313, Vergil, *Georg.* iv. 504.

Nacti cursorem noctuque dieque uolacem,   385
Mandauere duci quam ferrent asperitatem.
Protinus exertis percusso pectore pugnis
Ingemit et grauibus dampnat sua facta querelis,
Et nisi succurrat se causam mortis eorum
Deputat atque reum proclamat sanguinis horum,¹   390
Et quia forte aderant astan[tes Cesar]iani,ᵃ
Non bene pugnatiᵇ quesiunt [. f . q . et . . . .]
Sumit materiem, properat [Godefridus] adesse
Condere se pacem, belli pre[. . . . .]
Constantinopolim uacuare [. r . c . . . . an]   395
Transmissisque fretis securam [. . . . . e . . m]
Finibus inque Asie procerum [. . . . . ertam]
Queue mali fuerat subuertere [. . ua . . e . . ll . . . m]
Si Domini pauper resolutus carcere miles
Amissisque datis sequeretur preuenientes,   400
Et si, uenali repetita condicione,
Copia proposite reddatur digna monetae.
Talibus auditis nihil esse libentius illi
Clamauere suo magis aut optabile regi,
Nec distare moram quin augustalia² sacra   405
Circumquaque uolent ad talia conficienda.
Sic igitur cunctis que conuenere peractis
Foederibusque etiam iusta uice conciliatis,
Deserit obtenta dux et freta transmeat alta,
Atque in deserta statuit Chalcedone castra.   410
Sarcit semiruta, dat lapsis culmina muris,
Et reparat fossas, ponitque repagula portis.
Hic hyemis ueniens decernit ducere tempus
Expectans procerum sparsos in Achaide³ coetus.

Vt primum placidi flatus caluere Fauoniᶜ   415
Verque nouum coepit glaciali obstare rigori,⁴
Iam dicti procerum mouerunt castra magistri
Iungere se cupidi ductori preuenienti,
Presul Haimarus, Boimundus Tancradiusque,
Hugo comes, Stephanus nec non Rotbertus uterque⁵   420
Et reliqui quos non per singula dinumerare
Est opus autᵈ totiens eadem repetendo referre.

happen. [385] *They found someone to run quickly day and night to the duke, and sent word to him of the harshness they were enduring. Straightaway he struck his breast hard with blows, groaned aloud, and cursed his deeds in bitter lamentation, decreeing himself to be the cause of their death if he did not help them,* [390] *and declaring himself to be guilty of their blood.*[1] *Now because some imperial envoys happened to be there, standing not far off, they asked to raise the subject of those who had been wrongly attacked. He seized on this matter, and hastened to say that he was ready to declare peace, and to give back the spoils of war;* [395] *he would at once depart from the terrified city of Constantinople and cross the seas, leaving it safe and sound, and the good faith of the nobles would be certain within the boundaries of Asia. He would overthrow any evil there so long as the poor soldiers of the Lord God were released from prison* [400] *with their losses made good, and could follow those who were going on ahead, and so long as good value was given for the money they offered, according to the terms of trading he again asked for. When they heard these proposals, those envoys declared loudly that nothing was more pleasing to them or more desired by their emperor,* [405] *and that without delay the imperial servants*[2] *would hurry to and fro to get all these things done. And so, therefore, when all that was fitting had been done, and the agreement had been properly sworn, the duke abandoned the position he had occupied and crossed over the deep seas,* [410] *and pitched his camp in the ruins of Chalcedon. He repaired what was dilapidated and rebuilt the fallen walls, cleared out the ditches, and put bars on the gates. He decided to spend the coming winter-time here, waiting for the bands of nobles scattered in Achaia.*[3]

[415] *As soon as the breezes of the pleasant west wind blew warm, and a fresh spring began to oppose the harsh cold,*[4] *the noble masters whom we have mentioned broke camp, eager to join up with the leader who was going on ahead: these were Bishop Adhémar, Bohemond, Tancred,* [420] *Count Hugh, Stephen, and both Roberts,*[5] *and the rest, whom there is no need to list or mention individually, repeating the same things so many times. They left the*

---

[a] astantes Cesariani *Sirmond*   [b] prognati *Riant;* pugnanti *sugg. Hall*
[c] Fauonii *cod.*   [d] et *Sirmond;* ac *Riant*

---

[1] This description is reminiscent of the actions of the priest at mass, and there are literary parallels with the image of the dying Roland in the *Chanson de Roland*, ll. 2368–70.

[2] *Augustalia* is normally used to refer to the festival celebrated on 12 Oct.; here it must mean 'members of the imperial entourage'.   [3] Ovid, *Met.* v. 477.

[4] *Pervigilum Veneris*, 2; Vergil, *Georg.* i. 43.

[5] i.e. Stephen of Blois, Robert of Flanders, and Robert of Normandy.

Moenibus egressi Constantinopolitanis,
Mox [........f..] proprios assciti[a] Cesarianis,
Qui [....ras] ductor que bello uincere possent,   425
Que sibi non iuste gentilia bella tulissent,
Vt sibi gratanter sub pacis pignore reddant,
Quo sua consilia simul auxiliumque capescant
(Hec fore Nycenam urbem sed et Antiochenam
Et circumpositam quoquouersus regionem).   430
Declaraturum super his que digna fuissent,
Vtilia ut cuncta sibi nusquam defore possent.
Insuper et[b] tantum terre omni parte daturum,
Quatuor ut spatio peragraret mula dierum.
Haec sibi iurando firmari denique iure   435
Per bis septenos proceres sine fraude iubere.
Illi nil contra refragari, nam sibi certe
Aut fore parendum norant aut morte perire.
Iurauere tamen quia sic sua pacta ualerent,
Inuiolata sibi si regia sponsa manerent.[1]   440
His actis abeunt fretaque Hellespontica calcant,
Adiunctique duci pariter socia agmina miscent,
Militeque instructo pergunt Nychomedis ad urbem,[2]
Quam pretergressi simul obsedere Nyceam.[3]

fo. 78[r]   Haec de principiis callis Hierosolymitani   445
Scripsimus, ut nostrae permissum rusticitati.
Cetera describit domnus Gilo Parisiensis,
Cuius turpatur nostris elegantia nugis.[4]

Explicit liber tercius. Incipit quartus a domno
Giloni Parisiensi cum ceteris sequentibus eleganter
conditus

[a] asciri Riant   [b] Sirmond and Riant have a lacuna where the cod. reads insuper et

---

[1] For other accounts of the oath and the conditions imposed by the Byzantine emperor, see *Gesta Francorum*, p. 12; Peter Tudebode, pp. 47–8; Raymond of Aguilers,

city walls of Constantinople, and were soon welcomed by the emperor's guard
in this manner: [425] *** *their leader? What lands they could conquer by*
fighting, which the heathen wars had unjustly taken from him, they should
willingly hand over to him as a pledge of peace; by this they could gain his
good counsel and assistance (these places would be the city of Nicaea, Antioch,
[430] *and the lands around them in every direction). He would moreover*
decree to them what they deserved, so that no useful thing could ever be lack-
ing to them. Over and above this, he would grant them in every province as
much land as a mule could traverse in the space of four days. [435] *He*
ordered fourteen of the nobles to confirm these arrangements to him by lawful
oath and without treachery. They made no objection to this, for they knew for
certain that they had either to obey or to meet their end in death. However,
they took the oath on such terms that their agreement was binding [440] *only*
so long as the emperor's promises remained unbroken.[1] *When this was done,*
they departed, and crossed over the waters of the Hellespont; they joined forces
with the duke, and mingled the allied forces together, and then with lines
drawn up they headed for the city of Nicomedia;[2] *going beyond this, they at*
the same time besieged Nicaea.[3]

[445] *We have written these things about the beginnings of the journey to Jer-*
usalem as best our uncouth style has allowed us. My lord Gilo of Paris writes
about the rest; his elegant style is marred by our trifling efforts.[4]

Here ends the third book, and the fourth begins, with the rest of those that fol-
low, elegantly composed by my lord Gilo of Paris.

p. 42; Robert of Rheims, p. 749; Albert of Aachen, p. 312. See also R. J. Lilie, *Byzantium*
and the Crusader States, trans. J. C. Morris and J. E. Ridings (Oxford, 1993), pp. 9–11, 19–
28, for a detailed analysis of the nature of the oath and the ways in which it was
perceived by the different parties. Again the Charleville Poet emphasizes Godfrey's role
as hero of the crusade, making him the first leader both to arrive in Constantinople and
to cross over into Asia Minor. He is also the only one not to swear an oath to Alexius.
  [2] By contrast, Gilo does not mention the capture of the Muslim-held city of Nico-
media in his account of the siege of Nicaea. According to the *Gesta Francorum*, pp. 13–14,
however, Godfrey's forces remained there for three days and then proceeded to Nicaea.
  [3] See Albert of Aachen, pp. 313–28; Raymond of Aguilers, pp. 42–5.
  [4] Gilo makes no mention of events prior to the capture of Nicaea, and here as else-
where, the Charleville Poet fills in the gaps.

GILONIS PARISIENSIS HISTORIA VIE HIEROSOLIMITANE

LIBER IV (GILONIS LIBER I)[a]

Prologus[b]

Hactenus intentus leuibus puerilia dixi[1]
    Materia puero conueniente leui.[2]
Nec Turno dedimus carmen, nec carmen Achilli,[3]
    Sed iuuenis iuueni carmina multa dedi;[c]
Materiamque grauem penitus mens nostra refugit   5
    Et leuibus nugis dedita tota fuit.
Etas mollis erat teneris et lusibus apta,[4]
    Queque grauant mentem ferre nequibat ea.
Ausus eram, memini,[5] de bellis scribere; sed ne
    Materia premerer, Musa reliquit opus;[6]   10
Nam quamuis modicas mea ludere cymba per undas[7]
    Non dubitet, magnas horret adire tamen.
Nunc anni surgunt et surgere carmina debent;
    Tempora cum numeris conuenienter eunt.
Iam, positis remis, uelo concussa per equor   15
    Euolet ex humili littore[d] pulsa ratis.[8]

Errat ut ille rotam qui per decliuia motam[e]
    Nititur ut teneat cum rota missa ruat,
Sic miser inmundum qui non uult perdere mundum
    Errat; dum sequitur quod ruit, obruitur.[9]   20
Ergo quisque moram, quia mundus habetur ad horam,
    Pellat, et hoc querat quod mora nulla terat.
Detineat fundus nullum, domus optima, mundus,
    Quin querat lucem suscipiendo[f] crucem.

---

[a] *Titles: B reads* historia uie nostri temporis Jherosolimitana*; C has* historia Gilonis cardinalis episcopi de uia Ierosolimitana*; F reads* incipit proemium in historia iherosolimitana   [b] *ADG do not have the Prologue*   [c] plura dedi *BC*   [d] ex humili littore *BC;* littore ex humili *F*   [e] *BC read* 'comp' *in the margin; F reads* incipit hortatio in historia iherosolimitana   [f] suscipiendo *Grocock;* suscipiendo *B, C m. alt., F;* suppiciendo *C m. pr.*

GILO OF PARIS, *HISTORY OF THE JOURNEY TO JERUSALEM*

BOOK IV (GILO BOOK I)

Prologue

Thus far I have spoken of childish matters,[1] my mind set on things of no weight, with subject-matter fitted to a feckless boy.[2] I wrote no poem for Turnus, no poem for Achilles,[3] but many poems as one youth to another, and my mind shrank utterly from serious subjects [5] and was wholly given over to mere trifles. My age was tender and suited to playfulness,[4] and whatever weighed heavily on the mind, it could not bear. I had dared, I remember,[5] to write about wars, but lest [10] I be overwhelmed by the subject, my Muse departed from the task:[6] for though my little boat is not afraid to frolic over the gentle waves,[7] it shudders to face the large breakers. Now my years advance, and my poems must advance too; my time of life goes well with my verses. [15] Now, with oars set aside, let my ship be driven by its sail over the seas, and fly from the low-lying shore.[8]

As the man errs who strives to hold back a wheel set in motion down a slope, when it gains speed,[9] so errs the wretch who will not forsake the unclean world: [20] he is ruined while he pursues what is doomed to ruin. And so let every man shake off hesitation, because the world is ours for but an hour, and seek that which no length of time eats away. Let no man's farm, his fine house, or the world hold him back from seeking the light by taking up his

---

[1] Vergil, *Georg.* iii. 1; Ovid, *Am.* ii. 11. 16; Avitus, *Carm.* v. 1. The Prologue is similar to others found in medieval literature: cf. Walter of Châtillon's *Alexandreis*, Marie de France's *Lais*, and many others. As is noted in the Introduction, pp. xlvi–xlix, the present prologue is very valuable in determining the composition of the work.

[2] Ovid, *Amores*, i. 1. 2; on Ovidian influence generally in Gilo, see C. W. Grocock, 'Ovid the Crusader', pp. 62–5.

[3] Ovid, *Amores*, ii. 1. 29. [4] Ibid. 4.

[5] Ibid. 11. [6] Ibid. iii. 1. 6.

[7] Ovid, *Ars Amat.* iii. 26. [8] *Ilias Latina*, 1064.

[9] Matt. 16: 26.

Christus processit, Christo uictoria cessit: 25
    Crux quam sustinuit nostra medela fuit:[1]
Ergo lege pari qui Christum uult imitari
    Subdat ceruicem, suscipiatque[a] uicem.[2]
Securi pugnant qui sub tali duce pugnant;
    Huic qui pugnabit, dux bonus era dabit.   30
Vere securi pugnant quia sunt habituri
    Eternam requiem perpetuamque diem.[3]

[b]Est ope diuina Turcorum facta ruina:
Hoc pro laude Dei, licet impar materiei,
Carmine[c] perstringo facili[4] nec ludicra fingo.
Christe, mee menti tua bella referre uolenti[5]
Adsis, laus cuius series est carminis huius,   5
Vt bene proueniat et te duce carmina fiant.

Christicole gentes, gladioque fideque nitentes,[d]
Vt sacra purgarent a sordibus et superarent
Turcos insanos, fedentes fana,[e] profanos,[f]
Coniurauerunt et Iherusalem petierunt.[6]   10
Ast ubi iam lassus, iam multa pericula passus,[g]
Equoreum litus[h] tetigit chorus ille beatus,
Transiit equoream rabiem petiitque Niceam,[i]
In qua ter centum ter quinque triumque potentum[j]
Conuentus mores struxit[k] docuitque minores.[7]   15
Sed male mutata[8] Christique fide uacuata
Christum spernebat, gentilia monstra colebat,
Et, quoniam Christum prius hec coluisse putatur,
Ad Christum corrupta prius merito reuocatur.[9]

[a] suscipiatque *Grocock;* suspiciatque *BCF*   [b] *Before the text AD read* textus gesto-
rum memorandus Christicolarum; *F has* incipit argumentum; *G reads* incipit quartus a
domno Gilone Parisiensi cum ceteris sequentibus eleganter conditus   [c] carminis
A m. pr.   [d] *F reads* incipit historia Gilonis *in the margin*   [e] faena *D*
[f] prohanos *A*   [g] perassus *D*   [h] letus *D*   [i] rabiem . . . Niceam]
rabiem rabiem petiitque *A*   [j] parentum *A*   [k] finxit *D*

_____

[1] Prudentius, *Cath.* 10. 83; Fulgentius, *Aet. mund.* xiii. 23.
[2] Matt. 22: 5, 16: 24, and also Robert of Rheims, pp. 729–30; *Gesta Francorum*, p. 1. For
the symbolism of the Cross, which was regarded as a sign of the crusaders' spiritual as
well as physical pilgrimage to the Holy Land, see Siberry, *Criticism of Crusading*, pp. 95–
8; Riley-Smith, *Idea of Crusading*, pp. 24, 114.
[3] Rev. 3: 21, Dan. 12: 13. Participants believed that those who died during the expedi-

cross. [25] Christ has gone before, and the victory has fallen to Christ: the cross he carried was our healing.[1] Therefore let him who wishes to imitate Christ on equal terms bow his neck and take up the cross in his turn.[2] They fight in safety who fight under such a leader; [30] that good leader will repay the man who will fight for him. Truly they fight in safety because they are destined to possess eternal rest and the light of day for ever.[3]

The destruction of the Turks was brought about by divine aid; to the praise of God, though I am not equal to my subject-matter, I tell this briefly in straightforward verse,[4] and I relate no frivolous fiction. Christ, may you be present in my mind, [5] which desires to recount your wars[5] (for the narrative of this poem is your praise), so that my verses may turn out well, and be written with you as my guide.

The Christian peoples, bright with sword and faith, swore together to cleanse the holy places of all filth and to vanquish the maddened Turks, ungodly men who were desecrating the shrines, [10] and strove to reach Jerusalem.[6] But when that blessed company, already weary from enduring many dangers, reached the seashore, it crossed the raging sea, heading for the city of Nicaea. In this city a gathering of three hundred and eighteen powerful men of the church [15] established customs and instructed posterity.[7] But that city, changed for the worse,[8] was emptied of Christian faith, and rejected Christ, worshipping the prodigies of heathendom. Since it was thought to have worshipped Christ before, this formerly wicked city was justly called back to Christ.[9]

tion were granted the eternal reward of martyrdom. See H. E. J. Cowdrey, 'Martyrdom and the First Crusade', *Crusade and Settlement*, pp. 46–56; Riley-Smith, 'Death on the First Crusade', in *The End Of Strife*, ed. D. M. Loades (Edinburgh, 1984), pp. 14–32.

[4] On *carmen facile*, see Introduction, 'Metre and Rhyme', pp. xxviii–xxix. For the sense of *ludicra*, cf. Horace, *Ep.* i. 1. 10.   [5] Cf. the Charleville Poet, i. 16 and n.

[6] It is striking that Gilo makes no mention of the council of Clermont, or of the journey to Constantinople and events there. These omissions were later made good by the Charleville Poet in the books which precede Gilo's own work. See above, p. xv.

[7] A reference to the first council of Nicaea in 325, which dealt primarily with the Arian controversy. It is not known how many bishops attended: the number in the text is traditional. See above, ii. 240 n.

[8] For the metre here, see above, pp. xxxiii–xxxv.

[9] Nicaea had been captured by the Seljuk Turks in 1078; see above, ii. 244 n. It was regained by the crusaders in June 1097, after a siege lasting over a month.

Ergo disponunt acies, tentoria ponunt,   20
Vndique conueniunt et bello congrua fiunt.[1]
Partem quam mundus uocat occasum Boimundus
Occupat et contra[a] muros statuit sua castra;
Qui locus est Plaustro[b] iunctus, contrarius austro,
Ille tue forti datus est, Godefride, cohorti.   25
In loca succedunt[c] alii que congrua credunt.[d]
Cunctorum portus uertuntur solis ad ortus.[e2]
Militibus densi Raimundus cum Podiensi,
Hugo comes Magnus, leo seuis, mitibus[f] agnus,
Et satis expertus per prelia dira[g] Robertus   30
Dux quoque Flandrensis, cuius non fallitur ensis,
Et Stephanus muros expugnabant[h] ruituros.
Tuta sed a turbis pars una remanserat urbis,
Nec timet assaltus[i] pars quam sol respicit altus,
Nam lacus immensus, multaque[j] putredine[k] densus,   35
Hos defensabat,[l] nostros transire negabat.
Sed tamen hanc partem nostri tetigere per artem:
Namque superiectis ratibus multis quoque tectis,
Quas Caesar[m] dictus iunctis per terrea bobus[3]
Fecerat adduci uoto tunc auxiliandi.[4]   40
Sic quasi per pontes[n] potuerunt tangere sontes.[o]
Frustra securos petierunt denique muros:[p5]
Acriter insistunt nostri, Turcique resistunt,
Acriter impellunt illos,[q] illique repellunt.
Seua[r] uenenatas gens mittit ab urbe sagittas,[6]   45
Cuique sagitta dabat leue uulnus, eum perimebat,
Et, dum successit, per turpia dicta[s] lacessit
Christi cultores, cane dicens deteriores.
Vocibus ingratis nostris satis exagitatis,

---

[a] contar *D m. pr.*   [b] aratro *G*   [c] suncedunt *A;* succendunt *DG*
[d] cedunt *A*   [e] *Riant wished to place this line after l. 32*   [f] militibus *A*
[g] dura *D m. pr.*   [h]pugnabant *F m. pr.*   [i] assultus *ADG*   [j] multa *BC*
[k] uligine *A;* hirundine *B;* hirudine *C*   [l] defensebat *A;* defendebat *DG*
[m] Caesare *G*   [n] pontos *D m. pr.*   [o] fontes *AD*   [p] *ADG place this line*
after l. 34   [q] illosque *D m. pr.*   [r] sana *A*   [s] uerba *ADG*

---

[1] Godfrey and Tancred reached Nicaea on 6 May; Raymond's army arrived on 16
May, and Robert of Normandy and Stephen of Blois on 3 June. A Turkish relieving
force led by Kilij Arslan was repulsed on 21 May, but the city held out until 19 June.
Before the crusaders mounted a final assault, it surrendered to the Byzantine com-
mander.

[20] Therefore they drew up their forces, pitched their tents, gathered together from all parts, and the necessary preparations for war were made. Bohemond[1] took up position on the side which men call the west, and settled his camp opposite the walls; that side which is nearer the Plough, opposite the south, [25] was given to your mighty army, Godfrey. Other men occupied those places they thought suitable. The gates of all their camps were turned to face the rising of the sun.[2] Raymond and Adhémar of Le Puy, thronged about with soldiers, Count Hugh the Great, a lion to the fierce and a lamb to the gentle, [30] and Robert, well experienced in hard fighting, as well as the Duke of Flanders, whose sword never missed, and Stephen, all these overthrew the walls that were destined to fall. But one side of the city remained safe from the masses of troops, the side on which the sun looks down from on high, and it feared no attacks, [35] for a huge lake, full of deep slime, protected them and denied our men a way across. But our men reached this side too, by means of their skill, for they threw across a bridge of boats, many of them with canopies. *The afore-mentioned emperor had had these dragged overland by yoked oxen,*[3] [40] *hoping then to help them.*[4] And so they were able to reach the wicked as though crossing a bridge. In vain did they aim for the impregnable walls;[5] our side pressed hard their attack, the Turks fought back, they drove on at them hard, and the Turks drove them back again. [45] From the city the cruel people shot poisoned arrows,[6] and an arrow which gave a man even a slight wound was the end of him. While they held the upper hand, they hit out at the worshippers of Christ with filthy words, saying they were worse than dogs. When our men were thoroughly roused by their hateful speech,

For other accounts of the siege of Nicaea, see *Gesta Francorum*, pp. 14–17; Raymond of Aguilers, pp. 42–5.

[2] Robert of Rheims, p. 756, has a very similar account to this one.

[3] Ovid, *Met.* xiv. 3.

[4] This detail added by the Charleville Poet is also found in *Gesta Francorum*, p. 16; Fulcher of Chartres, p. 187. Alexius had set up his camp at Pelecanum. The chronology here is confused. The arrival of the Byzantine boats postdated the defeat of Kilij Arslan and occurred shortly before the final assault on the city.

[5] A reference to the Byzantine fortifications, which at the time of the crusaders' arrival were still in good repair. See above, ii. 246 n. The aim seems to have been to cut off the supplies which were reaching Nicaea via the lake. See *Gesta Francorum*, p. 16; Albert of Aachen, pp. 322–4; Raymond of Aguilers, p. 44. A 'bridge of boats' is also referred to during the siege of Antioch.

[6] Cf. Robert of Rheims, p. 756.

Altior ad duros*a* portatur machina muros.*b1*   50
Gentiles miseri tandem cepere uereri:*c*
Nostri non segnes lapides iaculantur et ignes,
Turres impellunt, affixaque tela reuellunt
A clipeis, hostes proprio telo*d* ferientes.
Vtque cadit spissus imber cum grandine missus,*e2*   55
Sic non uitate mittuntur ubique sagitte.
Tela cadunt, miserique gemunt, moriuntur utrinque;*f*
Hi gladiis, alii baculis*g* pugnant sudibusque.
Magnus erat turbe clamor trepidantis*h* in urbe.*3*

Ergo plorantes manibus quoque significantes   60
Orarunt pacem, clararunt deditionem,
*Expediunt dextras uaduntque recludere portas.*4
*Exultant nostri, laudant magnalia Christi.*5
Primum purgari censent a sordibus urbem
Et consignari per aquam prece sanctificatam;   65
Cumque ymnis crucibusque intrant reconciliatam.
Mittuntur sacri portantes sacra ministri,
Lustrant securos benedicta aspergine muros,
*Cantantes modulos diuinis ritibus aptos.*6
Talia cum ciues uisu audituque capescunt,   70
Protinus irati in gentilia monstra recurrunt:
Cuncta profanari magica uertigine dicunt,
Et proturbantes extra sacra agmina trudunt.
Sic irritantur legiones Christicolarum,
Et delusa dolent mysteria celicolarum.   75

fo. 79*v*   *Acrius insurgunt, celeres et in arma recurrunt,*
Deque profanatis poenas cum sanguine poscunt.
Acrius incumbunt: balistas, fundibula aptant,
*Prefodiunt*i *portas,*7 *miseros quasi carcere uallant.*
Excubias statuunt noctuque dieque cauentes   80
Ne quis colloquio exterior iuuet interiores,
Dumque instant uigiles sibi succedendo per horas
Repperiunt quendam per nigras ire tenebras

---

a muros *D m. alt., FG*   *b* duros *D m. alt., F m. alt., G*   *c* uerere *D m. pr.*
d telo proprio *ADG*   *e* C reads 'comp' *in the margin*   *f* ubique *G*
g gladiis *F m. pr.*   *h* trepidantes *AD*   *i* perfodiunt *Riant*

---

[1] Fulcher of Chartres, p. 186, refers to siege-engines, battering-rams, and mangonels.
For *machina muros* cf. Vergil, *Aen.* ii. 46, 237.

[50] a lofty war-engine was carried to the unyielding walls.[1] The wretched heathen at last began to be afraid: our men were not idle, but threw stones and firebrands, and charged at the towers, tearing from their shields the missiles caught there, and striking at the enemy with their own weapons. [55] Just as a heavy shower falls, sent down with hail,[2] so everywhere were arrows shot with accuracy. The missiles fell, the wretches groaned, and there were deaths on both sides; some fought with swords, others with sticks and staves. The shouting of the terrified crowd in the city grew loud.[3]

[60] *Therefore they begged for peace as they wailed and made signs with their hands, shouting their surrender, and throwing their weapons down they hurried to open the gates.[4] Our men rejoiced, and praised the mighty works of Christ.[5] They resolved first to cleanse the city of all filth, [65] and to sign it with the cross with water made holy through prayer. And so they entered the city, now at peace, singing hymns and carrying crosses. The holy priests were sent on, carrying the holy objects, and they cleansed the strong walls by sprinkling holy water, singing canticles befitting the divine service.[6] [70] When the citizens saw and heard these things, and realized what was going on, they immediately had recourse to their heathen marvels: they said that everything was being defiled by whirling witchcraft, and pressing forward they drove the holy procession outside. In this way the Christian armies were roused to anger, [75] and were grieved that the mysteries of heaven had been mocked. They rose up more keenly, ran swiftly to arms, and demanded a bloody penalty from the ungodly. They attacked harder, made ready their catapults and siege-engines, dug trenches before the city gates,[7] and shut the wretches in as though in a prison-cell. [80] They posted a watch by night and day, making sure that no one from outside might speak to and help those inside, and while the sentries were on guard, taking over from each other through the watches, they caught someone going through the dark shadows*

---

[2] The simile is also found in Vergil, *Aen.* xii. 284, *Ilias Latina*, 359, Lucan, *Bellum ciuile*, ii. 501–2, iv. 776.

[3] Cf. Robert of Rheims, p. 756, *unde fragor turbe clamorque sonabat in urbe*.

[4] There are no close parallels to this interpolated section by the Charleville Poet in the other sources; Albert of Aachen, p. 319, and the *Chanson d'Antioche*, 1248–50, describe the capture of a spy, as at iv. 83, below, but their narratives are otherwise dissimilar.

[5] Cf. Acts 2: 11 (*magnalia Dei*).

[6] For other references to this ritual of penance outside the walls of Nicaea, see Albert of Aachen, pp. 317, 320.

[7] Vergil, *Aen.* xi. 473, and Servius ad loc. The mining of the walls is also mentioned in the *Gesta Francorum*, p. 15, and Raymond of Aguilers, p. 44.

Querentemque locum uel portas ingrediendi
Vel per foramina cum clausis sermocinandi.[1]　　85
Illi [correptum][a] grauiter manicisque ligatum
Cogunt aut citius que nosset cuncta profari
Aut dure mortis grauia experimenta lucrari.
Ille metu uictus nimio nec longa moratus
Dicere seruata se deuouet omnia uita.　　90
Hinc ubi fecit eum pia conuenientia fidum[b]
Exponit missum se ciuibus insinuatum
Ne desperarent, sed se in[c] uirtute tenerent:
Namque sequente die plenum solamen haberent,
Quando obsessores[d] obsessi mortificare　　95
Possent atque opibus cum libertate uacare.
Milia nam propius plus consedisse trecenta
Sultanno ducibus Solimannoque[2] coacta,
Que sic de propriis se uiribus exhylararent,
Et quasi uictores iam facti glorificarent,　　100
Agmina Christicolum quo iam deleta putarent,
Solaque de spoliis inter se bella pararent,
Mane etiam primo statuissent castra mouere,
Illa quoque ante urbem uacua statione locare,
Que fuerat tibi, dux Raimunde, tuisque relicta　　105
Quando ibi prima duces coeperunt figere castra;
Qui retrorsus adhuc aberant ad milia bina,
Pro quibus est missum citius iussique uenire,
Ipsa in planitie tentoria disposuere.[3]
Legatus porro iam factus sponte fidelis　　110
Purgari sese expetiit babtismatis undis.[e4]
Quod dum fit citius concursu presbiterorum
Egregius fulsit uir in ordine Christicolarum.
Mane igitur primo nostri uertuntur ad[f] arma
Vrbis perfidiam punitum sorte suprema.　　115
Fit clamor multus, uariatur in urbe tumultus
Istinc pugnantum atque illinc extrema gementum.
Tormentis, iaculis, gladiis quoque bella geruntur,
Haud multum distat quin protinus ingrediantur.

fo. 80[r]

---

[a] correptum Sirmond　　[b] fidum G m. alt., over an erasure　　[c] rem Sirmond,
Riant　　[d] ……et Sirmond, Riant　　[e] unda Sirmond, Riant　　[f] in Sirmond,
Riant

and looking for an opportunity either of getting through the gates [85] *or of talking with those inside through a hole in the wall.*[1] *They seized the man roughly, bound him with chains, and forced him either to tell them all he knew straight away or to earn himself the experience of painful death. He was utterly overcome with fear,* [90] *and was not long in swearing that he would tell everything if his life were spared. Then when holy accord had made him faithful, he revealed that he had been sent to intimate to the citizens that they should not despair, but keep themselves in good heart, for they would receive complete relief the following day,* [95] *when the besieged could put to death the besiegers and enjoy their wealth in freedom: for positioned very near there were over three thousand men gathered under the command of Sultan and Suleiman;*[2] *they were rejoicing so much in their own strength and glorifying themselves,* [100] *as though they had already been declared the victors, that they considered the Christian forces to be destroyed already, and the only fighting for which they were preparing was amongst themselves, over the spoils. They had moreover decided to break camp at first light, and to pitch it in an unoccupied position in front of the city* [105] *which had been left to you, Raymond, and to your men, when the leaders had first begun to pitch their camps there. They were still two miles behind this position; word was quickly sent to them, and they came as ordered and pitched their tents in the plain itself.*[3] [110] *Moreover, the envoy became a believer of his own free will, and asked that he be cleansed through the waters of baptism.*[4] *This was quickly done by a throng of priests, and the noble fellow shone outstandingly in the ranks of the Christians. At first light, therefore, our men took up their weapons* [115] *to punish the treachery of the city with final destruction. There was much shouting, and in the city were heard the cries of men fighting and of men groaning in death. War was waged with ballistas, spears, and swords, and they were not far off making a swift entry.*

---

[1] Albert of Aachen, p. 319; *Chanson d'Antioche*, 1248–55.

[2] Kilij Arslan ibn Sulaiman. For this confusion between the title and the patronymic, see above, ii. 263–6.

[3] Godfrey of Bouillon's army arrived outside Nicaea on 6 May; Raymond of Toulouse joined them on 16 May; Bohemond followed a few days later, and Robert of Normandy and Stephen of Blois took up their places outside the walls of Nicaea on 3 June.

[4] Arator, *Hist. apost.* i. 626. According to the *Chanson d'Antioche*, 1256–8, the spy was killed and his body catapulted into the city. In Albert of Aachen, p. 319, his conversion to Christianity is not accomplished. For other examples of the conversion of Muslims during the crusade, see *Gesta Francorum*, p. 71; Raymond of Aguilers, p. 112. See also B. Z. Kedar, *Crusade and Mission: European Approaches toward the Muslims* (Princeton, 1984), pp. 57–67; Riley-Smith, *Idea of Crusading*, pp. 109–10.

Dum sic instarent*a* nostri, miseri trepidarent,   120
Et iam*b* constricti*c* sua uellent reddere uicti,
En*d* sexaginta Turcorum milia structa
Ensibus et clipeis ad opem uenere*e* Niceis.*f* 1
Gens tua, Christe, nimis*g* metuens,*h* suspirat ab imis
Pectoribus: clari bello cepere precari   125
Supplice uoce Deum, quod eis daret*i* ipse tropheum.
Vt conspexerunt Turci nostros, fremuerunt.
Mox, ubi fecerunt*j* tres turmas, disposuerunt
Quod pars*k* intraret*l* muros inopesque*m* iuuaret
Viribus et telis, et opem prestaret*n* anhelis;   130
Ipsi munirent portas, nostrosque ferirent.
A gemina*o* parte, comperta protinus arte,
Noster in hostiles multo*p* ruit impete miles.

Pugnatur dure, sed non par actus utrimque,
Sed perimunt nostri, pereunt enormiter illi.   135
Franguntur rigide ualidis impulsibus haste,
Pectora rupta sonant riuosque cruoris inundant,
Trunca uolant capita tremula uelut arbore poma,
Nec qui descendit montem post hac repetiuit.

Et quod de nostris stolide predixerat hostis,   140
Hoc patitur uictus, nec duros sustinet ictus,
Sed celeres fugiunt*q* et tardi funera fiunt.
Dimissa parma fugit hic: sua dum capit arma
Alter prostratus cadit, in capiendo moratus.
Singula quid*r* dico?2 Nullus succurrit amico.*s*   145
His pietate Dei uictis timuere Nicei,
Atque metu tacti tandem cessere coacti,
Perque duos menses obsesse gentis habene,
Dux, tibi traduntur, Constantinopolitane.3
Ducuntur plena Pictum4 quoque milia naui.   150

---

a instabant *F*   *b* etiam *D*   *c* cum stricti *A;* cum strati *D;* constrati *G*
d ens *A*   *e* temere *D*   *f* For ll. *122–3, G has:* ecce repentino clamore ululante
Nycea | milibus auditis montana uidentur operta | que dum desiliunt hinc per decliuia
montis | altera contigue properant per concaua uallis   *g* satis *D*   *h* memens
G   *i* claret *A*   *j* struxerunt *G*   *k* par *F*   *l* intrarit *D*
m inoresque *A*   *n* preberet *G;* prebere *A;* preberte *D*   *o* agmina *B m. pr.*
p cuneos *G*   *q* finniunt *A m. pr.*   *r* quod *D*   *s* succurrit amico nullus
D m. pr.

[120] While our men were on the attack in this way, and the wretches were smitten with fear, hemmed in, and wished to surrender their possessions in defeat, suddenly sixty thousand Turks drawn up in battle-formation came to the aid of the Nicaeans with sword and shield.[1] Your people were afraid, O Christ, and sighed from the bottom of their hearts: [125] those men distinguished in war began to raise humble voices in prayer to God to give the prize to them. When the Turks caught sight of our men, they raised a war-cry. They divided into three squadrons and decided that one group should enter the walls and give succour to the beleaguered [130] with force of arms, and give respite to the exhausted; the rest would strengthen the gates and attack our troops. Our soldiers, discovering the strategy, at once charged in a massive attack against the army from both sides.

The fighting was hard, but both sides did not act in the same way, [135] our men cut theirs down, and they suffered heavy losses. Stout lances were shattered as they hit home hard, chests were ripped loudly open and poured out rivers of blood, and heads were cut off and flew like apples shaken from a tree; the men who came down from the mountain did not go back there after this.

[140] The enemy endured in defeat what he had stupidly predicted for our men, and did not stand up under the heavy blows: the swift ran away and the slow met their death. One threw his shield away and ran off; another fell, cut down as he gathered his weapons, and delayed as he gathered them. [145] Why should I go into every detail?[2] No man came to the help of his friend. With these men defeated by the goodness of God, the Nicaeans were terrified, and smitten with fear they were at last forced to surrender. The governance of the besieged for two months was given to you, O leader of Constantinople.[3] [150] *A thousand Picts[4] also were transferred there in well-laden ships.*

---

[1] The Muslim relieving army was led by Kilij Arslan. See Raymond of Aguilers, p. 45; Albert of Aachen, p. 319; Fulcher of Chartres, pp. 192–3.

[2] Ovid, *Amores*, i. 5. 23.

[3] *Gesta Francorum*, p. 17, and Raymond of Aguilers, p. 44, attribute the capture of Nicaea entirely to the Byzantine emperor. See also Albert of Aachen, p. 327. There are varying descriptions of the length of the siege. Fulcher of Chartres, p. 189, states that it lasted five weeks; the author of the *Gesta Francorum*, p. 17, claims seven weeks and three days.

[4] The sense of this verse is far from clear: *pictum*, the clear reading of the manuscript, seems to be a contracted form for *pictorum*. Perhaps the poet means the emperor's Varangian Guard, which at this time included a number of Englishmen and

His ita deuictis, uictis sub rege relictis,[1]
Successu leti nostri, nec cedere certi,
Castra mouent Dominoque uouent ieiunia, cuius
Auxilio uicere pio gentis scelus[a] huius.[2]
Sed, quoniam per dura uiam fuerant habituri,   155
Ne populi languore, siti[b] caderent perituri,
In turmas cessere duas. Tibi traditur una,
Dux Boimunde,[c] tibi, comes Hugo,[d] traditur una,[3]
Sicque graues colles nostri, licet ad mala molles,
Transiuere[e] tribus non absque[f] labore diebus,   160
Inque die quarta,[4] postquam uia facta per arta,
Illi securi, quasi gens ignara[g] futuri,
Quos sibi commissos Boimundus ab agmine[h] scissos[i]
Duxit, letantes, graue nil restare putantes.
Dum male se iactant[5] et dum bene facta retractant,   165
Turcis insultant, ter centum milia[6] spectant
Turcorum; mesti tanteque resistere pesti
Non ausi dubitant.   Prius ergo prelia uitant.
Sed nullam mortem metuens, Boimunde, cohortem
Instruis, ut uiles depellat[j] cuspide miles,   170
Et ponis iuxta[k] riuos ex ordine[l] castra,
Quos nimis exosos uocat incola turba lutosos.[7]
Sed nondum[m] nostri fuerant ad bella parati,
Cum quinquaginta centum ferrugine tincta[n]
Milia Turcorum cursu portantur equorum,   175
Et non paulatim ueniebant siue gradatim,
Sed cito, more canum quiddam grassando profanum,[o]
Sese commiscent nostris et prelia miscent.
Noster commixtos miles ferit eminus istos,

---

[a] et scelus *A m. pr.;* celus *D m. pr.*   [b] sitti *A m. pr.;* sitis *BC*   [c] Boamunde *B*
m. pr.   [d] Hugo *om. A*   [e] transiliere *G*   [f] abque *D*   [g] ignata *A*
[h] acmine *C*   [i] cissos *F*   [j] depellati *G*   [k] iusta *F*   [l] ordina *D*
[m] nundum *A*   [n] cincta *DG*   [o] *G omits this line*

Scandinavians. See J. Shepard, 'The English and Byzantium: a study of their role in the
Byzantine army in the later eleventh century', *Traditio,* xxix (1973), 53–92; S. Blondal, *The
Varangians of Byzantium,* rev. and trans. B. S. Benedikz (Cambridge, 1978), pp. 129–36,
141–7.

[1] Kilij Arslan's family and nobles were taken to Constantinople. See Albert of
Aachen, p. 327; *Gesta Francorum,* p. 17.

[2] Stephen of Blois and others wrote letters home after the capture of Nicaea full of
optimism about the future success of the crusade: *Die Kreuzzugsbriefe,* pp. 140, 145; Ray-
mond of Aguilers, p. 45.

With these forces thus defeated, and the vanquished left in the
emperor's charge,[1] our men rejoiced at their success and, certain
that they would not yield, they broke camp and declared a fast to
the Lord God, by whose holy help they had conquered this foul
people.[2] [155] But because they were going to be making a difficult
journey, they divided into two companies so that their people
might not fall down and die of exhaustion and thirst. One group
was given to you, Duke Bohemond, and one, Count Hugh, to you,[3]
and in this way our troops, though not used to hardship, crossed
over the steep hills [160] in three laborious days. On the fourth
day,[4] when a road had been made through a pass, Bohemond led
those separated from the main column and entrusted to him; they
exulted, feeling safe and secure, like a people ignorant of what will
happen, thinking that no difficulties remained in their path, [165]
and while they boasted stupidly,[5] recounting their own good deeds
and abusing the Turks, they saw three hundred thousand[6] Turks,
and with downcast hearts they wavered, not daring to oppose such
a pestilential might. At first therefore they avoided combat. But
you drew up your men, Bohemond, not fearing death at all, [170] so
that your troops might drive off those wretches with the sword, and
you pitched camp with precision beside some brooks, which the
natives called the 'loathsome muddy' brooks.[7] Our men were not
yet ready for war when one hundred and fifty thousand dark-
skinned Turks [175] rode at them on horseback, and they were not
approaching gradually or slowly, but quickly, like dogs being up to
no good. They joined in the attack on our men and opened the fight-
ing. Our soldiers struck at their mingled throng from a distance,

[3] Here Gilo displays his preference for Bohemond. He is alone in stating that the army
was divided into two companies, led by Hugh of Vermandois and Bohemond, when it
resumed its march. The *Gesta Francorum*, p. 18, records that the second army was led by
Raymond of Toulouse, rather than Hugh. After Nicaea, the next objective was Dory-
laeum.

[4] Robert of Rheims, p. 759, also states that they came upon the Turks after four days.
Raymond of Aguilers, p. 45, and the *Gesta Francorum*, p. 18, maintain that it was three;
Fulcher of Chartres, p. 190, says it was two. The author of the *Gesta Francorum*, pp. 18–19,
at this point makes Bohemond address the frightened army and encourage them to fight
the Turks.

[5] The idle jesting of the knights recorded here is paralleled in the *Voyage de Charle-
magne*, 448–628.

[6] Robert of Rheims, p. 759, also gives a figure of 300,000, as does the Charleville Poet,
above, iv. 97; Raymond of Aguilers, pp. 45, says the number was 150,000.

[7] Robert of Rheims, p. 760; Fulcher of Chartres, p. 192, refers to a nearby marsh. In fact
the crusaders encamped in the valley of the Bathys. For the precise location, see Runci-
man, *Hist. Crus.* i. 186 n. 1.

Et fidei*a* parma[1] protectus*b* non timet*c* arma.   180
Turci*d* uallabant nostros, cursuque uolabant,
Et nunc instabant, nunc*e* Christicolas fugiebant:*f,g*
Dumque fugit Turcus, sinuatus soluitur arcus
(Arcu quippe magis pugnant, et non sine plagis).
Dum*h* graue cum Turcis bellum Boimundus haberet,   185
Inque uicem Turcus nostros fugiendo fugaret,*i* [2]
In fugiendo quidem uulnus facit et fugit idem.
Nam modo qui Turci ueteri sunt nomine Parthi,
*Fidere quis*j *uersis mos est fugiendo sagittis.* [3]
Magna cohors Magni non huius conscia dampni   190
Gente sub ignota quasi milibus octo remota
Colles girabat, nec tam prope bella putabat
Sed per legatum bellum scit adesse paratum,
Consilio nitidus quem misit ei Boimundus. [4]
At*k* dum pugnatur, dum turba*l* uocata moratur, [5]   195
Pars ea Turcorum quos altera ripa tenebat,
Vt faceret cedem de nostris quam sitiebat, [6]
Per loca nota parum tentoria Christicolarum
Attigit et cedes facit hostis*m* et occupat edes,
Datque neci lassos*n* et plurima uulnera passos,   200
Oppida seruantes nec martem ferre ualentes,
Qui,*o* si marte mori possent, mors*p* esset honori.
Matribus herentes illic truncare uideres
Infantes, gladioque dari miseras mulieres.*q*
Hoc*r* ubi cognouit Boimundus, castra petiuit,   205
Sub duce Normanno*s* dimittens prelia dampno,
Hosque*t* iuuare parat quos gens mala pene necarat.

---

a fidi *G*   *b* ? proteutus *D*   *c* ? times *D*   *d* Turcii *D m. alt.*
e modo *C*   *f* fugitabant *C*   *g* *This verse omitted by B m. pr. and added m. alt.*
h cum *F*   *i* fugarat *G m. pr.*   *j* quis *Grocock;* quos *G*   *k* et *F*
l turma *F m. alt.*   *m* hostis facit *D m. pr.*   *n* passos *D*   *o* quis *F*
p mos *D m. pr.*   *q* *A has this verse after l. 230*   *r* hec *BC*   *s* noemanno *F*
t hos *AD*

---

[1] Eph. 6: 16.
[2] For the tactics employed by the Turkish horse-archers, see Smail, *Crusading Warfare*, pp. 76–83; Raymond of Aguilers, p. 50; Fulcher of Chartres, p. 194.
[3] Vergil, *Georg.* iii. 31.
[4] The second contingent, led by Raymond of Toulouse and including Godfrey and Hugh, arrived at midday, when the fighting was well under way. For other accounts of the battle of Dorylaeum, see *Gesta Francorum*, pp. 19–21; Fulcher of Chartres, pp. 194–7; Albert of Aachen, pp. 331–2; and also Smail, *Crusading Warfare*, pp. 168–9. In his

[180] and protected by the shield of faith[1] they did not fear their weapons. The Turks hemmed in our men, and then rode off swiftly, now attacking the Christians, now fleeing from them, and while the Turks ran away they let fly with their curved bows (for they fight more with the bow, and to great effect). [185] While Bohemond was struggling in this action with the Turks, and the Turks were by turns putting our men to flight and fleeing from them, in their flight they both ran away and inflicted wounds,[2] *for those who are now called Turks are the Parthians of old, and trusting in their arrows while fleeing away is their custom.*[3] [190] A massive force under Hugh the Great, not knowing of the losses being suffered, was skirting round the hills some eight miles away, right beside the hordes of whom he was unaware, and he did not think the fighting was so close to him. But he discovered that the fighting was actually already happening, by means of an envoy whom Bohemond,[4] who shone in counsel, sent to him. [195] While the battle raged and the host that had been summoned was delaying,[5] that group of Turks who were occupying the other bank of the river reached the Christians' tents through the region they little knew in order to carry out the slaughter of our men for which they thirsted.[6] The enemy made great slaughter and took hold of the buildings, [200] putting to death the weary and those who had suffered many wounds, those who were working in the settlement, and those who were not strong enough for fighting, who would have found an honourable death if they could have died fighting. There you could see them hack at babes-in-arms clinging to their mothers, and their poor mothers put to the sword. [205] When Bohemond learned of this he made for the camp, leaving the battle as a lost cause under the Duke of Normandy, and made ready to help those whom the evil

description of the battle, another historian, the biographer of Tancred, Ralph of Caen, declared that Roland and Oliver, the heroes of the *Chanson de Roland*, were reborn (Ralph of Caen, p. 627).

[5] Cf. Robert of Rheims, p. 760: 'dum sic pugnatur, dum sic pars prima necatur | pars ea Turcorum que riuum transiit, illa | protinus inuasit tentoria Christicolarum.' Robert includes a number of hexameters in his account, but only one is identical with anything in Gilo (*partim predati partimque fuere necati*), found in Robert of Rheims, p. 776, and Gilo, v. 38; see also Introd., n. 104. It is impossible to say whether one is dependent on the other; it is more likely that both are drawing from an independent source.

[6] Raymond of Aguilers, p. 45, and Fulcher of Chartres, p. 193, also refer to the Turkish attack on the Christian tents. Fulcher states that it was the second contingent, rather than Bohemond, which drove them away. This again may be an attempt by Gilo to underline Bohemond's personal role and bravery.

Protinus elegit paucos paucisque subegit
Hanc gentem fedam, recipit tentoria, predam,
Armatosque uiros*a* circum tentoria ponit,*b*   210
Castraque terribili pro uallo milite munit.

Dum duplices pugnant acies, illic*c* Boimundus,
Ex hac parte comes Normannus in arma timendus,
Francigene tacti nimio*d* terrore,*e* coacti[1]
Cum duce Normanno fugiunt, sed*f* non sine*g* dampno,   215
Marte, calore, siti crudeliter excruciati.
Et nisi, dum fugerent, dum palmam pene tenerent
Turci, uincentes se conuertissent*h* in hostes
Dux Normannorum, signum clamando suorum,
Lux ea plena malis nostris foret exitialis.[2]   220
Nec mora,[3] Francigene ducti spe*i* sedis amene,[4]
Despiciendo*j* mori bene pro uita meliori,
Ad sua*k* conuersi, circa*l* tentoria sparsi,
Facti castellum[5] permiscent denuo bellum.
Dum nimis insistunt Turci, nostrique*m* resistunt,   225
Tela legunt pueri, cantant ex ordine cleri,*b*
Fortes pugnabant, mulieres collacrimabant:
Altera prostratum portabat in oppida natum,
Altera de riuis tendebat pocula uiuis.*n*[7]
Est aliquid*o* quod quisque facit: tegit alter amicum,   230
Hic fugit, hic sequitur, captum rapit*p* hic inimicum.
Pene triumphantes nostros, te, Christe, uocantes,
Turci prosternunt, et eorum prelia spernunt.
Vtque lupus, uillas circumdans, querit ouillas,*q*
Et, quas deceptas stabulis non esse receptas   235

---

a uiros *omitted by F m. pr.*   *b* predam *D m. pr.*   *c* illinc *BC*   *d* nimi-
oque *AD*   *e* timore *ADG*   *f* et *ADG*   *g* sic *A*   *h* conuestisset *D*
m. pr.   *i* spe ducti *ADG*   *j* respiciendo *G*   *k* se *F m. pr.*
l circum *ADG*   *m* Turcique nostri *D;* nostri Turcique *G*   *n* *G omits this*
verse   *o* aliquis *D*   *p* raptum capit *ADG*   *q* *C reads* 'comp' *in the mar-*
gin against this line

---

[1] This tactic of feigned flight was employed by both the Turks and the crusaders. See
Smail, *Crusading Warfare*, pp. 78–9; B. S. Bacharach, 'The feigned retreat at Hastings',
Mediaeval Studies, xxxiii (1971), 344–8. It was a favourite tactic of the Normans, and is
highlighted by Guy of Amiens, *Carmen de Hastingae proelio*, ed. C. Morton and H. Muntz
(OMT, 1972), 26–8, ll. 424–34.

race had almost killed off. Straight away he chose a few men, and with these few he subdued this foul race, recaptured his tents and the plunder, [210] and placed armed men round the tents, fortifying the camp with fierce soldiers for a rampart.

While the twin battle-lines were fighting, Bohemond on one side and the count of Normandy, terrifying at arms, on the other side, the Franks were smitten with a great terror, and under compulsion they fled,[1] not without loss, [215] with the Duke of Normandy, for they were cruelly tortured by the fighting, by the heat, and by thirst. And if, while they were running away and the Turks had almost carried off the prize, the Duke of Normandy had not wheeled round his men to face the triumphant enemy, shouting his men's rallying-cry, [220] that day, full of misfortune, would have been deadly for our men.[2] Without delay[3] the Franks were spurred on by the hope of a lovely dwelling-place,[4] and thinking nothing of dying well in exchange for a better life, they turned to their tents, and spreading around them they drew themselves up in a defensive square[5] and renewed the fighting again. [225] While the Turks pressed on the attack very hard, and our men repulsed them, the children collected missiles, the clergy sang in proper order,[6] the brave men fought, and the women wept as one carried her prostrate son into the camp, and another proffered cups of water from the flowing streams.[7] [230] Everyone was busy at some task or other: one man covered up his friend, one ran away, another pursued him, another despoiled the enemy he had caught. Almost victorious over our men, who were calling on you, Christ, the Turks threw them down and disdained to fight with them. As a wolf, circling round farms, seeks out the lambs, [235] traps those that it sees are not shut up in the pen, casts the wretched creatures

---

[2] See also Robert of Rheims, p. 761.

[3] Ovid, *Met.* i. 221.

[4] *sedis amene* in this line is a very obscure phrase; it seems to refer more to Jerusalem than to 'heaven' or 'paradise' in the present context.

[5] The phrase *facti castellum* is the most perplexing phrase in the whole poem. *castellum* cannot mean 'fort' or 'camp', but 'defensive square', taking *facti* as passive, functioning as a middle; see also *Gesta Francorum*, p. 19 n. 1. Fulcher of Chartres, pp. 195–6, however, says that at this point the army was close-packed and in confusion.

[6] Cf. also Fulcher of Chartres, pp. 196–7; Siberry, *Criticism of Crusading*, pp. 73, 90.

[7] *Gesta Francorum*, p. 19.

Aspicit, has fundit*a* miseras et in ora recondit,[1]
Sic quoque uallantes Turci nostros*b* trepidantes
Hunc quem spectabant extra castella*c* necabant.
Nostri quid facerent nisi tanta pericula flerent?
Non poterant dorsum dare, nec pugnare seorsum.   240
Quod fuerant clausi nostri, pugnare nec ausi,*d*
Non satis est genti de palma non dubitanti,
Sed monuit mille*e* Turcos dux*f* prouidus ille[2]
Vt que*g* transierant nostri montana requirant.
Hac*h* etenim de re dubia suspecta*i* fuere: 245
Quod tegerent aliquos montana mouebat iniquos.
Ast eques armatus*j* nichil*k* ad precepta moratus
Montes lustrauit, crudeliter ense necauit
Mille uiros ferme, mulieres, uulgus inerme,
Exanimes factos,*l* nimioque metu stupefactos,*m*   250
Multum tardatos rebusque suis oneratos,
Qui male sub caueis*n* latitantes non latuerunt
Exploratores, sed turpiter interierunt.[3]

Ecce nichil timidus comes Hugo, dux Godefridus,
Hortati fortem precibusque minisque cohortem[4]   255
Cursu certabant sociosque iuuare parabant.
Vtque uident flentes socios iam deficientes,
Dimittuntur equi; quamuis non uiribus equi
Essent, non dubitant, nec tela uolantia uitant.[5]
Ergo ducum sydus cum paucis dux Godefridus   260
In medium dense gentis stricto uolat ense
Et, ueluti diram sus*o* postquam colligit iram
Dente canis lesus, baculo uel arundine cesus,*p*
Dente canes angit, ruit, et uenabula frangit,
Hos ita conculcat Godefridus et agmina sulcat.   265
At comites comitis dant multis Tartara Ditis
Trans ripam riui pugnantibus,*q* in pede cliui.*r*
Istis*s* prostratis, de cliuo precipitatis,
Ascendit cliuum comes, implet sanguine riuum:*t*

a fundas *D m. pr.*   *b* nostros Turci *ADG*   *c* castra *B*   *d* *ADG put*
this line after l. 242   *e* ille *D m. pr.*   *f* grex *AC*   *g* utque *A;* atque *F*
h hec *ACF*   *i* dubii timidique *DG*   *j* armatos *D*   *k* nil *DG*
l facti *DG*   *m* stupefactus *D m. pr.;* stupefacti *G*   *n* rupibus *AD;* saxis *G*
o diramen *D*   *p* *B m. pr. omits this line*   *q* pugnabant *G*   *r* in pede cliui
pugnantibus *B*   *s* illis *G*   *t* murum *G*

to the ground, and swallows them in its jaws,[1] so the Turks
hemmed in our terrified men and killed him they saw outside the
camp. What could our men do, save weep over such dire peril?
[240] They could not turn their backs, nor go out and fight. It was
not enough for this race which did not doubt that the victory was
theirs that our side were shut in and did not dare to fight, but their
leader, a man of foresight,[2] advised a thousand Turks to make for
the mountains our men had crossed over. [245] For the mountains
were suspect, because of this puzzling achievement, and he was
concerned that they might be hiding some traitors. The armed
horsemen wasted no time in executing these commands, but
scoured the mountains, and cruelly slew with their swords a good
thousand men, women, and unarmed, common folk, [250] driven
out of their wits and horror-struck, much slowed down under their
heavy burdens; they tried to hide in caves, but could not hide from
the enemy scouts, and died a shameful death.[3]

But behold, the utterly fearless Count Hugh and Duke Godfrey
[255] encouraged their brave squadrons with prayers and threats,[4]
and made ready with all speed to come to their allies' aid. When
they saw their allies weeping, and already falling back, they sent
their horses to the rear, and although they were not equal in
strength, they did not hesitate at all or shrink from the flying mis-
siles.[5] [260] Therefore the star of dukes, Godfrey, took a few men
and rushed with drawn sword into the midst of the densely-packed
people, and, as a boar when it musters its terrible wrath, hurt by a
dog's bite or struck by a staff or an arrow, harries the dogs with its
tusks and charges and breaks down the hunting-spears, [265] so
did Godfrey trample those men down and plough through their
lines. The count's companions too allotted the infernal regions of
Hades to many who were fighting across the bank of the river at the
foot of the hill. The count threw these back and drove them from
the hill, and then went up the hill, filling the river with blood:

[1] Fulcher of Chartres, p. 195, writes that the army was huddled close together, like
sheep in a fold.
[2] Kilij Arslan. As a result of the battle of Dorylaeum, the crusaders came to respect
the Turks as skilled fighters. See *Gesta Francorum*, p. 21.
[3] The episode recounted in ll. 243–53 is unparalleled in any other sources.
[4] Lucan, *Bellum ciuile*, v. 480–1.
[5] Robert of Rheims, p. 762.

Milia nam quinque morti dedit ipse, decemque   270
Si[a] quod iuncta manus fecit[b] comiti[c] referamus.
Omnibus accensis ad pugnandum, Podiensis
Atque comes fortis Raimundus duxque cohortis
Audacesque uiri, uelut ad bellum solet iri,
Paulatim ueniunt, et ab his[d] noua prelia fiunt.[1]   275
Hi cornu dextrum cedunt, aliique sinistrum
Qui prius inclusi fuerant, formidine fusi.[2]
Fit strepitus[e] multus, fit magnus utrinque tumultus,
Nec sonitu minimo dissoluitur arcus equino
Neruo constrictus, sine quo satis est leuis ictus   280
Horum, spes quorum non est nisi cursus equorum.
Cum serpentino iaculatur tela ueneno[f3]
Vt uulnus geminum iactum det Turcus in unum.[g]
Dum sic pugnatur, nostri ter[h] ab hoste fugantur,
Terque fuge dantur[i] gentiles, sed reuocantur,[j]   285
Et solitos cursus faciunt et uulnera rursus.
Nec puto cessissent[k] nec bella pati potuissent
Ni circa montes quidam Turci latitantes
Acriter artarent nostros pluresque necarent:
Quos ubi senserunt nostri comites, statuerunt   290
Vt magis audaces,[l] committere bella sagaces,
Ad latebras irent, necopino[m] marte ferirent
Hos qui pugnabant furtim[n] multosque necabant.
Protinus ingentes animis annisque[o] uigentes
Mille uiri laudis cupidi, sub tegmine[p] fraudis[4]   295
Bella relinquentes,[q] uelut e bello fugientes,
Ascendunt taciti montem,[r5] sed[s] monte potiti[t]
Non tacuit Christi miles, fugit hostis: at isti
Ensibus hos angunt, arcus et spicula frangunt.
Non prodest domino neruo constrictus equino   300
Arcus, non pharetra de cruda condita pelle,
Non equus aut cursus, non illita spicula felle,

[a] sed *DG*   [b] cofecit *F*   [c] comiti fecit *ADG*   [d] abis *D m. pr.*
[e] trepitus *F*   [f] *ADG put this line after l. 283*   [g] iactu . . . uno *ADG*
[h] tibi *A*   [i] dantur sed *D m. pr.*   [j] *A omits this line*   [k] pressissent *DG*
[l] audacter *D*   [m] nec opinio *B m. pr.*; nec primo *A*; inopino *DG*   [n] furtis
ADG   [o] animusque *B*; animisque *C*   [p] tuctmine *D*   [q] relinquentes
bello *D m. pr.*   [r] montes *ADG*   [s] sunt *C*   [t] petiti *D*

---

[1] Only Robert of Rheims's account is at all similar to Gilo's narrative in these verses.

[270] for he himself gave five thousand over to death, and ten, if we ascribe to the count all the exploits of the band of men accompanying him. With all their men stirred up for war, Adhémar and the brave Count Raymond, and the leader of their squadron, bold men indeed, such as are accustomed to go to war, [275] advanced gradually, and fresh fighting was begun by them.[1] These men cut down the right wing, while the others, who before had been shut in, terror-stricken, cut down the left.[2] There was a lot of shouting and a great tumult on both sides, and their bows made a loud sound as they were loosed, [280] being strung with horse-gut, without which these men whose sole hope is in the speed of their horses could strike only feeble blows. The Turks hurled weapons smeared with snake-venom,[3] so that they put a twofold wound into one cast. While the fighting was going on like this, our men were put to flight by the enemy three times, [285] and the heathen likewise were three times routed, but regrouped, again making their accustomed charges and inflicting wounds. But I think they would have yielded and could not have been able to endure the fighting if some Turks hiding round the mountains had not pressed savagely on our men and killed many of them. [290] When the counts on our side became aware of them, they decided that the more daring warriors, who were skilled in waging war, should make their way to the hiding-places and make a surprise attack on those who were fighting in secret and killing many of our men. [295] Straight away a thousand stout-hearted men, in the prime of their years and all desirous of renown, left the fighting under the cloak of deceit[4] as though fleeing from the fight, and silently made their way up the mountain.[5] But when they reached the mountain-top the soldiers of Christ were not silent, and the enemy fled, while those men of ours pressed home their attack with swords, breaking their bows and spears. [300] The bow strung with horse-gut was of no help to its master now, nor the quiver made from untanned leather, nor the swift horse, or the spears smeared with poison: they were

---

[2] The various contingents in fact formed a long front, with Bohemond, Robert of Normandy, and Stephen of Blois on the left wing; Raymond of Toulouse and Robert of Flanders in the centre; and Godfrey of Bouillon and Hugh of Vermandois on the right wing. Adhémar of Le Puy led a separate detachment, which acted as a diversion.

[3] Lucan, *Bellum ciuile*, viii. 304; Arator, *Hist. apost.* i. 361.

[4] Avitus, *Carm.* v. 507.

[5] Adhémar of Le Puy in fact descended from the mountains and surprised the Turks from the rear. See *Gesta Francorum*, p. 20.

Sed male turbantur, moriuntur, precipitantur.
His ita dispersis, multis in Tartara mersis,
Attoniti, belli subiti formidine tacti,   305
Post illos reliqui fugiunt, dare terga coacti.
Ergo resumentes animos nostri fugientes
Turbant: funduntur Turci, fugiunt, moriuntur;
Tardius egressi uel belli turbine fessi
Acrius insurgunt et equos calcaribus angunt;   310
Francigene pronos faciunt ad pectora[a] conos,
Cornipedes spumant, aspersi sanguine fumant,[b]
Frena terunt,[c] dominosque ferunt[d] non impete paruo,
Dumque ruunt stratos feriunt, nam multus in aruo[e]
Turcus erat stratus, iaculis[f] aut ense necatus.   315
Exuperare[g] pares certant, flant non leue nares,
Albet[h] et intinctus tabo cum[i] puluere rictus.
Hostem quisque premit, sed nox obscura[j] diremit
Gaudia nostrorum tristemque fugam miserorum,
Et, quod non poterat[k] leuis arcus et inresolutus,   320
Nec sonipes[l] uelox et longis[m] cursibus aptus,
Hoc importuna potuit nox turpis et una.
Quippe per exosam noctem,[n] diram, tenebrosam,
Gens inimica Deo, Christi subdenda tropheo,
Inuenit latebras: fugit ergo secuta tenebras,   325
Atque per hanc noctem gens Christi perdidit hostem,
Et tandem[o] tutus sub eadem nocte secutus
Seuos gentiles redit[p] ad tentoria miles[1]
Vestibus et telis diues multisque camelis.
Mox proceres leti sua membra dedere quieti.[2]   330

Solares ortus ubi lucifer attulit ortus,
Surgunt. cognatos[q] quondam, modo funera, natos[3]
Euertunt; fundunt gemitus, sua pectora tundunt,
Quisque breui fossa cognati collocat[r] ossa.
Sepe dabant aliqui tumulo caput hostis iniqui,   335
Esse caput notum sperantes inde remotum;

[a] pectore A   [b] spumant D   [c] ferunt D   [d] dominumque ferunt D
m. pr.   [e] nam multus in aruo om. D m. pr.   [f] gladiis AD   [g] exsuper-
ares D m. pr.   [h] ? albit G   [i] non A   [j] obcura F m. pr.
[k] poterat om. F m. pr.; potuit A   [l] sonipnes A   [m] legis D   [n] noxtem D
m. pr.   [o] etandem F   [p] rediat A m. pr.   [q] congnatos D   [r] col-
ligit ADG

utterly routed, slain and overthrown. With these men scattered, and many plunged to the depths of Hades, [305] the rest of the heathen were dumbfounded, struck with fear at the sudden attack, and were forced to turn tail and flee after them. The spirits of our men revived, and they routed the fleeing horde: the Turks were thrown back, fled, and died; those who were late in reaching the fray or exhausted from the whirling of the fight [310] pressed on with greater heart and spurred on their horses; the Franks lowered their visors to their chests, their horses foamed at the mouth and steamed with spattered blood, straining at the reins and bearing their masters on a headlong charge, while they rushed in and struck at the fallen; for many a Turk [315] had fallen in the field, slain with spear or sword. They strove to outdo their equals with nostrils snorting, their muzzles glistening with a covering of gore and dust. Each man bore down on the enemy, but the darkness of night put a halt to the joy of our men and the sad flight of the wretched Turks, [320] and what the light, tautly-strung bow could not bring about, nor the swift steed used to running long distances, one ill-timed, wretched nightfall achieved. That race of men hateful to God, that must be brought under Christ's victorious sway, [325] found refuge through that foul, terrible, dark night; they fled, chasing the shadows, and through this night the people of Christ lost contact with the enemy, and our soldiers pursuing the savage heathen through the same darkness did so in safety, and then finally returned to camp,[1] enriched with garments and weapons and many camels. [330] Then the happy nobles laid their bodies down to rest.[2]

When the rising of the morning star brought the sunrise, they got up. They turned over the bodies of those who had been their kinsmen and children,[3] now mere corpses; they let out loud cries and beat their breasts, and every man gathered the bones of his kinsman together in a shallow trench. [335] Often some of them would put the head of an enemy soldier in the grave, hoping this head was the one they knew, though it had been torn away; they

---

[1] Lucan, *Bellum ciuile*, iii. 496.

[2] Proba, *Cent. Verg.* 124, = Vergil *Aen.* i. 691, iv. 5. No other source describes the fighting in such vivid detail. For some parallels, however, see Raymond of Aguilers, p. 45; *Gesta Francorum*, p. 20.

[3] Amongst those killed was Tancred's brother William. See *Gesta Francorum*, p. 20.

Vulnera contrectant, infixaque spicula[a] spectant
Vulneribus, plorant, et de pietate laborant,
Aspiciuntque bonos equites in puluere pronos,
Qui dum uiuebant super aurea strata iacebant,   340
Inque die tota non sunt tentoria mota.[1]
Interea lassi recreantur uulnera passi.
Cure traduntur medicorum, tela leguntur
Et fiunt plene pharetre, solidantur habene.
Cuncta reformantur quorum monet[b] usus egere.   345

Altera lux oriens ubi noctis depulit astra,
Castra mouens miles sequitur gentilia castra.
Miles at ille Dei cuiusdam planiciei
Dum loca transiret et tutus ab hostibus iret,
Peste, calore, siti[2] moriuntur in agmine multi.   350
Inde recedentes securi, nil metuentes,
Omine felici loca uastabant inimici.
Hostis iter tutum dabat illis, tela tributum.
Sicque metu mota[c] patuit Romania tota,[3]
Nec sensit[d] penam quis donec ad Antiochenam[4]   355
Vrbem, famosam[e] muris, opibus speciosam.[f][5]

Denique tam rite caruit uia cetera lite
Vt quidam proceres paucis comitantibus irent,
Egregiasque urbes et fortia castra subirent:
Sicque per extentas[g] terrae Pamphylidos[6] oras   360
Et Cylicum[7] fuit his spatiandi tuta uoluptas,
Sicque metus gentes perterruit exanimatas,
Vt, cum Tharsenses nostrorum pauca uiderent
Agmina de muris, se in ca[.....] reportant;[8]

[a] spicla *B*   [b] monet *Grocock;* manet *G*   [c] meta *D*   [d] sentit *D m. pr.*
[e] formosam *D; ?* fecundam *A m. pr.*   [f] spaciosam *C*   [g] extensas *Sirmond,*
Riant

---

[1] Robert of Rheims, p. 764.
[2] Cf. iv. 216. The army rested at Dorylaeum for two days, then set out on the road for Philomelium and Iconium. The suffering endured by the crusaders as they crossed the desolate land between Philomelium and Iconium is described graphically by *Gesta Francorum*, p. 23. They then reached the fertile valley of Meran.
[3] Fulcher of Chartres, p. 199; *Gesta Francorum*, pp. 22–3.
[4] The ellipsis in the Latin text is spectacular to say the least, but is supported by all the manuscripts, including G. The Charleville Poet corrects errors in both sense, where

examined their wounds, looked at the spears stuck in their wounds, wept, and went on with their toil out of godly respect; they saw good knights laid low in the dust, [340] men who when they lived lay on golden coverlets; throughout the whole day they did not move their tents.[1] Meanwhile, the weary and wounded regained their strength. These were given up to the charge of the physicians, weapons were gathered up, quivers filled and reins repaired. [345] *All things were put right which experience showed needed to be done.*

As dawn broke the next day, driving off the stars of night, the soldiers broke camp in pursuit of the heathen camp. But as those soldiers of Christ crossed a certain plain and proceeded in safety from the enemy, [350] many of their company died of pestilence and of heat and thirst.[2] Withdrawing from there in safety, fearing nothing, they laid waste the enemy's land, a happy omen. The enemy gave them a safe journey, their weapons gave them tribute. And thus all Rūm was stricken with fear and lay wide open,[3] [355] and none of them met any hardship as far as the city of Antioch,[4] renowned for its walls, notable for its riches.[5]

Indeed the rest of the journey was so utterly free from strife that some of the nobles went on ahead with a few companions to conquer some notable cities and mighty forts: [360] *thus they took pleasure in passing in safety through the broad regions of the land of Pamphylia,*[6] *and through the land of the Cilicians.*[7] *Fear gripped the terrified peoples so much that when the people of Tarsus saw from the walls a few columns of our men, they fled in the open plain;*[8]

the manuscript he was working from was missing verses contained elsewhere in the tradition, and also in prosody, and it is notable that he apparently saw no deficiency in the text here, but rather continued with a fresh sentence, instead of making up what seems to be lacking. There is a similar expression in Vergil, *Aen.* ii. 100.

[5] See *Gesta Francorum*, pp. 76–7. The original fortifications of Antioch, built by Justinian, were repaired by the Byzantines when they reconquered the city from the Muslims in 969.

[6] *Pamphylidos* (gen. sg.) appears to be a new coinage. It lay on the coast of Asia Minor between Lycea and Cilicia.

[7] According to Robert of Rheims, pp. 767–8, and Albert of Aachen, p. 342, only Tancred and Baldwin took the route described here. The Charleville Poet, however, is always anxious to underline Godfrey's role in the expedition and he therefore links the journey through Cilicia with the episode of the bear which follows it. The main army proceeded via Heraclea, Caesarea, Comana, Coxon, and Marash. See *Gesta Francorum*, pp. 22–7.

[8] The inhabitants of Tarsus surrendered to Tancred, but he was forced to hand the city over to Baldwin.

Sed quedam magni intercessu*a* omina pericli[1]   365
Egregioque duci fors aspera †signat ab hosti†
Nam dum per quedam carecta cacumine celsa
Mixtim transiret peditumque equitumque caterua,[2]
Quidam monstrose molis uel roboris ursus
Pandebat rabidos in funera plurima rictus   370
Dumque intercoeptum peditem laceraret acerbe,
Nullus ut auderet pesti obuius ire maligne,
Vicit iter durum pietas ad cuncta parata,
Ire uel in cladem properat, succurrere certa:
Desilit alipede, procurrit et obuius hosti   375

fo. 84ᵛ

Ductor, et extemplo*b* prefulgurat ense potenti.
Ille uidens*c* contra predam dimittit inermem
Erigiturque super partem stans posteriorem.
Dux celer aduerso mucronem pectore figit,
Non tamen [.....] spina, timente recondit.   380
Ille ducem [strictum ualidis]*d* amplectitur ulnis.[3]
Dux nihilominus*e* acrius artando lacertis
Sub se prosternit atque innodatus inhesit,
Et dum [constrictis bracchiis]*f* utrimque tenentur,
Dum timuit [trepidans dux]*g* ante timente iuuatur,   385
Exterior[a cutis ursi]*h* pars uulnerat ensis,
Osque [ferae nudi laniat]*i* super edita cruris.
Tandem nobilium concursibus hoste perempto
Aegre sub ingrato [iacet urso]*j* uulnere duro.
Haec dedit interea [...] per castra cohortem   390
Merorem nimium, [ni]mium*k* quoque causa timorem.
Nam quidam [credunt miseri]*l* ductori affore mortem,
Quidam p[langebant],*m* metuebant debilitatem.
Quorum ut rum[ores]*n* integro de culmine cunctos
Deiceret, ta[ndem monstrauit]*o* lumine cassos,   395
Namque in[ualidum]*p* gestauit*q* uectus equorum,
Per menses aliquot ductum dedit omnibus unum.

Tandem diuinam [sanatus]*r* per medicinam
Cum sociis urbem pertendit ad Antiochenam,
De qua nobilium complures hystoricorum*s*   400
Multa reliquerunt dictorum scripta suorum,
Sed neque se scriptis digne potuisse profari
Que dicenda forent sunt inter dicta professi.

[365] *but harsh fortune gave certain signs, the occasion of great peril, to the noble duke,*[1] *for while the mingled band of infantry and knights*[2] *was crossing over a certain heath high on a summit, a bear of horrendous size and strength* [370] *opened its savage jaws to the destruction of many, and while it was tearing wildly at a foot-soldier it had seized, and no one dared to go to face this pestilence, the godly duke, ready for anything, overcame the difficulty of the road and made haste to go and bring sure aid, even if it meant death:* [375] *that leader leapt from his steed and ran straightway to meet the foe, blazing like lightning as he brandished his mighty sword. Seeing him approaching, the bear threw aside his helpless prey, standing on its hindquarters. The duke swiftly thrust his sword in the animal's chest, but the blow was timid,* [380] *and it plunged only into the skin, like a thorn. It seized the duke, gripping him with its powerful forelegs.*[3] *The duke gripped it even more tightly with his arms, forced it down beneath him, and clung tightly to it, and while each held the other in a powerful grip,* [385] *while each feared the other would be helped by his fearing, the outer edge of the sword wounded the bear's chest, and the bear's mouth bit the duke at the top of his thigh. At last the hostile beast was done to death by the attacks of the nobles, and he lay in pain beneath the foul bear, with a terrible wound.* [390] *This event gave rise to a host of rumours in the camp, grief, and also reason for great fear, too; for some of our men believed that death was close by their leader, and some wept, fearing a permanent injury. So that he could cast down utterly all the rumours of these men,* [395] *at last he showed that they were blind, for a horse-drawn cart bore him along, sick as he was, and he gave them all a single leadership for several months.*

At last through divine healing he recovered, and made his way with his allies to the city of Antioch, [400] *about which many notable historians have left many records of their observations, but as they spoke they admitted that they found themselves unable to express in writing what should be said about it.*

[a] intercessit *Sirmond, Riant*   [b] extemplo *Grocock:*extempto *G*   [c] autem *Sirmond, Riant*   [d] strictum ualidis *Sirmond*   [e] nihil attonitus *Sirmond, Riant*   [f] constrictis bracchiis *sugg. Grocock*   [g] trepidans dux *Grocock*   [h] [a cutis ursi *Holford-Strevens*   [i] ferae nudi laniat *Holford-Strevens*   [j] iacet urso *sugg. Grocock*   [k] nimium *Holford-Strevens;* omnium *Grocock*   [l] credunt miseri *Grocock*   [m] planxissent *Grocock*   [n] rumores *Grocock*   [o] tandem monstrauit *Grocock*   [p] inualidum *Grocock*   [q] gestauit *Grocock;* gessauit *G*   [r] sanatus *Grocock;* recreatus *Sirmond*   [s] hystoricorum *Sirmond, Riant;* historiarum *cod.*

---

[1] The story of Godfrey's fight with a bear is also found in Guibert of Nogent, p. 230; Albert of Aachen, p. 341; William of Tyre, i. 219–20.

[2] Cf. ii. 4, above; Sidonius Apollinaris, *Carm.* ii. 90.

[3] Ovid, *Met.* viii. 818; *Ilias Latina* 571.

Huius nam meminit Moyses, rex hystoriarum,
Quarta in fine libri cui nomen dat Numerorum,[1]   405
fo. 85ʳ *Dum Domini narrat tribubus precepta ferentem,*
Quo sibi promissam discernant ordine terram.
Huius et insignis Hieremias[2] *cum Sedechiam*
Narrat ibi ductum poenam dare iudicialem,
Quando suis natis sese inspectante necatis   410
Luminibus petiit Babylonis menia fossis.
Huius Hiezechihel,[3] *cum templum spirituale*
Scribit, quod reputant Iudaei materiale,
Hanc Machabeorum liber[4] *asserit [ap]paruisse*ᵃ
Quando secus Daphnen[5] *uat[es fertur peri]isse:*ᵇ   415
*Daphnes quippe fuit nemus [halans]*ᶜ *suauibus herbis,*
Fontibus egregiis, lauris simul ac cyparissis,
*Quod nunc accipimus a nostra gente [diremptum]*ᵈ
Propter discursus ibi [..]t[.................]
Alluit hanc fluuius cui nomen priscus Orontis,   420
Qui modo uulgatur uocitari [..]men[.....]eti[.][6]
Imminet huic quoque mons equus [..]pro[..]ans[7]
Vnde ferunt solem specie[...........]as
Illius populus qui sit tamen [...........]
Dicitur ex scripto reliquis [...........]   425
Illius atque locos reliquis [......] plures
Dicunt ob Zephyros circum spirando frequentes
Tercia maiores inter fuit hec prius urbes[8]
*Quam res acciperet Byzantica [tollere]*ᵉ *uires.*
Haec etiam Christi in primis insignia sumpsit   430
Christicolum nomen quando hic primordia coepit.[9]
Hic et apostolica Petro residente cathedra
Floruit ante foret quam [...].pre[.....]a Roma.[10]
Ergo profanatam male Christi turma dolentes
Ad recoaptandam Christo uenere frequentes.[11]   435

Explicit liber quartus. incipit quintus.

ᵃ apparuisse *Grocock*   ᵇ uates fertur periisse *Holford-Strevens;* uates Onias peri-
isse *Grocock*   ᶜ halans *Sirmond*   ᵈ diremptum *Holford-Strevens*
ᵉ tollere *Holford-Strevens*

[1] Num. 34: 11. Here Antioch is equated with Riblah or Riblath, south of Hamah. The same connection is made by Fulcher of Chartres, pp. 216, 709, and by William of Tyre,

Moses, the king of historians, mentions the city [405] *at the end of his fourth book, called Numbers,*[1] *when he speaks of the Lord God giving instructions to the tribes as to the order in which they should divide the promised land for themselves. The famous Jeremiah*[2] *also mentions it when he tells how Zedekiah was led there to be executed,* [410] *when his own sons were killed before his very eyes, and then with his eyes gouged out he travelled to the mighty city of Babylon. Ezekiel*[3] *mentions it too when he writes about the spiritual temple, which the Jews think is a physical one. The book of Maccabees*[4] *asserts its existence,* [415] *when the priest is said to have perished, next to Daphne:*[5] *Daphne, incidentally, was a grove with sweet-scented grasses, notable springs, laurels and cypress trees, and we understand that it had been destroyed by our people, on account of the raids there . . .* [410] *This grove is watered by a river which of old bore the name Orontes and is now commonly said to be called by the name* ⟨Farfar⟩;[6] *over it there looms a table-topped mountain*[7] *. . . from which they say [you may see the sun from its splendour at dead of night].* [425] *It is written that the character of its people is . . . in the rest . . . and . . . its regions . . . because of the west wind, which often blows around there. This ranked third among the great cities*[8] *until the Byzantine empire took its strength.* [430] *It was also among the first to take up the marks of Christ, since the use of the name 'Christian' first began here.*[9] *Here too the apostolic seat flourished under St Peter, before . . . by Rome.*[10] *And so the armies of Christ, grieving that it was so wickedly profaned,* [435] *came in great numbers to recapture it for Christ.*[11]

The fourth book ends. The fifth begins.

viii. 1–4. See P. W. Edbury and J. G. Rowe, *William of Tyre, Historian of the Latin East* (Cambridge, 1985), p. 36.

[2] Jer. 39: 5–7, 52: 9–27. See also below, vi. 331–9.

[3] Perhaps Ezek. 47: 15–18.

[4] 2 Macc. 4: 33.

[5] See Baldric of Dol, p. 46; Orderic Vitalis, v. 78. *Daphnes* was the name given to a tributary of the Orontes, now the river Doueir. In Num. 34: 11 it is a fountain.

[6] The Orontes was usually known as the 'Farfar' or 'Ferreus' by the crusaders: see below, v. 3; *Gesta Francorum*, p. 28 n. 1; Fulcher of Chartres, p. 216. William of Tyre, p. 243, however, referred to this as a vulgar mistake. Cf. 4(2) Kgs. 5: 10.

[7] The city of Antioch lay on the SE bank of the Orontes, in a plain bordered by Mount Silpius, upon which stood its citadel. See Raymond of Aguilers, pp. 47–8.

[8] Cf. Josephus, *Bellum Iudaicum*, iii. 29. Antioch was the third city of the Roman Empire and as a patriarchal see ranked after Rome and Alexandria, until it was eclipsed by the rise of Constantinople and Jerusalem.

[9] Acts 11: 26.

[10] *Gesta Francorum*, p. 76; Guibert of Nogent, p. 204; Baldric of Dol, pp. 13, 40; Fulcher of Chartres, p. 216. See also Riley-Smith, in *Outremer*, pp. 50–1.

[11] Cf. Guibert of Nogent, p. 169. Antioch had been captured by the Seljuks in 1085. Yaghi Siyan was subsequently installed as governor by the sultan in 1090, and Ridvan of Aleppo became his overlord in 1095.

Vrbis ut inmense tetigerunt menia mense
Octobris, turbis pars maxima cingitur urbis.[1]
Pons tamen in Ferro fit peruius antea ferro,[2]
Multaque predati licet et multis honerati[3]
Essent, disponunt acies, tentoria ponunt   5
Inter inexhaustum*a* fluuium murumque leuatum,[4]
Et, quia munite genti bellique perite
Si contendissent per uires nil nocuissent,
Ingenio querunt quod per uim non potuerunt,
Ingenioque fugant quecumque uident nocitura,*b*[5]   10
Accelerat*c* que proficuo scit quisque futura.
Ergo super flumen pontem[6] Christi facit agmen,
Per quem transisset, si grex malus inualuisset.
Fiunt res plures, fiunt ex ere secures,
Fiunt balliste, plumbata, phalarica, talpe,   15
Falces, tela, faces, aries fundeque minaces;[7]
Multa per artifices celsas equantur ad arces.[8]

Vtque parauerunt quecumque paranda fuerunt,
Muros*d* impugnant*e* frustra Turcique repugnant,*f*
Queque parare uident nostros ut inania rident.[9]   20
Nam quis speraret*g* quod gens hec exuperaret
Militibus plenam non paucis*h* Antiochenam

a exhaustum *B m. pr.*   *b* *A m. pr. omits this line; it is added m. alt. after l. 77*
c accelerant *AD*   *d* moros *D m. pr.*   *e* expugnant *C*   *f* resistunt *F*
g sperarte *D*   *h* tam multis *ADG*

[1] The main crusading army arrived at the Iron Bridge, where the roads from Maraş and Aleppo met to cross the Orontes, on 20 or 21 Oct. 1097. See *Gesta Francorum*, p. 28; Robert of Rheims, pp. 771–2; Albert of Aachen, p. 361.

[2] The Iron Bridge, which was flanked by two towers, was already in existence and formed part of Antioch's defences, covering the road to Aleppo. Its capture, soon after the crusaders' arrival, was directed by Bishop Adhémar of Le Puy. See Albert of Aachen, pp. 358–64. For the play on words, see above, iv. 421 and n.

[3] The crusaders captured horses, camels, and mules laden with supplies for Antioch. See *Gesta Francorum*, p. 28.

[4] The army took up its position on the narrow strip of land between the Orontes and the city walls, facing the three main gates, those of the Duke, Dog, and St Paul. See Albert of Aachen, pp. 365–6.

They reached the walls of the massive city in the month of October, and the greatest part of the city was surrounded by the throng.[1] First they constructed a bridge of iron[2] to make a passage across the Farfar, and though they had gathered much booty and were heavily laden,[3] [5] they drew up their battle-line and pitched their tents between the ever-flowing river and the raised wall;[4] and, because they would have inflicted no harm on this well-defended race who were experienced in battle if they had attacked them by force, they sought to effect by ingenuity what they could not achieve by force, [10] and by ingenuity they put to flight whatever they saw would be dangerous;[5] each of them hurried to complete what he knew would be advantageous. And so Christ's army built a bridge[6] over the river, over which they would have crossed, if the evil horde had grown stronger. They made many things, axes from bronze, [15] ballistas with lead shot, and catapults, sapping-engines, grappling-irons, missiles, firebrands, battering-rams, and threatening slings;[7] a multitude of engines were raised level with the lofty citadel by the craftsmen.[8]

When they had prepared everything that needed to be prepared, they assailed the walls in vain, and the Turks fought back; [20] they laughed at all the preparations they saw our side making as being useless.[9] For who would have expected that this race of men would overcome the city of Antioch, filled as it was with not a few

[5] See Robert of Rheims, p. 775. The Turks had only succeeded in capturing Antioch in 1085 through treachery and, on hearing of the approach of the crusaders, Yaghi Siyan had sought to rid the city of 'disloyal elements', in particular the Greeks and Armenians. This passage looks ahead to the betrayal of the city to Bohemond by a renegade Christian, Fīrūz. See below, vii. 7–19.

[6] The purpose of the bridge was to provide a link with the opposite bank of the Orontes and thus to open the road to the sea and the port of St Simeon. Raymond of Aguilers, p. 49, and Fulcher of Chartres, p. 219, both state that the bridge was built of boats, but given the width of the Orontes it cannot have been very substantial.

[7] See Robert of Rheims, p. 775.

[8] The citadel was in fact on the summit of Mount Silpius, 1,000 feet above the town.

[9] After some initial caution, the Turks led forays from the town to ambush the crusaders. See *Gesta Francorum*, p. 29; Albert of Aachen, p. 369.

Vrbem, quam^a clerus^b aliquis sapiens^c uel Homerus[1]
Si modo uixisset describere non potuisset?
Christicole fessi sunt ad sua castra regressi,   25
Et se securos intra^d sua castra futuros
Nocte putauerunt. sed et hostes nocte fuerunt
Et male tranquilli nocuerunt pluribus illi.
Nec^e semel hac fraude nocuit gens callida ualde:
Nocte lacessebant^f nostros et nocte petebant   30
Non clausis portis munite^g castra cohortis.
Sed leuis interea bellum fortuna regebat,^{h}
Inque uicem miseram gentem gens nostra premebat,
Sepe super nostros^i Turcorum dextra ualebat,
Iamque fatigatis nostris opibusque minutis   35
In predam pedites Christi misere quirites,
Qui dum^j predari loca uellent hostis auari
Partim^k predati^l partimque^m fuere necati.[2]
Sed tamen[3] illorum pauci mortem^n sociorum
Narrando tristes faciunt socios quoque tristes,   40
Vnde^o nimis tristis Boimundus[4] rebus in istis
Supplex^p diuine rogat auxilium medicine
Insidiasque parat genti que fraude necarat
Victum querentes, nil per montana timentes.
Ad uictus igitur querendos ut prius itur;   45
Cum duce Flandrensi Boimundus consociatur,^{q}
Armigeris^r—res armigeris predicta dabatur—[5]
Premissis mille sequitur dux prouidus ille.[6]
Hos ubi predantes uiderunt insidiantes,
Protinus e latebris salientes undique crebris   50
Vocibus insultant et equorum pectora multant,
Armigeros feriunt. dum talia prelia fiunt,
Cum parua gente Boimundus bella repente
Turbauit, multos perimit, socios nec inultos

---

^{a} quem A ^{b} clarus G ^{c} sapiens aliquis ADG ^{d} intra F *m. alt. over
an erasure* ^{e} ne F ^{f} lacessabant F ^{g} inimice ADG ^{h} gerebat
A ^{i} muros DG ^{j} cum ABC ^{k} p.partim F ^{l} predari F *m. pr.*
^{m} partim et A ^{n} mortem pauci ADG ^{o} inde A ^{p} suppelx D
^{q} cum sociatur F ^{r} armigeros F

---

[1] This is an example of the 'topos of inexpressibility' referred to by Curtius, *European
Literature*, p. 159. For medieval writers, 'Homer' was not only the author of the *Ilias
Latina*, but also the supreme poet known to the writers of the classical world.

soldiers, which no clerk, nor even wise Homer,[1] if he lived now, could depict? [25] The Christians returned exhausted to their camp, and thought that they would be safe in their camp by night. But the foe was there by night too, and through their restless activity they caused great harm to many of our men. Nor did that most cunning race harm our men once only by such deceit, [30] but night after night they wounded our men, seeking out the camp of a squadron not protected by closed gates. In the meantime fickle fortune ruled over the fighting, and by turns our people harried that wretched people, and the Turks' right hand often prevailed over our men. [35] Our side was already wearied and short of supplies, when the knights sent the infantry off to plunder; while they wanted to plunder the area belonging to the greedy enemy, some of them were plundered themselves, and some were slain.[2] However,[3] a few of them, sadly relating the death of their comrades, [40] made their allies sad too in the telling, so that Bohemond,[4] very sad at this situation, begged and prayed for the help of divine relief, and prepared an ambush for that race of men who had deceitfully killed the men out foraging, who feared nothing as they wandered in the mountains. [45] And so they went to look for provisions as they had before; Bohemond joined with the Duke of Flanders, and sending a thousand squires on ahead (the action just mentioned had been entrusted to the squires),[5] the far-seeing duke followed behind.[6] When their enemy, lying in wait, saw them plundering, [50] they leapt out straight away from the mass of hiding-places all around, and reviling them loudly and whipping their horses' sides they struck at the squires. While the battle proceeded in this way, Bohemond suddenly threw it into turmoil with his small force, slaying many; he did not permit his allies to go unavenged

---

[2] This verse is found *verbatim* in Robert of Rheims, p. 776. Although there are close links between the two works, this is the only occasion on which a precise correspondence occurs. It seems more likely that they are both drawing on a shared source than that one copied the other. See introduction, 'Relationships with Other Sources', pp. lviii–lx.

[3] See above, iv. 37, for a previous instance of the otiose padding *sed tamen*.

[4] Gilo, like the author of the *Gesta Francorum*, depicts Bohemond as a major figure in the First Crusade. By contrast, the Charleville Poet's hero is Godfrey of Bouillon, and Bohemond is mentioned only twice in his account (i. 243, iii. 419).

[5] Smail, *Crusading Warfare*, pp. 108–9, claims that the squires (*armigeri*) were not normally employed in fighting: 'during the engagement they had charge of the baggage'.

[6] See Robert of Rheims, p. 776; *Gesta Francorum*, p. 30. Bohemond and Robert of Flanders set out on 28 Dec.

Amplius esse sinit gemitusque suos ibi finit.[1]   55
Hic quoque Flandrensis plures[a] necat horridus ensis.
Sic Turci telis populi cessere fidelis.
Oppida uictores repetunt, priscosque dolores
Ponere precipiunt. ponunt, sollempnia fiunt.[b]
Tempora tranquilla uictoria prebuit illa.   60
Victus de uillis[c] non insidiantibus ullis
Portabant gentes ad castra, nichil metuentes.

Ast ubi plena malis aduenit hiemps glacialis,[2]
Venit tempestas, nostros afflixit egestas,
Imbribus et multis niuibus[d] montana tumebant,[e]   65
Armeniique[f 3] cibo qui castra iuuare solebant
Per nimios[g] fluctus[h] nimios extinguere[i] luctus
Non poterant. flebat populus quem grando premebat.[j]
Non inopes tantum glacies sed tela[k] premebant.
Non aliqui portum Sancti Symeonis[4] adibant,   70
Qui nauale forum[l] dabat omni[m] merce[n] decorum.
At[o] fidei pugiles nimias penas[p] fore uiles
Corporeasque putant, nec penis gaudia mutant,
Nec bona tormentis titubat[q] constantia mentis,
Quamuis pressuras patiuntur corpora duras: 75
Sed quicunque pati potuerunt arma[r] parati,
Paruam nec fortem uix extruxere[s] cohortem,
Atque manu parua predam rapuere per arua.

Quos tulit euentus Gallorum clara iuuentus[t]
Enumerare licet: sed quis[u] tot acerrima[v] dicet   80
Prelia, pressuras, ieiunia,[w] frigora, curas?
Pauca quidem dico tristis, nec lumine sicco.[5]
Milia ter centum fuerant: tunc, estimo, centum[x]

---

[a] multos *ADG*   [b] finut *D*   [c] illis *D*   [d] nimbis *D*   [e] time-
bant *A; F m. pr. omits this line*   [f] Ermenique *BC*   [g] mimios *D*   [h] fluc-
tos *D m. pr.*   [i] exungere *A*   [j] grauabat *G*   [k] grando *F*   [l] ferum
D m. pr.   [m] omnia *D*   [n] mercedo *D*   [o] ad *D*   [p] penas nimias
ADG   [q] titubant *D m. pr.*   [r] tela *ADG*   [s] extruxe *BF*   [t] iu-
uentes *D m. pr.*   [u] quis *om. D.*   [v] arerrima *A*   [w] ienunia *D*   [x] *A
m. pr. omits this line*

---

[1] This is probably a reference to Bohemond's destruction of the Turkish garrison of
Hārīm, which lay to the east of Antioch, and had mounted several attacks on foraging
parties from the crusaders' camp. The *Gesta Francorum*, pp. 29–30, states that
Bohemond launched this attack after two knights, who had been sent to reconnoitre the

[55] any longer, and put an end to his grief there.[1] The terrible sword of the Duke of Flanders killed many here, too. Thus the Turks gave way before the weapons of the faithful. The victors made for their camp once again, and began to lay aside their grief of old. This done, the customary religious services were held. [60] That victory led to some times of peace; the people brought provisions from the villages to the camp with no attacks made on them, and with nothing to fear.

But when icy winter came, full of hardships,[2] and bad weather arrived, then want beat down our men. [65] The mountains were swollen with rain and heavy snow, and the Armenians[3] whose custom it was to supply the camp with food were unable to put an end to the enormity of sadness because the rivers were in flood. The people beaten down by hail could only weep; and it was not only the cold which beat them down helplessly, but armed attack as well. [70] None of them went to the port of St Simeon,[4] which provided them with a maritime market-place furnished with all good merchandise. But those fighters for the faith regarded their excessive pains as merely bodily suffering, a small price to pay, and their joy was undiminished by such pains; nor was their good and constant mind shaken by their agonies, [75] although their bodies suffered burdensome hardship: but all who were able to bear it made ready for war, hardly making up a small squadron, and not strong at that. They foraged through the fields for plunder in a small band.

The exploits of the noble young men of Gaul deserve to be listed: [80] but who can speak of so many bitter battles, agonies, fasting, cold, and anxiety? I tell of just a few, with sadness, and not with a dry eye.[5] They had been three hundred thousand: but by then, by

garrison, were killed. See also Fulcher of Chartres, p. 222. The crusaders built a castle, known as Malregard, to guard this flank.

[2] Winter usually saw an enforced cessation of military activity; see Smail, *Crusading Warfare*, p. 71, and also Robert of Rheims, p. 777 (*Glacialis hiems mercatum afferentes ad ipsos uenire non licebat*), Albert of Aachen, p. 375, *Gesta Francorum*, p. 30.

[3] For the role of the Armenians during the siege of Antioch, see *Gesta Francorum*, pp. 29, 33; Matthew of Edessa, p. 33; Smail, *Crusading Warfare*, pp. 46–8.

[4] St Simeon is the modern Mağaracık. It lies at the mouth of the Orontes, some 14 miles from Antioch. In mid-Nov. 1097, a Genoese fleet had arrived at St Simeon with reinforcements. Gilo's allusion here is unclear, but some contemporaries considered that the road from Antioch to St Simeon was very unsafe.

[5] Cf. Lucan, *Bellum ciuile*, ix. 1044; Statius, *Siluae*, v. 3. 35; Arator, *Hist. apost.* i. 356.

In bello clari uix possent annumerari.
Sepe quidem leti sua membra dedere[a] quieti[1]   85
Et[b] nil solliciti gaudebant aere miti;
Sed sub momento surgente per aera uento
Aeris ingrati commotu precipitati
Vix subite pesti poterant obsistere mesti,
Cunctaque lustrabant imbres et castra natabant.[2]   90
Quique locarat equum nocturno tempore secum
Flebat eum mane corpusque trahebat[c] inane;
Militibus mille qui cinctus[d] erat prius, ille
Pro nimia peste nec nomen habebat honeste
Militis, atque pedes factus plorabat in edes.   95
Turpe quidem dictu, sed miles inops sine uictu
Armigerum flentem flens ipse fame pereuntem
A se pellebat,[e] quia nec sibi sufficiebat.[f][3]
Proh dolor! ipse pater nato, fratri quoque frater
Quos sibi seruabat uictus in morte[g] negabat.   100
Attonitis[h] ducibus quos miserat undique mundus,
Cum duce Flandrensi solatur eos Boimundus
Et bellatores iubet armari meliores;
Ter decies[i] mille[4] pedites dux eligit ille,[j]
Armatique fere galeati mille fuere,   105
Hique suos enses conuertunt ad Syrienses:
Oppida predantur Syrie, nostri recreantur.[5]
Telluris grate dum gaudet[k] fertilitate
Diripiendo sata Syrie gens illa beata,
Tres ammirati[l] (sic reges quippe uocati[6]   110
Iherusalem,[m] Scalapi[n] ductores atque Damasci)[7]
Ipsos inuadunt, sed et hi nostris sua tradunt.[8]
Quippe recesserunt uicti, plures perierunt.
Hac palma freti repetunt tentoria[9] leti.

[a] dederunt sua membra ADG   [b] e D   [c] trahabant A   [d] cunctus A
[e] pellabat D   [f] suffiebat D   [g] motre F   [h] attentis A   [i] trede-
cies D   [j] ipse D m. pr.   [k] gaudent DG   [l] admirati AD; ammiraldi G
[m] Iherusalem om. F   [n] Calapi ADG

[1] Cf. iv. 330.   [2] See Robert of Rheims, p. 777: *ipsa tentoria innatabant.*
[3] See Fulcher of Chartres, pp. 255–6; Robert of Rheims, pp. 780–1.
[4] *Gesta Francorum*, p. 30, mentions 20,000 participants, but Robert of Rheims, p. 776, gives the same figure as Gilo.
[5] Bohemond and Robert of Flanders set out on 28 Dec. to raid the Turkish villages in the Orontes valley. In their absence the crusading camp was attacked by Yaghi Siyan,

my reckoning, hardly a hundred could be counted who were famous for fighting. [85] Often indeed they happily laid themselves down to sleep,[1] and without a care they rejoiced in the gentle air; but as the wind suddenly stirred the air, they were buffeted by a blast of foul weather and in their wretchedness could hardly stand up to this sudden misfortune; [90] the rain poured down on everything, and the camp was awash.[2] The man who stabled his horse with him at nightfall wept over it in the morning, dragging its lifeless body; the man who formerly had been attended by a thousand knights did not even fairly have the name of knight himself because of the dreadful pestilence, [95] and reduced to being a footsoldier, he wept in his dwelling. It is shameful to say it, but a helpless knight with no food would drive from him his weeping squire who was dying of hunger, and would weep himself, because there was not enough to feed even himself.[3] What suffering there was! A father would refuse his own dying son food he was keeping for himself, and brother did the same to brother. [101] The dukes whom the whole world had sent were astounded; Bohemond, along with the Duke of Flanders, comforted them, and ordered the better warriors to be armed; that duke picked out thirty thousand infantry,[4] [105] and there were about a thousand helmed knights. These turned their swords against the Syrians: they plundered the towns of Syria, and our men were made strong again.[5] While that blessed people rejoiced over the bountiful produce of that fine land, plundering the cornfields of Syria, [110] three emirs[6] (for that is what the kings and leaders of Jerusalem, Aleppo, and Damascus are called)[7] attacked them, but then they too handed over their possessions to our men;[8] in truth they retreated in defeat, and many died. Heartened by this victory they joyfully returned to their tents.[9]

but saved by the alertness of Raymond of Toulouse, who pursued the Turks almost to the city walls. See *Gesta Francorum*, p. 32; Raymond of Aquilers, pp. 50–1. Amongst those who perished in the fray was Adhémar of Le Puy's standard-bearer.

[6] Gilo's *rex* is not in fact the precise equivalent of 'emir'; see A. A. Duri, art. 'Amīr', in the *Encyclopaedia of Islam*, ed. B. Lewis *et al.*, 2nd edn., (Leiden/London, 1960), i. 438–9.

[7] The rulers of these three cities are also listed by the *Gesta Francorum*, p. 30, and Robert of Rheims, p. 778. In fact Ridvan of Aleppo at first refused to assist his former vassal Yaghi Siyan of Antioch, who had deserted to the side of his brother and rival Dukak, emir of Damascus. It was the latter, together with his regent (*atabeg*) Tughtigin and the emir of Homs, Janāḥ ad-Daulah, who arrived at Antioch in Dec. 1097. After Dukak had returned to Damascus, Ridvan and Sokman ibn Artuk, the emir of Jerusalem, led a second Turkish army to relieve Antioch in Feb. 1098. See *Gesta Francorum*, p. 35, and below, v. 152 and note.

[8] See *Gesta Francorum*, p. 31; Albert of Aachen, pp. 373–4.

[9] Cf. Lucan, *Bellum ciuile*, iii. 496.

Dantur opes, gaudent inopes, meliusque[a] futurum   115
Esse putant, credunt non posse resistere murum.
Optima creduntur bona que mala prima secuntur.
His ita transactis[b] mons extans menibus altis
Desuper equatur et castello decoratur
De quo spectaret[c] speculator, si qua pararet   120
Vrbs armata dolis, de culmine[d] peruia molis.[1]
Hic consumpserunt uim multam, nec potuerunt
Castrum natura munitum uellere plura
Agmina, nam nati[e] Christi satis exagitati
Pellebant contis[f] ciues de culmine montis.[2]   125

Viribus interea fractis ex urbe Lycea[3]
Auxilium[g] querunt, quod non tamen optinuerunt.
Normanno[h] comiti dederant hanc, urbe potiti,
Angli uictores paribusque suis meliores;
Nec gens[i] Anglorum gessit pugnas aliorum,   130
Marte sed equoreo fuit illa potita tropheo.[4]
Hoc genus oratum[j] non est his partitipatum
Mentis turma bone que gessit in obsidione:
Nam grex Turcorum, diuortia nota locorum
Obseruans, nostris castella[5] propinqua tenebat,   135
E quibus auxilium dare Christicolis[6] prohibebat.
Auxilii[k] postquam fiducia non fuit usquam,[l]
Hos inuaserunt metus et pudor, obriguerunt
Audaces animi, trepidant et[m] in agmine primi;
Penitet auctores rerum tot inisse labores,   140
Penitet incepti. Mox in sua castra recepti,
Dum perscrutantur quid agant, magis attenuantur

---

[a] melusque *D*   [b] transsactis *F m. pr.*   [c] spectaret et *D*   [d] culmine
A; culmina *BCDFG*   [e] fidi *DG*   [f] comptis *F*   [g] auxilia e *G*
[h] non manno *A;* Hermanno *BC*   [i] glus *A*   [j] ornatum *BC*   [k] auxil-
ium *D, A m. pr.*   [l] unquam *A*   [m] et *om. A*

---

[1] This is probably a reference to the castle known as 'Malregard', established to the
NE of the city. See *Gesta Francorum*, p. 30; Peter Tudebode, p. 65; Raymond of Aguilers,
p. 58, and above, v. 55n.
[2] Cf. Ovid, *Met.* xii. 337.
[3] *Lycea* is probably to be identified as Latakia, a port on the coast, some 40 miles S. of
the mouth of the Orontes.
[4] See Albert of Aachen, pp. 500–1, who states that Latakia was captured from the
Turks by Guynemer of Boulogne and his fellow pirates (Flemings, Danes, and Frisians)

[115] The wealth was handed out and the poor rejoiced, thinking that what was to come would be better; they believed the walls would not be able to withstand them. The good things which first follow after bad are thought to be the best. When this business was concluded, a prominent hill was raised to the level of the high fortifications and graced with a tower on top, [120] from which scouts could see if the city armed with deceit, now visible from the summit of the mound, was preparing anything.[1] They spent a great deal of energy here, and even many companies were unable to tear down the castle, strengthened as it was by its location, for the sons of Christ, repeatedly attacked, [125] drove the citizens from the top of the hill with poles.[2]

With their strength meanwhile exhausted, they sought help from the city of Latakia,[3] but did not, however, obtain it. On its capture this city had been given to the Count of Normandy by the conquering English, better than their peers; [130] the English race did not join in any of the battles fought by the others, but this prize was won in a naval battle.[4] This race of men, though asked, played no part in all that the stout-hearted army did in the siege: for the Turkish hordes kept a watch on the well-known tracks in that area, [135] and occupied a fort[5] close to our men, from which they prevented them from giving help to the Christians.[6] After all confidence that help was coming had gone, fear and shame overtook them, bold hearts became inert, and the front-line troops quaked with fear. [140] The instigators of the whole enterprise regretted embarking on so much toil, and regretted their undertaking. Soon they withdrew to their camp, and while they explored what they should do, resolve weakened yet more in those who thought that

---

in the autumn of 1097. According to some sources, Edgar Atheling then arrived with his fleet and took it over in Mar. 1098, and it eventually came into the possession of Robert of Normandy. See David, *Robert Curthose*, pp. 230–44; Runciman, *Hist. Crus.* i. 255, n. 2; F. Chalandon, *Essai sur le règne d'Alexis 1er Comnène, 1081–1118* (Paris, 1900), pp. 205–12. William of Malmesbury, *De gestis regum Anglorum*, ed. W. Stubbs (Rolls Series: 2 vols., London, 1887–90), ii. 310, maintains that Edgar did not arrive in the East until much later and took part in the battle of Ramle in 1102. For Guynemer's 'pirate fleet', see P. Riant, *Expéditions et pélérinages des Scandinaves en Terre Sainte au temps des croisades* (Paris, 1875), pp. 134–7.

[5] Robert of Rheims, p. 731, and *Gesta Francorum*, p. 29, call this castle Aregh. If this identification is correct, it is the same as the place mentioned below at v. 194.

[6] The reference here must be to the occupiers of Latakia, i.e. the Normans.

Illorum mentes mala queque futura putantes[a]
Que poterant fieri. Sed mens est inscia[b] ueri,
Mens sapit humanum.[1] Proceres dant denique uanum   145
Consilium turbe quod[c] quisque recedat ab urbe,
Et se tutetur ne turpi morte necetur.
Dum sunt attonite tot gentes, fama[d] repente
Rem docet ingratam, pugnam prope castra paratam.[2]
Nam tres predicti primo certamine uicti,   150
Turba collecta, castrorum soluere tecta
Haud diffidebant, et ad hec[e] taciti ueniebant.[3]
Hec ubi torpentes, quasi de somno redeuntes,[f]
Auribus hauserunt, alios alii monuerunt,
Albescunt uultus, auditur ubique[g] tumultus,   155
Et ueluti uentus cum fit[h] subito uiolentus,
Murmura parua freti, sed non omnino quieti,
Turbat, at[i] inflatum resonat mare, reddit hiatum,
Res referens subitas, sic aspera fama iacentes
Attollit mentes,[j] animos agit ira[k] furentes.   160
Protinus e castris acies procedit equestris,
Que quadringentis armata simulque trecentis
Quatuor, exemptis paucis in castra retentis,[l4]
Examen dire[m] gentis non horret[n] adire.
Deinde[o] uigens[p] dextris, pede prompta caterua pedestris,   165
In numero paruo renitens exponitur aruo,
In qua quingenti pedites ibant numerati.
Nec simul incedunt, sed in agmina quinque recedunt,[5]
Emensisque tribus leugis aliisque duabus,
Eminus optatos hostes uidere paratos   170
Ad pontem Ferri:[6] nequeunt numerando referri
Agmina Turcorum, nec uis capit hec oculorum.
Hostes absque[q] mora sub eadem scilicet hora

---

[a] timentes *G;* sperantes *F m. pr.*   [b] nescia *BC*   [c] quo *G*   [d] fame *A*
[e] hoc *ADG*   [f] redientes *BC*   [g] utrinque *BC*   [h] sit *A*   [i] et *BC*
[j] gentes *D m. pr.*   [k] ipsa *g*   [l] *This line is not in ADG*   [m] *A reads* perfi-
ciam *for* examen dire   [n] audet *G*   [o] inde *ABC*   [p] rigens *A*
[q] abque *D*

---

[1] Cf. Prov. 16: 9, 21: 2; Isa. 55: 8.
[2] The allusion is unclear. Morale was low in the crusader camp, however, and both
Stephen of Blois and Anselm of Ribemont wrote letters home noting the shortage of
food, appalling weather, and loss of horses: *Die Kreuzzugsbriefe*, pp. 150, 157. Adhémar of
Le Puy ordered a three-day penitential fast and Fulcher of Chartres, pp. 222–3,

all that was to come, and all that could possibly happen, would be
bad. But the mind does not know the truth, [145] the mind
possesses only human wisdom.[1] At last the nobles gave this useless
counsel to the mass of people, that each of them should leave the
city, and should take care for himself so that he did not die a
shameful death. While so many races of men were still astonished
at this, a report suddenly made known the unpalatable fact that the
enemy were ready to fight, near the camp.[2] [150] For the three we
mentioned earlier, who were defeated in the first battle, had
gathered their men, and were not lacking spirit to strike camp, but
were silently approaching ours.[3] When, as though awakening from
deep sleep, the sluggards heard and understood this, they gave
advice to one another, [155] their faces grew pale, uproar could be
heard everywhere, and just as when a powerful gust of wind
suddenly blows, it ripples the shallow murmurs of the strait, not
altogether at rest, but the swollen sea crashes and gapes wide, so
the bitter report bringing news of this sudden development [160]
lifted their hearts, and anger drove on their frenzied minds.
Forthwith the line of mounted men led the way out of the camp,
with seven hundred and four men-at-arms, less a few kept behind
in the camp,[4] and did not shrink from meeting the swarm of this
fearful race. [165] Next the company of infantry, strong of arm and
fleet of foot, shone forth in a small band in their ranks in the field;
their company numbered five hundred infantry. They did not adv-
ance together, but drew apart into five columns,[5] and marching
three leagues and another two [170] they saw in the distance the
hoped-for foe all prepared by the bridge over the Farfar;[6] the
Turkish columns could not be numbered, and eyes were not able
to encompass them all. Without delay, that is, at the same time, the

attributed the army's suffering to its sinful behaviour. See Siberry, *Criticism of Crusading*,
pp. 73–4; Raymond of Aguilers, p. 54. At this point Peter the Hermit made an attempt to
escape from the camp, but was pursued and brought back; Bohemond threatened to
leave unless he was granted the lordship of Antioch, and other lesser crusaders planned
to flee 'by land and sea'. See *Gesta Francorum*, pp. 33–4; Raymond of Aguilers, pp. 53–4.

[3] See v. 111 n.

[4] Peter Tudebode, p. 72, mentions a force of 700; the *Gesta Francorum*, p. 34, notes that
there were fewer than 1,000 knights who had managed to keep their horses in good con-
dition. See also *Die Kreuzzugsbriefe*, p. 157.

[5] According to the *Gesta Francorum*, p. 36, the crusading army was divided into six
columns. Five of these advanced to attack the Turks, and one under Bohemond's
command remained in reserve.

[6] The Orontes. See above, iv. 420–1.

Nostros uiderunt, et in ipsos[a] se rapuerunt.
Spicula mittuntur, clamores tela secuntur.[1]   175
Instant pagani, iactu frustrantur inani.
Turcus equo gaudens nec prelia comminus audens
Expectare, tonat uerbis nostrosque coronat.[b2]
Nostri uallati stant in medio glomerati,
Et Turcis obstant: clipei[c] galeeque resultant   180
Ictibus immensis,[d] ensemque reuerberat ensis.
Iamque fatigati Turci lateque necati
Non[e] spe uincendi contendunt sed fugiendi.
Mox uersis scutis petitur fuga causa salutis.
Turcus[f] equum frenis indulgens urget habenis.[g]   185
Preceps ille fugit, tellus pede concita mugit.
In campo lentus iacet arcus puluerulentus.
Iste iacit[h] pictas pharetras, capit ille relictas,
Alter currendo[i] se liberat orbe rotundo.[3]
Singula quid dicam?[4] Gentem superant inimicam,   190
Vix euaserunt aliqui, plures[j] perierunt,
Qui dum luctantur superare uadum, superantur.[5]
In bello strati pauci sunt ense necati.

Hanc stragem quidam gentiles prospiciebant,
Quoddam castellum[k] qui non procul inde tenebant;   195
Illi[l] fugerunt et castrum[6] deseruerunt.
Huic proceres nostri custodes imposuerunt
Qui custodirent pontem. Post hec redierunt
Auxilio fulti[m] diuino, fortiter ulti.
Hos exceperunt socii letique fuerunt   200
Conflictu duplici quod[n] conciderant inimici.
Nam dum predicti pugnant,[o] ad castra relicti
Insignem palmam de ciuibus optinuerunt,
Et multi uirtute Dei paucos timuerunt.[7]

---

[a] ipsis A   [b] coronant A m. pr.   [c] glipei B   [d] in mensis D
[e] nonque D m. pr.   [f] Tucus D m. pr.   [g] habenis urget D m. pr.
[h] iacet A m. pr.   [i] curendo F   [j] plures aliqui D m. pr.   [k] castellum
quoddam ADG   [l] ilico ADG   [m] freti BC   [n] quia CF   [o] pug-
nant predicti F

---

[1] *Gesta Francorum*, p. 36, refers to a storm of missiles darkening the sky. For other
accounts of the fighting, which took place on 9 Feb. 1098, see *Gesta Francorum*, pp. 36–7;
Raymond of Aguilers, pp. 56–7.

enemy saw our men, and hurled themselves upon them. [175]
Spears were thrown, and shouts followed the missiles.[1] The
heathen attacked, but were of no effect with their useless hurling of
weapons. The Turks, exulting in their horsemanship, did not dare
to wait for combat at close quarters, but uttered thunderous cries,
and surrounded our men.[2] Our side stood packed close together,
hemmed in at the middle, [180] and held firm against the Turks:
shields and helms rang out with mighty blows, and sword crashed
against sword. Already the Turks were tired, and were slain far and
wide; they struggled in the hope not of winning, but of fleeing.
Soon they swung their shields on to their backs and fled for safety.
[185] The Turks slackened their bridles, and urged their horses on
with the reins. They fled headlong, and the earth echoed with
hoofbeats. The pliant bow lay covered in dust on the plain. One
man threw down his painted quivers, another snatched them up.
Another freed himself from his round shield[3] as he ran. [190] What
need have I to speak of every detail?[4] They trounced the hostile
race, scarcely a few got away, and many died, overcome as they
struggled to overcome the shallow river.[5] A few were laid low in the
fighting and slain by the sword.

Watching this slaughter were some heathen who were [195] occu-
pying a fort not far from there; they made a swift escape, and aban-
doned the stronghold.[6] Our nobles set guards there to guard the
bridge. After this they returned, strengthened by divine help and
bravely avenged. [200] Their comrades welcomed them and
rejoiced that their enemies had fallen in the twofold struggle, for
while those mentioned above were fighting, those left in the camp
gained a noble victory over the citizens, and by God's power the
many feared the few.[7]

[2] For the Turkish tactic of encircling an enemy, see Smail, *Crusading Warfare*, pp. 79,
171.
[3] *orbe rotundo* is an accurate description of a Turkish shield (Smail, *Crusading Warfare*,
p. 78). The Franks used a kite-shaped shield.
[4] Ovid, *Amores*, i. 5. 23.
[5] The fighting took place on the narrow plain between the Orontes and the lake of
Antioch.
[6] This castle was called Aregh; see *Gesta Francorum*, pp. 29, 37; Robert of Rheims,
pp. 784–5; and above, v. 135. Gilo may have confused his source material and inadvert-
ently created a 'doublet' here.
[7] Yaghi Siyan had led an attack upon the crusaders' camp, but retired when he saw
the main army returning from its victory over Ridvan of Aleppo. See Raymond of
Aguilers, pp. 57–8.

Nec[a] tamen audaci populo fiducia cessit,   205
Nec sociis aduersa suis fortuna repressit.
Ergo repente cauis de turribus egredientes
Turci turbabant uictus ad castra ferentes.
Neue dolo tali paterenter sepe ruinam
Inuenere duces nostri super hoc medicinam,   210
Atque super montem, preter[b] fluuium, prope pontem,
Castellum[1] fieri statuunt pontemque tueri.
Sed[c] res difficilis non[d] perficeretur[e] ab illis
Bello quassatis et uiribus attenuatis;[2]
Mox Boimundus equo celer insilit et quasi preco   215
Euocat[f] e castris aliquos[g] surgentibus[h] astris;[3]
Egidii Sancti comes associatur eunti.[4]
Ensibus ergo bonis fisi Sancti Symeonis
Ad portum properant ut ab his suffragia[i] querant
Qui sua uendebant illic nostrisque fauebant: 220
Hi sunt Genuenses,[5] Angli,[6] Venetumque colentes,
Pisani,[7] cuncti nauali marte periti.

Dumque[j] duces aberant, reliqui torpescere sperant,
Si non impeterent ciues urbique nocerent.
Protinus afflatis animis[k] uento leuitatis   225
Vrbanum temere pontem nostri petiere.
Sic inconsulte gentis facto grege stulte
Prouocat hostiles Turcos prope menia miles.[8]
Funduntur portis subito clamoribus ortis
Nudati pedites, quorum uix spicula uites,   230
Prosiliuntque citi iuuenes uittis redimiti[9]
Et procul exertis[l] iaculantur[m] utrimque lacertis.

[a] non *ADG*   [b] iuxta *ADG*   [c] si *BC*   [d] ne *DG*   [e] conficer-
etur *A*   [f] euolat *BC;* conuocat *ADG*   [g] aliquot *BC*   [h] uergentibus
ADG   [i] uires sibi *BC*   [j] cumque *F*   [k] annuis *A*   [l] excertis *D*
m. pr.   [m] iaculant *A;* iaciuntur *D*

---

   [1] This fortress was built near a Muslim cemetery and mosque, which stood opposite
the city and fortified bridge, and was subsequently known as 'La Mahomerie'. See *Gesta
Francorum*, p. 39; Raymond of Aguilers, p. 62. Its purpose was to guard the vital road to
the coast and the port of St Simeon.
   [2] The crusaders in fact lacked both the materials and the skilled craftsmen to build
this castle, but ships carrying both had arrived at St Simeon in March. See *Gesta Fran-
corum*, p. 39; Raymond of Aguilers, pp. 57–8.
   [3] Vergil, *Georg.* i. 440.
   [4] According to the *Gesta Francorum*, p. 39, Raymond of Toulouse was the first to

[205] However, confidence did not depart from that brazen people, and that fortune which checked their allies did not hold them in check. And so the Turks made swift forays from the hollow towers and threw those carrying supplies to the camp into disarray. So that they should not often suffer defeat by such trickery, [210] our dukes found a remedy for this, and agreed that on a hill beside the river, near the bridge, a fort[1] should be built to watch over the bridge. But the project was difficult, not one to be undertaken by men who were weakened by fighting and in a state of exhaustion.[2] [215] Bohemond at once leapt swiftly on his horse, and, like a herald, summoned some men from the camp as night was falling;[3] the Count of Saint-Gilles went with him.[4] So, trusting in their excellent swords, they made haste to the port of St Simeon to ask support from those [220] who sold their goods there and who were on our side: these were Genoese,[5] English,[6] inhabitants of Venice, and Pisans,[7] all well versed in maritime warfare.

While the dukes were away, the others felt they would be wasting time if they did not attack the citizens, and do damage to the city. [225] With their spirits raised by a breezy spirit of levity, our men rashly made straight away for the bridge to the city. Massing together in such an ill-advised and stupid way, the troops stung into action some Turks who were near the fortifications.[8] The gates were suddenly flung open, and shouts rang out loud. [230] The infantry, who scarcely had vine-branches for spears, were left defenceless, and swift youths crowned with chaplets[9] leapt forward and from both sides threw weapons with mighty casts at a distance.

suggest that they should go to St Simeon for supplies and assistance. Bohemond then agreed to accompany him. Neither of them was prepared to set out for St Simeon alone, each mistrusting the other. The account given here by Gilo is a further indication that he wished to portray Bohemond as a key figure in the expedition.

[5] See Raymond of Aguilers, p. 49. A Genoese squadron of 13 vessels set sail in July 1097 and arrived at the port of St Simeon in mid-November.

[6] On 4 Mar. 1098, an English fleet with some Italian pilgrims on board put in at St Simeon. It had called at Constantinople, where the exiled Edgar Atheling had assumed command. See above, v. 129; David, *Robert Curthose*, pp. 236–7; A. Grabois, 'Anglo-Norman England and the Holy Land', *Anglo-Norman Studies*, vii (1984), pp. 132–41.

[7] Italian ships played an important part in the later stages of the First Crusade. See Albert of Aachen, p. 668. Baldric of Dol, p. 18, however, refers to Venetians, Genoese, and Pisans who had taken the cross much earlier. See also above, i. 167 and n.

[8] According to the *Gesta Francorum*, pp. 39–40, the Turks attacked the crusaders as work on the rebuilding was just beginning; Robert of Rheims, p. 785, suggests that the Seljuk Turks initiated this attack.

[9] The young men did not wear normal protective leather caps or metal helmets.

Ille sudes iacit, hic lapides, hic tela: sed ille
Dum trahitur[a] gemit, hic petitur per spicula mille.
Lumina nostrorum nubes hebetant[b] iaculorum,   235
Atque coartati crudeli cedere marti
Qui tot uicerunt totiens prius[c] hic didicerunt.
Laxatis loris fugiunt multumque cruoris
Amittunt;[d] Parthus[e] confractos[f] proterit[g] artus.
Hic pedis, hic oris uulnus gemit, ille cruoris   240
Exactas[h] uenas dum respicit inter habenas
Labitur et plenam defunctis[i] mordet harenam.
Nullus equi frontem uertit donec fuga pontem
Repperit, ut dixi quem dudum nauibus ipsi
Struxerunt.[1] Sed ibi restant animi melioris   245
Agmina que nondum[j] fuerant oblita[k] decoris,
Et se defendunt clipeis hostesque[l] retardant.
Plures dum trepidi pontem conscendere[m] tardant[n]
Turpiter oppressi moriuntur flumine mersi.
Turci letantur, flent[o] nostri, castra petuntur.   250
Nec sic[p] lassatur ferus hostis, et insidiatur
Dum succedit ei,[q] male callidus,[r] huic[s] aciei,
Que ducis hortatu ueniebat cum comitatu
Forti, multiplici. Sed et hunc[t] superant inimici[2]
Atque necant peditum[u] tria milia. Turma quiritum[v]   255
Euasit latitans per colles, prelia uitans.
Nec[w] mora,[x] gaudentes de turribus illa uidentes
Perse ridebant nostris[y] qui castra tenebant
Remque docent signis, strepitu, clamoribus, ymnis.

Ergo uir intrepidus Flandrensis, dux Godefridus,   260
Robertus, Stephanus, Tancretius, Hugo, Statinus[3]

---

[a] trabitur *D*   [b] hebebant *D m. pr.;* hebetant nubes *A*   [c] post *G*
[d] omittunt *F;* emittunt *G*   [e] Parthos *G*   [f] fugientes *G*   [g] preterit *D*
[h] exhaustas *ADG*   [i] defunctus *BC*   [j] necdum *ADG*   [k] ablita *A*
[l] hostemque *G*   [m] cum scendere *F;* concerndere *D*   [n] parant *F*
[o] flen *D*   [p] si *A*   [q] ei succedit *A*   [r] caldidus *D m. pr.*
[s] huic *om. A.*   [t] hanc *A*   [u] pedites *ADG*   [v] quiritu *A*
[w] hec *D m. pr.*   [x] mora *om. D m. pr.*   [y] nostros *ADG*

---

[1] In fact, Gilo has not previously stated that this bridge was built of boats, though his source may well have done. See above, v. 12 and n.

[2] *Gesta Francorum*, p. 40; Raymond of Aguilers, pp. 59–60; Robert of Rheims, pp. 785–6. The Latin text at this point is very convoluted. *hunc* in line 254 refers back to *comitatu* in line 253, which probably refers to the nobles who formed a mounted escort to the

One threw sticks, another stones, another spears; on the other side one groaned as he was dragged off, another was pursued by a thousand missiles. [235] The cloud of spears obscured the vision of our men, and, packed together, those who had been victorious so often before learnt here to yield to cruel fighting. They slackened off their armour straps and fled, shedding torrents of blood; the Parthians trampled over their shattered limbs. [240] One groaned over a wound to his foot, another to his mouth, one looking at his gashed veins gushing with blood slipped down between the reins and bit the sand strewn with corpses. None of them wheeled his horse about until his flight had brought him to the bridge, which as I said they constructed themselves from boats a short time before.[1] [245] But there were marshalled there columns of better spirit, who had not yet forgotten their honour, and they protected themselves with their shields, holding up the enemy. Many who were fearful and slow in climbing over the bridge were foully trampled down and met their death by drowning in the river. [250] The Turks were overjoyed, our men wept and made for camp. Nor was the wild enemy wearied by this, but lay in wait for the arrival of that company of men—how cunning he was—which at the duke's urging was approaching with a brave and numerous escort. The enemy routed this band as well,[2] [255] and killed three thousand infantry. The squadron of knights got away, sheltering in the hills and avoiding the fighting. Without delay the Persians rejoiced as they saw those events from their towers, jeered at our men who were occupying the camp, and noised it all abroad with waving, yelling, shouting, and singing.

[260] Therefore the fearless man of Flanders, Duke Godfrey, Robert, Stephen, Tancred, Hugh, and Statin[3] (who was noseless

whole column. As they fled, so the *pedites* were open to attack. The ambush of Bohemond and Raymond of Toulouse took place on 6 Mar. as they were returning from St Simeon.

[3] Statinus is called 'Tatikos' by Anna Comnena, 'Tetigus' in *Gesta Francorum* and Robert of Rheims, 'Tatic' by Raymond of Aguilers, and 'Tatice' or 'Estatins l'Esnané' by the *Chanson d'Antioche*. He was the representative of Alexius Comnenus and accompanied the crusading army to Antioch. In Feb. 1098, when the army was suffering from shortage of food, he sailed from St Simeon to Cyprus, stating that he would arrange a better system of supply for the army, but he was accused of cowardice by those who remained behind, particularly Bohemond: see *Gesta Francorum*, pp. 34–5; Raymond of Aguilers, p. 54; Robert of Rheims, p. 782; Albert of Aachen, pp. 366, 417. It is therefore interesting that Gilo should list him here amongst the 'fearless' leaders of the crusade, and in this respect he comes close to the *Chanson d'Antioche*, where he is regarded

(Qui dum uiuebat naso, non laude carebat)
Et reliqui fortes armantur; et ecce cohortes
Procedunt, plorant quia frustra sepe laborant.
Optat quisque mori nisi[a] bellum cedat honori: 265
Mors ingrata, grauis, foret illis grata, suauis.
Integrat[b] illorum mentes solator[c] eorum
Et rogat intensis precibus presul[d] Podiensis
Ne desperarent, quia credentes superarent,[e1]
Ceruicesque gregis signat summi[f] cruce regis.   270
Pluribus hortati mortemque subire parati
Aut superare, boni proceres fideique patroni
Illuc accelerant, ubi se concurrere sperant
Hostibus, et tacite graditur prior et sine lite
Corripit ignarum Hugo ductor[g] Francigenarum,   275
Amotique parum cursores[h] Christicolarum
Stantia[i] summa[j] ducum uexilla uident quasi lucum.[k]
Nec mora, per scalas Godefridus segregat alas.
En modo deuictus dux et[l] de strage relictus[2]
Emersit[m] subito de montibus, et repetito   280
Milite signa gerens demissa, fugam sibi querens,
Visa recognouit[n] uexilla metumque remouit.
Precipit et stare sua signa[o] tubisque[p] sonare.[q]
Alterutrum gaudent sociorum scuta[r] uidere,
Alterutrumque uiris[s] resides animi rediere.   285
Exacuit Persas[t] uictoria parta recenter,
Erigitur sonipes, dominum gerit impatienter.
Arcus lunantur, clipei galeeque parantur,
Iam resonant nerui, iam Turci tela[u] proterui
Intorquent, iam cornipedes saliunt quasi cerui,   290
Iam tubicen[v] teter lituis[w] sonat, obstrepit ether,
Iam caua saxa datas uoces reddunt geminatas:
Vndique pugnatur,[x] belli fortuna[3] uagatur.

[a] ni B   [b] interga D   [c] solatur D   [d] presul precibus D m. pr.
[e] superaerent D m. pr.   [f] summi signat ADG   [g] doctor D   [h] cursores
B m. alt.   [i] stantis DG   [j] signa DG   [k] lucem D m. pr.   [l] et om.
D   [m] emisit BC   [n] recogniuit ACDFG   [o] siga D m. pr.
[p] turbisque D m. pr.   [q] tubisque canare sonare A   [r] sociorum signa scuta A
m. pr.   [s] uires C   [t] Perses BCF   [u] pila BC   [v] tybicen D m. pr.
[w] lituus ABCD   [x] bellatur ADG

in a favourable light, and defends the Franks in their absence against the emperor.
Statinus' physical description may also have recalled the character *Guillaume as cortes nes*

but not worthless while he lived) and the other brave men armed themselves, and see! there were the cohorts, weeping as they advanced because they so often toiled in vain. [265] Each of them chose to die if the war did not bring him honour: unwelcome and grievous death would be pleasant and sweet to them. Their comforter, the Bishop of Le Puy, strengthened their hearts and besought with earnest prayers that they should not lose hope, because those who believed would overcome,[1] [270] and he signed the bowed heads of the throng with the cross of the highest of kings. Encouraged by his many words, and ready to meet their death or conquer, the good nobles and lords of the faith made haste to the place where they hoped they would meet the enemy, and proceeding silently in front without any commotion, [275] Hugh, the leader of the Franks, caught his enemy unawares, and the Christian troopers who were a little way off saw the tops of the dukes' raised banners standing erect like a thicket. Without delay Godfrey divided his ranks into battalions. Then suddenly the duke who had just been defeated and abandoned after the fray[2] [280] charged from the mountains, and sought out his troops again with his standards held low, looking for a way of escape for himself, but when he saw the banners and recognized them, his fear vanished. He ordered his standards to be raised aloft and his trumpets to sound. The allies rejoiced to see each others' shields, [285] and good heart returned to downcast men on both sides. The victory that they had not long before gained sharpened the zeal of the Persians, and the horses reared up, bearing their masters with impatience. Bows were bent tight, shields and helms were made ready, and already bowstrings twanged, already the shameless Turks were [290] hurling missiles, already their steeds were leaping like stags, already the brazen bugler resounded his horn-calls, and the air was full of noise, already the hollow rocks re-echoed their doubly sounding voices. There was fighting everywhere, and the fortune of war[3] wandered far and wide: for

in the Old French epic Le Charroi de Nîmes, ed. J.-L. Perrier (Paris, 1966), ll. 5, 139–47, 533, 847, etc.

[1] 1 John 5: 4.
[2] This is presumably a reference to either Bohemond or Raymond, whose forces had fled into the mountains after being ambushed by the Turks on their way back from St Simeon. See also above, v. 256, Gesta Francorum, p. 40.
[3] Cf. above, v. 32.

Nam modo terga dabant hostes,*a* modo nostra fugabant[1]
Agmina; per bellum uersat Bellona flagellum.[2]   295
Diuersum iacitur*b* nec eisdem missile uotis:
Destinat*c* hic iaculum presentibus, ille remotis.
Cedere*d* crinitus iuuenis non pellere doctus
Funditur in plano, iactu terit aera uano.
Neue petat palmam gens conspicienda capillis[3]   300
Libertate fuge, libertas clauditur illis.[4]
Ergo Dei proceres, umbonibus*e* ordine*f* iunctis,
Sic cinxere*g* uiros ut silua cacumina montis.
Vndique stant turbe; Godefridus pugnat ab urbe,
Imminet a tergo Boimundus.[5] Comminus ergo   305
Pugna fit immitis,*h* tanto minus apta sagittis.
Flectit equum Parthus*i* nusquam, uetat hoc locus artus;
Tinguit*j* Persarum cruor enses Francigenarum.
Ensis inexperti*k* studio conantur inerti
Turci per minimam campo se reddere rimam.*l*   310
Vt pateant aditus et possint*m* tangere litus
Se satis exercent, sed eos stipata cohercent
Agmina, constrictus nequit hostis cedere*n* uictus.
Stat stupidus furor eous, uia nulla*o* saluti,
Non iaculis licet aut solitis anfractibus*p* uti.   315
Audax et timidus pereunt simul: hic*q* prohibetur*r*
In pugna pugnare, sed huic fuga fida negatur.
Non modice*s* turbe modico capiuntur*t* ab orbe.
Turcus in oppositum dum sepius erigit ictum
Confossis*u* costis socii partem iuuat hostis.   320
Pectora pectoribus et membris membra teruntur.
Soli*v* bella gerunt nostri, Turci patiuntur.[6]
Parthus,*w* Arabs*x* proni succumbunt*y* ultro mucroni,
Nec nostri tantum possunt prosternere,*z* quantum*aa*
Agmina densa mori.*bb* Claudit*cc* madefacta*dd* cruori   325

---

a Perse *G*   *b* tacitur *D m. pr.*   *c* detinatque *F*   *d* credere *F*
e uerbonibus *D m. pr.*   *f* cedine *A*   *g* succinxere *G;* sic cincere *D m. pr.*
h inmittis *D*   *i* partus *F*   *j* tingit *A*   *k* inexpertis *G;* inherti *A*
l ripam *ADG*   *m* aditus rimam possit *A*   *n* nequit hos procedere *A*
o nulla uia *A*   *p* anfratibus *A*   *q* hic *Grocock:* huic *all MSS*   *r* pro-
betur *D m. pr., corrected to* proibetur *m. alt.*   *s* inmodice *ADG*   *t* capuntur *B*
u confessis *A*   *v* sola *ADFG*   *w* partus *DF*   *x* Araps *D*   *y* suc-
cubunt *B*   *z* prosternunt *D*   *aa* quantis *A*   *bb* moret *D m. pr.*
cc cadit *F*   *dd* malefacta *D*

now the enemy turned their backs, now they put our columns to
flight;[1] [295] Bellona turned her whip about through the fighting.[2]
All kinds of missiles were thrown, with varied intentions: this man
aimed his spear at those near him, that one at men far off. The
long-haired youths who had learned to give way, not to drive the
enemy back, were brought low in the field and wore the air thin
with their futile throwing. [300] And lest that race so conspicuous
for their long hair[3] should try to gain the victory by having the free-
dom to flee, that freedom was cut off from them.[4] Therefore the
nobles of God joined their shields by ranks, and surrounded those
men as a wood does a hilltop. The throng stood on every side;
Godfrey fought from the city, [305] Bohemond pressed on in the
rear.[5] Therefore the harsh fighting came to close quarters and all
the less suitable for firing arrows. At no point did the Parthians
wheel round their horses; the narrowness of the place prevented
this; the blood of the Persians stained the Frankish swords. In-
experienced at sword-play, the Turks tried with unskilled zeal
[310] to reach the open plain through the narrowest of gaps. They
laboured hard to force an opening and be able to get to the shore,
but the troops packed all round hemmed them in, and the defeated
foe was encircled and could not retreat. The frenzy of the east
stood dumbfounded, with no way of escape, [315] and no room to
deploy their spears or their usual wheeling manœuvres. The bold
and the fearful perished together: one was prevented from fighting
in the fray, the other was denied a sure escape. Large throngs were
captured by a small circle of men. Quite often as the Turks struck
blows at their opponents [320] they cut into a comrade's ribs, and
helped their enemy's cause. They were packed chest to chest and
limb to limb. Only our men waged war: the Turks endured it.[6] Par-
thian and Arab helplessly fell forward on to the sword, and our men
could not kill to the same extent as the close-packed host could
die. [325] The sodden earth closed off the way out for the gore,

---

[1] On this tactic, see Smail, *Crusading Warfare*, pp. 78–9, and above, iv. 219–20.

[2] Lucan, *Bellum ciuile*, vii. 568.

[3] This reference to long hair may stem from the vernacular tradition: it is a distin-
guishing feature of Chernubles de Munigre, one of the Saracens described in the
Chanson de Roland, ll. 975–8.

[4] Raymond of Aguilers, p. 60, states that the Turks were trapped because those inside
the city, fearing that the crusaders would surge inside, closed the gates against them.

[5] The Turks were trapped between the two forces of crusaders as they tried to reach
the fortified bridge, and thereby the safety of Antioch.

[6] Robert of Rheims, p. 786: *nostri tantum pugnabant, illi patiebantur*.

Terra uiam, rimas quia*a* iam compleuerat imas
Sanguis cognatus,*b* nec habet quos pandat*c* hiatus.
Puluis ubi cessit quem sanguinis unda repressit,*d1*
Vincendi certum signum campum per apertum
Conspiciunt nostri factos de sanguine riuos*e*   330
Et sustentantes erecta*f* cadauera uiuos.*g2*
Et quoniam tantum licuit pro strage nocentum
Se stolide gentes reputabant esse nocentes.

Miles ut eoo uidet arua cruore natare
Cessit et exactas*h* uoluit uires*i* renouare.   335
Rupit ut ille*j* chorum, nubes glomerata uirorum
Conuersis frenis in se ruit, urget habenis
Lassos cornipedes, caruitque modo noua*k* cedes.
Hic fratrem terit, ille patrem; ciuilia bella*3*
Exercent dominumque premit super obruta sella.   340
Et, uelut in stagnis, cum sepe recluditur amnis,*l*
Vnde detente disrupto fonte repente
Prosiliunt, prime fugiunt reliqueque secuntur,
Impediunt alias alie, certare uidentur,
Haud secus ad planum properat uulgus male sanum   345
Et fugit ad pontem. Calcans dux Bullicus*m* hostem
Occupat ingressum pontis prohibetque*n* regressum
Ense cruentato populo grauiter superato.
Ira, locus, gladius pugnant, uim quodque*o* duci dat:
Hec*p* subigit*q* uires,*r* hic impedit,*s* ille trucidat.   350
Dux, spes nostrorum, Turcis confusio, luctus,
Truncat equos, equites, recipitque cadauera fluctus.*4*

---

a qui *C*   *b* conatus *D m. pr.*   *c* pandet *C*   *d* recessit *A*   *e* riuos
de sanguine factos *F m. pr.*   *f* erepta *A m. alt. written over an erasure*   *g* *A m. pr.*
omits this line   *h* exhaustas *ADG*   *i* uires uoluit *ADG*   *j* illa *DG*
k fera *BC*   *l* annis *F;* anguis *A*   *m* bellicus *BC;* publicus *DG*
n proibitque *D*   *o* quoque *BCF;* queque *G*   *p* nec *F*   *q* animos *ADG*
r firmat *ADG*   *s* inpedit *D*

---

[1] Alcimus Avitus, *Carm.* i. 167.
[2] See Robert of Rheims, p. 786: 'inter uiuos mortui stabant, quia suffulti densitate
uirorum cadere non poterant.'
[3] Lucan, *Bellum ciuile,* i. 1.
[4] For other accounts of this episode, see Peter Tudebode, p. 75; Robert of Rheims,
pp. 786–7; Albert of Aachen, p. 385. There are also close similarities between Gilo's ver-
sion of events and a vernacular account, the *Chanson du Chevalier au Cygne: Cycle belge*, ed.

because kinsman's blood had already filled the deep crevices, and the earth had no more clefts to open up. When the dust settled, held down by the wave of blood,[1] [330] our men saw a sure sign of victory over the open plain, streams made of blood, and live men holding corpses upright;[2] and since they were permitted so much slaughter of dangerous men, the foolish people reckoned themselves dangerous too.

When our soldiers saw the fields swimming with blood from the east, [335] they left off, wanting to replenish their exhausted strength. As they broke off the engagement, a cloud of men gathered, wheeled round their steeds, and rushed at them, driving their tired horses on with their reins, and the new slaughter lacked all moderation. One man trampled on his brother, another on his father; they waged a civil war,[3] [340] and dislodged saddles pressed down hard on their masters. And, just as often when a stream is dammed to form ponds, the waters held in check suddenly leap out when the pond is disturbed, the first currents tumbling down and the rest following, and they get in each other's way and seem to be at odds, [345] just like that the ill-advised common folk rushed for the open field and fled to the bridge. The duke of Bouillon trampled down the enemy, took possession of the approach to the bridge, and stopped their retreat, vanquishing the people savagely with his bloody sword. Anger, the locality, and his sword fought together, and each gave strength to the duke: [350] anger subdued their might, the locality hindered them, and his sword slew them. The duke, the hope of our men, but disaster and grief for the Turks, slew horses and knights, and the river bore away the corpses.[4]

F. A. F. T. de Reiffenberg (Monuments pour servir à l'histoire des provinces de Namur, Hainault, Luxembourg; Brussels, n.d.), ll. 6322–32:

> La avient Godefroy une cose avenant,
> Chou c'onques mais n'avint a nul homme vivant:
> Ung Sarrasins aloit Godefroy enkauchant,
> Arme souffisament, sur le destrier courant,
> Godefroys le fery du travers du talent,
> Par itel covenant, on le trouve lisant,
> Que le Sarrasin va parmy le corps trenchant.
> Une moitiet chey sur le pret verdoyant,
> Et ly aultre moitiet demoura sur Baucant;
> Et ly avans s'en va en le porte fuiant
> Ou Garsions estoit avoecques Solimant.

See also the *Chanson de Roland*, ll. 1367–78.

Quod non de Tideo*a* legitur nec de Capaneo,*b*
Quod non Eacides,*c* non Hector, non Diomedes,*d* 1
Dux potuit, neque nos latuit res digna*e* relatu:*2*   355
Mole sua terrens proceres multoque paratu
Dirus Arabs gladium uoluens radiante rotatu
Precipiti portatus equo celerique uolatu
Constitit*f* ante ducem, putat hanc extinguere lucem,
Et super inuictum caput erigit altius*g* ictum.   360
Precauet iratus dux sub clipeo replicatus,
Moxque*h* choruscantem gladium leuat*i* et*j* ferit*k* hostem:
Os, caput illidit, uitalia tota cecidit,*l*
Spargit et aruinam, rupit*m* cum pectore*n* spinam;
Sic homo prostratus*o* cadit in duo dimidiatus   365
Atque super scutum partes*p* in mille minutum
Pars cecidit, pars heret equo trahiturque*q* supina,
Estque sui moderator equi non iusta rapina.
Ictu sic uno fit magna nec una ruina.*r*

Dicere succincte si uellem funera uicte*s*   370
Gentis, quas mortes sunt passe mille cohortes,
Aut*t* quid Normannus comes egerit aut Hugo Magnus
Flandrensisue manus, essem*u* me iudice uanus:
Non*v* Maro, non Macer*3* quid ibi Tancretius acer*w*
Fecerit*x* exprimerent et uerbis facta carerent.   375

Hic decus*y* eoum*z* cecidit, nullumque tropheum
Hoc magis afflixit ciues. Hic dextra*4* reuixit
Mortua nostrorum, satiata cruore uirorum,
Hic ammirati*aa* primates*bb* sunt iugulati,*5*
Hic urbis magne fracte cecidere columne,*cc*   380
Hic quoque consilio rex designatus inani

---

a Tudeo *G;* Thideo *BC*   *b* Canapeo *BC*   *c* Eatides *D*   *d* siue
Titides *BC*   *e* digne *A*   *f* constuit *A*   *g* altius erigit *ADG*
h mox *G m. pr.*   *i* fecit *A*   *j* se *A*   *k* leua *A*   *l* cecidit *Grocock;*
cicidit *all MSS*   *m* rumpit *ADG*   *n* spectore *A*   *o* truncatus *ADG*
p atque scutum gladio partes *BC*   *q* traditurque *D*   *r* *D m. pr.* puts this line
after l. 367, corr. by m. alt. to put it after l. 366   *s* uite *D, A m. pr.*   *t* at *A*
u ensem *BC*   *v* nam *D*   *w* cacer *D m. pr.*   *x* fecerint *D*
y c.cecus *D m. pr.; ?* hic detus *A*   *z* euum *D m. pr.*   *aa* admirati *ABCD*
bb principes *B m. pr.*   *cc* columbe *A*

What is not read of Tydeus, nor of Capaneus, what neither Achilles, nor Hector, nor Diomedes[1] could do, [355] the duke did, and his exploit, worthy to be told,[2] is not hidden from us: terrifying the nobles with his massive bulk and his sumptuous equipage, an awe-inspiring Arab whirled his glittering sword about, and carried forward by the rapid flight of his steed, he halted before the duke, thinking he would extinguish this light, [360] and raised his sword high over that unvanquished head to strike. The angry duke took guard, bending back beneath his shield, and then straight away raised his gleaming sword and struck his enemy: he smashed his mouth and head, cut right through his vitals, strewed his fat about, and shattered his spine and chest; [365] thus was the man laid low, and he fell in two parts, sliced in half, and half of him fell on to his shield, which was shattered into a thousand pieces, and half of him stuck to his horse and was borne off lying flat on its back; the rider was his horse's unjust plunder. Thus with one blow came about massive defeat, and not a single one.

[370] Were I to wish to speak concisely of the ends met by the conquered race, what deaths those squadrons suffered, or what the count of Normandy achieved, or Hugh the Great, or the hand of the duke of Flanders, I would judge myself vain: not Vergil, not Macer[3] could describe what bold Tancred [375] did there, and would lack the words to fit their deeds.

Here fell the glory of the east, and no victory-prize shattered the citizens more than this. Here the long-dead hand of our men[4] came back to life, sated with the gore of men, here the noble emirs had their throats cut,[5] [380] here fell the broken columns of the great city, here too by useless counsel the crown prince, son of the

---

[1] The variant in *BC* is explained by the gloss on Statius, *Achilleid*, i. 844: 'Tydides, Diomedes uel Ulixes'; see *The Medieval Achilleid of Statius*, ed. P. M. Clogan (Leiden, 1968), p. 106.   [2] Sidonius Apollinaris, *Carm.* vii. 221.

[3] 'Macer' is the poet Odo of Meung, who wrote the *De uiribus herbarum*, a study of plants which became widely studied as a schooltext (see Manitius, *Geschichte der lateinischen Literatur*, ii. 539–47). See also Robert of Rheims, p. 787; *Gesta Francorum*, p. 44, for other expressions of inability to describe adequately the events during the siege of Antioch.

[4] See Robert of Rheims, p. 788; Peter Tudebode, pp. 76–7. In the *Chanson de Roland*, l. 597, Roland is referred to as the 'destre braz del cors' of Charlemagne.

[5] *Gesta Francorum*, p. 41, Robert of Rheims, p. 788, and Albert of Aachen, p. 386, say that twelve emirs were killed in this battle.

Filius occubuit magni regis Casiani.[a1]
Corporibus plenum flumen stetit Antiochenum[b]
Vndaque pallorem mutans imitata[c] ruborem.[d]
In pontis strata sunt milia quinque[2] necata,   385
Dextraque cedentum deforme facit pauimentum.[e]
Iamque fatigati, multis spoliis onerati,[3]
Nocte duces leti[f] redeunt, dant[g] membra quieti,[4]
Sed uigilant sensus, hostesque fugare uidentur
Quique suos, capuloque[h] manus absente mouetur.   390
Postquam[i] clara dies nituit nostri nituere
Vestibus, era suis uictores distribuere.
Tunc[j] capti numerantur equi, septemque fuere
Milia, tunc[k] equites totidem proceres statuere.
His ita transactis[l] castellum turribus altis   395
Et solido fundo stabilitum dant Raimundo.[5]

Dum bene succedit, dum sepius alea fati[6]
Mergit gentiles, sunt extra castra uocati
A ducibus magnis audaces meliusque parati.
Quilibet hostili gaudens occurrere dampno   400
Ducitur in[m] predam, sed non hortamine magno,
Qui festinantes fluuiumque sub urbe uadantes[n]
Mulas et mulos capiunt multosque camelos
Et subito rapiunt animalia milia quinque
Cum totidem, licet urbani[o] iaculentur[p] utrimque.[q]   405

Huc[r] quoque quo iuuenes predam cepere nouatur
Quoddam castellum uallumque uetus reparatur.[7]
Illud Tancreto committitur omine leto,
Nam[s] premonstrabat minimi custodia muri

[a] Cassiani *BDF*   [b] Antiochenu *B pr. m.*   [c] mutata *A*   [d] ruborem
est *B m. pr.;* cruorem *D*   [e] *This line reads* fitque pauimentum de corporibus
morientum *ADG;* de iugulis flentum miserabile fit pauimentum *F*   [f] leti *om. BC*
[g] sua reddunt *BC*   [h] scapuloque *F*   [i] post ubi *G*   [j] nunc *F*
[k] tunc pro *F*   [l] tranactis *D*   [m] ad *ADG*   [n] uadentes *D m. pr.*
[o] urbanna *A*   [p] culentur *A*   [q] utrumque *F*   [r] hic *ADG*   [s] iam
CF

[1] Robert of Rheims, p. 788, also refers to the death of Yaghi Siyan's son, Shams ad-
Daulah, who had accompanied the first Turkish army to Antioch. See above, v. 111 and
n. In fact, however, while his father was killed as he fled to the hills, Shams ad-Daulah
gained control of the citadel, which he held against the Christians until relieved by
Kerbogha.

great king Cassianus, met his end.[1] The river by Antioch stood
still, full of bodies, and its waters exchanged their pale colour for
red. [385] On the planks of the bridge five thousand men[2] were
killed, and the right hands of the slaughterers made foul its surface.
Already exhausted and laden with a mass of booty,[3] the dukes
returned full of joy at night, and laid down their bodies to rest,[4] but
their senses were still awake, [390] and each of them seemed still to
be routing his enemies, and moved his hand, though it held no
sword. After radiant daybreak shone clear, our men too were
radiant in their clothing, and the victors shared the spoils among
their men. Then they counted the horses they had captured, and
there were seven thousand, so then the nobles promoted the same
number of men to be knights. [395] When all this was done, a fort
with high towers and built on solid ground was given to Raymond.[5]

With things going well, and the dice of fate[6] more often over-
whelming the heathen, the bold and better-prepared men were
summoned out of the camp by the great dukes. [400] Whichever of
them delighted in causing loss to the enemy was led off to plunder,
and did not need a great deal of encouragement; they made haste,
forded the river below the city, and captured donkeys and mules
and many camels, and then quickly snatched a total of ten
thousand beasts, [405] even though the men in the city threw
weapons at them from both sides.

In addition, a certain fort to which the young men could take their
plunder was renovated, and an old rampart was made good again.[7]
This was entrusted to Tancred—a happy omen, for the custody
of this tiny part of the city wall betokened that he would have

[2] The *Gesta Francorum*, p. 41, refers to 1,500 casualties.
[3] Gilo does not specifically mention the gold and silver which was taken from the
Turkish corpses. See *Gesta Francorum*, p. 42.
[4] Proba, *Cent. Verg.* 124, 599 = *Aen.* ii. 691, and Gilo, iv. 330.
[5] See Peter Tudebode, p. 78; *Gesta Francorum*, pp. 30, 42. The castle known as 'La
Mahomerie' was completed on 19 Mar. and entrusted to Raymond of Toulouse. See
Raymond of Aguilers, p. 62. The author of the *Gesta* claims that it was built with stones
taken from Turkish tombs.
[6] Lucan, *Bellum ciuile*, vi. 7, 603.
[7] A second castle was built on the site of the monastery of St George, opposite the
gate of that name, its purpose being to block off the route whereby supplies continued to
reach the city. See Peter Tudebode, pp. 81–2; *Gesta Francorum*, p. 43.

Vrbis custodem, prenuntia facta futuri.[1]   410
Iam[a] timet obsessus ciuis, clamorque repressus
Est insultantis populi de se meditantis.
Pluribus afflictus[b] dolet, at penuria uictus
Acrius[c] angebat[d] quia uix exire licebat.[2]
Post hec inter se statuerunt talia Perse   415
Vt pax ad tempus cum Christicolis habeatur,
Qualiter interea se reddant discutiatur.[e]
Sic igitur coram pax confirmatur ad horam.[3]
Porte celate[f] sunt interea reserate,
Muros hostiles posita formidine miles   420
Circuit et tuto Parthi[g] tandemque soluto[h]
Arcu ridebant nostris et castra petebant.

At Gualo[i] uir fortis,[4] dum lumina pascit[j] in hortis,
Perfidie gentis nimis immemor hec simulantis
Dum delectatur, male fida fides uiolatur:[k]   425
Occubuit nempe loca dum uidet emula Tempe.[5]
Iura fidesque data sunt morte uiri temerata,
Quem simul elusit se ciuis[l] in urbe[m] retrusit.[n]
Audiit ut funus Humberga[o6] decens et Hugonis
Filia, nupta prius comitis, tunc[p] nupta Gualonis,[q]   430
Palluit atque genas secat unguibus illa proteruis
Et sustentatur matrum[r] stipata cateruis.
Dextra comas lacerat; sed que lacerat laceratur,
Subtilisque manus subtili[s] crine secatur.

[a] nam F   [b] afflictu D m. pr., corr. to afflictis m. alt.   [c] arcrius F
[d] urgebat F   [e] discuciatur F   [f] scelate F   [g] Pathi A; parti C m. pr., F
[h] solutos D   [i] Galo CF   [j] pacit D m. pr.   [k] A m. pr. omits ll. 425–8; m.
alt. puts them after 460, with the rubric questio uxoris Galonis uitio scriptoris pretermissa.
hac xiiii cartum   [l] cuius A   [m] ab urbe F m. pr.; in orbe D m. pr.   [n] D
reads planctus Huncberge super Galone coniuge after this line   [o] Huncberga D;
Hunberga   C;   Umberga   A   [p] nunc   AD   [q] Galonis   CF
[r] neruis D m. pr.   [s] subtilique F

---

[1] Tancred became ruler of Antioch in Mar. 1101, after Bohemond was captured by
the Turks (cf. Runciman, Hist. Crus. i. 325–6). This is Gilo's only reference to an event
which took place after the First Crusade.
[2] Tancred himself captured a large consignment of food destined for Antioch. See
Gesta Francorum, pp. 43–4.
[3] Only Robert of Rheims, p. 794, and the Chanson d'Antioche, 5689–733, appear to
mention this truce. In reality it may have been simply a lull in the fighting after the
crusaders' victory and amidst rumour that a third Turkish relief force was on its way

[410] the custody of the city, and these happenings were forebodings of the future.[1] By now the beleaguered citizens were afraid, and the shouting of this insolent people was held in check as they considered their own interests. Affliction hurt many, but the lack of food hurt more bitterly because they had scarcely an opportunity of going out.[2] [415] After this the Persians came to an accord amongst themselves of this nature, that peace should be observed for the time being with the Christians,[3] and that meanwhile they should discuss the terms of their surrender. And so peace was affirmed in their presence until a given time. Meanwhile the decorated gates were opened, [420] and the soldiers laid aside their fear and walked round the enemy walls, and the Parthians at length slackened their bows in safety, smiled at our men, and headed for their camp.

But there was a brave man, Gualo,[4] who went to look at the gardens, and forgot too soon about the treachery of this race who were feigning these things; [425] while he feasted his eyes, their untrustworthy faith was broken, for he was slain as he was looking at places as lovely as Tempe.[5] The terms of faith which had been given were violated by the death of this man, and the citizen who deceived him at once hid himself away in the city. When the worthy Humberga[6] heard of his death—[430] she was the daughter of Hugh, and had earlier been the wife of a count, but was then the wife of Gualo—she grew pale, wildly scratched her cheeks with her nails, and was supported by a band of ladies gathered round her. Her right hand tore at her hair, but in tearing she tore herself, and her graceful hand was cut by her graceful hair.

to Antioch. Ibn al-'Athīr, i. 193, however, notes that the crusaders sent an abortive embassy to Dukak of Damascus, asking for his neutrality.

[4] The death of Gualo is also mentioned by Guibert of Nogent, p. 252, and by Anselm of Ribemont in a letter to Archbishop Manasseh of Rheims (*Die Kreuzzugsbriefe*, pp. 159, 323–4). Albert of Aachen, p. 363, states that he was the French standard-bearer, and in fact he can be identified as Gualo II, lord of Chaumont-en-Vexin, the constable of Philip I of France. See *Cartulaire de l'Abbaye de Saint-Martin-de-Pontoise*, ed. J. Depain (Pontoise, 1895), pp. 350–1. The editors are indebted to Professor Riley-Smith for this reference.

[5] 'Tempe' was a common term for a beautiful place: cf. Statius, *Thebaid*, x. 119.

[6] Robert of Rheims, pp. 795–6, also describes the grief of Gualo's wife, but only Gilo mentions her name. Humberga was the daughter of Hugh of Le Puiset and sister of Everard, himself a crusader. She had previously been married to Count Robert of Meulan. See J. La Monte, 'The lords of Le Puiset on the crusades', *Speculum*, xvii (1942), 100–18, at pp. 100–2. The passage from this point to the end of book v is treated in depth in Grocock, 'Ovid the Crusader', pp. 55–69, esp. at 65–8. As might be expected, it owes much to Ovid's treatment of suffering women in the *Heroides*.

Exanimemque[a] diu uox pressa dolore[b] relinquit,[c]   435
Sed[d] tandem uoci uia uix[e] laxatur et inquit:
'Tantane sustinuit Deus infortunia genti
　　Occurrisse sue, plus inimica mihi?
Occubuitne decus[f] Francorum, maximus hostis
　　Hostibus, ille meus, spesque salusque suis?   440
Languet morte graui bello non languida dextra,[g]
　　Languet et occubuit uir Gualo,[h] uita mea.
Me miseram! non obsequium miserabile feci[i]
　　Vir, tibi: cum caderes, compariter cecidi.
Hei mihi! non foui, non clausi, non ego laui   445
　　Os, oculos, uulnus, ueste, manu, lacrimis.
Lux mea, cui moriens morituram deseruisti?
　　Vt tecum morerer dignior ipsa fui.[j]
Tu[k] mihi tu, certe memini,[l] iurare solebas[l]
　　Te uitaturum cautius insidias.   450
Sed quam[m] non poterat gens[n] perfida demere bello
　　Est sublata tibi uita beata dolo.
An sine te uiuam patris a patria procul absens?[o]
　　Absque uiro uiuet femina castra sequens?
Figite[p] me quibus est pietas, opponite[q] telis[r,s]   455
　　Parthorum miseram, mors mihi pena leuis,
Mors mihi[t] pena leuis si iungar morte Gualoni,[u]
　　Si non sim[v] Turco preda futura truci.'
Hos leuat Eurardus[w] frater[2] solamine questus
　　Et reprimit blanda uoce graues gemitus.   460

Sic apud hostilem uariis euentibus urbem
Ducebant longam nostrates obsidionem.
Inter Christicolas et Christi nominis hostes
Pugna trahebatur prope denos aspera menses;[3]
Instabant isti fisi uirtute superna,   465
Obstabant illi nitentes fraude paterna,
Sperabant siquidem nostros uel deficientes
Deserere in medio frustratos sepe labores,

---

[a] e.exanimemque *A*   [b] delore *F m. pr.*   [c] reliquit *AC;* reliquid *D*
[d] e *D*   [e] lux *D*   [f] ? detus *A*   [g] *D omits this line; G completes the couplet*
with eheu quis mihi det misera decedere uita   [h] Galo *ABCF*   [i] fecli *D m. pr.*
[j] *ADG omit ll. 447–8*   [k] en *G*   [l] solebat *F m. pr.*   [m] quia *BC;* quam
ADG   [n] gens non *A m. pr.*   [o] *DG omit ll. 453–4; A has* quid faciam procul a
patria procul a patre degens | quid faciet fragilis femina castra sequens   [p] fugite *A*

[435] For a long time her voice was checked by grief, and left her lifeless, but eventually the path of her speech was loosened sufficiently for her to speak: 'Has God allowed such great misfortunes to afflict his own people, misfortunes yet more hateful to me? Has the glory of the Franks perished, the greatest of enemies to [440] his enemies, my own husband, hope and salvation for his own? The right hand that was not idle in war lies idle in grievous death; my husband Gualo, my life, lies still and is slain. Alas, poor me! I have performed no service of pity for you, husband; when you fell dead, I likewise fell. [445] Ah me! I have not wiped your mouth with my dress, nor closed your eyes with my hand, nor washed your wounds with my tears. O my light, for whom have you left me in death, me who must also die? I was more worthy myself to die with you. You used—I remember it well[1]—you used to swear to me [450] that you would be wary and very careful of ambushes. But your blessed life, which this treacherous race could not take away in war, has been taken from you by a trick. Am I to live without you, far away from the land of my father? Shall a woman live, following the camp without a husband? [455] You who know your godly duty, strike me down! Stand me against the Parthian spears; death is a slight pain for me, yes death is a slight pain for me if I am joined with Gualo in death, if I am not to be enslaved by the savage Turks.' Her brother Everard[2] comforted these laments with soothing, [460] and put an end to her deep sobbing with sweet words.

And so with various outcomes our side carried out a protracted siege at the enemy city. Between the Christians and the enemies of Christ's name, bitter fighting dragged on for about ten months;[3] [465] one side attacked, trusting in the virtue from on high, the others defended, relying on the treachery of their fathers, and indeed they hoped either that as our men grew weak they would abandon their oft-frustrated toil unfinished, or that the myriads of

[q] apponite D   [r] Partis A m. pr.   [s] D m. pr. puts this line after l. 456; m. alt. corrects   [t] mors A   [u] Galoni AD; Galonis BC   [v] sum B; si A   [w] Euuradrus F; Euardus A

[1] Ovid, *Amores*, ii. 10 (11). 1.
[2] Everard of Le Puiset; see below, vii. 428 n.
[3] *Gesta Francorum*, p. 77, states that the siege lasted for eight months and one day. Robert of Rheims offers both ten months, like the Charleville Poet (Robert, p. 836), and also eight months and one day (p. 844). The final stages of the siege are described by Gilo of Paris below, in book vii.

Vel sibi myriadas Persarum gentis adesse,
More locustarumque obstantia cuncta uorare.   470
Tali comperto rumore beata caterua
In conspectu urbis producit pignora sacra:
Illic obsidio septem[1] *iuratur in annos,*
Rursus et in totidem nisi uirtus celica muros
Panderet ante sibi, que spem resecauit inanem   475
Ciuibus immodicumque incussit causa timorem.

---

[1] This repetition of seven may have an additional significance, an echo of vernacular

the race of Persians would come to them, [470] devouring all that stood in their way like locusts. When the blessed company heard such reports, they brought holy tokens out in the sight of the city, and there the siege was sworn for seven years,[1] and for another seven, too, if the valour of heaven [475] had not breached the walls for itself before then; this event removed empty hope from the citizens and struck them with terrible fear.

poetry and an attempt to draw another parallel between the crusade and Charlemagne'scampaigns against the Muslims. Charlemagne reputedly spent seven years fighting in Spain. See the *Chanson de Roland*, ll. 1–2.

fo. 93ᵛ *Incipit liber sextus*

> *Talia apud Syriam uaria dum sorte geruntur*[1]
> *Nuncque hinc nunc illinc mala uel bona distribuuntur,*
> *Venit ad heroas supplex legatio nostros*
> *Consilii poscens simul auxiliiique ministros,*[2]
> *Precipueque ducis compellat nobile nomen*   5
> *Vulgatum fama terram uolitante per omnem.*
> *Vnde tamen uel cur legatio uenerit ista*[3]
> *Restat ut expediat narratio suppeditata.*
>
> *Terra inter geminos ditissima clauditur amnes,*
> *Tygrin et Eufraten, populos famosa per omnes,*   10
> *In greco retinens que Mesopothamia nomen*
> *Ex habitu cause*ᵃ *conseruat nominis omen.*
> *A fluuio ad fluuium tantum distare uidetur*
> *Quantum †ac†*ᵇ *pedibus septena luce meatur.*
> *Haec inter plures gremio quas continet urbes,*   15
> *Vrbs antiqua, potens, speciosa et diuite uena*
> *Eminet antique Babyloni nempe coeua;*
> *Nam quo Chaldeam pharetrata Semyramis arcem*[4]
> *Tempore construxit, simul hec quoque condita fulsit,*
> *Nomine corrupto que nunc Rohasia*ᶜ *dicta,*   20
> *Temporis antiqui possedit nomen Edyssa.*[5]
> *Haec secus Assyrias iacet ad sex milia Charras*
> *Romanis ducibus Crassorum morte perosas,*[6]
> *In quibus antiquus degebat Abram patriarcha*

ᵃ terrae (?) (*sic*) *Riant; Sirmond prints a lacuna*   ᵇ ac *cod.; Sirmond and Riant print a lacuna; Holford-Strevens sugg.* hominis   ᶜ Rahasia *Sirmond, Riant*

---

[1] The style of this book, and the emphasis upon Godfrey of Bouillon, as well as the manuscript tradition, make it clear that it is in its entirety the work of the Charleville Poet. See Introd., Sect. I.

[2] After the Cilician diversion recounted above in iv. 360–4, Baldwin of Boulogne rejoined the main crusading army at Marash, but when it began the march to Antioch, he led a small force to the east and the valley of the Euphrates. In the course of the journey he established contact with local Armenian princes, and it was in Feb. 1098 at

Book six begins.

While such actions as these were being carried out in Syria,[1] *with varying results, and good or bad fortune was being dispersed now here, now there, an embassy came in supplication to our heroes, asking them to provide counsel and assistance;*[2] *[5] they were driven to do this particularly by the noble reputation of the duke, noised abroad as reports of him winged their way through the whole earth. But as to where this embassy came from and why,*[3] *it remains for the following detailed account to relate.*

A very rich land lies closed in between twin rivers, [10] the Tigris and the Euphrates; it is well known to all nations, and still bears the name Mesopotamia in Greek, keeping from its situation the significance of the cause for that name. It seems that it measures from river to river as far as a man may walk in seven days. [15] Among the many cities which this land cherishes in its bosom is an ancient and powerful city, beautiful and famous for its gold deposits, and coeval with ancient Babylon: for at the same time that quivered Semiramis built the Chaldean citadel,[4] *this city was founded and shone forth, [20] the city now called Rohas, its name corrupted, but which in ancient times bore the name Edessa.*[5] *It lies roughly six miles from Assyrian Carrhae, odious to Roman generals for the death of the Crassi,*[6] *where in ancient times the patriarch Abram lived,*

Tell Bashīr rather than at Antioch, as the Charleville Poet implies, that he received the embassy from Thoros, the Armenian ruler of Edessa. See below, vi. 50 and n.

[3] For other accounts of the embassy from Edessa, see Fulcher of Chartres, pp. 209–10; Guibert of Nogent, p. 165; Albert of Aachen, p. 352. As his chaplain, Fulcher accompanied Baldwin to Edessa and is therefore an eyewitness of events there. The reliability of Albert of Aachen as a source for this aspect of the First Crusade is discussed by A. A. Beaumont, 'Albert of Aachen and the county of Edessa', in *The Crusades and Other Essays: Presented to D. C. Munro by his Students*, ed. L. J. Paetow (New York, 1928), pp. 101–23.

[4] Juvenal, *Sat.* ii. 108. The Charleville Poet makes use of a number of Juvenalian quotations elsewhere: cf. above, iii. 380.

[5] According to Pliny, *Hist. Nat.* v. 105, Rhoas was the ancient name of Latakia, not Edessa. In this period, however, Roais (or Rohais) was commonly used for Edessa; both spellings are forms of the Arabic *al-Ruhāʾ*. See C. Cahen, *La Syrie du Nord à l'époque des Croisades* (Paris, 1940), p. iii.

[6] The Roman general Crassus was defeated and killed by a force of Parthians at Carrhae (modern Harran), a city some 25 miles SW of Edessa, in 53 BC. See Lucan, *Bellum ciuile*, i. 105–6. The reference to *Crassi*, i.e. 'Crassus and his son' derives from Orosius, *Historia aduersum paganos*, vi. 13. 3–4; cf. also Ovid, *Fasti* v. 583.

fo. 94^r

Cum de Chaldaica diuino numine flamma   25
Erutus euasit, fuerit qua frater adustus,
Vnde et uoce Dei mox est excedere iussus.[1]
Sed iam premisse textus repetatur Edysse,[2]
In qua regna tenens fuit Abgaerus ille beatus
Ex Domini Christi rescripto magnificatus   30
Ac morbi ueteris cruciatibus exoneratus.
Haec ibi temporibus permansit epistola multis
Atque ea ab aduersis tutauit menia cunctis,[3]
Nam si barbaricus furor illuc adueniebat,[a]
Babtisatus eam puer alta in arce legebat,   35
Moxque uel in pacem gens ex feritate redibat
Aut terrore fugam diuino tacta[b] *petebat.*
Hic quoque Thaddeus in septuaginta probatus
Et fidei normam contradidit et requieuit,[4]
Hic etiam Thome, qui Christi uulnera sensit   40
Et dubitans nobis dubitandi[c] *crimen ademit,*
Corpus ab Indorum regionibus esse relatum
Creditur et magnis hic honoribus accumulatum.[5]
Haec semel in Christi postquam direxit amorem,
Numquam sustinuit frigescere religionem   45
Sed neque scismaticis patiens concedere ad horam
Catholici tenuit moderaminis integritatem,[6]
Vnde et gentilis mala plurima conditionis
Et tulit heretice feritates impietatis.[7]
Maxima sed fuit hec odiorum primaque causa   50
Que super hanc grauius commouit finitima arma,
Quod Syrie ueniens Christi chorus in[d] *regionem*
Antiochi quateret uariis conflictibus urbem,
Et nec eos magno ualuissent uincere bello

---

[a] *perueniebat Sirmond, Riant*   [b] tacta *Sirmond;* tactu *cod.*   [c] dubitandi
Sirmond; dubitande *cod.*   [d] ad *Sirmond, Riant*

[1] Gen. 11: 27–8, Acts 7: 2–4. Abraham journeyed from Ur of the Chaldees to Harran and finally Canaan. The reference here must be to Abraham's brother Haran, whose death is mentioned in Gen. 11: 28.

[2] This and vi. 15 are the only leonine verses in all the complete books by the Charleville Poet.

[3] For the story of King Abgar V, who ruled Edessa 4 BC–AD 7, 13–50, see L. J. Tixeront, *Les Origines de l'église d'Édesse et la légende d'Abgar* (Paris, 1888), pp. 82–91. The miraculous properties of the letter from Christ were noted by Etheria, a Spanish abbess or nun, who made a pilgrimage to the Holy Land, Edessa, and Constantinople, probably at the end of the fourth century. See her *Peregrinatio*, ed. H. Petrie (Sources chrétiennes, xxi; Paris, 1948), pp. 158, 166–8.

[25] *when by the divine spirit he escaped, plucked from the Chaldean flames,*
in which his brother was burned, and whence he was ordered to depart in
haste by the voice of God.[1] *But let our story return to Edessa, mentioned*
above,[2] *in which that blessed Abgarus held sway* [30] *who was glorified by a*
letter from our Lord Christ, and was healed from the agonies of a disease
which had long afflicted him. This letter remained there for many years, and
it preserved the city from all its enemies.[3] *For if the crazed barbarians came to*
it, [35] *a baptized boy would read it out loud high on the citadel, and that*
race would either recover from its raging and be at peace, or would be smitten
with divine fear and run away. Here too Thaddeus, tested as one of the
seventy, handed over the rule of faith and rested,[4] [40] *and here too the*
body of Thomas, who felt the wounds of Christ and by his doubting removed
the charge of doubting from us, is thought to have been brought from the
lands of the Indians and here had great honours heaped upon it.[5] *After this*
city had once given itself over to the love of Christ, [45] *it never allowed its*
religious fervour to grow cold, neither did it allow itself to give way to
heretics for an instant, but held fast to the wholeness of Catholic governance.[6]
For this reason it suffered many evils from the heathen regime and the wild
attacks of ungodly heretics.[7] [50] *But the foremost, indeed the principal*
reason for their hatred, which brought down on it with greater danger the
arms of its neighbours, was that the company of Christ, advancing into the
region of Syria, was shaking the city of Antioch with attacks of varying
kinds, and they were not strong enough either to defeat them in war,

[4] Thaddeus is traditionally identified as Jude, brother of James and one of Christ's
twelve apostles: see Matt. 10: 3, Mark 3: 18; cf. J. A. LeFrançois, art. 'Jude Thaddeus, St',
in the *New Catholic Encyclopaedia*, (Washington, DC, 1967), viii. 16–17. J. Stevenson, *A
New Eusebius* (London, 1957), pp. 152–3, identifies him with Addai the Apostle, one of
the seventy (so Eusebius, *HE* i. 13. 10; the story as the Charleville Poet tells it here is
taken from this chapter).

[5] See John 20: 24–9. Thomas is reputed to have died whilst conducting a mission at
Mylapore, near Madras. See L. W. Brown, *The Indian Christians of St Thomas* (Cam-
bridge, 1956), pp. 43, 54–5. His remains, however, were subsequently taken to Edessa,
where they were being venerated at the end of the 4th c. See Etheria, *Peregrinatio*, ed.
Petrie, pp. 158, 162; Gregory of Tours, *In Gloriam Martyrum*, cc. 31–2 (*MGH, Rer. Merov.*
i. 307–8).

[6] In his crusading bull *Quantum praedecessores* dated Mar. 1146, Pope Eugenius III
described Edessa in similar terms: 'It is said that [Edessa] alone under Christian rule
had respect for the power of God at that time when all the land in the East was held by
the pagans.' See P. Rassow, 'Der Text des Kreuzzugsbulle Eugens III.', *Neues Archiv*,
xlv (1924), 302–5.

[7] The ruler of Edessa was Thoros (T'oros), who had started his career as an imperial
official. He subsequently became one of the chief lieutenants of the Armenian Philare-
tus, who ruled the territory from Cilicia to Edessa between 1078 and 1085. In that year
Edessa was taken by the Seljuk Turks and, although Thoros became governor in 1094,
he had to accept the presence of a Turkish garrison. See J. Laurent, 'Des grecs aux
croisés: Étude sur l'histoire d'Édesse entre 1097 et 1098', *Byzantion*, i (1924), 367–449.

Sed nec ab obsesso saltem depellere muro;   55
Inde graues irae contra genus omne piorum
Et desiderium delendi nomen eorum.¹
Propterea celsam circa concursus Edyssam
Vastabat totam regionis fertilitatem.
Illuc uicini cuncta de parte gregati,   60
Illuc longinqui fama stimulante uocati
Oppida, rura, casas, castellaque concutiebant.
Matres, prata, uiros, animalia diripiebant.
Nonnumquam portis quoque pugnabatur in ipsis.ᵃ
Mutua coniectis feruebant uulnera telis,   65
Ciuibus [obsidio]ᵇ fessis non futile uisum
Auxilium contra perquirere Christicolarum.²
Hac igitur causa legatio iam memorata
Missa superueniens penetrauit Gallica castra.³
Monstrant et socios in Christi relligione,   70
Et conseruata semper fidei integritate,
Et, quia [propter eos]ᶜ grauia hec sibi proueniebant,
Auxilium per eos sibi dandum iure ferebant,
Precipueque ducis personam sollicitabant,
Namque [illo nihilum]ᵈ plus formidabile norant.   75

Talia mouerunt procerum miserantia corda,
Quid sit opus facto tractant indagine multa.
Credunt proficuum sibi deinceps esse futurum
Si per se columen prestatur rebus eorum;
Hinc sibi iuncturos socialia foedera multos   80
Quos fors †ab hilaratis† non paterentur inultos.ᵉ
Magnam uero sibi super hoc accrescere laudem
Spargendumque suum longe lateque timorem
Si, cum presentem retinerent obsidionem,
Largirentur opem longinquis auxiliarem.   85

His aliisque modis dicta ratione probata,
Ardor inest cunctis citius gnauare precata.
Sed quia presentis domitandi fulmina gentis
Maior cura ducem socialibus abstrahit armis,
Quod pignus pro se dare carius esse probauit,   90

ᵃ ipsis *Grocock;* istis *cod.*   ᵇ obsidio *sugg. Hall in the lacuna*   ᶜ propter eos
Grocock in the lacuna   ᵈ illo nihilum *sugg. Hall in the lacuna*   ᵉ *Both Sirmond*
and Riant omit this verse

[55] *or at least to drive them from the besieged wall; from this came their deep-seated anger against all races of godly men, and their desire to destroy their name.*[1] *For that reason a marauding band was laying waste all the rich crops of the region around lofty Edessa.* [60] *Neighbouring peoples assembled there from every nearby part, and men who lived far off were summoned there by rousing reports. They were striking at their towns, their lands and farms and fortresses, making off with their women, their crops, their men, and their beasts, and occasionally there was even fighting right at the city gates.* [65] *They were afflicted on both sides with burning wounds from the weapons they threw, and it did not seem useless to the citizens exhausted by the siege to summon the help of the Christians as a counterweight.*[2] *For this reason, therefore, the embassy already mentioned was sent, and on its arrival entered the Gallic camp.*[3] [70] *They showed that they were their allies in the religion of Christ, that they had always held firmly to the soundness of the faith, and, because these hardships were overtaking them because of the Crusaders, they asserted that by right help should be given them by the Franks. Above all they attempted to convince the duke,* [75] *for they knew nothing more formidable than him.*

All this moved the hearts of the nobles to pity, and with much questioning they discussed what needed to be done. They believed that it would be advantageous to the Franks thereafter if through this action they were to prove a bulwark in their situation; [80] *then, many would join forces with them in sworn allegiances whom they perchance would not allow to go unavenged . . . and moreover they would gain great glory for themselves on this account and would spread fear of themselves far and wide if, while they continued their current siege,* [85] *they were to bestow help and assistance on men far away. When the said case had been demonstrated in this and other ways, they were all straight away set ablaze to fulfil what had been asked of them. But, because quelling the thunderbolts of the present race was a greater concern which kept the duke from joining arms with his allies, he gave to those who asked of him a surety* [90] *which he judged to be the dearest thing he could give on his own behalf,*

[1] This is a reference to Kerbogha, who paused on his way to relieve Antioch at Edessa and besieged the city unsuccessfully for three weeks in May 1098. See Albert of Aachen, pp. 356–7; Fulcher of Chartres, pp. 242–3.

[2] News of Kerbogha's plans to relieve Antioch and fears that he might attack Edessa *en route* prompted the Armenians to appeal to Baldwin for assistance in Feb. 1098. See above, vi. 5 and n.

[3] This embassy offered Baldwin not only the government of Edessa, but also the succession-rights to it. An earlier appeal from Thoros for aid, which Baldwin had rejected, had merely asked him to serve as a mercenary. See Laurent, 'Des grecs aux croisés', at pp. 420, 422.

Fratrem quippe suum,[1] poscentibus associauit,
Cum quo militie partem quam mittere dignum
Credidit, emisit populatis suppetiatum.[2]
Iste minor natu fuit eius denique frater,
Qui post se rexit Solimorum sceptra decenter.[3]   95
Tunc proficiscentes longarum strata uiarum,
Nempe decem spatiis interdiuisa dierum,
Tandem perueniunt memoratam sepius urbem.[4]
Conficiunt stragem de uastatoribus acrem.
Arsacide[5] uicti neque comminus arma ferentes   100
Diffugiunt, arcus ut inutile reicientes,
Dum non expertam nequeunt [con]tendere[a] [gen]tem,[b]
In pedibusque citis totam posuere salutem.[6]
Nec nisi qui latuit Francorum uulnera fugit,
Nec qui desiluit sella post hanc repetiuit,[7]   105
Nec ueniens uulnus cutis exteriora peregit[c]
Sed cesim punctimque anime uitalia[d] adegit.
Non fuit his mirum Gallorum tela pauere,
Et collisa nimis post pectora terga fouere,
Dum, quorum fuerant uirtutibus omnia prona   110
Solaque habebatur gentilis gloria pugna,
Cum Gallis sueti pro sola bella salute
Ducere, sepe fugam sibi pro uictoria habere;[8]
Quos a se Crassi[9] meminissent funere uictos
Sublatisque etiam signis sua sub iuga missos   115
Cum Romanorum per plurima nomina gentis
Obruit Eufrates et multa cadauera Tygris
Detulit in terras ac reddidit. Ergo repulsis
Hostibus et cecis condentibus ora cauernis,
Omni pacata regione et constabilita,   120
Nulla se letis specie miscente maligna,[10]

fo. 95[v]

---

[a] contendere *Grocock;* protendere *Sirmond, Riant*   [b] gentem *Grocock;* [.....]tem *cod.*   [c] peregit *Grocock;* pepegit *cod.; Sirmond and Riant print a lacuna*   [d] uit-alia *Grocock;* penetralia *sugg. Hall;* ?uenalia *cod.; Sirmond and Riant print a lacuna*

---

[1] Fulcher of Chartres, p. 210, and Albert of Aachen, p. 352, state that the people of Edessa asked specifically for Baldwin, rather than Godfrey, but again this emphasis is consistent with the Charleville Poet's theme. Baldwin had previously acted as a hostage at the Hungarian court for the good behaviour of Godfrey's army. See above, iii. 136 and n.

[2] In fact Baldwin was accompanied by only a small number of knights when he departed from Edessa. Matthew of Edessa (p. 219) says there were 60, Albert of Aachen (p. 352) 200.

namely his own brother,[1] *and sent with him a section of his forces he judged proper to bring help to those who had been devastated.*[2] *This was his younger brother,* [95] *and he ruled Jerusalem worthily after him.*[3] *Then they set out over the long roads for the space of a full ten days, and at last they came to the oft-mentioned city.*[4] *They brought about a bitter slaughter of its assailants.* [100] *The sons of Arsaces,*[5] *unable to withstand the close combat, were defeated and fled, throwing aside their bows as useless; since they could not fight off a race they had not encountered before, they put all their hope of safety in a rapid escape.*[6] *Only those who hid escaped the Frankish wounds,* [105] *and the man who leapt from his saddle did not return to it afterwards.*[7] *The wound as it came did not graze the surface of their skin, but cut and pierced right to their vital organs. It was not surprising for them to quake at the weapons of the Gauls, or to look after their backs when their fronts had been so battered,* [110] *since everything had bowed before Gaul's courageous exploits, and their only glory was reckoned in fighting the heathen; they were accustomed to wage war with the Gauls only for their survival, and often to consider running away as good as victory;*[8] *they remembered that Franks were defeated by Arabs at the death of Crassus,*[9] [115] *and they also placed them under their yoke when they lost their standards; then the Euphrates overwhelmed the races of Romans under many names, and the Tigris carried many corpses downstream and cast them up on shore. And so the Franks drove off the enemy and stopped up the mouths of the pitch-dark caves,* [120] *and brought peace and stability to the whole region. No setback was seen amidst these successes.*[10]

[3] Baldwin was crowned ruler of the Latin kingdom of Jerusalem on Christmas Day, 1100, having taken the title on Martinmas, and died on 2 Apr. 1118. The use of the past tense, *rexit*, implies that this part of the poem was written after his death. See Introd., Sect. III.

[4] Baldwin arrived at Edessa on 6 Feb., having set out from Tell Bashīr a few days earlier.

[5] i.e. the Parthians. The epithet *Arsacidae* is found mainly in Lucan: see, for example, *Bellum ciuile*, viii. 217–18.

[6] Baldwin did not engage Kerbogha's army, but on his journey to Edessa he escaped an ambush by a local Turkish force.

[7] Cf. Charleville Poet, iv. 139.

[8] For an earlier reference to Frankish bravery by the Charleville Poet, see i. 11.

[9] See above, vi. 24 and n. The text at this point is very confusing; the lines from vi. 110 are dependent on *non fuit his mirum* in 108; at vi. 118, the subject changes without warning to the Franks.

[10] Shortly after his arrival in Edessa, Baldwin led a small force against the Turkish Emir of Samosata, whose troops were continually raiding the outskirts of Edessa. The Christian army was defeated and forced to withdraw, but Baldwin subsequently captured a small village near the emir's capital and installed a small garrison there, which controlled some Turkish movements and thereby reduced the number of raids on Edessa. See Matthew of Edessa, pp. 218–21; Albert of Aachen, pp. 353–4; Fulcher of Chartres, p. 211.

Vrbis regnator fratrem ductoris adoptat,
Vtque pater natum penitus sibi nectere certat.[1]
Delegat terram, regionem subiugat omnem,
In sua pacta manus facit ipsam iungere plebem.   125
Leta coronatur facies et concinit urbis.
Diuersis modulis iubilatio consonat astris.[2]
Cotidie celsam feruet concursus ad aulam,
Vnanimes nostram certant addiscere legem.
Funditur in cunctos pax et concordia ciues.   130
Iura docent nostri, componunt undique lites.
Militiam exercet sub certo iudice tyro.
Hinc eques hincque pedes recto mouet agmina gyro.
Pellitur atra fames, opulentia regnat in omnes,
Non aliquos patitur bonitas communis egentes.   135
Ductoris nostri nimio plebs ardet amore,
Nec satis expleri uisu ualet alloquioque,
Felices sese reputant fore iudice tali,
In quo non nisi pax poterat bonitasque uideri,
In quo militie decor et uirtutis honeste   140
Omnibus [exemplo poterat][a] communiter esse.
Nam ueluti Paulus sic omnibus omnia factus,[3]
Sic erat in cunctos moderanter morigeratus,
Fortibus ut fortis, infirmis poene sodalis,
Gauderet letis et compateretur amaris,   145
Largus erat largis, quasi parcus denique parcis,
Mitibus et mitis, feritate tumentibus aspis,[b]
Sic se conformans cunctis moderamine uiro
Vt uelut in speculo se quisque uideret in illo.

Hoc inspectanti diuini plasmatis hosti,   150
Inuidie patri, non esse ualebat amori,[4]
Vnde sibi ingeniti liuoris[5] fomite moto
Collectoque sue impietatis in arma ueneno,
Regnatorem urbis, prius hoc se letificantem,
Mouit in inuidiam mentis nimiumque dolorem.[6]   155
Crescere quicquid huic cernit de plebis amore
Diminui sibimet sperat, dictante timore,
Vnde in dogma cadens peruersum Herodis[c] iniqui[7]

fo. 96[r]

---

[a] exemplo poterat sugg. Sirmond   [b] asper Sirmond, Riant   [c] haeredis Sirmond, Riant

Then the ruler of the city adopted the duke's brother, and strove to draw him close to himself as a father his son.[1] *He delegated the land to him and placed the whole region in his charge,* [125] *and made even the common folk join hands in allegiance with him. The city's appearance was joyful, and there was singing as their rejoicing reached to the stars in its many-sounding strains.*[2] *Every day people thronged to the lofty palace, and with one heart they strove to learn our laws.* [130] *Peace and harmony were bestowed richly on all the citizens. Our men taught them our laws, and resolved all their disputes. The novice soldier practised under a sure judge; on this side knights, on that infantry performed their manœuvres in precise movements. Black hunger was driven away and plenty ruled over all,* [135] *and mutual goodwill did not allow any to go without. The common folk burned with great affection for our leader, and they could not see or hear enough of him. They reckoned that they would be happy with such a man to judge them, in whom only peace and goodness could be seen,* [140] *in whom the grace of military courage and upright character could serve as an example to all. For just as Paul was made all things to all men,*[3] *so this man behaved with moderation towards all: brave towards the brave, almost a fellow-sufferer to the weak,* [145] *he rejoiced with the happy and had pity on the grieving; he was generous to the generous, and gave short shrift to the mean, was gentle to the gentle, a viper to those swollen with fierce anger, and he thus adapted himself to all, conducting himself in such a way that everyone saw himself reflected in him as though in a mirror.*

[150] *As the enemy of the divine creation, the father of jealousy, looked on this,*[4] *he had not the strength to love what he saw, but it lit the kindling of his natural malice*[5] *and roused the poison of his ungodliness to arms:* [155] *he moved the ruler of the city, hitherto happy at the situation, to be jealous and very sad at heart.*[6] *Whatever increase he saw in the love of the common folk for our leader, he believed it meant a lessening of love for himself, as fear ruled his thoughts, so that he fell into the foul ways of wicked Herod,*[7]

---

[1] This adoption ceremony is described vividly by Albert of Aachen, p. 353. See also Beaumont, 'Albert of Aachen', p. 108.

[2] See Albert of Aachen, pp. 352–3.

[3] Cf. 1 Cor. 9: 22.

[4] Once again the Latin is very convoluted. vi. 150–3 make up an extremely obscure ablative absolute. vi. 151 recalls John 8: 44.

[5] Cf. Gen. 37: 8.

[6] Albert of Aachen, p. 353, claims that Thoros was jealous of Baldwin from the very beginning.

[7] Cf. Matt. 2: 3.

Et metuens ab eo de regni culmine pelli,
Hunc quem summissis precibus sibi muneribusque   160
Ad succurrendum rogitauerat ante uenire,
Cuique sibi patriam penitus tutore carentem
Poene et ab hoste malo ferro flammaque ruentem,
Cedibus et predis omni de parte gementem,
Reddiderat summo conamine, nil metuentem,   165
Querit quo genere specieque modoque uel arte
Possit ad interitus casum foueamque rotare.
Si faciat, sceptri fructum putat esse retenti,
Si non, desperat uite momenta lucrari,
Et tam peruerse mentis fuit inuidiaeque   170
Vt, cum Christicolam se dici uellet et esse,
Duxerit indignum se Christicolas adiisse,
Et tristaretur per eos sua tuta fuisse,
Optans idolatris potius sine honore subesse
Quam Christi famulis foedus sociale dedisse.   175

fo. 96ᵛ

Sed quia plebis amor nimio feruore fauebat,
Illi cui malus hic placitum loetale parabat
Demonstrare palam timuit quod mente gerebat.
Ergo legatos similes sibi nactus iniquos,
Hostes uicinos, a Christi milite pulsos,   180
Inuitat proprios ueniant ut rursus in agros:
Poeniteat quod se socios cepisseᵃ alienos,
Hos se missurum bellandi nomine ad illos
Iussurumque suis ut primo limine belli
Destituant illos fugiendo in terga regressi;   185
Hos permansuros fugiendi obstante pudore;
Sic omnes posse simul una morte perire.¹
Exultant Parthi capientes quod cupiebant,
Et celeres assunt, ut uota maligna capescant.
Ille acuit nostros penitus nil tale cauentes,   190
Donat eis comites sibi proditione sodales.²
Non tamen associat saltem de ciuibus unum
Ne pateat coeptum pacto quocumque nefandum.
Extra quesiti subeunt ea castra manipli
Indigenis ducibus concedere ad omnia iussi.   195
Procedunt alacres consueta ad ludicra nostri,
Occurrunt contra structis legionibus illi.
Primo congressu penetrant media agmina Galli,

and fearing that he would be driven from his high place as king [160] *by the very man he had earlier asked again and again with humble prayers and gifts to come to his aid, to whom he had handed over his fatherland, utterly lacking in leadership as it was, and on the point of collapse because of the wicked enemy's attacks with fire and sword, lamenting its depredations and slaughter on every side,* [165] *fearing nothing at the height of the fighting. He wondered by what sort of means or kind of plot he could bring about his downfall and destruction. If he were successful his reward, he thought, would be the retention of the crown; if not, he despaired of enjoying another moment of life,* [170] *and he was in such a wickedly jealous frame of mind that although he wished to say he was a Christian and to be one, he considered it unworthy of himself to have gone to the Christians, and was saddened that his realms had been made safe by them, choosing rather to be under the sway of idolators without honour* [175] *than to have entered into an alliance with the servants of Christ. But because the love of the people burned very strongly in support of him for whom this criminal was preparing his deadly plan, he was afraid of disclosing openly what he had in mind. Therefore he found some envoys who were wicked like himself,* [180] *and invited the neighbouring foe who had been driven off by the soldiers of Christ to enter his own lands once again; he said that he was sorry he had taken on foreign allies; he would be sending these allies against them under the pretext of waging war, and would order his own men to turn around at the edge of the fighting,* [185] *run away and leave them; the Franks would remain, shame preventing them from running away; thus they could all meet their end at the same time in one bloodbath.*[1] *The Parthians were overjoyed as they received what they desired, and swiftly presented themselves to fulfil his evil prayers.* [190] *The king spurred on our men, who had absolutely no fear of anything like this, and he gave them his comrades in treachery to be their companions.*[2] *He did not however join even one of the citizens with them, lest his unspeakable enterprise should somehow be revealed. The troops sought from outside approached the camp,* [195] *and were ordered to comply with the native leaders in everything. Our men sallied forth swiftly to their usual sport, and the Parthians ran forward against them in close formations. At the first clash the Gauls pierced the middle of their line,*

---

[a] cepisse *Grocock;* coepisse *cod.*

---

[1] This deceit recalls the betrayal of Uriah by King David. See 2 Kgs. (2 Sam.) 11: 15. There is no other evidence that Thoros sought Turkish aid against Baldwin.

[2] Some years previously, Thoros had sought help from the Turk Alpyaruk and then, once the immediate danger had passed, had him murdered.

Cedunt, prosternunt, uia fit calcaribus et ui,
Sed postquam infestis terebrarunt obuia telis   200
Inque eadem uersis referuntur prelia frenis, [1]
Ecce uident socios manifesta proditione
Diffugere et retro dare nemine terga fugante.
Tunc intellecta per signa patentia fraude,
Mutua adhortati in manibusque animas posuere: 205
Amplexi clypeos stringunt animosius enses,
Dant ualidos ictus in comminus atque secentes. [a]
Norunt in manibus uitam consistere et armis,
In pedibus uero stipendia mortis inermis.
Malunt nobiliter pugnando occumbere plagis   210
Quam paganorum trucibus dare colla cathenis.
Non parcunt dextris, non parcunt denique telis:
Nullus hic est iaculis leuibus locus atque sagittis.
Aspiciunt Parthi circum iaculando uagantes
Pro tutela anime nostros rem rite gerentes.   215
Perpendunt quod erat, quia laus sibi nulla canatur
Si morientibus his ipsi quoque commoriantur.
Vincere quod nequeunt, dimittunt[b] aufugientes,
Dimittuntque uiros dampnata luce feroces.
Desperata salus sic est pugnando redacta[c]   220
At[d] spes nequitiae in nihilum stercusque reducta. [2]

Egregius ductor[3] fortes affatur amicos
De fouea mortis propria uirtute reuersos:[e]
Non bene barbaricis umquam permixta cateruis
Agmina que fidei sint enutrita tropheis;   225
Esse sibi tutum comitatum linquere gentis
Que specie blanda propinet pocula mortis.
Monstrari tamen hec collectis foedera turmis
Vt nosci ualeant, [f] placeant si talia cunctis.
Cum dicto factum celeratur, contio tota   230
Cogitur, et fit eis mox hec querimonia nota;
Ob que sint missi se compleuisse perorant:
Tempus adesse sibi ut castra Antiochena reuisant;

[a] secentes *Grocock;* sedentes *cod.*   [b] dimitturt *cod.*   [c] reducta *Sirmond,*
Riant   [d] at *Grocock;* et *or perhaps* est *sugg. Hall;* ut *cod.*   [e] remersos *cod.;* reu-
ersos *Sirmond*   [f] ualeant *Grocock;* ualeat *cod., Sirmond, Riant*

[1] The poet, if he is not following an eye-witness account of the battle, shows a vivid

cutting and slaying, and making a path with the strength of their spurs, [200] but after they had drilled through the opposition with their fierce weapons and wheeled round to head back to the same affray,[1] *look! they saw their allies running away in open treason, turning their backs with no one pursuing them. Then through obvious signs they understood the deceit, [205] urged one another on, and put their lives in their hands; they gripped their shields and drew their swords more boldly, dealing mighty blows at those close by and to their rear. They knew that they held their lives in their own armed hands, and the only reward for running away would be a coward's death. [210] They preferred to die from wounds fighting nobly, instead of bending their necks to the savage chains of the pagans. They gave no respite to their right hands, nor yet to their lances: there was no room here for lightweight javelins and arrows. The Parthians chasing round throwing their missiles saw our men [215] conducting the fight with fitting courage for their own lives' sake. They considered the situation, reflecting that no praise would be sung for them if they too died with these who were dying. With no chance of victory, they turned from the fleeing men of Edessa, and also from the men who fought so fiercely on that accursed day. [220] Thus their unhoped-for escape was wrought by fighting, but the hope of evil was brought to nothing, reckoned as dung.*[2]

The outstanding leader[3] *addressed his brave friends, returned from the pit of death through their own courage. He said that warriors nourished by the victories of faith had never mingled successfully with barbarian troops, [226] and that the safe course was now for them to part company with a people that, while appearing kindly disposed, handed them the cup of death. These plans should, however, be set before the assembled troops, so that it might be known whether they found common acceptance. [230] As soon said as done, the whole force was assembled together, and they quickly made this complaint known to the assembly, stating clearly that they had carried out the task for which they had been summoned, and that the time had come for them to return to their camp at Antioch.*

sense of the realities of military tactics. As was often the case, the Frankish cavalry smashed right through the enemy lines, but on turning to regroup could see the Armenians on the far side of the Turks retreating from the field.

[2] The imagery recalls Phil. 3: 7.

[3] Baldwin of Boulogne. In the following passage, the Charleville Poet adapts the events of Feb./Mar. 1098 so as to absolve Baldwin from any guilt for the deposition and subsequent murder of Thoros. He is portrayed as befits the brother of the poet's hero, Godfrey of Bouillon. Fulcher of Chartres, who was an eyewitness, makes only a brief reference to these events. Matthew of Edessa's account is, not surprisingly, biased against Baldwin, who is quite clearly accused of treachery. See Beaumont, 'Albert of Aachen', p. 103.

Post hac auxilia si poscant, nec mereantur,
Hoc sibi pro meritis fieri non diffiteantur: 235
Propter opem, nece tractata, se poene perisse.
His quod adhuc uiuant se nullam gratiam habere:
Per Christum et dextras restare superstite uita.
Ergo recedere se melioraque querere pacta.

His dictis onerant que deportanda fuerunt,   240
Queque graui bello per se sua facta fuerunt.
Dispositi in turmas dant agmina bellica retro
Et male mercato celerant abscedere regno.
Protinus in tota fit lamentatio plebe
Vtpote que fuerat non huius conscia culpe.   245
Se miseros clamant, inopes, rationis egenos
Et uice crudeli sine defensore relictos.
Postquam dicta satis que dici digna fuerunt,
Que dolor atque timor comites dicenda dederunt,
Protinus in belli rationem questio transit,   250
Que sibi causa fuge feruens querimonia poscit;
Ac primo tacitis gladium mortemque minantur
Ni responsa sibi ueracia mox referantur.
Nemo sponte luit peccata aliena silenter:
Regem sic fieri*a* memorant iussisse potenter.   255
Tunc quecunque mali istius*b* commenta fuerunt
Et qua de causa concorditer edocuerunt.
Nec mora, fit celsam populi concursus ad aulam
Et cum rege agitant rationem iudicialem.
Non bene purganti facinus*c* crimenque retectum   260
Mox est purpurea caput a ceruice resectum. [1]
Tunc oratores mox ad tentoria mittunt,
Vt sibi consultum redeant lacrimando reposcunt.
Quamuis inuitus, ductor multa prece uictus
Consilii causa est ad menia celsa reductus,   265
Vtque fuit primum portis murisque receptus,
Omnis eum propere circumstat turma senatus. [2]
Omnes se purgant de crimine proditionis,
Omnes deplorant mala praue suspicionis
Que sibi ductoris animum per cuncta benignum   270
Abstulerat, cum nil foret a se perpere gestum.
Omnes poscere se precibus lacrimisque profusis

fo. 97ᵛ

fo. 98ʳ

If those people were to ask for assistance again after that, they would not merit it, [235] *and they should admit that this refusal was just what they deserved. Their death had been planned, and because of their assistance they had almost met their end. It was no thanks to those people that they had survived thus far: they remained in the land of the living through Christ and their own right hands. Therefore they were withdrawing and looking for better alliances.*

[240] *With these words they loaded up what they had to take away, all that had been made their own in the grievous fighting. They drew up their warlike columns in squadrons, turning back, and made haste to leave the kingdom where they had done such bad business. Straight away a shout of grief rose up among all the common folk,* [245] *for they were utterly unaware of this guilty action. They wailed that they were helpless wretches lacking in sense, abandoned by a cruel turn of fate without a defender. When enough that deserved saying had been said, all that those companions, grief and fear, prompted them to say,* [250] *the subject of the war was immediately raised, and in a frenzied complaint they demanded what was the cause of their running away, and when they at first said nothing they threatened them with death by the sword if they did not quickly give them truthful replies. No man willingly atones for the sins of another in silence:* [255] *and thus they recalled that the king had ordered most strongly that this should be done. Then they amicably disclosed all the stratagems that wicked man had planned, and why. Without delay the people rushed to the lofty palace, and they proceeded to put the king on trial.* [260] *Since he did not properly clear himself of the crime which had been disclosed, they at once cut his head from his purple neck.*[1] *Then they quickly sent spokesmen to the tents, to ask them with tears to return to them and discuss the matter. Although he did not wish to, the general was overcome by their many prayers* [265] *and was brought back to the lofty city for discussions. As soon as he was received within the city's wall and gates, the whole council quickly thronged round him.*[2] *They all cleared themselves of the charge of treachery, and all deplored the evil of foul suspicion* [270] *which had estranged them from the general, ever-kind, since they had done nothing wicked; all with entreaties and profuse tears begged him not to let foul infamy*

---

[a] nostri *Sirmond, Riant*   [b] illius *Sirmond, Riant*   [c] fraudis *Sirmond, Riant*

---

[1] Albert of Aachen, pp. 354–5, maintains that Baldwin refused the Edessenes' request to kill Thoros and warned him of their evil intention. Whilst he was doing so, the people attacked the palace and Thoros was killed trying to escape. See also Fulcher of Chartres, pp. 213–14; Beaumont, 'Albert of Aachen', pp. 109–12.

[2] Baldwin was invited to assume the government of Edessa on 10 Mar. 1098.

Ne se dedecoret post hec infamia turpis,
Ne se destituat tutela sue pietatis,
Neu se mortiferis uelit obiectare periclis. 275
Eius primatum super omnia uelle et[a] *amare.*[1]
Non indignetur secum regnando manere.
Ille negat sese super illum prefore posse
Quo se contigerat urbem inuitante petisse.
Quod se purgarent satis illis gratiam[b] *habere;* 280
Illius porro consortia nolle tenere.
Illi continuo monstrant que gesta fuissent,
Que pro perfidie sibi crimine dona tulissent.
Ostendunt caput, hocque sui dant pignus amoris,
Quod fidei lesae tulerat uindicta fidelis. 285
Hinc uotis uota iungunt precibusque precata,
Vimque parant nisi flectatur sententia fixa.
Obstipuit ductor tanto se foedere queri
In dominum populi pro se hac feritate seueri.
Quid sit opus facto sociorum consulit agmen;[1] 290
Collaudant omnes oblatum scandere culmen.
Ingreditur celsam cunctis letantibus arcem.
Iuris iurandi capit undique conditionem.
In sua sic totam componit foedera gentem
Defensamque regit propriis uirtutibus urbem. 295

fo. 98ᵛ

His ita compositis et fama notificante
Nostros obsidio dum detinet urbis amoene,[2]
Altera ad heroas legatio[3] *de Babylonis*[4]
Arcibus aduenit, non expers proditionis.[5]
Hec autem Babylon, que nunc habitabilis extat, 300
Longe a Chaldaice Babylonis climate distat:

ᵃ uellet *Sirmond, Riant* ᵇ gratiam *Riant;* grani *or perhaps* gramen *cod.*

---

[1] Cf. vi. 77.

[2] On hearing of Baldwin's success, a number of knights abandoned the protracted siege of Antioch and travelled to Edessa. See Albert of Aachen, pp. 441–2. Amongst them was Drogo of Nesle, who had been a member of Emicho of Leiningen's ill-fated contingent, then joined Hugh of Vermandois, and finally transferred his allegiance to Baldwin. See Riley-Smith, 'The motives', p. 736.

[3] The first embassy was of course the one from Edessa. See above, vi. 5 and n. As is frequent in medieval literature, the author 'signposts' the outcome of this part of the story, making clear from the outset that this legation's evil nature stemmed from the evil character of the Egyptian ruler. See J. Crosland, *The Old French Epic* (Oxford, 1956), pp. 144–5, 277, for similar instances of stock traitors in vernacular epic.

bring subsequent dishonour on him, nor to let the safeguard of his goodness
abandon them, [275] *and not to wish to hurl them into mortal danger. They*
said that they desired and loved his primacy over all, and that he ought not to
refuse to remain with them as their ruler. He maintained that he could not
hold sway over a man by whose invitation he had come to the city. [280] *He*
was glad enough that they had cleared themselves, but he did not wish to carry
on in a partnership with that man any more. Straight away they showed him
what they had done, and what gift they had brought him to atone for the
charge of treachery: they held out the king's head, and handed it over as a
pledge of their love for him, [285] *a pledge which faithful vengeance of good*
faith betrayed had taken. They piled vow on vow and prayer on prayer, and
made ready for violent action if his obstinacy did not yield. The general was
staggered that a treaty with him was being sought on such haughty terms by a
people who had acted so savagely on his behalf against their own lord. [290]
He took counsel with the company of his own allies to see what should be
done;[1] *they all exhorted him to ascend to the exalted position offered him.*
Everyone rejoiced as he entered the lofty citadel. He accepted terms from all
parties, sworn on oath. Thus he established peace on his own terms with the
whole people, [295] *and ruled the city which with his natural virtues he had*
defended.

When news that this whole matter had been settled reached our men, while
the siege of the lovely city was still detaining them,[2] *a second embassy,*[3] *not*
lacking in treachery, came to the heroes from the mighty city of Babylon.[4,5]
[300] *This Babylon, which even today is inhabited, is a long way from the*
region of the Chaldaean Babylon: that one is reckoned to lie towards the

---

[4] All the crusading chroniclers refer to Cairo as Babylon. The Charleville Poet seizes
the opportunity to display his knowledge of geography and history.

[5] The Charleville Poet's account of the Egyptian embassy in Mar. 1098 and the
subsequent Frankish legation to Cairo is unique. Raymond of Aguilers, p. 58, and the
Gesta Francorum, p. 37, attest the presence of envoys from Egypt in the crusaders' camp,
as does a letter from Anselm of Ribemont to Manasseh, archbishop of Rheims. See *Die
Kreuzzugsbriefe*, p. 160. Robert of Rheims, pp. 791–2, records that the Egyptians offered
the crusaders a safe passage to the Holy Sepulchre if they went unarmed, and Albert of
Aachen, p. 380, refers to a letter which wished the crusaders success against their
common enemy, the Turks. The closest parallel to the Charleville Poet's account is,
however, William of Tyre, i. 267–8. The actual purpose of the Egyptian embassy is
unclear and still a matter of debate. It may have been to negotiate the partition of Syria
with the crusaders, a proposal which they rejected, or simply to use their presence as a
counterpoise to the ambitions of the Turks. See Hamilton A. R. Gibb, 'The Caliphate
and the Arab states', in Setton, *History of the Crusades*, i. 81–98, at p. 95; Runciman, 'The
First Crusade: Antioch to Ascalon', ibid. i. 308–42, at pp. 315–16.

Illa etenim uersus Aquilonem ducitur,[a] *ista*
Euronothum spectans tangit Memphytica regna.
Alluit Eufrates illam torrentibus undis,
Fertilis hanc Nilus nigris foecundat harenis.   305
Illam post Nemroth[1] *fundamina preiacientem*
Inque polos turrim sustollere percupientem
Struxit Semyramis,[2] *quadro latera equa tenentem,*
Perque latus quodque sex denaque milia habentem,
Milia circuitus sic sexagena ferentem   310
Atque quaterna simul tota ambitione replentem.
Vndique coctilibus[3] *forma hec circumdata muris*
Atque gyganteis pedibus fuit alta ducentis,
Et cum uicenis pariter spissata tricenis.
Preterea portis tantum stridebat aenis   315
In medio turrim gremio complexa superbam,[4]
Quam scriptura refert gentem struxisse proteruam
Cum post diluuium ueniens orientis ab axe
Repperit hunc campum medio telluris apertae,
Cuius planitie mox delectata capaci   320
Hanc statuit turrim facere usque ad culmina celi,
Cumque euasisset iam milia ad usque quaterna
Atque foret totidem spatiosius[b] *undique lata,*
Hanc ita stulticiam pietas diuina recidit:
Vniloquam linguam per multas extenuauit.   325
Sic intermissa est operum presumptio cassa,
Non intellecta alterutrum currente loquela.
Taliter exstructa uiguit per tempora multa
Regibus ac populis compluribus imperiosa,
Multa mala exercens, crudelia cuncta frequentans,   330
Reges excecans,[c5] *proceres populosque cathenans,*
Templa Dei uiolans, sacra uasa per idola foedans,
Ignibus atque feris sanctorum corpora dedens,
Donec sub Cyro Moedos Persasque regente
Summo regna Deo sibi plurima subiciente   335
Capta et destructa quod fecerat est quoque passa,
Predans predata, captiuans exiliata,[6]
Atque, prophetarum iuxta predicta sacrorum,[7]
Monstrorum facta est habitatio multimodorum.
At postquam Cyrus Scytico fuit ense necatus,   340

north, while this one is to the south-east and borders on the realms of
Memphis. The Euphrates enriches that one with its raging waters, [305] *the*
enriching Nile makes this one fruitful with its black sands. After Nimrod[1]
laid its foundations, and desired to raise up a tower to heaven, Semiramis[2]
completed its construction, with four sides of equal length, each side being six-
teen miles long; [310] *it was thus sixty-four miles round its entire circumfer-*
ence. On all sides the city thus shaped was set about with walls of burned
brick[3] *which were two hundred giants' feet high and likewise fifty feet thick.*
[315] *Its creaking gates, moreover, were made of nothing but bronze, and at*
the centre it embraced a proud tower,[4] *which the scripture says a reckless race*
of men built, when on their arrival from the east, after the flood, [320] *they*
came across this plain in the midst of a wide-open land, and delighted by its
spacious openness they at once decided to raise this tower right up to the vaults
of heaven, and when it had reached four thousand feet, and on all sides was as
wide again, nay wider, the goodness of God put an end to this folly in this
way: [325] *he ended the unity of speech, dividing it into many languages.*
And so their presumptuous labours were unfinished and in vain, for they did
not understand one another's language. Built in this way, the city flourished
for many years, dominant over many kings and peoples, [330] *executing*
many evil deeds, repeatedly indulging in all kinds of barbarity, blinding
kings,[5] *putting nobles and nations in chains, desecrating the temple of God,*
polluting the holy vessels with their idols, giving the bodies of godly men over
to the flames and to savage wild animals, until, when Cyrus was king over the
Medes and Persians, [335] *the supreme God subjected many kingdoms to*
him, and the city, captured and destroyed, suffered what it had itself inflicted,
the plunderer plundered, the captor himself now in exile,[6] *and, in accord with*
the words of the holy prophets,[7] *it became the dwelling-place of all kinds of*
hideous beasts. [340] *But after Cyrus was killed by the sword of the Scythians,*

    ª dueitur *cod.*   ᵇ spatiosius *Grocock;* spatiosus *cod.*   ᶜ execcans *cod.*

    [1] Cf. Gen. 10: 8–9; 1 Chr. 1: 10; Mic. 5: 6. For the foundation of Babylon (Cairo), see
Eusebius, *Onomastikon of Biblical Place-Names*, in Jerome's translation: *Babel... erat autem
ciuitas regni Nemroth, in qua eorum . . . linguae diuisae sunt*, ed. E. Klostermann (Leipzig,
1904, repr. Hildesheim, 1966), p. 41.
    [2] The legendary queen of Assyria, consort of Ninus and his successor.
    [3] This detail is probably derived from Ovid, *Met.* iv. 58. The detail on dimensions
seems to be a conflation of Orosius, *Historia aduersum paganos*, ii. 6. 8–9 and Pliny, *Hist.
Nat.* vi. 121.
    [4] The tower of Babel. Cf. Gen. 11: 1–9.
    [5] Cf. 4 Kgs. (2 Kgs.) 25: 7; Jer. 52: 19–27. The reference is to the blinding of Zedekiah
by the Assyrians.
    [6] Cf. 1 Esd. (Ezra) 6: 1–15.
    [7] Jeremiah must be intended; see Jer. 50: 13, 51: 37.

Filius ipsius Cambyses[1] patrem imitatus
Que nunc incolitur Babylonem condidit, atque
Iudeos Arabes sibi subdidit Ethyopasque.
Sic ex tunc et nunc Babylon Egyptia regnat
Et circum circa famulantia regna coartat.   345

Huius regnator nostris apud Antiochenam
Insignes misit legatos perfidus urbem.[2]
Horum primus erat qui tunc fuit alter ab illo,
Vir bonus et prudens, non ingenioque maligno.[3]
Nescius ergo doli neque conscius insidiarum   350
Simpliciter dixit sibi quod fuit imperitatum:
Regem namque suum nostrorum gesta legentem
Exposuit multam nostris mandare salutem;
Vrbem Hierusalem sibi nunc ditione subactam,
Huius causa istos tantum sumpsisse laborem.   355

fo. 99ᵛ   Velle aliquos sibi nostrorum properanter adesse
Visu, colloquio, uictu sibi participare:
Si sibi uel ratio uel honestas relligionis
Suadeat ut faueat sua conuersatio nostris,
Iam fieri posse ut gentilia monstra refutet,   360
Vt posito Christum diademate pronus adoret.
Tunc sibi Hierusalem fieri per cuncta patentem,
Tunc sacrum tumulum, cunctum quoque cedere honorem,
Tunc palmeta suis insontes suggerere hastas,[4]
Inque Dei laudes habiles concedere spicas.   365
Exultant nostri, nihil hic hostile cauentes,
Sed nomen Domini hinc celebrari suspicientes:
Ille etiam princeps aliorum mente benigna
Perstat,[a] et hortatur, spondens fore prospera cuncta:
Hos etenim incolumes deducere se fore certum,   370
Rursus honorifice reduces dare pectore fixum.
Ergo inter primos bellorum laude potentes
Interque eximios insignia clara ferentes
Ductores uocitant complures, digniter ornant,
Cunctis militie simul utilitatibus armant   375
Et cum legatis legatos pergere mandant,

[a] constat Sirmond, Riant

[1] This figure has been identified with several characters in the Bible: the king who

his own son Cambyses[1] followed his father's example and founded that Babylon which is now inhabited, bringing Jews, Arabs, and Ethiopians under his sway. Thus from that day to this, the Egyptian Babylon has reigned [345] *dominant over all the subject kingdoms round about.*

The treacherous ruler of this city sent distinguished envoys to our men at the city of Antioch.[2] In charge was he who was ranked second after the ruler, a good and wise man, not of wicked character.[3] [350] *Not knowing of his deceit, and unaware of a trap being set, he therefore spoke straightforwardly as he had been ordered; he explained that his king had read of the deeds of our men and sent hearty salutations to them, and that the city of Jerusalem, on whose account they had undertaken such great toil,* [355] *had at that time been put under his authority. He desired that some of our men should present themselves quickly before him, to see him and to share in talks and food with him; if the good sense and upright character of their religion persuaded him to favour our men in his way of life,* [360] *it might even be that he would turn away from the horrors of heathendom, lay aside his crown, and falling on his face worship Christ. Then Jerusalem would lie wide open for them, and the holy sepulchre too, and every honour would be given them;* [365] *then the palm-groves[4] would provide innocent spears for his men, yielding up nimble spear-points to the glory of God. Our men were overjoyed, fearing nothing dangerous in this, but rather suspecting from it that the name of the Lord would be worshipped; the leader of the other embassy also persisted in his well-meaning, and encouraged them, promising them that all would be well:* [370] *he would be sure to lead them there in safety, and in his heart he was certain that he would bring them back with honour. Therefore the leaders summoned several of the first rank, mighty men, praised for their fighting, who bore signs renowned among the famous, fitted them out worthily,* [375] *armed them with all the equipment necessary for soldiery, and instructed them to go as envoys with the envoys, asking them to speak and act as was*

will devastate Israel (Ezek. 38–9); Ahasuerus (1 Esd. (Ezra) 4: 6), and Nebuchadnezzar (Judith). Orosius (*Historia aduersum paganos*, ii. 8. 1–2) refers to Cambyses, son of Cyrus, but does not mention the founding of the new Babylon.

[2] The anonymous author of the *Historia belli sacri*, p. 181, states that the crusaders had already sent an embassy to Cairo from Nicaea, on the advice of the Byzantine emperor.

[3] The envoys were sent by Al-Afḍal, the vizier to the Fatimid caliph, al-Mustaʿlī.

[4] The palm branch, collected from the banks of the Jordan, was the sign of a completed pilgrimage to Jerusalem. See J. Sumption, *Pilgrimage: An Image of Medieval Religion* (London, 1975), pp. 173–4, and below, vi. 475.

Dicere uel facere que sint se digna perorant.[1]
Quid multis opus est? Sociali foedere iuncti
Nostri et non nostri subeunt naualia cuncti,
Perque maris magni diuortia plurima uecti   380
Tandem sunt propius Babylonica menia ducti.
Princeps officii quosdam premittere curat,
Atque suo regi que gesserat ordine narrat.
Ille dolos uersans preceptum tale remandat:
Ne lucente die Francos in menia ducat,   385
Neue situs urbis cernens manus extera noscat.
Sicque animos in se gens bellis aspera tollat.
Ille dolum metuens paret, sed pectore tristi,
Inducitque uiros in menia nocte silenti,
Nec malus hos princeps patiens assistere coram   390
Omnes in quandam deduci precipit aulam:
Illuc inclusos et nusquam progredientes
Tempore non modico tenuit, suspiria dantes.
Iussit habundantem tamen illis affore uictum,
Sic celare uolens infandi pectoris astum.   395
Tandem conductor, questu pulsatus ab illis
Et grauiter motus pro crimine suspicionis,
Regnatorem adiit, querit que causa sit ista
Quod se legatum Francorum accedere castra
Iusserit atque uiros illinc deducere claros,   400
Quos a conspectu proprio uelit esse remotos;
Siquid forte mali contrudere[a] cogitet illis,
Non se posse pati consortia proditionis,
Sed conaturum toto discrimine uite
Vt sua procedat penitus legatio rite;[2]   405
Aut det magnificos coram se stare quirites
Et patria dignos illis concedat honores,
Aut se de proprio donatos ac renitentes
Efficere ut repetant sociorum castra canentes.
Talia per socios illo monstrante potentes   410
Obstupuit rector, metuens offendere plures:
Imperat acciri personas, colloquioque
Participans illos (interprete sed mediante)
Querit de sociis qui sint, que nomina gestent,
Quidue potestatis propria in regione retentent.   415
Illi responsa digna et ueracia reddunt,

fitting for them.[1] *No need for many words. Joined by a treaty of alliance, all our men and those who were not ours came to the docks,* [380] *and borne over the mighty sea they tacked hither and thither until at last they were brought close to the city of Babylon. The leader of the delegation had some men sent on ahead, and related all that he had done to his king; he, plotting trickery, gave him back this instruction:* [385] *he was not to bring the Franks into the city in the daytime, lest the foreign band should see the city's location and become familiar with it, and should thus raise their spirits against him, for they were a hardy race at fighting. He obeyed, but feared some trickery, and with a heavy heart he led them into the city at dead of night,* [390] *and the evil ruler did not allow them to meet him in person, but gave orders that they should all be led off to a certain hall; he kept them shut in there, and did not let them come out for some considerable time, which made them sigh deeply. However he did order plenty of food to be brought to them,* [395] *wishing in this way to hide the unspeakable cunning of his heart. At last their guide, driven from them by their complaints and deeply moved by their suspicious accusations, went to the ruler and asked him for what reason he had ordered him to gain access to the Frankish camp as an envoy* [400] *and to bring those outstanding men from there, when now he wanted them kept out of his sight; if the king was planning to devise any evil against them, he could not endure being a party to the treachery, but would endeavour, even at risk to his own life,* [405] *to see that his embassy was properly and rightly fulfilled;*[2] *the king should either grant that those magnificent knights should stand in his presence, and bestow on them honours worthy of their country, or should enrich them splendidly with gifts of his own and see that they made their way back to their allies' camp with rejoicing.* [410] *As this man recounted such acts as were performed by the mighty allies, the ruler was dumbfounded, and was afraid of offending more of them; he ordered those persons to be summoned, and shared in discussion with them through the offices of an interpreter. He asked them which of the allies they were, what names they bore,* [415] *and what positions of power they held in their own lands. They gave him worthy and truthful replies,*

---

^a contradere *Sirmond, Riant*

---

[1] The members of the Frankish embassy are unnamed. They were laden with gifts and booty captured from the Turks. See above, v. 387.

[2] See above, vi. 370–1. The Egyptian envoy had sworn that the Franks would return safely and with honour. Such conflicts of loyalty are a common theme in contemporary vernacular poetry such as the *Chanson de Roland* or Marie de France's *lai* called 'Equitan'.

Et pauide menti crementa timoris inurunt.
Ille metum celans, uultu fictoque[a] renidens,
Et gestus habitusque uirum spectando pererrans
Suadet ut armati campis potiantur apertis,   420
Et sua demonstrent quid Gallia possit in armis.
Paretur; capiunt celeres insignia et acres
Scandentes in equos geminas statuere cohortes:
Aspectus galeis, loricis corpora tecti,
Ardentes clypeos et spicula lucida nacti,   425
Aspera corripiunt imitantem prelia martem,
Et uariis monstrant patriam discursibus artem.
Confligunt dociles relegi docilesque relinqui;[1]
Nunc procul absentes a se, nunc uero propinqui,
Et nunc terga fuge dantes, nunc uersa fugantes,   430
Impediunt cursus concursibus, orbibus orbes.
Nunc uelut infestis in mutua funera[b] telis
Itur, at in rerum sunt omnia tuta peritis.[c]
Spectant Nilicole, spectat rex ipse malignus,
Atque hebetantur eis gelida formidine sensus   435
Sollicitis, quia si gens talis Francigenarum
Hierusalem capta fines peruadat eorum,
Nil fore uirtuti quod eorum obsistere possit,
Cum uehemens bellum quasi quidam ludus eis sit.
Tunc sibi dissimilem[2] post se loca summa tenentem   440
Conuocat, et gestit facere ex ratione furentem;
Orat ut hos Francos, quos iussus duxerat ad se,
Quos perpendebat sensu sua cuncta notasse,
Ne reduces facti socios huc affore cunctos
Procurent, sibi clam procuret decapitandos.   445
Ille uelut gladii per pectus acumine fixus
Pessima mandantem tali mox uoce secutus:[3]
Quenam uesani compellat[d] causa furoris
Vt sanctum nomen populis per secula cunctis
Nomine sub pacis[e] legatos euocet ad se,   450
Quos mactare uelit sub operta proditione?

fo. 101[r]

---

[a] fictuque cod.   [b] uulnera Sirmond, Riant   [c] potitis Sirmond, Riant
[d] compellant cod.   [e] pacisu cod., first hand

---

[1] Cf. Valerius Flaccus, Argonautica, vi. 236–7: uaditque uirum ui, uadit equum, docilis relegi docilisque relinqui. The Charleville Poet repeats this verse almost verbatim, but his source is likely to have been indirect, probably a florilegium. For the use of such

and burned the seeds of fear into his timorous mind. He covered up his
fear, smiling with a false expression, and carefully observing the behaviour
and manners of the men, [420] *he exhorted them to arm themselves and*
make for the open plain, to show him what his Gauls were capable of in
warfare. Obeying him, they quickly took up their emblems, and eagerly
mounting their horses they set themselves up in twin columns, covering
their faces with helms and their bodies with armour; [425] *they grasped*
their burnished shields and their glittering lances and set to in battle,
feigning bitter fighting, and showed off their native skill with various
manœuvres. They skirmished, skilfully withdrawing and skilfully linger-
ing;[1] *now far apart, now close to one another,* [430] *now turning their*
backs in flight, now pursuing in turn, they checked charges with charges,
shield with shield. Now they went at each other viciously with their
weapons as though to each other's destruction, but all they did was safe, for
they were well used to it. The Nile-dwellers looked on, and so did the
wicked king himself, [435] *and a chill of fear gripped their senses and*
numbed them, for if such a race of Franks were to capture Jerusalem and
then invade their territory, there would be nothing that could withstand
their courage, since passionate fighting was almost like a kind of game to
them. [440] *Then the king summoned the man unlike himself,*[2] *who held*
the second place in the government, desiring to turn him from rational to
frenzied thought; he begged him to see to it that the Franks whom he had
been ordered to bring to him, whom he considered had taken stock of all
his realm, should not be returned to their allies so they could bring it about
that they all came there, [445] *but should secretly be beheaded for him.*
The man was smitten as though a sword had struck him in the chest, and
responded to him who commanded such things as follows:[3] *he asked what*
the cause of his raging frenzy was that forced him to summon to himself
under the guise of peace envoys, a name holy to all peoples throughout
the ages, [451] *and now to slaughter them in covert treachery? Good*

collections in the Middle Ages, see R. H. Rouse, 'Florilegia and Latin classical
authors in twelfth- and thirteenth-century Orleans', *Viator*, x (1979), 131–60, and
L. D. Reynolds and N. G. Wilson, *Scribes and Scholars: A Guide to the Transmission of
Greek and Latin Literature* (3rd edn., Oxford, 1991), p. 113; *Texts and Transmission: A
Survey Of The Latin Classics*, ed. L. D. Reynolds (Oxford, 1983), p. xxxviii; M. D.
Reeve notes in this work (p. 427) that over seventy lines from the poem are found
in the *Florilegium Gallicum*, a detail substantiated by B. L. Ullman, 'Valerius Flaccus
in the medieval florilegia', *Classical Philology*, xxvi (1931), 21–30. None of the
excerpts noted by Ullman include this line, however.

[2] See above, vi. 350 and n.

[3] Contrary to the feudal ethic, strictly understood, the vassal here takes a stand
against his lord. This speech is interesting in that it is put in *oratio recta*, at least to
begin with, rather than the Charleville Poet's preferred *oratio obliqua*.

Nusquam tuta fides post hac, nil gentibus equum,
Hoc si contingat fieri dampnabile iussum.
Pacis in hoc equidem se processisse ministrum,
Nequitie nunquam consortem se fore uiuum.   455
Si sic complaceat quo[a] Franci decapitentur,
Ceruix ante sua gladio grassante secetur,
Sed perpendendum, quocumque hec fama uolaret,
Incurabiliter se infamia tanta notaret.
Esse quidem dampnum probitatis militieque   460
Si paucos istos contingeret oppetiisse.
Sed tamen amissis inter tot milia paucis,
Non multum Gallos sensuros debilitatis,
Sed tamen inmenso dolituros esse dolore,
Atque in uindictam maiore calere furore.   465
Non iam gentilem legatio sumpta iuuaret,
Dum res facti huius exempla sequenda probaret.
Quin potius tales magno cumularat honore,
Ditatosque opibus permitteret in sua abire.

Talibus inflexus rationibus ille tyrannus   470
Consilium mutat, sequitur que dictat amicus.
Sic post immensum, miles generose,[1] timorem
In tua terga redis, claro duce fretus eodem,
Ac per Iordanem redeuntes Hierusalemque
Accipitis palmas,[2] petitis loca sancta domosque: 475
Omnia lustratis, pascentes lumina uisu,
Discitis ignota, referentes digna relatu;
Et bonus ille comes non uobis defuit, usque
Dum uos securos sociis dedit incolumesque.
Sic igitur celeri repetentes castra recursu   480
Letantes comites proprio fecere regressu.
Sed quia iam textus capiende texitur urbis,
Hoc melius referet libri textura sequentis.[3]

Explicit liber sextus. Incipit septimus

[a] quo *Cod., Sirmond;* quo(d) (*sic*) *sugg. Riant*

fo. 101[v]

*faith would not be safe anywhere after this, there would be no justice among
the nations, if it happened that this damnable order of his were carried out. He
said that, for himself, he had set out on this mission as a minister of peace,*
[455] *and while he lived he would never be a party to wickedness. If it was his
wish that the Franks should be beheaded, his own neck ought to be cut
through first with the raging sword, but he ought to consider that, wherever
news of this spread, a terrible reputation would mark him out without re-
dress.* [460] *It would in truth be a loss to honour, and to chivalry, if it hap-
pened that those few should meet their end, but on the other hand the Gauls
would not feel much weakened by the loss of a few among so many thousand;
they would rather be saddened with intense grief,* [465] *and would burn with
greater fury for revenge. It would not have helped the heathen to have
received the legation, since the perpetration of this crime would show them
what action to take in future. Why did he not rather heap such men with
honour, enrich them with wealth, and let them go back to their own?*

[470] *That tyrant was swayed by this way of thinking, and changed his plan,
following the advice of his friend. Thus, noble knight,*[1] *you retraced your steps
after terrible fear, trusting in that same distinguished leader, and returning
through Jordan and Jerusalem you* [475] *received the victor's palm*[2] *and
sought out the holy places and dwellings: you saw it all, feasting your eyes on
the sight, learning things you did not know, reporting back things worthy to be
told; and that good companion did not leave you until he gave you safe and
sound to your allies.* [480] *And so they made their way back to the camp at a
swift pace, and made their comrades rejoice at their own return. But because
the text now concerns itself with the taking of the city, the contents of the book
which follows will better relate this.*[3]

The sixth book ends. The seventh begins.

---

[1] This is an unusual instance of apostrophe, in that the poet uses his own persona to
address his heroes, after the classical manner, rather than his audience. Note also the
switch from the collective singular to the plural.
[2] See above, vi. 364 and n., on the significance of the palm-branch.
[3] After the failure of the embassy, al-Afdal's forces marched north and captured
Jerusalem in Aug. 1098. The poet picks up the threads of Gilo's work, preparing the
reader for the next part of the story whose narrative he has broken in order to insert
these episodes.

Nunc age, uirtutem solitam, rex Christe, reuela,
Quam neque uis hominum tibi dant nec[a] plurima tela.
Nunc age, Christe, tuis da sepe datum Machabeis[1]
Diuinum munus, tot milia uincat ut unus,
Milia famose gentis, ciues populose   5
Vrbis. Christe, faue, uim[b] turbe[c] comprime praue.[2]

Ergo Dei pietas, per pondera tanta malorum[3]
Inspiciens animos non defecisse suorum,
Inspirat cuidam Turco,[4] miserata laborum,[d]
Vt nostris urbem tradat[e] murumque decorum   10
Turribus et capiat pro munere culmen honorum.[5]
Ista diu secum uir uersans iudicat equum
Vt prius hec pandat Boimundo.[6] Nec mora, mandat
Illi quanta paret. Sed, ne quicquam dubitaret,
Precipit ut capiat missum[7] dum res ea fiat,   15
Neue parando moram producant. Tempus et[f] horam
Hic designauit. Sed in hoc dux participauit
Consilio procerum; comitum pars maxima uerum
Missum ferre putat, dubitans pars altera nutat.[8]
Dicta nocte tamen Boimundus colligit agmen   20
Pulcrius armatum, belli sudore probatum.

[a] neque *BC*   [b] ui *B*   [c] gentis *ADG*   [d] miserendo laborum *A;* miserendo suorum *DG*   [e] tradat urbem *BC*   [f] ad *D*

---

[1] Both Fulcher of Chartres, p. 116, and Raymond of Aguilers, p. 53, compare the deeds of the crusaders with the wars of the Israelites and Maccabees. See also Y. Katzir, 'The conquests of Jerusalem, 1099 and 1187: historical memory and religious typology', in *The Meeting of Two Worlds: Cultural Exchange between East and West during the Period of the Crusades*, ed. V. P. Goss and C. V. Bornsteinn (Kalamazoo, 1986), pp. 103, 106–7; J. Dunbabin, 'The Maccabees as exemplars in the tenth and eleventh centuries', in *The Bible in the Medieval World: Essays in Memory of Beryl Smalley*, ed. K. Walsh and D. Wood (*SCH*, Subsidia iv; Oxford, 1985), pp. 31–41.

[2] Christ is invoked in the same manner as a pagan classical poet would have invoked the Muses. See also above, iv. 4–6.

[3] See above, v. 148–9 and n.

[4] Other sources name this man Fīrūz, and give conflicting descriptions of his race and position. *Gesta Francorum*, p. 44, describes him as an emir of Turkish descent; Anna Comnena, ii. 19, says that he was an Armenian; Raymond of Aguilers, p. 64, calls him a 'Turca-

Come, Christ the King, reveal now the accustomed prowess which
neither the strength of men nor many weapons give to you. Come,
O Christ, grant now that divine gift often granted to your Macca-
baeans,[1] that one man may trounce thousands upon thousands, [5]
the thousands of the infamous race, the citizens of the populous
city. Christ, have mercy, and check the violence of the foul host.[2]

And so the goodness of God, seeing that the hearts of his people
had not grown weak through their terrible burdens of suffering,[3]
took pity on their toil and prompted a certain Turk[4] [10] to hand
over the city and its wall adorned with towers to our side, and to
receive the utmost honour for his service.[5] The fellow mulled his
intentions over in his mind for some time, and thought it fitting to
reveal them to Bohemond first.[6] Without delay he sent word to him
about the great enterprise he was planning. But so that he should
have no doubts at all, [15] he instructed him to keep his messenger[7]
until the deed was done, lest they should cause delay by their prepar-
ations. The man himself decided the time and place. But in this
matter, the duke took counsel with the leaders; the majority of the
nobles thought that the messenger was telling the truth, the rest
wavered in doubt.[8] [20] Even so, on the appointed night Bohemond
drew up his splendidly armed forces, tested in the sweat of battle.

---

tus' or renegade Christian, and Ralph of Caen, pp. 651–2, states that he belonged to a
family of armour-makers.

[5] Fīrūz was in charge of three towers on the walls of Antioch, near the gate of St George
and opposite the towers entrusted to Tancred. See above, v. 407 and n.

[6] Robert of Rheims, pp. 796–7, sets the first encounter between Bohemond and the
Turks at the time of truce. See above, v. 418. The *Gesta Francorum*, p. 44, implies however
that Fīrūz had known Bohemond for some time, and the *Chanson d'Antioche*, ll. 5501–15,
begins the story with the capture of Fīrūz's son, and his father's gratitude for the good
treatment that he received from the Christians.

[7] Fīrūz sent his son to Bohemond as a pledge of good faith. See *Gesta Francorum*, p. 45.

[8] According to the *Gesta Francorum*, pp. 44–6, the other leaders were initially reluctant
to accede to Bohemond's proposal that, if successful, he should rule Antioch. They
changed their minds when reports reached them of the advancing Turkish army, which
had abandoned the fruitless siege of Edessa. See above, vi. 67 and note. The treachery of
Fīrūz was not disclosed to the other leaders until the last moment.

Dux animo flagrat, diuortia nota peragrat.
Quisque pari[a] uoto suspirat pectore toto.
Per tenebras dux carpit iter galeaque nitenti
Deposita silet, et graditur sub nocte silenti.   25
Est uia militibus timidis, iuga deuia, ualles,
Queque per occultos[b] lucebat[c] semita calles.[d1]
Ne male res caderet ductor licet ipse timeret,
Quod[e] tamen angebat mentem[f] frons leta tegebat,
Dat spem tardanti, tristemque serenat ouanti   30
Vultu,[g] uirtutem stimulat, populoque salutem
Hactenus[h] optatam nunc innuit esse paratam.
Vtque locum uotis[i] multoque labore[j] petitum
Prospiciunt, hostemque uident uigilare peritum,[k]
Stant procul et[l] latebris tuti[m] noctisque tenebris   35
Collucere[n] faces spectant arcusque[o] minaces,
Et discurrentes per propugnacula Turcos,
Purpureos cristis, gladios uersare choruscos,
Qui loca mutantes commissa, uices uariantes,
Excubias noctis succedenter faciebant,[p]   40
Vocibus assuetis terrores[q] incutiebant
Militibus clamando 'quis[r] es?', nec adesse sciebant.
Nec mora, dat dux magnanimus dignas duce uoces,
Instimulando uiros uerbis[s] animosque feroces:[2]
'Pluribus optatum uotis, satis inuigilatum,   45
Tempus adest, proceres, Domini pietate paratum.
Tempus in hoc protracta[t] fuit uictoria sera,
Perque nouem menses Domini uindicta seuera[u3]
Nos castigauit. Sed sunt prope gaudia uera.
Ergo, uiri fortes, forti persistite mente,   50
Vosque, citi iuuenes, muros[v] superate repente.
Vincite, sed celeres[w]—pudeat uos uincere lente.
Ille locus' (monstratque locum) 'prius aggrediatur;[x4]

[i] locum spectant uotis *BC;* locum noctis *D*   [j] *BC omit* labore, *then add it in the margin*   [k] periclum *D m. pr., corr. to* peritlum *m. alt.*   [l] et *om. A m. pr.*   [m] tecti *ADG*   [n] pollucere *F*   [o] acusque *D m. pr.*   [p] et faciebant *A*   [q] terroribus *F;* clamores *D*   [r] quid *B*   [s] hortans *BC*   [t] prostrata *DF*   [u] serena *F m. pr.*   [v] murum *B*   [w] sceleres *D m. pr.*   [x] *F m. pr. omits this line*

[1] Probably a reference to a ruse suggested by Fīrūz. The crusaders marched east, as

His courage aflame, he made his way along the well-known tracks.
Each of his men sighed the same prayer with all his heart. The
duke made his way through the darkness, his burnished helm [25]
laid aside, and made no noise as he proceeded through the noise-
less night. There was a path there for the fearful soldiers, and
trackless heights and vales, and a track which gleamed amidst the
hidden ways.[1] Even their leader was afraid that things would turn
out badly, but his face was cheerful, hiding that which grieved his
mind, [30] and he gave hope to the hesitant and soothed the sad
with his joyful expression. He urged them to be courageous, and
signalled to the people that the salvation they had hoped for thus
far was now ready. As they looked over to the place they had
prayed and laboured much to reach, and saw their experienced
enemy on watch, [35] they halted at a distance, safe in the shadows
and darkness of the night, and gazed at the blazing torches, the
threatening bows, the Turks running to and fro along the battle-
ments with their purple crests and twirling their glittering swords;
exchanging the places entrusted to them and taking their turns one
after another, [40] they carried out the watches of the night, caus-
ing terror to the soldiers with their usual cries of 'Who goes there?',
though they did not know men were at hand. Without delay, the
stout-hearted duke spoke as was worthy of a duke, stirring the
fierce hearts of his men with these words:[2] [45] 'Noble men, the
time for which you have waited with many a prayer, and watched for
long enough, has now arrived, made ready by the goodness of the
Lord. Victory, late in coming, has been delayed until this time, and
for nine months the harsh rod of the Lord has chastised us.[3] But true
joys are close at hand. [50] So, brave men, stick to your firm resolve,
and you, swift youths, climb up the walls at once. Be victorious—
but quickly!—you should be ashamed to be slow in conquering.
That place' (he pointed the place out) 'is to be attacked[4] first;

---

[1] if to plunder the Muslim camp, and then under cover of darkness turned back towards
the towers controlled by Fīrūz. See *Gesta Francorum*, pp. 45–6, and above, vii. 12.

[2] Gilo alone gives Bohemond such a lengthy speech. The latter's words of en-
couragement are much shorter, for example, in the *Gesta Francorum*, p. 46. Here, his
words are cast in a frame reminiscent of the pre-battle speeches in Lucan.

[3] The crusaders had arrived outside Antioch in late Oct. 1097; they captured the city
on 3 June 1098.

[4] Note that *aggrediatur* here must be passive in meaning. Priscian, *Gramm*. viii. 14,
notes that many writers (Jerome and Augustine among them) use the verb in this non-
classical sense.

Vos ibi palma sedens[a] uocat et prius inde petatur.[b]
Dona manent omnes, sed non mea dona uocabo[c]   55
Quod sibi[d] quisque dabit: uictori nulla negabo.
Sed moror. Ite, uiri! Cum paucis hic ego stabo.
Accelerate, boni proceres! Ego tardius ibo:
Si sit opus, pedes[e] ipse prior certamen inibo.'
Finierat dubiusque silet dux, atque uagantur   60
Per totam mentem quecunque futura putantur.
Accelerant iuuenes, Fulcherius[1] imminet ante;
Per tenebras[f2] legit ille[g] uias gressu titubante.
Illis temporibus radios ducente cometa[3]
Premonstrabatur regni mutatio leta;   65
Astra polusque[h] nouo sunt obfuscata rubore,
Cordaque sunt hominum nimio percussa[i] timore.
Noctis erat medium cum miles ad illa paratus
Constitit ad turrem[j] quam traditor ille beatus
Seruabat, stupuitque nimis[k] de turre uocatus.   70
'Eia', clamabat Turcus, 'conscendite muros.
Summa petat uirtus,[l] premat hostes iam ruituros;
Scalarumque modo funes huc ferte plicatos.'[4]
Mouit eos tandem latitantes, sepe rogatos;
Denique calcata formidine, ui reuocata,[m]   75
Vepribus extracti uix uincentesque coacti
Sese confortant, scalas ad menia portant;
Dantque retro gressus iterum, turpesque recessus
Frutectis mersi repetunt,[n] ad tuta reuersi;
Et, licet[o] instaret Turcus, lux appropiaret,   80
Nil tamen audebant, sed corda gelata stupebant.
Increpat[p] e muris uir uocibus agmina duris.
Iamque recedebat[q] nox et Matuta[r 5] rubebat

[a] sedes D   [b] putatur D m. pr.   [c] D m. pr. puts this line after l. 51; m. alt. puts it
after l. 59   [d] si D m. pr.   [e] opus pedester pedes D   [f] latebras BC
[g] ipse D   [h] polaque D m. pr.   [i] perculsa ADG   [j] turrim A; turres DG
[k] minus C   [l] uirta G m. pr.   [m] renouata BC   [n] referunt AD; redeunt
G   [o] licen D m. pr.   [p] hicrepat A   [q] recedebant F m. pr.
[r] Matura F. with the gloss Aurora above; matutina BCDG

[1] Raymond of Aguilers, p. 64, names Fulcher as the brother of Bartholomew Boel of
Chartres (see below, vii. 98), and the first to enter Antioch. He is also mentioned by
Orderic Vitalis (v. 90, n. 3), who probably had some direct information about him and his
family, since they were connected with his own monastery of Saint-Évroul. Fulcher had
been a member of Peter the Hermit's expedition, and was listed by Albert of Aachen as
one of the casualties at Civetot. In fact he joined Bohemond's forces and was ultimately

the victor's prize sits there calling you, and must first be sought from there. [55] Gifts await you all, but I shall not call gifts of mine what each man may give himself: I shall deny him nothing who conquers. But I am wasting time. Be gone, men! I shall stand here with a few soldiers. Make haste, good nobles! I shall proceed more slowly; if need be, I shall enter the fray before you on foot myself.' [60] the duke finished, and fell silent in doubt; every outcome that he could think of passed through his mind. The young men sped on their way, with Fulcher[1] pressing on ahead; with faltering steps he picked his way through the darkness.[2] About this time, a joyful change of rule was foretold by the rays of a comet;[3] [66] the stars of heaven were dimmed by the strange brightness, and the hearts of men were struck with terrible fear. It was the middle of the night when the soldier, prepared for this action, stood before the tower which that blessed traitor had in his charge, [70] and he was utterly astounded at being hailed from the tower. 'Hey', the Turk was shouting, 'climb the walls. Let your courage seek the heights and strike down the enemy destined to fall; bring your rope-ladders here.'[4] At length, having asked them many times, he moved them from their lurking; [75] at last they trod down their terror and renewed their strength; reluctantly emerging from the bushes, compelled to be conquerers, they encouraged one another and carried their ladders to the fortifications, then withdrew again, and made once more for their shameful refuge, skulking in the bushes, turning back to safety; [80] and although the Turk was insistent, and dawn was approaching, they dared not do anything, but their hearts were chilled and numb. From the walls the man rebuked the soldiers with harsh words. Already night was fleeing and dawn[5] was blushing red

rewarded with a fief in the county of Edessa by Baldwin of Boulogne. See Albert of Aachen, pp. 277–8, 281, 283, 286, 288, 357, 682; Riley-Smith, 'The motives', pp. 730, 736. There was at least one other person called Fulcher who took part in the First Crusade, namely the historian and chaplain of Baldwin of Boulogne; see Fulcher of Chartres, pp. 1–19.

    [2] Fulcher and a few other knights scaled a ladder on to the city walls and took the Tower of the Two Sisters held by Fīrūz.

    [3] The comet is also mentioned by Raymond of Aguilers, p. 54; *Gesta Francorum*, p. 62; Fulcher of Chartres, p. 224. Such phenomena were interpreted as portents of a Christian victory and placed the crusade in a supernatural context. See Riley-Smith, *Idea of Crusading*, pp. 33–4, 92.

    [4] The author of the *Gesta Francorum*, p. 46, makes Fīrūz call out that there were too few Franks, and appeal for Bohemond.

    [5] *Matuta* here is the goddess of dawn. See for example Lucretius, *De rerum natura*, v. 656 (which Gilo is unlikely to have known), Priscian, *Inst. gramm.* ii. 53, and also Siguinus, *Ars lectoria*, p. 26.

Cum[a] stans in medio reliquorum iunior unus
Sic ait: 'oblatum, iuuenes, ne spernite[b] munus.   85
Surgite! Primus ero.' Parent, Fulcherius ille
Natus Carnoti[1] proceres precedere[c] mille
Non[d] timet inuicte properans ad menia uille.
Non hunc tardat honus clipei sed ad[e] ardua pronus
Euolat arma gerens[f] scaleque uiriliter herens.   90
Illum Veneticus[2] sequitur. Stupet hostis iniquus
Vt stetit in muris Fulcherius: ense[g] necantur
Fulmineo uigiles et ad infima precipitantur.
Exultat uictor laniataque proterit ora.
Corpora[h] trunca cadunt, lacerantur membra decora.   95
Aspirat[i] fortuna uiro, plebemque solutam
Turbat,[j] que requiem trahit inter pocula tutam.
Euellit postes turresque subintrat et hostes
Opprimit incautos, prospectus[k] occupat altos,[l]
Tresque capit turres[3] propria uirtute Boellus   100
(Hunc natiua[m] uocat tali cognomine tellus).[4]
Germanos hic forte tuos, bone traditor urbis,
Sternit, quos nollet morientibus addere turbis,[n]
Et fratres geminos[o] impellit ab arce[p] supinos.[q5]

Iamque uiri fortes pendebant undique scalis   105
Nec dubitat quisquam niti per membra sodalis,
Ascensu superant muros, fastigia dextris
Prensant, obiciunt clipeos ad tela sinistris.
Instaurant animos Turci, detrudere primos
Frustra luctantur trepidaque manu iaculantur.   110

[a] tum F   [b] perdite D   [c] procedere D   [d] num A   [e] et F
[f] herens D m. pr.   [g] esse A   [h] corporea truncata D   [i] spirat F
[j] turbant A m. pr.   [k] prospectos D   [l] hostes D m. pr.   [m] natura A m.
pr.   [n] D m. pr. adds impellit ab urbe supinos, from l. 104, at the end of this line
[o] suos geminos D m. pr.   [p] urbe DG   [q] D m. pr. adds morientibus addere
turbis, from l. 103, at the end of this line. BC place this line after l. 101

[1] See above, vii. 62 and n.
[2] This Venetian is not mentioned in any other crusading narrative. *Gesta Francorum*,
p. 46 and Orderic Vitalis, v. 90, n. 3, however, say that a south Italian Lombard named
Pain led the ascent of the tower, and called out to Bohemond to follow.
[3] This is probably a reference to Fulcher of Chartres's brother Bartholomew Boel
(above, vii. 63 n.), who was a member of Bohemond's contingent. See Raymond of
Aguilers, p. 64; Orderic Vitalis, v. 90 n. 3; *Gesta Francorum*, p. 81; Riley-Smith, *Idea of*

when one of the younger men, standing in the midst of the rest, [85] spoke these words: 'Young men, do not spurn the gift we are offered. Come on! I shall go first.' They obeyed, and noble Fulcher, born in Chartres,[1] did not fear to go in advance of the thousand knights and hurry to the walls of the unvanquished city. The burden of his shield did not slow him down, [90] but he flew swiftly to the top, brandishing his weapons and clinging to the ladder in manly fashion. A Venetian[2] followed him. The wicked enemy was astounded when Fulcher stood on the walls; the sentries were slain by the lightning swiftness of his sword, and were cast down to the depths below. The conqueror rejoiced to trample on the mangled faces. [95] Bodies fell, dismembered, and handsome limbs were torn asunder. Fortune breathed on the man, and threw into confusion the heedless crowd idling away its safety and rest over the drinking-cups. Tearing open the doors, penetrating the towers and overwhelming the unwary enemy, Boel (his native land calls him by such a name)[3] took possession of the lofty lookout-posts [100] and captured three towers[4] by his own courage. By chance he cut down here your brothers, good betrayer of the city, though he would not have wanted to add them to the host of the dying, and he drove those twin brothers headlong from the citadel.[5]

[105] And now brave men were hanging everywhere from ladders, and none hesitated to heave himself up over the limbs of his comrade; they reached the top of the walls in their climb, gripping the summit with their right hands and with their left setting their shields against the enemy's weapons. The Turks renewed their efforts and [110] struggled in vain to dislodge the front rank, throwing weapons with trembling hands. The

---

Crusading, p. 77. He was the same Bartholomew Boel as the man from Chartres who was grandson of Gerard, canon of Chartres. See Orderic Vitalis, v. 36 n. 1. There is a faint reminiscence of Vergil, *Aen.* ii. 480–1, in the phrase *euellit postes*.

[4] The three towers held by Fīrūz. See above, vii. 12 and note.

[5] According to the *Gesta Francorum*, p. 47, Fīrūz had one brother who was killed during the ascent of the tower. There are, however, several other stories about his ultimate fate. William of Tyre, i. 299, maintains that Fīrūz himself killed his brother; the *Chanson d'Antioche*, ll. 6216–29, makes Robert of Flanders responsible. According to Robert of Rheims, pp. 800, 805, Fīrūz had two brothers who were killed by Fulcher of Chartres. By using the imperfect subjunctive, Gilo seems to imply that the killing of Fīrūz's brother was a case of mistaken identity: Fulcher would have spared him had he been able to distinguish him from other Turks.

Fratrum fata dolens Turcus[1] sed[a] de nece nolens[b]
Sumere uindictam pacemque resoluere fictam
Frena[c] dat huic ire, properat portas aperire,[2]
Educensque[d] graues gemitus de pectore, claues
Porte porrexit Boimundo, duxque reflexit[e]   115
Supplex ante uirum corpus uultumque seuerum.
Diffugiunt miseri ciues ubi morte teneri
Cuncta uident. Telis sternuntur menia tota,
Et sunt de muris Parthi[f] rubra signa remota,
Albaque pro rubeis illic uexilla locantur.[3]   120
Ad commune bonum sic agmina fida uocantur,
Clangoremque tube tulit ad tentoria uentus;
Impediuntur[g] equi frenis, fremit arma iuuentus.
Nec mora, prosiliunt de castris agmina densa,
Deseruere duces campis tentoria tensa.[h]   125
Dum sine lege ruunt ex urbe uiros fugientes
Excipiunt terreque premunt hos sponte cadentes:
Sponte cadunt quibus exciderant cum corpore mentes.[i]
Agmina per portas mox irrupere patentes,
Et pressere[j] uiri primorum terga sequentes.[4]   130
Protinus inuadunt urbem, dant uulnera multa,
Passim turba perit somno uinoque sepulta.[5]
Signa canunt,[k] matresque gemunt, est luctus ubique,
Perque uias omnes gentis cruor errat[l] inique.
Ore uomit cerebrum capitis compage soluta[m6]   135
Infans et fedant nutricem[7] sordida sputa.[n]
Ad matres tendunt captiue lumina nate—
Lumina, namque manus rigido[o] sunt[p] fune ligate;
Flent herentque senes templis auro spoliatis
Duraque[q] percutiunt loca frontibus inueteratis.[8]   140

---

[a] se *G*   [b] dolens *D m. pr.*   [c] freno *D*   [d] producensque *F*
[e] dux quoque flexit *G*   [f] Parthi *Grocock;* parti *AF;* partim *BCDG*
[g] impeiliuntur (*sic*) *D*   [h] densa *F*   [i] *For this line, G reads* hos non sponte cadunt quibus et cum corpore mentes *F m. pr.*   [j] expressere *D m. pr.*   [k] cadunt *BC, F m. pr.*   [l] erat *F;* error *D*   [m] saluta *A*   [n] oscula muta *A*   [o] rigide *D m. pr.*   [p] sunt rigido *F*   [q] luraque *F*

---

[1] Again Fīrūz.

[2] *Gesta Francorum*, p. 47, describes how a small party, including its author, gained access to the city through a gate hidden by the darkness. The narrative here and in Robert of Rheims, p. 805, focuses on the gates opened by Fīrūz, the Gates of St George

Turk[1] grieved over the fate of his brothers, but not wanting to take revenge for their deaths or to undo the peace he had made, curbed this wrath and made haste to open the gates,[2] and uttering groans from deep in his breast, [115] he held out to Bohemond the keys of the gate, and the duke bowed as a suppliant before the man, lowering his stern gaze. The wretched citizens fled when they saw that all was held in the grip of death. All the fortifications were battered down by weapons, the red Parthian standards were taken down from the walls, [120] and white banners were raised in the place of the red ones.[3] Thus were the faithful columns summoned to the general triumph, and the wind carried the blare of the trumpet to the tents; the horses were bridled, and the youths clamoured for arms. Without delay the close-packed columns leapt from the camp, [125] and the leaders abandoned the tents pitched in the plain. They caught up the men fleeing from the city, rushing on in disorder, and crushed them to the ground as they fell down without a touch: for men whose spirit has failed them as well as their body fall down of themselves. The columns quickly burst in through the gaping gates, [130] and men following pressed on behind the first to enter.[4] Straight away they invaded the city, inflicting many wounds, and everywhere the host buried in a drunken slumber[5] met its death. Trumpets gave the signal, women wailed, there was grief everywhere, and the blood of the wicked race flowed in every street. [135] The infant with its head severed[6] puked its brains from its mouth, and the foul spittle made filthy its nurse.[7] Captured daughters cast longing looks to their mothers— looks only, for their hands were tied firmly with rope; old men wept and clung to the temples despoiled of gold, [40] and struck the hard ground with their aged foreheads.[8]

and the Bridge. Robert's wording is similar to Gilo here: 'cum graues gemitus ab imo pectore traheret longaque suspiria'.

[3] *Gesta Francorum*, p. 47. According to Fulcher of Chartres, p. 234, Bohemond himself had a red banner.

[4] For other accounts of the crusaders' entry into the city, see Albert of Aachen, p. 405; Raymond of Aguilers, p. 65; Fulcher of Chartres, pp. 233–5.

[5] Cf. Vergil, *Aen.* iii. 630, ix. 316.   [6] Cf. Lucan, *Bellum ciuile*, i. 72.

[7] See below, ix. 329–30 and n., for a similar account of the massacre of the inhabitants of Jerusalem. The imagery in ll. 137–18 is very close to that in Vergil, *Aen.* ii. 405–6.

[8] The description in this line is curiously suggestive of the characteristic Muslim attitude at prayer; perhaps this action was misunderstood by an uncomprehending observer.

Emicat ante uolans Godefridus,[1] inertia spernit
Corpora, quosque uidet torquentes spicula sternit.[a]
Loricas clipeosque simul secat ense nitenti,
Territat instantes hoc,[b] obicit hoc fugienti;
A nece uix gladium dux ipse potest inhibere,   145
Quosque mori nollet gladio multi periere,
Vulnere nam si quem modico[c] perstringere[d] captat,
Hunc rapido mucrone manus licet inscia mactat;
Dum quecunque suis suadet uictoria leta
Gens leuis exequitur licitis miscens inhonesta.   150
Celauit pannis regem rex obsitus annis,
Victorumque manus sic euasit Casianus.[2]
Non tamen est fatis ereptus, sed bene notus
Armenio[e] cuidam fugiens et ab urbe remotus
Perdidit annosis cinctum caput undique uillis   155
Atque reportatur ceruix[f] suspensa capillis.
Per uicos urbis caput applaudendo[g] secuntur
Armenii,[h] Turcique suo pro rege queruntur.[3]

Vrbi contiguus mons est montisque cacumen
Non leuiter ualet humanum comprendere[i] lumen.[4]   160
Stat super hoc[j] castrum, de quo patet Antiochena
Pulchra nimis regio, cum lux solet esse serena.
Illuc euadunt Perse, nostrosque sagittis
Inde premunt, nec tota uenit uictoria mitis.[5]
Cum legione sua Boimundus suscipit ictus   165
Illorum, petit hostis eum[k] per menia uictus.
Cumque super murum turrem[l] dux fortis haberet
Que munita parum castro uicinius heret,
Incumbebat ei seuissima turba resumptis
Viribus, amentant Arabes de culmine montis,   170
Ast alii conantur eum[m] depellere contis,
Perque globos densant cuneos et culmina prensant.

[a] strenit *A m. pr.*   [b] huic *G*   [c] quam paruo *AG;* quem gladio *glossed*
paruo *D*   [d] prestringere *G*   [e] Armeno *F;* Ermenio *BC*   [f] coniunx
BC   [g] applaudando *B;* ad plaudendum *D*   [h] Armeni *F;* Ermenii *BCD;*
Emenii *A*   [i] comprehendere *F*   [j] hunc *F*   [k] *?* cum *G*   [l] tur-
rim *ADG*   [m] cum *A*

---

[1] Only Gilo gives such prominence to Godfrey of Bouillon in his account of these
events.
[2] The escape of Casianus (Yaghi Siyan), the governor of Antioch, and his murder at

Godfrey shone forth,[1] flying in front, and he paid no heed to the lifeless bodies, but laid low those he saw throwing spears. With his glittering sword he cut through breastplates and shields in one blow; with it he terrified those pressing on him, and thrust it in front of those who fled. [145] The duke himself could scarcely keep his sword from the slaughter, and many whom he would not have wanted to perish died by his blade: for if he tried to touch any man with just a slight wound, his hand, though unaware of it, slew him with a rapid sword-thrust; whatsoever deeds his joyful victory encouraged his men to perform, [150] the unquestioning mob carried out, mingling unlawful deeds with lawful ones. The king, laden with years, hid his royal self in rags, and thus did Casianus escape the victors' clutches.[2] He was not snatched from the fates, however, but, being well known to a certain Armenian to whom he fled far from the city, [155] he was beheaded, and his head, covered all over with aged locks, was brought back suspended by the hair. Throughout the streets of the city Armenians followed the head, shouting their approval, while the Turks wailed for their king.[3]

Adjoining the city is a mountain whose summit [160] the eyesight of men cannot easily make out.[4] On top of this is a fort, below which the beautiful region of Antioch lies wide open, when the light is clear, as it often is. The Persians escaped to this place, and from there they harried our men with arrows, and complete victory did not come smoothly.[5] [165] Bohemond and his force received their blows, as the defeated enemy sought him out through the city, and since the brave duke had possession of a tower on top of the wall which was very lightly fortified and clung very close to the fort, the ferocious host fell on him with renewed vigour, [170] and the Arabs hurled weapons down from the moun-tain-top, but others strove to drive him off with pikes. They massed their formations in close ranks and laid hold of the heights.

the hands of Armenians, is also described by *Gesta Francorum*, pp. 47–8; Raymond of Aguilers, p. 66; Robert of Rheims, p. 806; Fulcher of Chartres, p. 235.

[3] *Gesta Francorum*, p. 48, says that Yaghi Siyan's head was brought to Bohemond by his captors as the price of their freedom, and that his belt and scabbard were worth 60 bezants.

[4] Mount Silpius, upon which stood the citadel. For other descriptions of Antioch, see Robert of Rheims, pp. 806–7; *Gesta Francorum*, pp. 76–7.

[5] Yaghi Siyan's son, Shams ad-Daulah, had taken control of the citadel and appealed from there for aid from Kerbogha. See *Gesta Francorum*, p. 50, and above, v. 382 and n. The Turkish relief force encamped before the city walls on 7 June, four days after the crusaders had entered the city.

Prelia committunt, uix primi spicula mittunt
Assimilanda[a] niui, calcantque cadauera uiui.
Dux equitesque ducis consistunt, et morientes   175
Turribus euoluunt, ciuesque necant subeuntes,
Nunc instant[b] sude, nunc saxo, per tela ruentes
Hos fugiunt, hos deiiciunt. Dux summa tenentes
Amputat ense manus clipeoque sonante furentes
Sustinet, hortatur proceres, telis honeratur.[1]   180

Dum certant acies, iaculum femori ducis hesit
Atque uirile femur grauiter uulnus leue lesit.[2]
Dux igitur reprimens fugientis sanguinis undam
Deseruit[c] primam turrem[d] petiitque secundam.
Vtque[e] sui uidere ducis procumbere mentem,   185
Apulus et Calaber[3] fugiunt uictam modo gentem.
Sed tamen amissa uir solus in arce remansit,
Cuius honesta satis Boimundus funera planxit.[f 4]
Hostibus hic[g] mediis ubi se uidet esse relictum
Exagitans clipeum circum sua timpora[5] pictum   190
Territat[h] instantes turbas sub turre uagantes.
Obruit[i] elapsis de summo culmine saxis,
Mille manus lassat manus una,[j] uiros sude quassat,
Frustaque[k] cementi decrustans ungue trementi[6]
Stantibus infligit, ferro caua timpora figit.   195
Hunc[l] sub pace uocant ciues, succurrit at isti[m]
Quam pulchrum sit marte mori pro nomine Christi.
Iamque superficiem clipei densauerat hostis
Missilibus, iacet orbis iners,[7] pondus graue costis.
Protinus haud timide sese super agmina iecit,   200

[a] assimulanda D   [b] instat G   [c] desereit F m. pr.   [d] turrim ABCDG
[e] atque A   [f] plansit D   [g] his F   [h] territant F   [i] obtulit B
[j] unaque G   [k] efrustaque D m. pr.   [l] tunc F   [m] illi D

---

[1] Gilo here exaggerates Bohemond's personal role in the ascent and capture of the tower. See Robert of Rheims, p. 805.
[2] Robert of Rheims, p. 807, is the only other source to mention the wounding of Bohemond. Wounds in the thigh were often associated with impotence in medieval literature, accounting for the epithet *uirile*: cf. Marie de France's *Lai* 'Guigemar', l. 99.
[3] Bohemond's companions from southern Italy are also mentioned by the *Gesta Francorum*, p. 78. See in addition G. A. Loud, 'Norman Italy and the Holy Land', in *The Horns of Hattin*, ed. B. Z. Kedar (Jerusalem, 1992), pp. 49–62, at 49–50. The phrase *Apulus et Calaber* is also found in Guy of Amiens, *Carmen de Hastingae proelio*, l. 259.

They had scarcely joined battle before the front rank sent spears
falling like snow, and the living trampled on the dead. [175] The
duke and the duke's knights held firm; they rolled the dying out of
the towers, killing the approaching citizens, and attacked now with
pikes, now with stones, putting some to flight as they rushed
forward through the falling spears, and casting others to the
ground. With his sword the duke cut off the hands of those clinging
to the top of the wall, and held off the raging foe with his resound-
ing shield, [180] encouraging his peers, and was weighed down
with missiles.[1]

While the two sides fought on, a spear stuck in the duke's thigh;
the wound was slight, but still gave his manly thigh much pain.[2]
For this reason he abandoned the first tower, pressing back the
wave of flowing blood, and made for the second tower. [185] As his
men saw their leader's spirits fall, Apulians and Calabrians[3] fled
from the people they had just vanquished. But there was one man
who stayed on alone in the now-lost citadel, and Bohemond greatly
bewailed his noble death.[4] When this man saw that he was aban-
doned in the midst of the enemy, [190] he swung his painted shield
wildly about his head[5] and filled with fear the attacking crowds scur-
rying below the tower, overwhelming them with rocks dislodged
from the topmost height; his one hand wearied a thousand hands; he
battered men with his pikestaff, and flaking off chunks of masonry
with his trembling fingernails[6] he hurled them [195] at those who
stood against him, and pierced their temples with iron. The citizens
called out to him in the name of peace, but he bethought him how
lovely it is to die in battle for the name of Christ, and already the
enemy had made the face of his shield thick with missiles; the round
shield lay there useless,[7] a heavy weight at his side. [200] Straight
away he threw himself without any fear upon the enemy columns,

---

[4] On 5 June, Kerbogha's army attacked one of the towers on the Iron Bridge gar-
risoned by the crusaders. All the defenders were killed, with one exception; he was later
found by the crusaders bound in iron chains. See *Gesta Francorum*, pp. 50–1. This
appears to be the incident described here.

[5] The spelling *timpora* is attested in Latham, *Revised Medieval Latin Word-List*, and is
widely distributed—though not with any consistency—throughout all six MSS; they use
it only in the sense 'temples of the head', not 'times'.

[6] Robert of Rheims, p. 807, has a similar description.

[7] In fact the crusaders generally used kite-shaped shields. See above, v. 189
and n.

Tormentumque nouum proprio*a* de corpore fecit,
Et fractus fregit multos. Hec Apulus egit.
Sed quis id expediet uerbis? Que lingua notare
Funera tot poterit,*b* tot captiuos numerare?
Ne*c* turbare quidem queat amplificatio[1] uerum;*d*   205
Sufficiat mihi summa sequi uestigia*e* rerum.

Vrbs antiqua, potens, Petri cathedra decorata,
Ecclesie sedes post Romam[2] iure uocata,
Vrbibus innumeris urbs assidue dominata
Muris, delubris felix, iocunda, salubris,   210
Ignorantis erat populi demersa tenebris.
Inde*f* sed erupit,*g* noua facta, magisque celebris.*h*[3]
Vestes gemmatas auroque domos laqueatas
Agmen habet nostrum, peregrinum possidet ostrum,
Vrbis et unius expleuit copia gentes,[4]   215
Pauperibusque*i* nichil possunt auferre potentes.
Seruus in hac seruos habet urbe, cliensque clientes;
Illam luce Iouis[5] tuus intrat, Christe, satelles,
Sed castellanos nequit*j* exuperare rebelles.
Ergo die tota pugnat, noctique laborem*k*   220
Continuat nullumque*l* capit sub nocte soporem.*m*
Ast ubi mane datur Venerisque dies reseratur,[6]
Stans eques in muris dum sustentatur*n* ab hasta
Sortitusque locum loca lustrat*o* lumine uasta,
Pulueris obscuram*p* prospexit in aere*q* nubem;   225
Tristia mox reliquam uocat ad spectacula pubem.
Suspensis animis per propugnacula stabant,
Diuersique uiri diuersa uidere putabant.
Appropiare quidem Turcos*r* pars uaticinatur,
Pars Bizantinos fore credit*s* quos speculatur.[7]   230

---

a ? porpore *D m. pr.*   *b* poterat *AD*   *c* nec *A;* non *D*   *d* *D, first hand,*
puts this line after l. 206   *e* fastigia *G*   *f* idem *A*   *g* eripit *B*
h salubris *BC*   *i* pauperibus et *D*   *j* nequid *D*   *k* labores *A*
l ullumque *A*   *m* saporem *BC*   *n* spectatur *A*   *o* uastat *D;* uisit *G*
p obseruam *A*   *q* aera *F*   *r* tucos *D*   *s* cediti *A m. pr., corr. to* crediti *m.*
alt.

---

[1] *Amplificatio* is a technical term from medieval poetics, referring to development at length, rather than stress on a particular point: cf. Faral, *Arts poétiques*, pp. 61–84. Gilo prefers to keep to the main points of his narrative, rather than let *amplificatio* distort the truth, a stance he also adopts at the start of book ix.

making a new kind of catapult from his own body, and though
shattered himself, he shattered many. It was an Apulian who did
this. But who could give fitting expression to that deed? What
tongue could tell of so many deaths, or count so many prisoners?
[205] Not even expansion[1] can distort the truth, let it be enough for
me to follow the most important steps in the course of events.

The ancient, powerful city, beautified by the seat of Peter, rightly
called the chief see of the church after Rome,[2] a city accustomed to
lording it over numerous cities, [210] blessed, joyous, and secure in
its walls and shrines, had been plunged in the darkness of an
ignorant people. But it escaped from that plight, made new and
more glorious.[3] Our troops possessed jewelled vestments and
houses with ceilings panelled in gold. They possessed its exotic
purple-dyed fabrics, [215] and the wealth of one city fully satisfied
our peoples[4]—and the powerful can take nothing from poor men;
in this city a slave has slaves, and a client clients. Your company, O
Christ, entered it on a Thursday,[5] but could not overwhelm the
rebels in the fort. [220] And so they fought all day, and carried on
with their toil by night, taking no rest during the night. But when
dawn broke and Friday was revealed,[6] a knight, standing on the
wall and leaning on his spear where he had been allotted a place,
was gazing over the wide-open spaces, [225] and saw a shadowy
cloud of dust in the air; he swiftly called the rest of the young
men to see this sorry sight. They stood on the battlements with
bated breath, and different men thought they saw different things,
for some predicted that the Turks were approaching, [230] and
some believed it was the Byzantines whom they were looking at.[7]

---

[2] See above, iv. 428 and n.; Riley-Smith, 'The First Crusade and St Peter', pp. 50–1.
St Peter was the first bishop of Antioch.

[3] After the capture of Antioch, Adhémar of Le Puy ordered that the churches should
be cleansed and the deposed patriarch, John, enthroned. See Albert of Aachen, p. 433;
Hamilton, *The Latin Church in the Crusader States*, p. 7.

[4] Other sources make no reference to booty at this point.

[5] 3 June 1098.

[6] Kerbogha's army arrived at the Iron Bridge on 5 June. See above, vii. 189 and n.
Robert of Rheims, p. 808, is very similar to Gilo: 'ecce illi qui stabant in turribus et
muris eminus contemplantur immensam nubem agitati pulueris'.

[7] Alexius Comnenus had set out from Constantinople at the head of a relieving force,
and reached Philomelium in the middle of June 1098. The description of the approach-
ing army, seen first from its burnished weaponry glinting in the sunshine, is paralleled
by that in the *Chanson de Roland*, ll. 1031–3. Cf. also below, vii. 503 and n.

Ardentes clipeos sol lumine percutiebat
Paulatimque frequens exercitus adueniebat.
Consedere tamen procul, expectando sequentes,
Corbana milite princeps reliquique potentes.[1]
Sed quidam Perse iam menia spe capientes   235
Vrbis in aspectu campos petiere[a] patentes,
Diuersisque modis gaudent ibi luxuriare,
Turpia non[b] cessant speculantibus improperare,[c]
Spumantes per gramen equos dimittere certant,
Nudatos enses iaciunt iterumque receptant,   240
Exululant, passim uolitant clausisque minantur,[d]
Telaque per uacuas auras temere iaculantur.
Tutius esse putant nostri loca certa fouere
Quam casus incerta sequi bellumque mouere.[e]
Sed cum iam Turci remearent uociferantes,   245
De Barna Villa sequitur Rogerus ouantes[f]
Cum tribus armatis,[2] quos postquam gens remorata
Respexit, facit insidias sub rupe cauata,
Dumque lacessentes aliquos nostri sequerentur,[g]
E latebris fures saliunt iuuenesque tenentur[h]   250
Inclusi, uersique stupent, animisque receptis
Vallantes penetrant clipeis ad terga reiectis.
Vt fit ubi canibus post cerui crura solutis
Hi pedibus predam, portum petit ille salutis,
His alas addit spes, fit celer ille timore,   255
Mox uoti compos ceruus canis exit ab ore,
Hos[i] ita Parthus[j] agit preceps, in uerbera pendens,
Sic fugit ista cohors ad uite premia tendens.
Instigat[k] socios Rogerus et excipit ictus.
Hunc tardare facit probitas et conscia uirtus.   260
Telorum siluam uix sustinet horrida parma,
Labentem sustentat equum, tinguit cruor arma.

[a] paciere *D m. pr.*   [b] nec *ABC*   [c] improperares *F*   [d] minatur *G m.*
pr.   [e] sequi Rogerus ouantes *D m. pr.*   [f] sequitur bellumque mouere *D m.*
pr.   [g] sequereneur *A*   [h] nostrique tenantur *A m. pr., corr. to* nostrique ten-
entur *m. alt.*   [i] nos *A*   [j] Partur *A m. pr., F m. pr.; both corr. to* Partus *m. alt.*
[k] istiga *A*

[1] See Robert of Rheims, p. 808; *Gesta Francorum*, p. 49; Raymond of Aguilers, p. 66.
[2] This episode is also described in Raymond of Aguilers, p. 66, Robert of Rheims, pp.
808–9, and the *Chanson d'Antioche*, ll. 6676–721, which is very close to Gilo's account.
Roger, who came from Barneville in the Cotentin, had been a baron of Count Roger of

The sun beat down with its rays on burnished shields as the great
army gradually approached. But they halted at a distance, waiting
for those following on behind—Kerbogha the leader of the army and
the rest of the nobles.[1] [235] Some of the Persians, already seizing the
battlements in hope, made for the plains that stretched out within
sight of the city; they rejoiced to relax in various ways there, and did
not cease from addressing foul words at our men who looked on at
them. They strove to disperse their foaming horses over the grass,
[240] threw their unsheathed swords in the air and caught them
again, they yelled out loud, flew all round threatening the
besieged, and threw spears wildly through the empty air. Our men
thought it safer to keep to sure and certain places than to follow the
uncertainties of chance and to open hostilities. [245] But when the
Turks were already withdrawing, uttering loud cries as they went,
Roger of Barneville pursued the exultant foe with three armed
men;[2] the enemy race lingered, looked back at them, and laid an
ambush beneath an overhanging rock. While our men were pur-
suing some men who were provoking them, [250] the scoundrels
leaped from the shadows and the young men were trapped, cut off;
they turned round in astonishment, then recovered their senses,
and cut their way into those hemming them in, their shields
thrown round on to their backs. Just as hounds seek their prey
when they are unleashed after the running stag, whereas it seeks a
way of escape, [255] and hope adds wings to the hounds, while the
stag is made swift by fear, and soon escapes the hound's jaws, its
prayer answered; just so did the Parthians drive these men head-
long, ever poised to strike them, just so did that company flee, grasp-
ing at the prize of life. Roger goaded on his men and received blows.
[260] His noble nature and courage which knew itself true made him
delay. His bristling shield scarcely held up the forest of missiles on
it; he rallied his flagging horse, and blood stained his weapons.

Sicily since at least 1086, and joined Robert of Normandy's contingent when the cru-
saders were wintering in Calabria or Sicily. He took part in the siege of Nicaea, and was
captured and beheaded by the Turks after leading a sortie from Antioch on 10 June 1098.
Tudebodus Imitatus et Continuatus, p. 198, says his horse stumbled in a swamp, Albert of
Aachen, pp. 407–8, that he was hit in the lung by an arrow. He was subsequently buried
in St Peter's church and referred to as a martyr (see above, Prologue, l. 32 and n.). See
Gesta Francorum, pp. 15–16; Orderic Vitalis, v. 54 n. 2, 102; E. Jamison, 'Some notes on
the *Anonymi Gesta Francorum* with special reference to the Norman contingents from
Italy and Sicily in the First Crusade', in *Studies in French Language and Medieval Literature
Presented to Professor M. K. Pope* (Manchester, 1939), pp. 183–208, at 207–8; David, *Robert
Curthose*, p. 227; Riley-Smith, *Idea of Crusading*, pp. 76, 115.

Oppressis fortuna nocet. Iam deficiebant
Instantes, Rogere, tui iam tuta*[a]* tenebant,
Cum*[b]* te precipitat sonipes male precipitatus,   265
Nec releuaris equi reuoluti mole grauatus.
Qui non parcebas hosti fedaris in alto
Puluere,*[c]* nec uoluit Turcus tibi parcere capto.
Estuat in muris confusa pudore iuuentus
Dum*[d]* premitur iaculis uir fortis*[e]* ab hoste retentus.   270
Auertunt oculos proceres qui prospiciebant
Cum*[f]* per saxa canes*[g]* insignia membra trahebant,
Raptatoque*[h]* uiro tandem*[i]* caput amputat ensis.
Tum*[j]* uero resonant clamoribus agmina densis.
Parthus*[k]* ouat digitisque*[l]* premit caput ille cruentum   275
Prefigensque*[m]* sudi madefactum sanguine mentum
Ora refert ad castra nigro rorantia*[n]* tabo.

Vrbis ad euentus*[o]* nunc ingenium reuocabo.[1]
Vrbi quaque*[p]* die Turci*[q]* sua castra propinquant,
Marte, minis*[r]* clausis suadent*[s]* ut adepta relinquant,   280
Et castrum plures ex illis ingrediuntur:
Intus et exterius ita nostros aggrediuntur.
Non igitur positis telis manus ulla uacabat,
Nec galea quisquam pressum caput*[t]* exonerabat.
Nocte cubant tecti clipeis in puluere uili,   285
Membraque deficiunt ipso cruciata cubili.
Vrbis turbabat loca discursus iaculorum:
Turres inde rigent hirsutaque tecta*[u]* domorum.
Se quoque gentiles in aperta pericula mittunt,
Et prope decertant gladiis, arcusque remittunt   290
Hostes, et nostri minimum*[v]* discrimen habebant.
Omnes quaque die sub castro*[w]* conueniebant.

Iamque opibus minimis a pluribus attenuatis
Vix aliquid uictus restabat in urbe beatis.

---

[a] tute *D m. pr.*   [b] dum *F*   [c] uulnere *F*   [d] cum *G*   [e] fortes *D m. pr.*   [f] dum *A*   [g] canes *om. A m. pr.*   [h] raptoque *A*   [i] subito *ADG*   [j] tunc *ADG*   [k] Partus *A*   [l] digitis *A m. pr., corrected m. alt. (a different hand)*   [m] profigensque *F;* prefigitque *D;* prefiguntque *G*   [n] rotantia *F m. pr.*   [o] euentes *D m. pr.*   [p] namque *F*   [q] turi *F*   [r] nimis *C*   [s] suadent clausis *F*   [t] capud *F*   [u] tela *BC*   [v] modicum *ADG*   [w] castra *F*

Fortune stood against the oppressed. Your attackers were already
weakening, Roger, and your men were already reaching safety,
[265] when your steed stumbled badly and threw you off, and
weighed down by the mass of the fallen horse you did not stand up
again. You who did not spare the enemy were made filthy, deep in
the dust, and the Turks did not wish to spare you when you were
captured. On the walls the young men were in anguish, filled with
shame [270] as that brave man in the enemy's clutches was finished
off with spears. The nobles looking on averted their gaze as the
dogs dragged his noble limbs over the rocks, and a sword at last cut
off the head of the man they had carried away. Then it was that the
column rang out with many a cry. [275] The Parthian was over-
joyed; he picked up that bloody head with his fingers, and fixing its
blood-soaked chin on a spear-point, he carried the head bedewed
with black gore back to the camp.

I shall now recall my attention to what happened in the city.[1] Every
day the Turks drew their camp closer to the city, urging the
besieged [280] with threats of war to leave what they had gained,
and many of them entered the fort: thus they attacked our men
from both inside and outside. Therefore no hand was idle, its
weapons laid aside, and no man relieved his weary head of its hel-
met's weight. [285] At night they lay down under the shelter of their
shields in the foul dust, and their bodies grew weak in agony from
this manner of sleeping. Showers of arrows caused havoc all over
the city, and the towers and roofs of the houses bristled stiff with
them. The heathen exposed themselves to overt danger too, [290]
and the enemy fought with their swords at close quarters, laying
aside their bows, while our men had but little danger to face. They
all gathered each day beneath the fort.

By now, with slender provisions eaten up by a large host,
hardly any food was left in the city for the blessed company.

---

[1] See *Gesta Francorum*, p. 56; Raymond of Aguilers, p. 67; Fulcher of Chartres, p. 243.
On 9 June a Turkish assault launched from the citadel was driven back, but the follow-
ing day Kerbogha's army encircled the city. On 10 June, William of Grandmesnil (who
had married Bohemond's sister Mabilla), his brother Aubrey, and Lambert, count of
Clermont near Liège, escaped from Antioch and made their way to St Simeon. See *Gesta
Francorum*, pp. 56–7; *Die Kreuzzugsbriefe*, p. 166; Raymond of Aguilers, p. 74. Gilo makes
no mention of this and only a brief reference to the earlier departure of Stephen of
Blois. See above, i. 213 ff. and nn., and below, vii. 503 and n.

Ergo fames crudelis adest, crudelior omni 295
Peste.[1] Viri uigilant, fugiunt ieiunia somni.
Deformat macies uultus, nigriora sepultis
Ossibus[a] ossa micant, apparent uiscera multis.
Vulgus iners herbas dubias letumque[b] minantes
Vellit et in duro fraguntur[c] cespite dentes. 300
Frondibus hi gaudent arbusta suis spoliare:
Illi more fere radices, prata uorare.
Multa quidem comedunt hominum non cognita[d] mensis.
Arida facta manus uix pondera sustinet ensis.
O referenda Deo uirtus! Circumdata peste 305
Nostra cohors saturo[e] ieiuna timetur ab hoste.
Res noua, crus asini libris tribus appretiatur,
Quisque dedit pretium, non prodigus inde putatur.
Ora mouent pueri matresque uocant morientes,
Aera pro[f] solitis[g] epulis aurasque terentes.[h] 310
Cursor equus quem uix nuper carcer retinebat
Nunc auido morsu uacuum presepe petebat
Et tandem posita feritate, furore remoto,
Labitur infelix[2] singultans corpore[i] toto.
Deuorat hunc etiam prestans uirtute iuuentus, 315
Et cibus iste placet populis, care[j] licet emptus.
Dum pereunt, dum qui[k] poterat persistere[l] fortis
Viuit, si uiuit quisquam[m] sub imagine mortis,[3]
Vir quidam data nocte sibi solacia sancta
In commune refert—fidei fiducia tanta est!—[4] 320
Ille refert palmam nostris post quinque paratam
Esse dies, hilaratque uiros plebemque uocatam.
Preterea mentes nostrorum letificauit
Lancea que Domini latus innocuum[n] penetrauit.[o]
Hanc Sancti Andree reserauit uisio certa, 325
Cuiusdamque[5] fuit precognitione reperta.[p]

---

[a] ossebus *G m. pr.*   [b] loetumque *G*   [c] luctantur *ADG*   [d] cognit *F*
[e] satiro *F*   [f] aera per pro *D m. pr.*   [g] solites *F m. pr.*   [h] tenentes *F*
[i] pectore *BC*   [j] quare *F*; caro *ADG*   [k] quis *F*   [l] resistere *F*
[m] quisque *F*   [n] innocium *A*   [o] penetriuit *D m. pr.*   [p] *A m. pr. and D m.
pr. omit ll. 325–6*

---

[1] The shortage of food is also noted by Robert of Rheims, pp. 814–15, *fames omni hoste crudelior nostros inuadit*; Raymond of Aguilers, p. 76; *Gesta Francorum*, pp. 57, 62.
[2] Cf. Vergil, *Georg.* iii. 498.   [3] Cf. Ps. 22 (23): 4 for a similar sentiment.

[295] There was cruel hunger as a result, more cruel than any plague.[1] Men stayed awake, and sleep fled from their hunger. Wasting disfigured their faces, and their bones shone darker than the bones of buried men; the insides could be seen on many men. The helpless common folk plucked plants of doubtful nature, threatening death, [300] and their teeth were broken on the hard turf. Some were happy to strip shrubs of their leaves: others ate roots, like wild animals, and consumed the fields. They ate many an item not known to men's dinner-tables. Their hands dried up and could hardly bear the weight of a sword. [305] What courage, thanks to God! Surrounded by plague our company was starving, yet feared by a well-fed foe. A happening without precedent, the leg of an ass was priced at three pounds, and anyone who paid it was not thought extravagant for doing so. Children moved their lips and, as they died, called to their mothers, [310] gnawing at the airy breezes, instead of the food they were used to. A charger which not long ago the stall could hardly hold, now scoured its empty pen, gnawing ravenously with its teeth, and at last abandoned its wildness, its frenzy gone, and slumped wretchedly,[2] heaving sighs with its whole body. [315] Even this charger was devoured by the young knights, and that sort of food was welcome to the people, though it was dearly bought. While they were dying, while he who could remain courageous yet lived—if anyone is alive with images of death all about him[3]—a certain man let it be known to all that, during the night, help from heaven had been vouchsafed them— so great was his trust in faith![4] [321] He recounted that victory was in store for our men after five days, and made cheerful the men and the common folk he had summoned. Moreover the lance which had pierced our Lord's innocent side brought joy to the minds of our men. [325] A sure vision of St Andrew disclosed this, and it was rediscovered by the foreknowledge of a certain man.[5]

[4] The enclitic *est* appears to break the caudate rhyme-scheme (and to introduce elision, a practice which Gilo is elsewhere at pains to avoid). It may have been swallowed up by the elision in the pronunciation of Gilo's day.

[5] Gilo here links the vision of Stephen of Valence, who claimed that Christ had appeared to him and promised that if the army repented he would send them aid, with Peter Bartholomew's revelation of the burial place of the Holy Lance. For other accounts of these visions, see *Gesta Francorum*, pp. 57–60; Raymond of Aguilers, pp. 68–72, 75; Fulcher of Chartres, pp. 244–7. See also C. Morris, 'Policy and wisdom: the case of the Holy Lance at Antioch', in *War and Government in the Middle Ages: Essays in Honour of J. O. Prestwich*, ed. J. Gillingham and J. C. Holt (Woodbridge, 1984), pp. 33–45; Runciman, 'The Holy Lance found at Antioch', *Analecta Bollandiana*, lxviii (1950), 190–207.

Post hec congressum castellanis uetuere,
Et*a* murum nostri gentilibus opposuere.
Pluribus exemplis ubi spes est reddita uite,
Tertio[1] ieiunant omnes*b* sicut Niniuite.   330

Tunc heremita ducem Turcorum Petrus adiuit,
Qui procerum portans mandata petenda petiuit.[2]
Corbana dux sublimis equo se forte ferebat
Ad portum,*c* lasciua cohors utrinque fremebat,
Cum subito Petrus turbam subit impedientem.   335
Nec timuit quendam Turcum*d* sibi*e* precipientem
Vt caput inflectat, uultumque potentis*f* adoret,
Pectore sic placido demissa uoce peroret.
Dum*g* negat hic homini deitatis reddere cultum,
Illius incuruat gentilis dextera uultum,   340
Illius a stolidis bona deridetur egestas,*h*
Sed tamen est illi fandi concessa potestas.
'Maxime dux', uir paruus ait, 'nos non aliena
Querimus, ad nostros urbs*i* pertinet Antiochena.
Cur igitur nos a propria uis pellere sede?   345
Si censura mouet te iuris, ab urbe recede,[3]
Aut, si credere uis, erroris*j* lege remota,[4]
Sit regno*k* transcripta tuo Romania tota:
Fies rex Syrie, rex istius regionis,
Tuque potens multum multis onerabere donis;   350
Aut,*l* si mente sedet pugnandi tanta uoluntas,
Si mauis spectare manus ad prelia iunctas,
In paribus sortem reliquorum precipe poni,
Quique pari bello cedent, cedant regioni;
Pugnent*m* cum totidem ter deni uel duodeni;*n*   355
Discedant, si forte*o* ualent discedere, uicti.'[5]

---

a at *A*   *b* ieiunant omnes triduo *G*   *c* portam *BC*   *d* Turcum
quemdam *B*   *e* sibi *om. G m. pr.*   *f* petentis *A*   *g* cum *G*
h honestas *Riant*   *i* urs *F*   *j* erroris erroris *F*   *k* regno *om. F*
l aud *F*; at *ADG*   *m* pugnant *D*   *n* triginta siue uiginti *ADG;* ter deni seu
duodeni *BC*   *o* sorte *Riant*

---

[1] This biblical allusion is puzzling, as there is no reference in the book of Jonah to the
time that the Ninevites fasted. There may be some confusion with Esth. 4: 16, where it is
the Jews who fast; and cf. also Bede, *Historia ecclesiastica*, ii. 2, *peracto ieiunio triduano*.
Gilo's use of *tertio* is also perplexing, as is shown by the rewriting of the verse found in
MS G. It may be a confusion with the three days and nights which Jonah spent in the

After this they prevented those in the fort from meeting together, and our men set a wall against the heathen. When hope of life was given back to them by many token happenings, [330] they all fasted three times,[1] like the Ninevites.

Then Peter the Hermit went to the Turkish general, carrying despatches from the nobles, and he sought what needed to be sought.[2] The haughty general, Kerbogha, happened to be riding to the harbour, and an insolent company was frolicking all around him, [335] when suddenly Peter met the throng in his way. He was not afraid of any Turk who instructed him to bow his head and worship the face of the ruler, but with a calm heart he spoke in a quiet voice. When he said that he would not give the worship due to God to a man, [340] a heathen hand forced his face downward, and his honest poverty was mocked by these fools, but even so he was given permission to speak. 'Great general,' the little man said, 'we do not ask for what is not ours; the city of Antioch belongs to our side. [345] Why therefore do you wish to drive us from our home? If you are swayed by considerations of justice, withdraw from the city,[3] or, if you will believe, and discard your law of error,[4] then let all Rūm be handed over to your kingdom: you shall become king of Syria, king of this region, [350] and you shall be laden with many gifts, as a mighty and powerful man; or, if the will to fight is so great in your mind, if you prefer to watch bands of men joined in the fight, then order the fate of the rest of your men to be placed on equally-matched warriors, and whoever shall give way in an even contest, let them leave the country; [355] let thirty or thirty-six fight with an equal number; the losers may depart,[5] if by chance they are well enough to depart.'

---

fish's belly (Jonah 2: 1, Matt. 12: 40). During the siege of Antioch, the crusaders took part in two three-day fasts and associated penitential rituals. See *Gesta Francorum*, pp. 67–8; Fulcher of Chartres, p. 257; Siberry, *Criticism of Crusading*, pp. 74, 90–1.

[2] For other accounts of Peter's mission to Kerbogha on 27 June, see *Gesta Francorum*, pp. 66–7; Raymond of Aguilers, p. 79; Fulcher of Chartres, pp. 247–50. He was accompanied by a Frank named Herluin, who spoke both Arabic and Persian. This is the first reference to Peter the Hermit in Gilo's own work. See above, ii. 5–6 and n. Riant's reading *honestas* in l. 341 is unsupported and spoils the sense. It was Peter's *egestas* that the Turks derided.

[3] For a parallel, see Robert of Rheims, p. 825: 'si ratio iuris tecum esset et censura aequitatis nobiscum agere uelles . . .'.

[4] *Gesta Francorum*, pp. 66–7, also refers to an offer of conversion, which was reciprocated by Kerbogha.

[5] See also Fulcher of Chartres, p. 248.

Inquit[a] ad hec ensem quatiens dux Corbana nudum
'Tune putas impune mihi talem dare ludum?
Hoc gladio caput amittes,[b] truncabitur isto
Gens que nescio cui studet obsequium dare Christo.'   360
Discedit Petrus dictis commotus acerbis.
Arma parant proceres[c] auditis ordine uerbis,
Illa nocte duces[d1] uigilant, errata fatentur,
Turba[e] gemens aras tenet, ecclesieque replentur.
Luce data[2] ter tres de tota gente statute   365
Sunt acies,[3] propriumque ducem sunt queque secute:[f]
Quas habeant in fronte manus ibi disposuere,
Quas medium uel quas[g] cupiant[h] extrema tenere.
Sistitur Hugo prior, medium robur tenuere
Magnanimi septem, Boimundo deseruere   370
Vltima, custodes per muros[i] instituere.[j]
Hic ducis officium presul Podiensis habebat[4]
Et populos egri Raimundi rite regebat;
Lancea sancta[k5] Dei preuecta uiros animabat,
Membraque pontificis lucens lorica grauabat.   375
Hic[l] populi uoces ubi uoce manuque repressit,
Dixit (eo dicente[6] solo gens prona silescit):
'Rebus in extremis uires effundite totas,
O proceres, renouate manus Turcis bene notas,
Ite per ignauos, gladiis disrumpite gentes   380
Quas[m] primi iactus exarmant deficientes.
Mittet in auxilium[n] Deus angelicam legionem,[7]
Opprimet hunc populum uelut oppressit Pharaonem.
O quanto rapitur gens insensata furore!
Hec emit infernum proprio malesana cruore,   385
Penaque lucratur penam, caro bis cruciatur,

---

[a] inquid *F;* dixit *ADG*   [b] amites *D, F m. alt.;* admittes *A, F m. pr.*   [c] hostes *BC*   [d] patres *ADG*   [e] turma *BC*   [f] statute *F m. pr.*   [g] quos medios uel quos *ADG*   [h] cupiunt *ADG;* capiant *BC*   [i] per muros custodes *BCG*   [j] constituere *BCDG*   [k] sancta lancea *D m. pr.*   [l] sic *F*   [m] quos *D*   [n] axilium *D*

---

[1] ADG's reading *patres* is curious, and must have meant something like 'elders'. The reading of BCF makes much better sense.
[2] The army prepared for battle on the early morning of 28 June.
[3] See Albert of Aachen, pp. 420–1; Fulcher of Chartres, p. 251; *Gesta Francorum,* p. 68. The *Gesta* maintains that the army was dra·vn up in six battle-lines: the first led by Hugh of Vermandois and the count of Flanders, the second by Godfrey of Bouillon, the

The general Kerbogha brandished his bared sword, and said in reply: 'Do you think you can make such sport of me and get away with it? You shall lose your head by this sword, [360] and by it the people shall be slain that is eager to pay homage to some Christ, whoever he may be.' Disturbed by these bitter words, Peter departed. When they had listened to all he had to report, the nobles made ready their arms, and that night the leaders[1] kept vigil, confessing their sins, while the weeping crowd held fast to the altars, and the churches were filled. [365] At first light,[2] nine battle-lines were drawn up from the whole people,[3] and each of them followed its own leader: there they drew up those bands whom they could position in the front, and those they wished to take the middle ground and the rear. Hugh took his stand in front, [370] seven stout-hearted leaders held the centre in strength, and they left the last positions to Bohemond, setting guards on the walls. Here the bishop of Le Puy did the duty of a general,[4] and duly governed the men of Raymond, who was ill; the holy lance of God,[5] carried before him, gave heart to the men, [375] and a glittering breastplate weighed heavily on his priestly frame. When he had stilled the people's voices with a word and a gesture, he spoke (and, as he spoke,[6] the people kept silence, prostrate on the ground): 'In these dire straits pour out all your strength, O nobles, refresh the hands that the Turks know so well, [380] and go through these cowards, shatter with your swords these weakling peoples whom the first shock of battle disarms. God will send his legion of angels to help,[7] he will overwhelm this people as he overwhelmed Pharaoh. Oh, how great is the frenzy with which this senseless race is seized! [385] In their madness, they are buying hell with their own blood, they earn pain with pain, their flesh is twice crucified,

---

third by Robert of Normandy, the fourth by Adhémar of Le Puy, the fifth by Tancred, and the sixth by Bohemond himself. Raymond of Toulouse, who was ill, remained behind to keep watch on the citadel. Raymond of Aguilers, p. 79, states that there were four divisions, each consisting of knights and infantry. See also Smail, *Crusading Warfare*, pp. 172–4. Note in this section that the abrupt changes of gender in ADG are altered to feminines throughout in BCF, referring back to *manus* in l. 367.

[4] For the role of Adhémar of Le Puy on the First Crusade, see above, i. 254–5 and n.

[5] The Holy Lance was carried into battle by the historian and chaplain to Raymond of Toulouse, Raymond of Aguilers (see his own account of the event, p. 82).

[6] Robert of Rheims, pp. 829–30, and the *Historia Gotefredi*, pp. 485–6, are the only sources to refer to this sermon. Even there, the details are different from Gilo's account. Cf. also Vergil, *Aen.* x. 101.

[7] Cf. Matt. 26: 53. *Gesta Francorum*, p. 69, describes the appearance of a heavenly army led by SS George, Mercurius, and Demetrius.

Atque per hanc mortem mortem sine fine meretur.[1]
At[a] nobis sit[b] siue pati postrema necesse,[c]
Siue Deus superat[d] gentiles, quod precor esse,
Exitus est felix: orietur morte corona,[2]   390
Militibus diuersa dabit uictoria dona.
Vincetis:[e] uirtutis erit uestre monimentum,
Parthorum cedes iam conspicio morientum.[f]
Ne[g] dubitate, suos equites[h3] Deus haud patietur
Plura pati[4] quam ferre queant,[i] ut glorificetur.   395
Letitie stimulis agitari sentio[j] gentem:
Supportate,[k 5] uiri, me gaudia uestra trahentem.
Sint rata, Christe, precor, nostris gratissima[l] uota
Vt uincamus.' 'Amen' respondit[m] gens prece mota.[n]

Interea mandat Persarum[6] dux[o] Boimundo   400
Primo suos equites duci,[p] nostrosque[q] secundo,
Nomen[7] et a reliqua iubet hoc abradere gente;
Neue decus mundi mittatur in arma repente
Precaueant, numeroque[r] pari pugnetur utrinque.[8]
Tunc ita legatum dux increpat 'ista relinque!   405
Desine uana loqui, nos ad maiora uocamur.
Vincamus simul, o comites, simul aut moriamur'
(Respexitque suos comites), 'bona uel mala uere
Proueniunt[s] sanctis.'[9] Nichil interea timuere
Nostri, sed portas egressi distribuere   410
Per loca certa uiros, dum tutus ab urbe recessit
Nuntius. Ista, Deus, tua dispensatio fecit.[t]
Presbiteri turres[u] rara[v] cinxere[w] corona,[10]

---

[a] et *F*   [b] sit *om. D m. pr.*   [c] necessit *F m. pr.*   [d] superet *AB*
[e] uinceris *D m. pr.;* uincentis *F m. pr.*   [f] *For this line BC read* uincere uos uideo tris-
temque necem morientum   [g] nec *F*   [h] pugiles *ADG*   [i] queat *C*
[j] senscio *A*   [k] sub portate *B*   [l] grauissima *F*   [m] respondet *G*
[n] nota *B*   [o] dux Persarum *ADG*   [p] dici *ADG*   [q] uestrosque *D m. pr.*
[r] numero *G*   [s] prouenient *BC;* prouenniunt *G*   [t] gessit *ADG*
[u] muros *DG*   [v] tara *A m. pr.;* parua *G*   [w] cinxtere *D m. pr.*

---

[1] This verse, added only in MS G, is merely a gloss on the previous line. The reason
for its addition may be that l. 386 is the sole leonine in a section of *caudati*, and the
Charleville Poet makes l. 386 into the first half of another end-rhymed couplet.
[2] Cf. 2 Tim. 4: 8; Jas. 1: 12; Rev. 2: 10. Those who died on the crusade believed that
they would become martyrs. See above, Prologue, ll. 31–2 and n.
[3] ADG's *pugiles*, attested in Latham as a 'champion', lacks the nobility of BCF's
reading.

and through this death they merit death without end.[1] But whether it is necessary for us to suffer the final fate, or God defeats the heathen—which I pray may be the case—[390] our end is a happy one: in death a crown will arise,[2] and victory will grant many kinds of gifts to you soldiers. You shall conquer: this will be the monument to your courage, and already I see the slaughter of the dying Parthians. Do not doubt, God will not permit his knights[3] [395] to suffer more than they can endure,[4] so that he may be glorified. I feel this people being stirred by the goads of joy: men, give me your support[5] as I bring joy for you. I pray, O Christ, that your most grateful prayers for our men may prove sure, that we may win.' 'Amen!', replied the people, moved by his prayer.

[400] In the meantime, the leader of the Persians[6] sent word to Bohemond that his own knights should be led out first, and then ours, and told him to put aside this honour[7] from the rest of the people, saying that they ought to beware lest the glory of the world be sent into battle at once, and that the fight ought to be undertaken by an equal number from each side.[8] [405] Then the duke spoke brusquely to the envoy in these words: 'Away with such talk! Desist from empty words, we are summoned to greater things. Let us conquer in one blow, fellow nobles, or let us perish in one blow' (he looked round at his comrades as he said this); 'truly even defeat proves a blessing for the saints[9] of God.' In the meantime our men were afraid of nothing, [410] but rather went outside the gates and posted men in sure positions, until the messenger had left the city in safety. Your direction, O God, brought these things about. The priests manned the towers in a sparse ring,[10]

---

[4] Cf. 1 Ccr. 10: 13.

[5] *Supportate* is a late usage, meaning 'support' in an abstract sense. There is also a hint at the image of Moses being held up by Aaron and Hur, in Exod. 17: 12.

[6] Raymond of Aguilers, pp. 80–1, stated that Kerbogha received news of the Frankish advance whilst playing chess.

[7] The sense of this line is very obscure: *hoc nomen* must mean something like 'the honour of, or renown of, the Christian force'; cf. Vergil, *Aen.* vii. 717, Lucan, *Bellum ciuile*, vi. 759, and *nomen Christi*, which has a similar sense, at viii. 183, below. See also Lewis and Short, *A Latin Dictionary*, 'nomen', B.4.

[8] The proposal to have individual armed combats, rather than a full-scale battle, was also made by Peter the Hermit on his mission to the Turkish camp. See above, vii. 333 and n.

[9] See *Gesta Francorum*, p. 68; Fulcher of Chartres, pp. 253–4.

[10] Cf. Vergil, *Aen.* x. 122.

Illorum iacet in muro*a* pars maxima prona,
Ornatique stolis quas*b* sumunt tempore misse   415
Altius hi psallunt, hi flent orantque remisse.[1]

At sonuere tube, populos prior Hugo feroces
Inuadit,*c* solitas emittunt*d* undique uoces,
Francorumque cohors longo distenta recessu*e*
In seriem coniuncta pari petit agmina gressu.   420
Stant infra iactum teli totoque uigore,
Inflectunt arcus Turci neruo meliore
Intensos: stridendo uolant per inane sagitte.*f*
Instat eis oblita breuis gens Gallica uite.
Paulatim dant pressa retro uestigia Parthi,   425
Vicinoque timent dextras committere marti.
Spicula Turcorum diuertit ab agmine uentus.
Eurardus[2] de Puteolo*g* feruensque iuuentus
In bello*h* querunt bellum, gladiosque leuabant
Percussi, quos percuterent non inueniebant.   430
Nuntius ecce celer missus uenit a Boimundo,
Qui, dum pauca refert, sua preterradit*i* harundo
Timpora, sed tamen hec inquit: 'Boimundus utrinque
Hostibus urgetur: fugitiuos, Hugo, relinque!'
Conuersis*j* mox Hugo suis Arabes speculatur   435
Hastatos circa Boimundum. Tunc ita fatur:
'Quod iuuenes optatis*k* adest! Huc*l* ferreus hastis
Horret ager, uertamur*m* ad hos, incumbite*n* uastis
Viribus!'[3] Ergo manus iungunt comes et Boimundus.
Hic etiam dux ille ducum stabat Godefridus,*o*   440
At*p* contra*q* tendunt Arabes*r* regesque potentes
Et rex Damasci Lucas;[4] illicque furentes
Stant*s* amici*t* duo (namque duos sic turba uocabat):

a muris *ADG*	*b* stolis pars per quas *F m. pr.*	*c* inuasit *BC;* inuadit et *A*
d inuadunt *DG*	*e* recursu *BC*	*f* *BC omit this line*	*g* de Pusiaco *ADG*
h bellum *F*	*i* perterradit *A*	*j* conuersus *D*	*k* obstatis *D m. pr.*
l hic *G*	*m* uertatur *F*	*n* incombite *BC*	*o* Boimundus *F m. pr.*
p et *F*	*q* cuncta *F*	*r* Arabes *om. D m. pr.*	*s* sunt *DG;* ssunt (*sic*) *A*
t proamici *A*		

[1] See *Gesta Francorum*, p. 68; Raymond of Aguilers, p. 81.
[2] Everard of Le Puiset, viscount of Chartres. He served with three of the leading figures on the First Crusade: Robert of Normandy, Hugh of Vermandois, and Bohemond. See Albert of Aachen, p. 362; Robert of Rheims, p. 833; Orderic Vitalis,

with the greater part of them lying flat on the wall, [415] and
dressed in the vestments which they put on at the time of mass,
some of them loudly sang psalms, while others wept and prayed
quietly.[1]

The bugles blared, and Hugh led the attack against the fierce
peoples; they uttered their accustomed cries all around, and the
band of Franks, over a considerable distance, [420] sought out the
ranks joined together in rows, stepping regularly in formation. They
held their positions within range with all their might, as the Turks
bent their bows strung with a better thong: arrows flew, whistling
through the void. Forgetful of brief life, the men of Gaul bore down
on them. [425] Little by little the Parthians gave way under pressure,
and were afraid of joining their right hands in combat at close
quarters. The wind blew the Turks' missiles away from the column
of men. Everard of Le Puiset[2] and his impetuous youths looked for
fighting in the fighting itself, and raised their swords, [430] but
though they were struck they found no-one to strike. Then suddenly
a swift messenger came, sent by Bohemond; arrows whistled close
by his head as he related his brief message, but none the less he
spoke these words: 'Bohemond is pressed by the enemy on both
sides: Hugh, let these runaways alone!' [435] Hugh quickly turned
his men about, and saw the Arabs armed with spears around
Bohemond. Then he spoke: 'Young men, here is what you are
hoping for! The field is bristling with iron spears here, let us turn to
these men, lay on with a mighty effort!'[3] And so the count and
Bohemond joined forces. [440] Godfrey, that leader among leaders,
was standing here too. But against them there advanced the Arabs,
and their powerful kings, and Dukak, king of Damascus;[4] the two
friends (for the throng called them two such) stood there, seething:

v. 30. Everard probably died in 1099 from wounds received at the battle of Ascalon. See
above, v. 429–30 and n.

[3] The reference here is unclear. Robert of Flanders, Hugh of Vermandois, and
Godfrey of Bouillon led the attack on the Turkish camp. In the midst of the battle, how-
ever, Bohemond prevented an encircling manœuvre by sending Rainald of Toul, in
command of a seventh division, to attack the Turkish flank. See *Gesta Francorum*, pp.
68–9.

[4] Kerbogha's forces included men provided by other Turkish princes and emirs such
as Dukak of Damascus. See above, v. 111 and n. Rivalries between the various con-
tingents and leaders led to desertions from the Turkish force as it waited outside
Antioch. See Ibn al-'Athīr, p. 194.

Dux Boimundus adhuc, Godefridus et ipse uacabat.
Bellum primus init Magnus frenumque furenti   445
Laxat*a* equo cuidamque uiros in marte monenti*b*
Hasta disrupit guttur, uitamque loquenti
Abstulit et uoces. Hastilis lancea lenti
Frangitur: ille gemens petit ore solum morienti.*c*
Concurrunt*d* Arabes et Francigene uiolenter.   450
Pugna grauis surgit, iaculis*e* obtexitur ether.
Hic Balgentiacus Odo*f* [1] primus*g* ubique ruebat
Vexillumque tenens se non retinere ualebat;
Cum degustasset*h* latus huic non uisa sagitta,
Stridula signiferum priuauit*i* lancea uita.   455
Lapsus at*j* ille cadens humectat sanguine signum
Et quo conciderat traxit*k* de uulnere lignum.
Mox succedit ei signumque leuat Beniensis*l,m*
Guillelmus,[2] fecitque uiam iuueni*n* suus ensis.

Non procul hinc ibat nostrorum parua caterua,*o*   460
Quos nimis urgebat*p* Turcorum turba proterua,
Turbaque fraude nocens ignes per gramina sparsit,
Quos aluit uentus, et sic ager*q* aridus arsit.
Ardor at ille dedit fumum tenebrasque*r* creauit,
Fumus in aduersos impulsus eos hebetauit,[3]   465
Perque cauam*s* nubem campo trahit hostis in equo
Atque necat pedites ter centum uulnere ceco.
Tunc cum Pagano Beluacensis Rainaldus,*t* [4]

a laxa *G m. pr.*   *b* mouenti *ADG*   *c* *A omits this line*   *d* concurrunt
om. A   *e* telis *DG*   *f* Obdo *F m. pr.*   *g* pronus *CDF;* prius *B*
h deglutasset *A*   *i* priualuit *F m. pr.*   *j* ad *A*   *k* taxit *A m. pr.*
l Bemensis *D;* Boemensis *A*   *m* *D m. pr. puts this line after l. 459*   *n* iuuenique
uiam fecit *ADG*   *o* catrrua *G m. pr.*   *p* angebat *BC*   *q* aer *D*
r dedit flammas fumumque *F*   *s* *?* causim *A*   *t* Tainaldus *BC*

---

[1] Odo of Beaugency was Hugh of Vermandois's standard-bearer. See Robert of
Rheims, p. 831, *Chanson d'Antioche*, ll. 8650–5. His brother Ralph was also a member of
the expedition, and was married to Hugh's daughter. See Baldric of Dol, pp. 17, 47, 65.

[2] See Robert of Rheims, p. 831; *Chanson d'Antioche*, ll. 8661–2; *Balduini III Historia
Nicaena uel Antiochena*, p. 171. William of Benium (Bény-sur-Mer) is otherwise unident-
ified.

[3] *Gesta Francorum*, pp. 68–9, notes that the burning of grass was a pre-arranged signal
by Kerbogha, a sign that he had been defeated and that the Turkish army should retreat.
Gilo seems to think it was a ruse by the Turks to appease the Franks, and then make it
easier to kill them (this seems to be the force of ll. 466–7).

[4] See, especially, *Chanson d'Antioche*, ll. 9145–62:

thus far, duke Bohemond and Godfrey too had been idle. [445] Hugh was the first to enter the fight, easing the reins of his frenzied horse, and with his lance he ripped out the throat of a man giving orders to men in the fray, taking his life and his speech while he was speaking. The lance with its pliant shaft was shattered; the man groaned, and fell face down, dying on the earth. [450] The Arabs and the Franks charged one another with a violent crash. A fierce fight ensued; the air was thick with spears. Here Odo of Beaugency,[1] who was everywhere the first to lead the charge, hold-ing the banner, could not hold himself back; an arrow, unseen by him, gave him a first taste of wounding in his side, [455] and then a whistling spear took his life away from the standard-bearer. He slipped and, falling, moistened the standard with his blood; and he dragged the wooden shaft from the wound by which he had fallen. William of Benium[2] quickly took his place, and raised up the stan-dard; his sword cut a pathway for the young man.

[460] Not far from here a small band of our men was proceeding, and a fierce host of Turks was pressing them hard. Harming them by deceit, the host scattered fires over the grass, the wind fanned them, and so the parched plain blazed, but that blaze gave off smoke, creating darkness, [465] and the smoke, driven against them, blunted the edge of their attack.[3] The enemy drew three hundred infantry though enveloping cloud across the flat plain, and killed them with an unseen wound. Then Rainald of Beauvais,[4] Pagan,

> A tant es vos Gerart molt tost esperronant,
> Nes fu de Meleun, tot ot le poil ferrant,
> Mais malades ot jut grant piece de devant;
> En la presse se fiert: jo le tieng pour enfant,
> Car tost l'orent ocis li cuivert mescreant.
> Estes me vos Evrart a esperon brocant,
> Nes estoit del Puisac, molt ot fier hardement,
> Droon et Clarembaut et Thomas le vaillant,
> Et Paien de Belvais sor un destrier ferrant;
> Quant voiant mort Gerart, forment en sont pesant;
> De lor ami vengier sont forment desirant.

See also *Balduini III Historia Nicaena uel Antiochem*, p. 172; Robert of Rheims, p. 833. Otherwise nothing is known about either Rainald or Pagan. Albert of Aachen, pp. 293–5, 299, 304–5, mentions Thomas of Marle, Drogo of Nesle, and Clarembald of Vendeuil as members of Emicho of Leiningen's contingent, who later joined the army of Hugh of Vermandois. They subsequently had very varied careers: Thomas died as count of Amiens in 1130 (Albert of Aachen, pp. 315, 332, 422, 464, 468; Riley-Smith, *Idea of Crusad-ing*, p. 51); Drogo followed Baldwin to Edessa and then Jerusalem (see above, vi. 298 and note); Clarembald distinguished himself in the crusade itself (Albert of Aachen, p. 398; Riley-Smith, *Idea of Crusading*, p. 51).

Cumque Drogone[a] Thomas et bellipotens Clarebaldus
Et reliqui subitis[b] se mortibus[c] eripuere,   470
Et rapido[d] cursu[1] belli robur petiere.
Fortis ut ista cohors se magno iunxit Hugoni,
Immenso ueluti cedunt[e] armenta leoni[f],
Sic[g] Arabes illis: uertuntur scuta reiecta,
Dorsum quisque tegit pudibunda fronte retecta.[h]   475
'Vicisti Deus omnipotens!' clamat Godefridus,
Instat ui patria[2] primusque uolat Boimundus.
Corrigiis agit hostis equos, insibilat ether,[i]
Puluis ad astra uolat morientum[j] sanguine[k] teter.[3]
Contigerant collem quemdam populi fugientes.   480
Tunc Parthi latus in leuum sese replicantes
Post longam restare fugam fortes uoluerunt,[l]
Arcu conuerso nostros iterum petierunt.[m]
Impiger ergo senex Geraldus[n] de Melione,[4]
Tempore qui longo fuit eger in obsidione,   485
Sicut inermis erat, medios irrupit in hostes
Et meruit pulchram mortem confossus. In hostes
De nostris aliqui[o] tribus inuasere diebus,[5]
Sed tantis non sufficiet mea pagina rebus.
Quinque camelorum[p] capiunt et milia dena.   490
Pluribus inueniunt spoliis tentoria plena.[6]
De Turcis equites decies sunt mille necati,
Cum totidem pedites miseri[q] non sunt numerati.
Preterea qui castellum ciuile tenebant
Castellum nostris reddunt quia mira uidebant.[7]   495
Regius[r] inter eos iuuenis de Perside natus
Est cum ter centum sacro de fonte leuatus.[8]
Deleo de nostro, de qualicunque libello
Hos quos non puduit sese subducere[s] bello:
Hec miseranda cohors uelut ad uomitum reuocata[9]   500

---

[a] drogene *D*   [b] subiti *G*   [c] moribus *D*   [d] e trapido *A;* et rabido
BC   [e] cedant *D*   [f] *C reads* 'comp' *in the margin here*   [g] hic *F*
[h] *A m. pr. omits this line; it is added at the foot of the page by a second hand*   [i] ether *D m.*
alt., written over an erasure   [j] morientium *B m. pr.*   [k] sangne *D m. pr., corr. to*
sangine *m. alt.*   [l] uoluere *AD*   [m] petiere *AD*   [n] Giraldus *BC;* Girar-
dus *F*   [o] manubias nostri *D*   [p] camalorum *A*   [q] miseri pedites *BC*
[r] reius *D*   [s] submittere *BC*

---

[1] The text of MS G breaks off abruptly in mid-page at this line.
[2] Cf. Vergil, *Aen.* ii. 491.

Thomas, and Drogo, and Clarembald the mighty warrior, [470] and the rest snatched themselves from their sudden deaths, and made for the main body of fighting with a rapid charge.[1] As that brave squadron joined itself to Hugh the Great, the Arabs fell before them just as herds of cattle fall before a massive lion: they turned tail, with shields swung round, [475] and every man of them covered his back, his face already covered in shame. 'Almighty God, you have conquered!', shouted Godfrey. Bohemond pressed on in his native strength[2] and flew ahead of them. The enemy thrashed their horses, the air whistled, and dust flew up to the stars, foul with the blood of the dying.[3] [480] As they ran away, the peoples had seized hold of a certain hill; then, turning themselves round to their left, the brave Parthians wanted to halt their lengthy flight, and with bows bent taut they again sought out our men. And so the elderly but active Gerald of Melion,[4] [465] who was ill for a long time during the siege, charged into the midst of the enemy, unarmed as he was, and was struck down, worthy indeed of a beautiful death. Some of our men assailed the enemy for three days,[5] but my page does not have space for such great matters. [490] They captured fifteen thousand camels; they found the tents full of many kinds of plunder.[6] Of the Turks, ten thousand knights were slain, and the wretched infantry were not reckoned with that number. Moreover those who were occupying the citadel [495] handed it over to our men, because they observed such wonders.[7] Among them a young prince, Persian-born, was raised up from the holy font of baptism with three hundred others.[8] I blot out from my book—from any book, indeed—those who were not ashamed to sneak away from the fighting; [500] this pitiable company, as though called back to their own vomit,[9]

---

[3] Robert of Rheims, p. 833, uses similar imagery.

[4] Gerard (or Gerald, as Gilo calls him) of Melion (Melun?) is also mentioned by Robert of Rheims, p. 833; *Balduini III Historia Nicaena uel Antiochena*, p. 172; and the *Chanson d'Antioche*, ll. 9145-9 (cited above, pp. 190-1, n. 4), but otherwise he has not been identified.

[5] The Turks were pursued up to the Orontes bridge and Tancred's castle: *Gesta Francorum*, p. 70; Albert of Aachen, pp. 425-7.

[6] See *Gesta Francorum*, p. 70; Albert of Aachen, pp. 421-9; Raymond of Aguilers, p. 83; Fulcher of Chartres, p. 256. Robert of Rheims, p. 834, parallels Gilo closely in mentioning the capture of 15,000 camels.

[7] See Raymond of Aguilers, pp. 82-3. The citadel was commanded by Aḥmad ibn-Tūtūn, one of Kerbogha's trusted lieutenants.

[8] The baptism of Aḥmad ibn-Tūtūn is also recorded in *Gesta Francorum*, p. 71. See also above, iv. 111 and n.   [9] Cf. Prov. 26: 11.

Pretulit exilium patrie, mundo sociata.[1]
Pretereo quare nostros timuere iuuare
Consilio Stephani Constantinopolitani.[2]

Prima cohors primique duces loca prima tuentur;
Vulgus in urbe*ᵃ* tenet medium murique replentur.   505
Tunc regalis Hugo,[3] qui Magnus iure uocatur,
Nomen dote replens, communi uoce rogatur
Vt Constantini*ᵇ* petat urbem nomine dictam.
Imperii domino*ᶜ*[4] regionem reddere uictam
Cura*ᵈ* fuit: lex, iura, fides data, pignora, pactum,   510
Vox populi iusteque*ᵉ* preces misere coactum.[5]

ᵃ inherme *AD*   *ᵇ* Constantin *A*   *ᶜ* imperio Domini *D;* induperatori *A*
ᵈ iura *F*   *ᵉ* iuxteque *A, D m. pr.*

---

[1] Cf. Jas. 4: 4, 1 John 2: 15.
[2] Fulcher of Chartres, p. 228, places Stephen of Blois's departure from Antioch on 2 June, the day before the capture of the city. The *Gesta Francorum*, p. 63, sets it after the city had been taken, but whilst the citadel was still in Turkish hands and Kerbogha's army was approaching. Stephen and William of Grandmesnil (above, vii. 279 and n.) met the Byzantine relief force at Philomelium when it arrived in mid-June. Painting a desperate picture of the crusaders' plight, they persuaded it to turn back.

were allied to the world, and put exile before their homeland.[1] I
pass over why the men of Constantinople were afraid of helping
our men because of Stephen's counsel.[2]

The foremost company and the foremost leaders watched over the
foremost places; [505] in the city, the common folk occupied the
middle ground and thronged the walls. Then princely Hugh,[3] who
is rightly called 'the Great' and endowed that name with lustre,
was asked by common accord to journey to the city named after
Constantine. It was his duty to hand over the conquered land to
the lord of the empire;[4] [510] law, justice, the oath they had sworn,
their pledges, their allegiance, the voice of the people and their
righteous prayers sent him, compelled to do this.[5]

[3] Hugh was commissioned to inform Alexius of the capture of Antioch. He set out in
early July 1098 and was accompanied on his journey by Baldwin of Hainault. See above,
i. 207 and n.; *Gesta Francorum*, p. 72; Robert of Rheims, p. 837.

[4] Both sides of the tradition attest the reading adopted, *imperii domino* (though D as
often reverses the case-endings, in error). A's *induperatori* is very rare, and if it is not to
be regarded as an interpolation, may perhaps (following the principle of *difficilior lectio
potior*, whereby harder readings are held to be correct, having been replaced with easier
ones by scribes) have been Gilo's first reading, but its rarity in the tradition makes it
likely that the reading printed is his own preference.

[5] On the oaths sworn to Alexius, see above, iii. 440 and n.

Ast alii proceres[a] uoto iam mente propinqui
Vtiliter statuunt ad tempus bella relinqui:[1]
Estus enim populos siccataque terra grauaret,[b]
Vreret estus eos, potum dare terra negaret.[c]
Est igitur requies lassorum reddita membris,   5
Dimittenda breui sub prima luce Nouembris.[2]
Turba partita, loca sunt diuersa petita,
Et quisquis lucro gaudebat[d] in urbe manebat.
Obsequiis erat hic studiosus et era merebat.[3]
Ex illis plures Raimundus miles alebat,[e]   10
Quem cognomento Piletum gens nostra uocabat.[4]
Otia cum multis hic non ignaua[f] secutus
Prouidet ut nequeat gentilis uiuere tutus.
Ergo duas urbes pertransit[g] et ad[h] Thalamana[i5]
Improuisus adest. Hoc castrum gens Suriana   15
Seruabat, que sponte uirum[j] recipit bene sana.
Itur et[k] ad castrum quoddam,[6] sed turba profana
Obstitit hic nostris intorquens spicula uana:
Sed tamen hoc[l] Domini manus obruit, et peregrini
Illic gentiles sunt ad baptisma uocati,   20
Quique reiecerunt illud[m] periere necati.
Captiuatur ibi puer; at[n] quicunque senescit
Occidit; ignotis regnum breue[o] parcere nescit.
Hostibus euersis, auro, spoliis honerati
Ad castrum redeunt cui[p] iam fuerant dominati.[7]   25

---

[a] proeeres *D m. pr.*   [b] grauabat *D*   [c] negabat *D*   [d] gaudebant *D*
[e] alebatt *D m. pr.*   [f] ignauia *D m. pr.*   [g] permansit *D*   [h] a *A*
[i] Talamana *D*   [j] uiris *D m. pr.; corr. to* uiros *m. alt.*   [k] *A omits* et
[l] hec *C*   [m] illic *D*   [n] ac *F*   [o] breue regnum *A;* brebe regnum *D*
[p] qui *A*

---

[1] Note that in this book, *caudati*, *catenati*, and *Tiradenreim* replace leonines almost completely in Gilo's rhyme-schemes.
[2] This decision was taken by the council of leaders. See *Gesta Francorum*, pp. 72–3; Raymond of Aguilers, p. 64; Robert of Rheims, pp. 837–8; Albert of Aachen, pp. 449–50.

However, others of the nobles by now felt close to fulfilling their prayer, and decided that it was pragmatic to leave off fighting for the time being;[1] for the heat and the parched earth were a burden on the people, the heat burning them and the land yielding nothing to drink. [5] For that reason rest was granted to the limbs of the weary for a short time, to be forsaken on the first day of November.[2] The host was divided up, making for different places, and whoever took his delight in gain remained in the city.[3] One man did his duty conscientiously, and was worthy of his pay. [10] This was Raymond, a knight who gave food to many of them; our people called him by the surname of Pilet.[4] He was not addicted to indolent pleasures, as so many were, but saw to it that the heathen could not live in safety. He therefore passed through two cities, [15] and arrived unexpected at Tell-Mannas.[5] The Syrian people, in whose keeping this town was, sensibly took the man in of their own free will. He made his way to a certain fortified town,[6] but a wicked host stood in the way of our men here, uselessly throwing their spears: however, the hand of the Lord overcame this obstacle, [20] and in that place the nomadic heathen were called to be baptized, and whoever refused it perished, cut down. Children there were taken prisoner, but any who were elderly were killed; their brief reign had no thought of sparing the base-born. With the enemy overthrown [25] they returned to the town, of which they were well and truly masters, laden with gold and booty.[7]

---

[3] Some knights joined Baldwin at Edessa; others took part in sorties and raids on neighbouring villages.

[4] Raymond Pilet was lord of Alès and a member of the army led by Raymond of Toulouse. He took part in the sieges of Tell-Mannas, Ma'arrat an-Nu'mān, Tortosa and Jerusalem. He also acted as a sub-commander and one of the members of his own contingent was probably the author of the *Gesta Francorum*. See *Gesta Francorum*, pp. 73–4, 83, 87–9; Baldric of Dol, pp. 81–2, 91–2; Orderic Vitalis, v. 130–2, 138, 146, 158, 160; *HGL* iii. 483.

[5] Raymond set out from Antioch on 17 July and occupied Tell-Mannas, which was situated E. of the Orontes, on 20 July. See *Gesta Francorum*, pp. 73–4, which also mentions (but does not name) the two cities.

[6] The Turkish castle captured by Raymond is also not named.

[7] See *Gesta Francorum*, pp. 73–4; Robert of Rheims, pp. 838–9; Albert of Aachen, p. 448.

Nec requie*a* detenta*b* diu uirtus animosa
Hostis ad interitum manet*c* assidue studiosa,
Gentilisque legens uestigia sparsa per orbem
Aggreditur Marram,[1] plenam gentilibus urbem.
Fluxerat*d* ad Marram, duce fama, turba remota,[2]   30
Fortis*e* Aleph,*f* Roboam rex et uicinia tota.
Gens ea non humili terrore repressa decenter
Disposito bello*g* ruit in nostros uiolenter.
Ferrea silua*h* cadit passim*i* campumque cruentum
Asperat, astra petit fragor et gemitus morientum.   35
Concurrunt per inane sudes, hi spicula iactant,
Illi protendunt hastas iterumque receptant;*j*
Fortius incursant ipsisque cadauera portis
Affigunt*k* nostri. Iam stabat in aggere fortis*l*
Miles, inundabant fosse, cum forte retortis   40
Vertitur*m* agmen equis. Quam perfida gratia sortis!
Christicole dant terga retro formidine mortis.
Turbat eos inimica cohors, agiturque*n* furore.
Tinnitum reddunt clipei*o* galeeque sonore,
Obtenebrant oculos*p* lapsi de uertice coni,   45
Loricas odiunt*q*[3] iuuenes ad uerbera proni.
Scindit labra sitis, non sufficit umbo*r* sagittis.
Vt Raimundus eos uidit rarescere, primus
'Respirate,*s* uiri!' clamat, 'quo,*t* proh pudor, imus?'
Taliter a trepido cursu proba gens reuocata   50
Gentiles agit ad muros, simul agglomerata.
Sed non uertuntur Suriani*u* deficientes
Nec socios iuuere suos sitis*v* impatientes;
Aeris illa*w* sui gens emollita tepore,
Non est marte, sed est martis superata calore.   55
Vt dare terga uident nostrorum castra secutos
Turci, Christicolas iam magna*x* parte minutos*y*
Inuadunt, dat eis uires animosque sequendi

---

a requiem *D*   *b* contempta *AD*   *c* manus *D*   *d* fruxerat *F m. pr.;*
duxerat *A*   *e* urbis *AD*   *f* Alep *BC*   *g* disposuit bellum *AD*
h turba *D*   *i* spassim *F m. pr.;* sparsim *BC*   *j* retentant *BC*   *k* affli-
gunt *F*   *l A m. pr. and D. m. pr. omit this line; A m. alt. adds it at the foot of the page, D m.
alt. at the top*   *m* uertuitur *D;* utitur *BC*   *n* agitata *AD*   *o* clipei red-
dunt *AD*   *p* occulos *F*   *q* odiunt *all MSS;* fodiunt *Riant*   *r* uebo *D m.
pr., corr. to* uerbo *m. alt.*   *s* respirare *D*   *t* quod *D, first hand*
u Suriatii *BC*   *v* sicitis *A m. pr.*   *w* ille *B m. pr.*   *x* manga *D m. pr.*
y minutas *A;* munitos *BC*

In their spirited courage they were not held back by resting for
long, but remained characteristically eager for the enemy's down-
fall, and following the heathen's tracks through the land, they
came to Ma'arrat,[1] a city full of heathen. [30] Drawn by this news,
there rushed to Ma'arrat a crowd from far and wide,[2] powerful
Aleppo with its king, Ridvan, and all the neighbouring lands.
That people was not restrained by humbling fear, as was fitting,
but drawn up for battle they rushed violently on our men. Every-
where the iron forest fell, spattering the field with gore; [35] the
crash of battle and the groans of the dying rose to the stars.
Stakes clashed in mid-air, some men threw spears, others lunged
back and forth with long lances. Our men pressed on more bravely,
and pinned corpses to the very gates. Our brave soldiers were
already standing on the earthworks, [40] and the ditches were
awash, when the column happened to wheel its horses about and
turned in retreat. Such is the treacherous favour of fate! In fear of
death, the Christians turned their backs in retreat. The enemy
force routed them, spurred on by frenzy. Resonant shields and
helmets clanged noisily, [45] visors slipped down from the tops of
helmets and darkened their wearers' gaze, and the young men,
bent as they were to receive blows, loathed their breastplates.[3]
Thirst split their lips, their shields did not have space enough for
the arrows. As soon as Raymond saw that their ranks were growing
thin, he first shouted out 'Get your breath back, men! For shame,
where are we heading?' [50] Called back from their terrified flight
by such words, the trusty people, all crowded into one space, drove
the heathen to the walls. But the Syrians, who were weakening, did
not turn back, and they could not help their comrades, who could
not endure their thirst; those people, made soft by the mildness of
their own climate, [55] were not defeated by fighting but by the
heat of fighting. When the Turks saw those who had followed our
men's camp turn tail, they attacked the Christians, who were now
severely depleted; the runaway race gave them the strength and

[1] Ma'arrat an-Nu'mān lies on the road from Hamah to Aleppo.

[2] A relief force was led by Ridvan of Aleppo. See Kemāl ad-Dīn ('Umar ibn 'Aḥmad),
Chronicle of Aleppo, in *RHC, Hist. Orient.* iii. 584, and above, v. 111 and note thereon.

[3] The reading *odiunt* is attested unanimously by all five MSS, and is a peculiar, post-
classical rendering of *oderunt*; Riant's suggestion *fodiunt*, 'they stab their breastplates', is
nonsense; Gilo's point is that the armour that should have assisted the young men got in
their way. Moreover, as Runciman points out (*Hist. Crus.* i. 252), Raymond Pilet's troops
were 'unused to bearing arms'.

Gens fugitiua, monet timidos fortuna nocendi.
Ordine non habito fugit agmen Christicolarum, 60
Non expectata reuocantum uoce tubarum.
Segnius haud fugiunt^a equites peditumque caterua
Quam fugit ante canes latratu^b territa cerua.
Sternitur heu felix^c populus^d per opaca uiarum,[1]
Expositusque^e Ioui fit martyr et esca ferarum. 65
Expirant^f animas multi,^{g} nec eos meus edet
Versus, uix equidem recolo que dicere tedet.[2]
Ad castrum rediit Raimundus et inrequieta^h
Perfruitur requie cum gente dolore repleta.
Hic aliquod^i tempus exegit ad omne paratus 70
Vtile uir fortis, per multa pericla probatus.

Interea nimius dolor accidit Antiochenis:
Vrbis enim rector, moderatus ad omnia, lenis
Presul obit, patremque suum dolet urbs^j obiisse:
Hanc^k cum capta fuit non credo magis gemuisse.[3] 75
Dum calet Augusti dictus^m de nomine mensis
Non sibi sed populo moritur presul^n Podiensis.
Pro Petro tracto de carcere dum tibi, Christe,
Vrbs canit, est tractus de carcere corporis^o iste,
Quaque die recolunt soluentem uincula Petrum,[4] 80
Illa luce uiri deplorauere feretrum.

Post nimios luctus,^{p} post infortunia plura,
Stans comes Egidii Sancti per tempora dura
Iuit ad Albariam,[5] quam multo milite cingens
Cepit, et huic urbi murus non profuit ingens. 85
Ensibus his incurua senum sunt colla secata,^{q}
Nec minus infantum rumpuntur timpora grata,
Nec uetulas^r reuerenda iuuat rugosaque pellis,^{s}
Nec facies prodest non ledi digna puellis,
Nec simplex uia mortis erat, quia mille necantur 90

---

^{a} figiunt D ^{b} latrantis A; latrantes D ^{c} A omits felix ^{d} populos
D m. pr. ^{e} expositus D ^{f} exspirat D ^{g} animos Turci F ^{h} iure
quieta A ^{i} aliquot B ^{j} hec D ^{k} hanc D m. alt., written over an erasure
^{l} doluisse AD ^{m} ? dicens A ^{n} presul moritur AD ^{o} corpore car-
ceris D; corporis carcere B ^{p} fluctus D ^{q} resecta A, D m. pr.; reserta D m.
alt. ^{r} uetulos D ^{s} persis A

spirit for pursuit, and fortune admonished the faint-hearted that
they too could inflict hurt. [60] The column of Christians fled in
utter disarray, and did not wait for the bugle's blast to call them
back. The knights and the band of infantry were no slower in their
flight than a hind flees before the hounds, terrified at their barking.
Alas! the happy people were slain in the shady paths,[1] [65] and
exposed in the open air became both martyrs and food for the wild
beasts. Many breathed their last; my poem will not set them forth,
for I hardly recall things which it is tedious to relate.[2] Raymond
went back to his camp, and enjoyed a restless rest along with his
people, full of grief. [70] The brave man spent some time here,
ready for every useful venture, his worth proven in many an
exploit.

In the meantime, a great misfortune befell the inhabitants of
Antioch: for the governor of the city, the gentle bishop, moderate
in all his ways, passed away, and the city was grieved that its father
had passed on: [75] I do not think it wept more even when it was
captured.[3] It was while the month named after Augustus was blaz-
ing that the bishop of Le Puy died, not for himself, but for his
people. While the city was singing to you, Christ, on account of
Peter's release from prison, he was taken from the prison of his
body, [80] and on the day that they recalled the loosing of Peter's
chains,[4] on that same day they wept over the bier of the great man.

After great sadness and many a misfortune, the count of Saint-
Gilles, who held firm throughout these hard times, went to Albara,[5]
which he surrounded with a large force [85] and captured; that city's
massive wall gave it no help at all. By their swords were the bowed
necks of old men severed, and the lovely heads of young children
were no less broken; venerable faces, all wrinkled, did not avail the
old women, nor their faces, undeserving of hurt, help young girls,
[90] and they did not all suffer a single death, for a thousand

---

[1] Cf. Proba, *Cent. Verg.* 273 = Vergil, *Aen.* vi. 633.
[2] *Gesta Francorum* states that the crusaders were defeated on 5 July, but this is obvi-
ously an error; 25 July would be a more likely date.
[3] *Gesta Francorum*, p. 74; Raymond of Aguilers, p. 84; Robert of Rheims, p. 839. Albert
of Aachen, p. 435, states that Adhémar died as a result of a plague which had spread
through the crusaders' camp.
[4] The feast of St Peter's Chains, 1 Aug. 1098.
[5] Albara was situated some 30 miles from Antioch.

Mille modis,[1] meritique uiri[a] merito lacerantur.[2]
Albarie sic ad Domini cultum reuocate
Preficitur presul, uite persona probate.[3]

Iamque uocabat hiemps proceres, noua bella mouendi
Tempus erat[4] ceptique[b] dabat spem perficiendi.[c]   95
Omnibus ergo[d] bonis[e] dum festum fit generale,[5]
Congregat absentes edictum spirituale;
Tam[f] uarius populus confluxit in Antiochena
Menia quam uarii pisces in retia plena,[6]
Dissimilique placet similis sententia genti.   100
Iherusalem loca sancta uident animo cupienti,
Vis[g] secura uirum[7] iubet ipsos esse paratos,
Deque suis abolent animis conubia,[h] natos.[8]
Vrbis[i] ad ignotos tractus[j] iam marte feruntur
Parthorumque pedes iam martis amore secuntur.   105

Conueniens comites dux interea Boimundus
Pactam querit ab his urbem.[9] negat hoc Raimundus,[k]
Regis et[l] aduentus Constantinopolitani[m10]
Expectare iubet, munitque domum Casiani.
Sic duce turbato comes impatiens[n] Rugiosam[11]   110
Transit ad Albariam, Marramque petit populosam.
Ne dolor irati ducis ad communia dampna
Forte redundaret,[12] procerum discretio[o] magna

---

[a] homines D; necem A   [b] cepitque A   [c] proficiendi BCD   [d] hinc
AD   [e] sanctis AD; bonis glossed sanctis BCF   [f] iam A; tunc BC   [g] his
F   [h] coniugia AD   [i] orbis A   [j] tractum D   [k] F omits this line
[l] A omits et   [m] D m. pr. omits this line   [n] impacies F   [o] discretia
D m. pr.

---

[1] Cf. Ovid, Amores iii. 14. 24.

[2] See Gesta Francorum, pp. 74–5; Raymond of Aguilers, p. 91; Albert of Aachen, p. 448.
Albara, a Muslim city, was captured in Oct. 1098. At the same time, other crusading
leaders including Bohemond led forays against Turkish towns in Cilicia. See Albert of
Aachen, pp. 435, 440–1 and above, viii. 9.

[3] Peter of Narbonne, a Provençal priest and chaplain of Raymond of Toulouse, who
was appointed bishop of Albara and given half the city and its territory. See Gesta
Francorum, p. 75; Raymond of Aguilers, pp. 91–2; B. Hamilton, The Latin Church in the
Crusader States (London, 1980), pp. 10–11, 22–3.

[4] Gesta Francorum, p. 72, says the crusaders had decided in the summer to leave any
action until the beginning of November.

[5] All Saints' Day, 1 Nov. 1098.

[6] Cf. Matt. 13: 47, for a biblical use of this image.

were slain in a thousand ways,[1] and men were deservedly cut down according to their deserts.[2] When it had thus been recalled to the worship of the Lord, a bishop was appointed over Albara, a person of trusty character.[3]

By this time winter was summoning the nobles, [95] and it was time to begin the war afresh,[4] giving rise to hopes of finishing off their enterprise. Therefore, while the common festival of All Saints was celebrated,[5] a spiritual summons gathered together all those who had been absent; as varied a people flowed into Antioch's walls as different kinds of fish into a full net,[6] [100] and a common feeling was shared by the different races. In their eager minds they saw the holy places of Jerusalem, their confidence in their strength bade them be ready,[7] and they shut out from their minds their wives and children.[8] Already they were being borne in battle to the unknown lands around the city, [105] already through love of battle they were following the steps of the Parthians.

Meanwhile Duke Bohemond met with his companions, and asked for the city,[9] as had been agreed. Raymond refused this, ordered them to await the arrival of the emperor of Constantinople,[10] and fortified the palace of Casianus. [110] With the duke thus displeased, the count would not wait, but crossed over to Rugia[11] and Albara, and made for the populous city of Ma'arrat. Lest the angry duke's ill-feeling should by chance cause general harm,[12] the nobles in their great wisdom took his

---

[7] Cf. Vergil, *Aen.* vi. 553.

[8] See above, Charleville Poet i. 154 and n., for a similar sentiment.

[9] The leaders of the crusade met to discuss their future plans in St Peter's cathedral on 5 Nov. The argument centred on Bohemond's claim to Antioch and Raymond of Toulouse's insistence on the rights of the Byzantine emperor. Bohemond was ultimately given three-quarters of the town and the citadel; Raymond remained in control of the fortified bridge and the palace of Yaghi Siyan. See *Gesta Francorum*, pp. 75–6; Raymond of Aguilers, p. 93; *Tudebodus Imitatus et Continuatus*, p. 208; Robert of Rheims, pp. 843–4.

[10] Hugh of Vermandois did not arrive in Constantinople until the autumn of 1098 (above, vii. 510 and n.), and it would therefore not have been feasible for any Byzantine relief force to reach Antioch until the following spring. See Albert of Aachen, pp. 434–5.

[11] Raymond of Toulouse and Robert of Flanders set out from Antioch on 23 Nov. Rugia had been captured by Raymond in October. See *Gesta Francorum*, p. 77; Raymond of Aguilers, p. 94.

[12] Ma'arrat presented a threat to the army's left flank on the march south from Antioch to Jerusalem.

Consulit hunc:[a] mens alta uiri multa prece mota
Preposuit uoto priuato publica[b] uota.   115
Protinus educens acies populi modo mesti
Ad Marram properat respectu uictus honesti.

Lux[c] Domini specialis erat cum signa replerunt
Vrbis circuitus et castra duces posuerunt.[1]
Externos homines[d] ubi uidit gens stupefacta,   120
Quis referet quanta fuerit formidine tacta?[e]
Omnis in urbe locus feruet[f] properante tumultu,[g]
Discurrunt matres timideque nurus[h] sine cultu.
Hostes plus iusto fore rumor publicus[i] edit,
Compluresque timor, nec mens sua lumina credit.[j]   125
Si quisquam somnum recipit, somno cruciatur:
Vexat et insomnem res uana diemque minatur.
Stant ad opus seruile duces cum gente minore,
Nec[k] pudor est seruire, carent extrema pudore.[2]

Exuit ut Phebus terras caligine nigra,   130
Surgit nostra cohors[l] sub pigro tempora pigra,
Excitique probi iuuenes[3] clangore tubarum,
Corporis immemores, haud immemores animarum
Ad muros[m] properant.[4] Iam circumfusus adaptat[n]
Neruo pila pedes, iam letus ad ardua iactat.   135
Iactant saxa, faces flammas per inane ferentes,
Quas[o] herere uolunt[p] ad culmina suspicientes.[q][5]
Desudant alii fossas implere patentes,
Per[r] prerupta[s] ruunt equites: transcurrere montes
Non sinit[t] horror equos in frena[u] retro redeuntes.   140
Iamque caua latitans testudine firma cauabat[6]
Menia leta cohors, iam scalas turba leuabat,

[a] huic BC   [b] pullica AD   [c] lex A   [d] F m. pr. omits homines
[e] properante tumultu D m. pr.   [f] ferice (?) A m. pr., corr. to feruce m. alt.
[g] formidine tacta D m. pr.   [h] matres D   [i] publicu D   [j] cedit B
[k] ne D   [l] cohos D m. pr.   [m] martem AD   [n] adeptat D m. pr.
[o] quos B   [p] uolent BC   [q] sufficientes D m. pr.; suscipientes F   [r] pre
A   [s] preruta D m. pr.   [t] sunt A m. pr.   [u] ffrena F

[1] The *Gesta Francorum*, pp. 77–9, states that the army arrived outside Maʿarrat on 28 Nov., which fell on a Sunday in 1098. See also Robert of Rheims, p. 845.
[2] Gilo makes no mention of the shortages of food and important supplies, including

counsel; moved by their many entreaties, that man of high prin-
ciple [115] put the interests of all before his own interests. He
immediately led out the host of his downcast people and hastened
to Ma'arrat, overcome by regard for what was proper.

It was the special day of the Lord that dawned when standards
filled the open spaces around the city, and the dukes pitched
camp.[1] [120] Who shall tell how great was the fear which struck the
amazed inhabitants when they saw those foreign men? Every local-
ity in the city seethed with the noise of men making haste, and
panic-stricken mothers and daughters-in-law ran about in disar-
ray. Common gossip had it that there would be more troops than
they could cope with, [125] and fear had it that there would be yet
more. Their minds did not believe their own eyes. If anyone had a
dream, he was tormented in that dream; empty fears plagued their
sleepless nights also, and threatened their waking hours. The lead-
ers performed menial tasks along with the lesser folk, and had no
shame in serving, for there is no shame when straits are dire.[2]

[130] When Phoebus stripped the lands of their murky blackness,
our forces rose up slothfully in that slothful hour, the upright young
men were awoken[3] by the blare of bugles, and forgetful of the body
but not forgetful of their souls they rushed to the walls.[4] By now the
infantry, pouring round, [135] set missiles to bowstrings, now with
joyful heart they were hurling them at the heights. They flung rocks
and torches that carried flames through the void; they aimed these
high, wanting them to stick to the battlements.[5] Others sweated at
filling up the gaping ditches. The knights rushed on over the rugged
ground; [140] sheer terror did not let horses cross over the high
hills, they reared back, struggling against the reins. By now the
joyful band was sheltering beneath a hollow protective shell, dig-
ging out the solid walls,[6] by now the host was raising ladders aloft,

---

wood to make the siege-engines, or the vision of Peter Bartholomew. See Raymond of
Aguilers, pp. 94, 97. Cf. Maximianus, *Elegiae*, i. 149.   [3] Cf. Vergil, *Aen.* ii. 313.
   [4] Shortly after the crusaders arrived at Ma'arrat, they made two abortive assaults on
the city walls. The main attack took place on Saturday, 11 Dec.
   [5] For a parallel, see Robert of Rheims, p. 847:

   Tela, sudes, lapidesque uolent, ignesque facesque,
   Ex quibus arderent introrsus tecta domorum.

   [6] Sapping operations are also referred to in the *Gesta Francorum*, p. 79; Raymond of
Aguilers, p. 97.

Cum*a* subito coeunt Arabes, grauibusque lacertis
Saxa rotant et uulneribus dant proxima certis;[1]
Et*b* ueluti nimbos*c* cum torquet hiemps odiosa,   145
Aera*d* grando*e* secat, uis austri seuit aquosa,
Imbribus insultant crepitantia tecta domorum,
Verberat unda sequens fugientia terga uirorum,
Sic miseri, quibus una salus inimica saluti*f*
Pellere tela, sudes iaciunt, clipeique minuti*g*   150
Dant sonitum,*h* fugiunt equites sub eis*i* male tuti.

Vt uidet*j* ex equo Raimundus bella parari,
Altum de lignis*k* castrum iubet edificari;[2]
Illud montis habens instar trabibus fit acernis;[3]
Huius ductores*m* imis latuere cauernis,   155
In summo*n* Venator erat cornuque strepebat
Eurardus,*o* [4] delecta*p* cohors in fronte*q* fremebat.
Ergo uiri pedibusque suis pedibusque rotarum
Adnixi,*r* licet impediant loca stricta uiarum,
Adiungunt alte turri castrum magis altum,   160
Atque*s* parant super attonitos subito dare saltum.
Tunc et ab urbanis fit machina que iaciebat
Immensos lapides*t* et castrum concutiebat,*u*
Grecorum*v* piceos ignes*w*[5] rotat insuper illa,
Et uolat ante uiros fetens*x* et nigra fauilla.   165
Seruat in igne suos diuina potentia uiuos,*y*
Et dedit ardores non posse nocere nociuos.

Murorum iaciunt per propugnacula fortes
Christicole, castrique cadunt de culmine mortes;
Pislerio*z* de Monte*aa* furit Guillelmus[6] ibidem,   170
Robora, saxa, sudes certatim mittit et idem
Oppositus tedis*bb* rubet et lustratur ab igne.[7]

---

a com *A*   *b* ac *AD*   *c* nimbes *D m. pr.*   *d* sera *F*   *e* grado *D*
f salutis *D*   *g* muniti *AB*   *h* crepitum *A;* strepitum *D*   *i* sub eis
equites *BC*   *j* tradet *A*   *k* lignat *D m. pr.*   *l* aceruis *F, D m. pr.*
m doctores *D*   *n* sumno *A*   *o* Euurardus *DF*   *p* dilecta *BC*
q fonte *A*   *r* atnixi *A*   *s* adque *D*   *t* lapidides *D*   *u*concutie-
bant *D*   *v* Gregorum *F m. pr.*   *w* lapides *F; D omits* ignes   *x* fecens *D*
y suos *D m. pr.*   *z* Pillerio *F;* Bislerio *C*   *aa* de mote *D*   *bb* tedit *F m.
pr.;* telis *BC*

when suddenly the Arabs rallied, and with a mighty heave they rolled down rocks, dealing inescapable wounds to those nearest to them;[1] [145] and just as hail cuts through the air when hateful winter swirls the clouds about, the squally south wind blows fierce, the roofs of homes are alive with the pattering of rain, and torrents beat against the backs of men, pursuing them as they flee, so those wretches, whose one hope of salvation was [150] to drive back the weapons hostile to the way of salvation, threw aside their staves; their battered shields rang out as the knights fled, barely protected beneath them.

When Raymond saw that each side's warlike preparations were equal to the other's, he ordered a high tower to be built of timbers;[2] this was made of beams of maple, and was as high as a hill;[3] [155] the captains of war hid themselves in its hollow lower parts, and on its top stood Everard the Hunter,[4] blowing his horn. A picked band of men fought furiously in the front. And so men pushed with their own feet against the foot of the wheels, and although the narrow tracks in that place impeded them, [160] they brought their higher castle up to the tower on high, and made ready to leap down suddenly on the astonished foe. Then a siege-engine was built by the men in the city also; this threw enormous stones, which shook our tower, and moreover hurled the fiery pitch that the Greeks use,[5] [165] so that stinking black ash floated in front of our men too. The power of God kept his own folk alive amid the fire, and granted that these harmful flames could do no harm at all.

The brave Christians cast their spears over the battlements of the wall, and the dead fell down from the top of the castle; [170] William of Montpellier[6] raged there, strenuously hurling timbers, rocks, and staves; he stood out against the torches, and was cleansed by the fire.[7]

---

[1] The Latin here is an imitation of the hypallage used in Vergil's *Aeneid*: cf. *Aen.* iii. 61.

[2] See *Gesta Francorum*, p. 78. The 'castle' was commanded by William of Montpellier. See below, viii. 170 and n.

[3] Cf. Vergil, *Aen.* ii. 15, ix. 87.

[4] Everard is also mentioned by Robert of Rheims, p. 847, and *Gesta Francorum*, p. 78.

[5] Greek fire was a form of liquid pitch which was ignited and poured on assailants.

[6] William was a leading member of Raymond of Toulouse's contingent. He took part in the sieges of Maʿarrat an-Nuʿmān and Antioch and remained in Palestine until c.1103. See *Gesta Francorum*, pp. 26, 78; Orderic Vitalis, v. 68, 138; Riley-Smith, 'The motives', p. 728.   [7] Cf. Rev. 3: 18; 1 Pet. 1: 7.

Huius ego nequeo uirtutes dicere digne.
Illum[a] non[b] retinet frangendis congrua muris
Machina, sed gaudet, gaudet patientia duris.   175
Non retro mollitus uite dulcedine[c] cedit,
Nec, quamuis decuisset[d] ibi fugisse, recedit;
Hos necat, hos quassat, se circuit, arma repellit,
Nunc muros nunc scuta ferit, nunc spicula uellit.
Non procul a castro nec ab[e] adiuncta procul arce   180
Turba sacerdotum clamabat: 'rex pie, parce,
Parce, Deus, fugiatque[f] tuum gentilis ouile,
Qui nomen Christi[g] conatur[h] reddere uile.'[1]
Ex alia iuuenes certant irrumpere parte,
Nec bello defessa manus, nec profuit[i] arte.[j2]   185
Si quis forte parat compagem soluere muri,
Illius excussa dampnatur dextra securi.
Hec[k] indignatus uir de Da Turre[l] uocatus
Gulferius,[m3] pulchrumque[n] diu facinus[o] meditatus,
Turbidus arripuit erecte[p] robora scale,   190
Quam uix sustulerunt[q] humeris sudantibus ale,
Perque gradus trahit[r] ipse[s] suis sua membra lacertis,
Solus et in medium populi portatur inertis;[t,u]
Hunc[v] sequitur quem pellit[w] ad hoc manus omnipotentis;
Quippe modum nostre transcendunt[x] talia[y] mentis.   195
Sed, dum turba frequens firmat gressus per inane,
Scalam frangit onus gentisque repulsa profane.
At[z] uir predictus, tollendus ad astra fauore,
Quo se iam tulerat[aa] uirtute grauique labore,
Inter eos quos uix potuit conducere sursum   200
Eminet: utque canes depascunt morsibus ursum,
Cui plebs incumbens preclusit iter fugiendi,
Sic non[bb] equa manus premit hunc populique premendi.
Ille per instantes fertur, iaculo[cc] uenienti.

[a] illis A   [b] num F   [c] F m. pr. omits dulcedine   [d] docuisset A
[e] A omits ab   [f] metuatque AD   [g] Christi nomen AD   [h] conantur AD
[i] proficit F   [j] AD omit ll. 184–5; m. alt. (different hand) adds them in A only
[k] hoc C   [l] de daturre BCF; deda turre D; de la Turre A   [m] Gulforius BC
[n] pulchrique A   [o] farinus D m. pr.   [p] erecta B   [q] sustulerant A
[r] trait F   [s] ille BC   [t] inermis BC   [u] A omits this line   [v] nunc A
[w] ducit A   [x] transcedunt CDF   [y] gaudia D   [z] at Grocock; et ABCF;
aut D   [aa] tolerat A m. pr.; contulerat BC   [bb] nec D   [cc] adculo A

---

[1] See Gesta Francorum, pp. 78–9.

I cannot speak worthily of his outstanding qualities. The siege-engine made for breaking down walls did not hold him back; [175] rather his patience rejoiced, it rejoiced in hardship. He did not shrink back, softened by the sweet things of life, and he did not withdraw, though he might honourably have fled from there; some he slaughtered, others he dashed down, he swung round and repelled their weapons, now striking the walls, now their shields, and now pulling out their spears. [180] Not far from the castle, and not far from the citadel close to it, the band of priests was crying out: 'Holy king have mercy, have mercy O God, let them flee before your flock, these heathen who are trying to make foul the name of Christ'.[1] From the other side the young men strove to break through, [185] and their hand was not exhausted by the fighting, though its skill brought them no advantage.[2] If any of them happened to begin to loosen the bonds of the wall, he lost his right hand, severed by an axe. Aghast at this, a man called Geoffrey of Lastours,[3] who had long thought of attempting some noble deed, [190] frenziedly seized a ladder which the groups of men scarcely raised aloft on their perspiring shoulders, and raising its frame up high, he heaved his bulk along its rungs with his arms, and he was borne up alone in the midst of that inactive people; a man followed him, prompted to do so by the hand of the Almighty; [195] for indeed such things surpass our own level of understanding. But while a whole host of them were treading their way through the void, their weight and the repulse of the wicked race broke the ladder. However, the man we have mentioned (and he deserves to be raised to the stars in acclamation), shone forth there where he had already borne himself by his courage and his hard toil, [200] among those whom he had barely managed to lead up there with him; and just as dogs nip at a bear when the people thronging about shut off its way of escape, so he was hemmed in by a force of men not his equals, who do not deserve mention. He was carried along through his assailants,

---

[2] The siege-tower was used to protect those undermining the city walls.

[3] Geoffrey, lord of Lastours in the Limousin, died c. 1126. For his role in the siege of Ma'arrat, see *Gesta Francorum*, p. 79; Raymond of Aguilers, p. 97; Orderic Vitalis, v. 138. One of the knights of his household was Gregory Bechada, author of a lost Provençal epic poem on the First Crusade. See G. Paris, 'La Chanson d'Antioche provençale', *Romania*, xxii (1893), 345–64, at pp. 358–9, 362.

Opponit clipeum, socio tutela*ᵃ* sequenti:*ᵇ*   205
Nunc prior est, nunc*ᶜ* posterior, similis fugienti,*ᵈ*
Nunc propriis telis populo nocet ille stupenti,*ᵉ*
Nunc gladios, nunc pila fugit, nunc mille molares.
Iam fumant artus, iam spumant sanguine nares:
Contra tot pestes manet unius integra uita,   210
Missilibus, iaculis, sude, fustibus, ense petita.

Dum quantum*ᶠ* deprensa*ᵍ* potest gens turma*ʰ* resistit,
Fida cohors iterum scalas ad menia sistit.
Mox oblita sui sed non oblita suorum
Conscendit*ⁱ* muros properans ad opem sociorum.¹   215
Nec mora, per turres sonitu concurritur orto.
Non riget his arcus contentus*ʲ* fune retorto,
Res agitur gladiis: de menibus*ᵏ* ordine fixa
Saxa trahunt,*ˡ* murisque suis urbs frangitur ipsa.
Terga dedere prius nostri, numeroque furentum   220
Cesserunt,*ᵐ* pressitque sonum gemitus morientum.
Ad terram missi plerique necem*ⁿ* fugiebant,
Quam tamen ad terram confracti repperiebant.*ᵒ*

Soluitur*ᵖ* interea murus, quem*�q* nostra iuuentus²
Castro tecta subit, solida nec rupe retentus   225
Est eques:*ʳ* ingrediens artata foramine stricto
Gens repit,*ˢ* tuba signa dedit tristissima*ᵗ* uicto.
Vt uidere suis hostes in menibus isti
Qui*ᵘ* super adstabant, nec eis iam posse resisti,
Per muros rapuere fugam, clipeisque reiectis   230
Merguntur subito diuersis agmina tectis.
Pars solo terrore perit, plebique cadenti
Mors ignaua*ᵛ* uenit*ʷ* non ense uocata rubenti:
Maxima turba ruit*ˣ* uenientum turbine pulsa,
Muris fixa rubent*ʸ* miserorum membra reuulsa.   235

ᵃ tutela socio *F*   ᵇ uenienti *F m. pr.*   ᶜ nec *C*   ᵈ figienti *D*
ᵉ stipenti *D m. pr.*   ᶠ quarta *D*   ᵍ depressa *F*   ʰ turba *AD*
ⁱ conscendunt *D*   ʲ intentus *F;* intensus *BC*   ᵏ munibus *A*
ˡ tenent *F m. pr.*   ᵐ cescerunt *A*   ⁿ *F m. pr. omits* necem   ᵒ temperie-
bant *A m. pr.*   ᵖ sternitur *D*   q qui *A m. pr., corr. to* quis *m. alt.*
ʳ equus *BC*   ˢ reppit *F*   ᵗ tristisima *F*   ᵘ cui *A*   ᵛ ignora *A*
ʷ p.uenit *F m. pr.*   ˣ perit *AD*   ʸ rulent *A*

[205] and held his shield out against the approaching spears as a shelter for his comrades following on behind; now he held it in front of him, now behind him, as when a man runs away, now he dealt wounds to the astonished people with his own weapons, now he escaped their swords, their spears, and the thousand stones they cast at him. By this stage his limbs were steaming, and his nostrils were foaming with blood: [210] the life of one man remained whole against so many plagues, sought out as it was by darts, spears, staves, clubs, and swords.

While the troops fought back as hard as a besieged people can, the faithful company once again placed their ladders against the walls. Putting aside thoughts of themselves, but not of their own, [215] they were soon scaling the walls, rushing to the aid of their comrades.[1] Without delay, men came running as the noise spread from tower to tower; the bow bent taut with its twisted string did not stiffen for them. It was a time for swords: they dragged firmly-fixed stones from the walls along each course, and the city itself was broken by its own walls. [220] Our side turned their backs first, giving way to the raging horde, and the groans of the dying drowned out their noise. Many threw themselves to the ground, fleeing death, and yet found death, shattered on the ground.

Meanwhile, the wall which our young men had sapped,[2] [225] covered by their 'castle', was breached, and the knights were no longer held back by the solid rock; the people advanced, creeping, hemmed in by the narrowness of the gap, and the bugle gave out its signals, bringing sorrow to the vanquished. When those who were standing on the heights saw the enemy within their walls, and saw too that they could no longer withstand them, [230] they took to their heels through the walls, and throwing their shields away the troops quickly sank into hiding in various buildings. Some died of sheer terror, and a base death, not one summoned by a crimson sword, met the falling people. The greatest part of the crowd rushed headlong, driven on by the whirlwind of the approaching men, [235] and the wretches' torn-off limbs dripped red, fixed to the walls.

---

[1] For a parallel, see Robert of Rheims, pp. 847–9.
[2] See above, viii. 143, 186, and nn.

Vrbis ad excelsas turres ita dum properatur,
Diuersis mors una modis hos*a* depopulatur.
Vesper erat*b* nostris minus illo tempore gratus,
Paganisque dedit latebras nimium*c* properatus:
Noctem pro lucro penas in luce daturus   240
Ciuis habet, multoque rubet iam*d* sanguine murus.
At*e* dum leta*f* cohors*g* urbem sine uindice uastat,
Ad miseras turres gentilis pallidus adstat.*h*
Tunc*i* monuit Boimundus*j* [1] eos interpretis ore
Vt sua lenirent mala consilio meliore,   245
Et*k* subeant turrem que presidet ardua porte;
Hos equidem teget in misera sua dextera morte,
Victorem uictumque*l* facit mox inrequietum.
Victa rapit uictor, uidet*m* hic accurrere letum,
Iamque diem luctusque nouos aurora uocabat,   250
Vicini*n* morti [2] se ciuis in urbe parabat.
Christicole stringunt enses et tecta cruentis
Corporibus complent populique cruore cadentis.*o*
Hic etiam uirtutis opus gladiis iniere
Corpore qui tenui modicas uires*p* habuere,   255
Dantque senes decollandi*q* penam grauiorem
Quam iuuenes: producit*r* enim uis parua dolorem,
Et ueluti minimum*s* potuissent ense*t* nocere,
Timpora quorundam laqueis sic implicuere
Vt laqueum baculus constringat, et interiora   260
Perforet ossa rigens funis,*u* cruor impleat ora:
Tunc*v* educta suis extabant orbibus horum*w*
Lumina,*x* fedabat*y* sanies*z* barbas miserorum.
Talia fingebat auri sitis effodiendi;
Nam quid*aa* non suadet amor immoderatus habendi? [3]   265
Viscera morte graui iam frigida dextra cruenta
Scindit, et ex ipsis manus haurit auara*bb* talenta. [4]
Ast alios, quos cura ducis seruare*cc* uolebat, [5]
Inreuocabile uulgus ad impia fata trahebat. [6]

---

a hos una modis mors *BC*   *b* uesperat *D*   *c* nimiumque *A m. pr.*
d *B omits* iam   *e* et *AD*   *f* lecta *D*   *g* cohor *F*   *h* astat *BD*
i tum *F*   *j* *F m. pr. omits* Boimundus   *k* ut *F*   *l* uictorem uictum uic-
tumque *A*   *m* rapit *D m. pr.*   *n* uicinie *or* uicime *A*   *o* cadentes *D*
m. pr.   *p* uires modicas *AD*   *q* decollandi *Hall;* decollandis *all MSS*
r iuuenes sed producit *D*   *s* nimium *D*   *t* esse *A*   *u* funus *F m. pr.*
v nunc *F*   *w* orum *A*   *x* fulmina *F*   *y* fedenbat *A;* fedabant *BC*
z sanguis *D*   *aa* qui *F*   *bb* haurit auara manus *F*   *cc* seruare ducis
quos cura *AD*

And so while a rapid advance was made to the lofty towers of the city, a single death ravaged them in many ways. The evening was less welcome to our men on that occasion, and, hastening on too soon, enabled the heathen to hide: [240] the citizens, who would have paid the penalty in the daylight, had night for their reward, and already the city wall was red with much blood. But while the joyful company laid waste the city without being avenged, the heathen stood pale-faced in their wretched towers. Then Bohemond[1] advised them, through an interpreter, [245] to alleviate their wretched plight with better counsel, and to come down to the tower which overlooks the steep approaches to the gate; his own right hand, indeed, was their shelter in the face of a miserable death, and at once deprived victor and vanquished of rest, and the victor snatched his booty, and the other saw the approach of death. [250] And now dawn was summoning the daylight, and grief was renewed. In the city the citizens prepared themselves for death, which was now near at hand.[2] The Christians drew their swords and filled the dwellings with bloodied bodies and with the gore of people falling in death. Here indeed [255] those who had little strength in their feeble frame proceeded to an act of courage with their swords, and the old men who were to be beheaded paid a heavier penalty than the young, for but a slight force prolonged their agony, and inasmuch as they could only inflict short-lived pain on them with the blade, they tied up the heads of some of them with thongs, [260] in such a way that a stick tightened up the thong, and the rope as it tightened cracked the bones inside, so that the blood filled their mouths; then their eyes popped out and stood proud of their sockets, and bloody gore befouled the wretches' beards. It was thirst for uncovering gold that devised such things; [265] for what does unbridled love of possessions not urge men to do?[3] Their bloodied hands tore asunder guts already cold in the grip of death, and from them their greedy fists ripped gold coins.[4] But the uncontrollable mob hastened others, whom it was the duke's concern to keep safe,[5] to an ungodly doom.[6]

---

[1] Bohemond arrived at Maʿarrat on 28 Nov. See *Gesta Francorum*, pp. 77–8.

[2] Bohemond had promised safety to the Muslim inhabitants if they took refuge in a building near the main city gates, but in its destruction no one was spared. See *Gesta Francorum*, pp. 79–80; Raymond of Aguilers, pp. 98–9.

[3] Cf. Prudentius, *Psychomachia*, 478, Proba *Cent. Verg.* 201 = Vergil, *Aen.* viii. 327.

[4] See *Gesta Francorum*, p. 80.   [5] See above, viii. 252 and n.

[6] Cf. Lucan, *Bellum ciuile*, i. 509.

Ima senes Herebi repetunt, uenduntur ephebi.[1]   270
Detinuit nostros in finibus his mora mensis;[2]
Mortuus interea presul fuit hic Oriensis.[3]
Nostra cohors paucis consumpsit multa diebus:[a]
Nescit enim partis[b] uictoria parcere rebus.[c]
Illic ergo famem gens[d] pertulit immoderatam,   275
Et susceperunt mortem plerique uocatam,
Et, quia non habuit populus quod habere licebat,
Tendit in illicitum, facit hoc quod ius prohibebat.
Proh pudor! heu[e] facinus! ueribus[f] posuere recentes[g]
Turcorum carnes, lassantque[h] cadauere dentes.[i4]   280

Tunc perscrutatur[j] Boimundi causa secundo,
Nec concordari potuit dux cum Raimundo:
Regem non recipi[k] Constantinopolitanum
Nec dare iuratum comes asserit esse profanum.[5]
Ergo uie curam sancte[l] ducis[m] ira reiecit;   285
Ira ducem, dux agmen iter postponere fecit.
Ille quidem cum principibus[6] repetiuit amata[n]
Menia, plebsque dolet tantis patribus uiduata.[o]
At[p] comes Egidii Sancti manet inrequietus,
Anxius in multis, curarum mole repletus: 290
Sit[q] modo salua fides, placet ut descendat ad ima
Quelibet, et procerum summetur res[r] ea lima,
Mandauitque uiris absentibus ut Rugiosam[s7]
Iuris[t] amore petant, rem discutiant odiosam.
Conueniant, rem discutiant, sed fraus ibi dira[u]   295
Demonis insedit, nec finem repperit[v] ira.[w]
Tunc Marram petiit comes, expectatio turbe,
Collegitque sua comites Boimundus in urbe.[8]

[a] paucis uictoria parcere rebus *D m. pr.*   [b] parcis *D*   [c] *D m. pr. omits this line*   [d] plebs *BC*   [e] hiu *D m. pr.*   [f] uerubus *BC*   [g] fetentes *BC*   [h] lassant *A*   [i] carnes *F m. pr.*   [j] perscrutantur *D*   [k] recipit *BC*   [l] ergo tue tua sancte *D m. pr.*   [m] duris *D*   [n] armata *D;* amena *BC*   [o] uidiata *D*   [p] sed *AD*   [q] si *AD;* qit *F. m. pr.*   [r] summe turres *BC*   [s] Ruginosam *gl.* ciuitatem *BC*   [t] muris *F*   [u] sed demonis ira *D*   [v] repperis *A*   [w] *D reads* insedit ira finemque boni non repperit ira *for this line*

---

[1] Some of the women and children were sold as slaves.
[2] *Gesta Francorum*, p. 80, states that the army remained in Ma'arrat for one month and four days.
[3] See *Gesta Francorum*, p. 80; Raymond of Aguilers, p. 152, and above, i. 150.

[270] The old men went down to the depths of Erebus, and the youths were sold off.[1] Our men were held up for a month in these regions;[2] and in the meantime, the bishop of Orange died.[3] Our troops ate up many provisions in just a few days: for victory does not know how to be frugal with her gains. [275] Because of this, the people suffered terrible hunger there, and many of them received the death which they called upon, and, because the common folk did not possess what it was right to possess, they veered towards what was not right, and did what common law forbids. For shame, the dreadful deed! They stuck freshly-sliced flesh from the Turks on spits, [280] and wearied their teeth on the dead.[4]

Then Bohemond's case was examined for a second time, and the duke could not be brought to agree with Count Raymond; the count asserted that not to receive the emperor of Constantinople and not to give his oath was a base act.[5] [285] And so the duke's wrath pushed concern about the holy journey into the background; for wrath made the duke delay his journey, and the duke delayed the troops: for he sought out his beloved citadel with the nobles,[6] and the poor folk were grieved at being bereaved of such leaders. But the count of Saint-Gilles continued to be restless, [290] anxious about many matters, weighed down and full of cares; provided good faith was kept, he was happy to go to any depths, so that the matter could be concluded through the diplomacy of the nobles. He therefore sent word to the absent men to make for Rugia[7] in their love of what is right, to discuss this loathsome affair. [295] For all that they met together and discussed the matter, the fateful deceit of the devil was present there, and their wrath found no end. Then the count, the awaited hope of the masses, set out for Ma'arrat, and Bohemond gathered together his comrades in his own city.[8]

[4] Fulcher of Chartres, p. 267; Raymond of Aguilers, p. 101.

[5] After the capture of Ma'arrat, the dispute between Bohemond and Raymond resurfaced (above, viii. 108). See *Gesta Francorum*, pp. 80–1; Raymond of Aguilers, p. 99; Fulcher of Chartres, pp. 267–8; Robert of Rheims, p. 849.

[6] Bohemond returned to Antioch in late December; Raymond went to Rugia, leaving the bishop of Albara in control of Ma'arrat. See Raymond of Aguilers, pp. 98–9.

[7] At Rugia, Raymond offered Godfrey of Bouillon, Robert of Normandy, Robert of Flanders, and Tancred money to accept his leadership. See Raymond of Aguilers, p. 100.

[8] After the abortive meeting at Rugia, Bohemond returned to Antioch and Raymond to Ma'arrat, where in an effort to force his hand, the starving army had started to destroy the walls. See Raymond of Aguilers, pp. 100–1.

Vt comes a cunctis se conspicit[a] esse relictum[b]
Et Marram populis minimum[c] iam reddere uictum,   300
Plus fidei[d] fisus quam uiribus, omnia Christo
Committit, fatique uices duce non timet isto.
Tunc pedibus nudis, solito cessante paratu,
Egreditur Marram cum plebeio comitatu.[1]
Quelibet huic populo cessura pericula iurat,   305
Nec secura fides regum consortia curat.
Cedere pauperibus fortes putat ille fidelis,
Audet et ipse ratem laceris[e] committere uelis.
Plebs aggressa uiam propter ieiunia tarda,
Et[f] comites comitis primum uenere Capharda.[2]   310
Consul Normannus Normannorumque cohortes,[3]
Quos reddit[g] sua terra[h] pigros, incognita fortes,
Hic animis et corporibus[i] nostris sociantur,[j]
Nec[k] fidei zelo mala queque subire morantur.

Rex quoque Cesaree[l] nostris pretendit amorem,   315
Et[m] specie pacis[4] male palliat ille timorem.
Denique Cesaream[n] serie firmata malorum
Turba petit, quia longa quies labor esset eorum,
Inseditque super fluuium Farfar,[o][5] quia tale
Nomen habet flumen huic urbi conlaterale.   320
Vt muris admota nimis tentoria uidit
Rex urbis, uetuit commercia,[p] pacta recidit.
Nocte sed exacta, populo iam progrediente,
His occurrentes[q] duo Turci, rege iubente,
Hostibus obsequium, licet hostes, exhibuerunt,   325
Et uada quos nollet euadere predocuerunt.
Venit et ad uallem[r] quamdam gens nostra duorum
Conductu, cepitque boues multos[s] et equorum
Predam[t] (nempe boues et equi per gramina late

---

[a] prospicit F   [b] relictam A   [c] nimium D   [d] fides A
[e] raceris C   [f] at F   [g] redit D   [h] turba BC   [i] corporis BC
[j] satiantur D m. pr., corr. to sotiantur m. alt.   [k] ne D; de A   [l] ceserie D m.
pr., corr. to cesarie m. alt.   [m] at BC   [n] cesariam D   [o] Pharphar CD
[p] tertia D m. pr.   [q] occurrerunt AD   [r] uallam D m. pr.   [s] multos om.
AD   [t] predia BC

---

[1] Raymond left Ma'arrat on 13 Jan. 1099. See *Gesta Francorum*, p. 81; Raymond of
Aguilers, p. 102; Robert of Rheims, p. 850. Bare feet were a sign of penitence. Accord-

When the count saw that he had been abandoned by them all, [300] and that already Ma'arrat was yielding most meagre provisions for his people, he put more trust in faith than in power, handed everything over to Christ, and with Him as captain he did not fear the twists of fate. Then, with bare feet, and laying aside his usual apparel, he departed from Ma'arrat with an escort of common people.[1] [305] His firm faith swore that all kinds of peril would yield before this people, and paid no heed to keeping the company of kings. That faithful man thought that the mighty would give way to the poor, and he himself dared to entrust his ship to tattered sails. The common folk set forth on the journey, slow on account of their starving, [310] and the count's companions were first to arrive at Kafarṭāb.[2] The count of Normandy and the forces of Normans,[3] whom their own land made sluggish but the strange land brave, joined themselves in body and soul to our men here, and they were not slow to endure any hardship in the zeal of the faith.

[315] The king of Caesarea also offered his love to our men, barely cloaking his fear under the guise of peace.[4] Then, strengthened by a series of mishaps, the host made for Caesarea, for a long respite would have been an onerous task for them, and they settled above the river Farfar;[5] [320] the river which flows alongside this city has such a name. As the king of the city saw their tents very close to the walls, he forbade any trading and rescinded his agreement. But when the night was over and the people were already moving on, two Turks ran on the king's orders to meet them, [325] showing co-operation to their enemies, enemies though they were, and, as he did not wish them to depart, informed them about the fords round there. Under the guidance of these two men, our people came to a certain valley, and captured many cattle, and plundered horses (for cattle and horses

---

ing to Albert of Aachen, p. 481, after the capture of Jerusalem, Godfrey of Bouillon processed around the walls of the city wearing the dress of a humble pilgrim.

[2] Kafarṭāb was twelve miles south of Ma'arrat an-Nu'mān. Raymond remained there till 16 Jan.

[3] See also *Gesta Francorum*, p. 81. Raymond of Aguilers, p. 102, says that Raymond of Toulouse was accompanied by Tancred.

[4] The emir of Shaizar, of the Banū Munqidh, sent guides to lead Raymond's army safely across the Orontes and offered to sell the crusaders food and horses. See Raymond of Aguilers, p. 103; *Gesta Francorum*, p. 81.

[5] See above, iv. 420–1 and n., for an explanation of this nickname. The army crossed the Orontes between Shaizar and Hamah.

Ibant graminea gaudentes fertilitate,   330
Vtque ferunt quibus illa fuit predatio certa,[a]
Depredatorum sunt milia quinque reperta).[1]
Aggere munitum fortique ualloque[b] rotundo[2]
Stabat ibi castrum, sed redditur hoc Raimundo.
Hostibus in mediis per quinque dies habitare   335
Profuit[c] et spoliis iumenta datis honerare.
Tunc gens illa fide firmat se[d] fedus habere
Perpetuum cum Christicolis, nullique nocere;
Nec[e] tamen huic fidei foret ulla fides adhibenda[f]
Nec leuis illorum[g] promissio suscipienda.[h]   340

Post Arabum petitur castrum, quod mox aperitur.[3]
Proximus hos labor[i] ad uallem perduxit amenam,
Fructibus innumeris hiemali[j] tempore plenam.
Vrbs ibi grata situ manet alto splendida muro,
Que quasi gemma micat auro circumdata puro;   345
Incola Caphaliam[k4] uocat hanc, qui tunc fugiebat,
Certius ut uidit[l] quos iam rumore uidebat.
Ciuibus egressis uictores ingrediuntur,[m]
Tres et in urbe dies complent opibusque fruuntur.
Nescia[n] gens herere dehinc[o] montes superauit   350
Immensos, in ualle De Sem[p5] sua castra locauit.
Hic quoque larga[q] Dei pietas dedit huic aciei
Fructus, frumentum uel sufficiens alimentum.[r]
Sed que proueniunt ad nutum[s] despiciuntur,
Interdicta placent magis,[t] interdicta secuntur,   355
Et castrum confine petunt. Tunc[u] hostis hianti
Proiecit populo predas, et[v] res ea tanti
Extitit ut castrum uictores fraude subacti
Desererent[w] mentis uitio, non ense coacti,[6]

---

[a] tenta *A*   [b] muroque *AD*   [c] affuit *F*   [d] sed *A*   [e] non *AD*
[f] adhibendo *A*   [g] eorum *F*   [h] suspicienda *F*   [i] *F m. pr.* omits hos
labor   [j] hic mali *A*   [k] Caphalia *A*   [l] ut ut uidit *A*   [m] regredi-
untur *D m. pr.*   [n] hostia *A*   [o] diu *AD*   [p] ualle desen *BCF;* ualle locus
est *D*   [q] laga *D m. pr.*   [r] alimentum sufficiens *F m. pr.*   [s] uotum *AD;*
nuptum *F*   [t] magis placent *F m. pr.*   [u] his *F m. pr., corr. to* hic *m. alt.*
[v] at *F*   [w] desenerent *F m. pr.*

---

[1] Raymond of Aguilers, p. 103, states that these men 'imprudenter' led the crusaders
to a valley where the local inhabitants had hidden their flocks.

[330] roamed widely over its meadows, rejoicing in the richness of.
its pasture; and according to the report of those who knew for
certain about that plunder, the captured beasts were found to be
five thousand in number).[1] A fort stood there too, fortified with a
strong rampart[2] and a palisade about it, but this too was handed
over to Raymond. [335] It profited them to shelter for five days in
the midst of the enemy, and to heap their pack-horses with the
spoils given to them. Then that race swore in faith to have an
everlasting treaty with the Christians, and to harm none of them;
but no faith was to be granted to this faith of theirs, [340] and their
fickle promise was not to be taken up.

After this they made for the Arabs' fort, which was soon opened up
to them.[3] Their toil next brought them to a beautiful valley, which
was full of countless fruits, even in winter-time. There was a city
there, beautiful from its location, and made glorious by a lofty wall,
[345] which sparkled like a jewel set about with pure gold; its
inhabitants call it Caphalia,[4] and they fled when they saw with
greater certainty those whom they had already beheld from
rumour. With the citizens gone the victors entered, and they
passed a full three days in the city enjoying its riches. [350] From
here, this race which did not know how to be still crossed over
enormous mountains, and pitched camp in the valley of De Sem.[5]
Here too God in his generous goodness gave this force fruit and
grain, that is, enough provisions. But the things which were theirs
for the asking were despised, [355] forbidden things were more
pleasing to them, and they pursued things forbidden, seeking out a
neighbouring fort. Then the enemy threw down plunder to the
greedy people, and this had such a great effect that the conquerors
were subdued by this deception and departed from the fort, not
compelled by the sword, but by the fault of their own mind.[6]

---

[2] The description is typical of bank-and-ditch earthworks, BCF's *uallo* replacing the
earlier *muro* in AD.

[3] Presumably Masyaf, whose lord made a treaty with the crusaders. See *Gesta Fran-
corum*, p. 82; Albert of Aachen, p. 451.

[4] Rafanīya. See also *Gesta Francorum*, p. 82.

[5] This place is usually identified as al-Buqaïah. The plain was commanded by the
fortress of Hisn al-Akrad, which stood on the site where Krak des Chevaliers was built.
See also Robert of Rheims, pp. 851–2; Raymond of Aguilers, p. 105.

[6] Raymond of Aguilers, p. 106, states that Raymond of Toulouse was almost captured
as the crusaders chased after the cattle let loose from the castle.

Et*a* tamen aggressi*b* castellum luce sequenti,   360
Defensore*c* suo uacuum patet aggredienti.[1]
Annua festa Dei genetricis ibi celebrantur,
Hec que candelis specialius*d* irradiantur.[2]

Munera tunc ducibus mittuntur ab urbe Camela,[3]
Aureus arcus, equi, uestes et lucida tela,   365
Legatique*e* sui regis mandata*f* ferentes
Exorant pacem; quos Christicole sapientes
Incertos faciunt, certum nichil instituentes.[4]
Rex*g* etiam Tripolis formidine*h* tactus ut isti
Septem mittit*i* equos et mulas quattuor hosti.*j*[5]   370
Dona duces capiunt, sed et hec suspecta*k* fuere,
Cumque uiris fedus quesitum non iniere.[6]
Post requiem letam*l* castellum deseruerunt,*m*
Quindecimaque die proceres iter arripuerunt.
Inde petunt Archas,*n*[7] castrum uetus equiparandum*o*   375
Vrbibus*p* et populo non absque labore uiandum.[8]
Hoc Arabes, Turci, Publicanique*q*[9] coronant,
Turres, arma, locus,*r* muri munimina donant.[10]
Sed tamen hec*s* nostri clauserunt obsidione,
Que*t* superare putant uel ui uel proditione.*u*   380
Precipiti*v* cursu muros nostri petiere,*w*
Precipitem cursum gentiles sustinuere.*x*
Percutiunt clausos*y* grauiusque repercutiuntur,
Nam*z* grauius ledunt que desuper eiciuntur;*aa*
Arcu, balista, tormento*bb*[11] gens furit ista.   385
Tormento lapis impulsus magnisque uirorum

---

a at *BC*   *b* aggressum *BF*   *c* defensorem *A*   *d* specialis *D*
e legati *A*   *f* mandanta *D*   *g* sex *F m. pr.*   *h* fortuidine *D m. pr.*
i mittunt *D*   *j* isti *BC*   *k* sed hec incerta suspecta *A*   *l* quindeci-
maque die letam *D, A m. sec.: A m. tert. corr. to* quindecima die   *m* *A m. pr. omits this
line; it is included at the foot of the page by A m. alt.*   *n* Arcas *D, F m. pr.*
o equiperandum *A*   *p* uiribus *A m. pr.*   *q* Pullicanique *A;* gentes Medique
BC   *r* loca *A*   *s* hoc *ADF*   *t* quod *AD*   *u* *B m. pr. puts this line
after l. 381*   *v* precipite *A m. pr.*   *w* pieciere *A*   *x* *A m. pr. omits this line;
it is added by m. alt. at the foot of the page*   *y* classos *D*   *z* iam *F;* non *A*
aa iaciuntur *B m. pr.;* initiuntur *D*   *bb* tormentos *D m. pr.*

---

[1] On the following day, 29 Jan., the army prepared an assault on the city, only to dis-
cover that it had been abandoned during the night.
[2] The Feast of Candlemas, 2 Feb. 1099.
[3] *Camela* was the crusaders' name for Homs. See *Gesta Francorum*, p. 83 and n.

[360] And yet, when they attacked the fort the following morning, it lay wide open to its attackers, empty of defenders.[1] The yearly festival of the mother of God, the one which is especially illuminated with candles, was celebrated there.[2]

Then gifts were sent to the leaders from the city of Homs,[3] [365] a golden bow, horses, clothes, and shimmering spears, and the envoys carrying their king's instructions begged for peace; the Christians wisely made them unsure, making no firm decisions.[4] Even the king of Tripoli was smitten with fear as they were, [370] and sent seven horses and four mules to his foe.[5] The leaders accepted the gifts, but these too were regarded with suspicion, and they did not enter with those men into the treaty that they desired.[6] After a joyful rest they left the fort behind, and on the fifteenth day, the nobles resumed their journey. [375] From there they made for ʿArqah,[7] an ancient castle which was the equal of the cities, and which the people could not reach without toil.[8] Arabs, Turks, and Paulicians[9] encircled this place, and its towers, its weapons, its location and its walls gave it sure protection.[10] But even so, our men shut all these in with a siege, [380] and thought they could overcome them either by force or by treachery. Our men made for the walls in a headlong charge, a headlong charge that the heathen withstood. They struck at the besieged, who struck back harder, for those things thrown down from on high inflict greater injury; [385] that people raged with the bow, the catapult, and the siege-engine.[11] Stones hurled by the siege-engines and backed up by massive human strength

---

[4] The emir of Homs was Janāḥ-ad-Daulah, an *atabeg* of Riḍvan of Aleppo (cf. v. 111 n.).

[5] See *Gesta Francorum*, p. 83; Raymond of Aguilers, pp. 106–7; Robert of Rheims, p. 853. The *Gesta* and Robert mention ten horses.

[6] Raymond in turn sent envoys to Tripoli. They returned impressed with the city's wealth and advised him to make a show of force against one of the emir's fortresses.

[7] According to the *Gesta Francorum*, p. 83, the crusaders arrived at ʿArqah, a stronghold at the foot of Mount Lebanon, NE of Tripoli, on 14 Feb. 1099. The settlement there was reputedly founded by Aracaeus, son of Canaan and grandson of Noah. See Gen. 10: 15–17, and also William of Tyre, p. 361.

[8] The siege of ʿArqah lasted twelve and a half weeks: see Albert of Aachen, pp. 451–2; Robert of Rheims, pp. 853–4; Fulcher of Chartres, pp. 268–9.

[9] See *Gesta Francorum*, p. 83. *Publicani* became the popular name for the Paulician heretics, who were absolute dualists. See R. I. Moore, *The Birth of Popular Heresy* (London, 1975), p. 73; M. Lambert, *Medieval Heresy* (London, 1977), p. 23. The crusaders had already encountered Paulicians on their journey across Asia Minor. See *Gesta Francorum*, pp. 20, 26; Baldric of Dol, pp. 54, 59.

[10] See *Gesta Francorum*, p. 83.   [11] See Robert of Rheims, p. 853.

Viribus adiutus[a] terit artus[b] oppositorum,
Funestum sibi pandit iter per scuta uolando,
Seminat[c] ille neces quicquid petit exanimando.[d]
Hic procerum decus, Anselmus[e] de Monte Riballo,[1]   390
Lustrat[f] anhelanti dum menia lata caballo
Mortiferum uulnus recipit, uir uiribus Hector,
Vir Cato[2] consilio, uir primus[g] in agmine rector.
Sepius aggressi muros sunt sepe[h] reiecti.

Post hec ad Tripolim[i] sunt quinque nouemque profecti
Vt predam caperent;[3] sexagintaque repente   396
Inueniunt Turcos, quos, Christo subueniente,
Inuadunt et sex perimunt, armentaque plura
Dum leti redeunt[j] cepere per hostica rura.
Non[k] procul urbs aberat, ripe uicina marine,   400
Fertilitate sua[l] promittens multa[m] rapine,
Nomine que celebris ipso[n] Tortosa uocatur.[4]
Impetit hanc Piletus Raimundus,[5] et associatur
Tentorie proconsul[6] ei, qui par paritate
Nominis,[o] huic non impar erat[p] mentis probitate.   405
Hi duo Tortosam cum paucis aggrediuntur,
Frustranturque diu nec prosperitate fruuntur.
Sed tamen[q] haud longe iam[r] nocte superueniente
Castra locant nimium populo strepitum faciente,
Accenduntque uiri non ad sua commoda segnes   410
Per iuga, per campos plures uigilantibus ignes;
Quos postquam ciues[s] lucere[t] procul speculantur,
Quod metuunt sperant,[u] quod sperant uaticinantur:
Christicolas castri procinctum[v] deseruisse,
Vrbis ad excidium tentoria iam posuisse.[7]   415

---

[a] impulsus F   [b] arcus D   [c] geminat F   [d] examinando ABCD
[e] Ansellus ADF   [f] fustrat A   [g] magnus BC   [h] sepe sunt F m. pr.
[i] Tripolum F   [j] leti reti redeunt F m. pr., corr. to dum leti leti redeunt m. alt.
[k] haut D   [l] sue D   [m] multa promittens F   [n] ipsa F   [o] hominis
F   [p] erat haud impar AD   [q] tamen om. F   [r] iam om. F   [s] ciues
om. F   [t] luere D   [u] superant D   [v] procintum F

---

[1] Anselm was castellan of Bouchain and the author of letters to Manasses, arch-
bishop of Rheims, which are an important source for the siege of Antioch. See *Die
Kreuzzugsbriefe*, pp. 63, 144–6, 155–66. Although he led his own force, Anselm served
with both Hugh of Vermandois and Raymond of Toulouse. His death is also recorded

ground the limbs of those who stood in their way, opening up for themselves a path of death as they flew among the shields, sowing the seeds of destruction as they crushed the life from whatever they smote. [390] Here Anselm of Ribemont,[1] the glory of the noblemen, received a deadly wound as he rode round the broad walls on his panting horse; he was a man as strong as Hector, as wise as Cato,[2] a captain in the front rank. They attacked the walls repeatedly, and repeatedly they were repulsed.

[395] After this, fourteen of them set out for Tripoli to capture some plunder,[3] and suddenly they came upon sixty Turks, whom they attacked, and with Christ's help killed six of them; and as they made their joyful return through the enemy fields, they captured many cattle. [400] There was a city not far away which lay beside the sea, promising a great deal of plunder because of its richness; famed for its very name, it was called Tortosa.[4] Raymond Pilet[5] attacked it, and the viscount of Turenne,[6] his equal in name [405] and not unequal to him in his worthy intentions, joined forces with him. These two attacked Tortosa with a small band, but were thwarted for a long time, and did not enjoy success. Even so, the people pitched their camp not far away as night fell, making a great din, [410] and men not slow to see their own advantage lit many fires on the hills and in the plains for those on watch; after the citizens had seen them burning brightly in the distance, they began to suspect what they feared, and gave voice to these suspicions, namely, that the Christians had left the area round the fort, [415] and had already pitched their tents, to bring down the city.[7]

by *Gesta Francorum*, p. 85, and by Robert of Rheims, p. 857. See also Riley-Smith, 'Death on the First Crusade', p. 27.

[2] Cato was regarded as an 'exemplary figure' of wisdom, familiarity with whom was a 'requisite for scholarly poetry in the Middle Ages' (Curtius, *European Literature*, p. 60), and was regarded by the Platonizing poets of the 12th c. as a pagan counterpart to Solomon as a recipient of divine wisdom.

[3] The same details are found in both Robert of Rheims, pp. 853–4, and the *Gesta Francorum*, p. 83. See also Albert of Aachen, pp. 456–7.

[4] Tortosa (Tartūs), some 28 miles north of Tripoli and important to the crusaders as the best harbour between there and the garrison at Latakia. See Raymond of Aguilers, p. 108.

[5] See above, viii. 12 n.

[6] Raymond, viscount of Turenne and a vassal of Raymond of Toulouse. See *Gesta Francorum*, pp. 83, 87; *HGL* iii. 484.

[7] This ruse, which made the army appear much larger than it actually was, is also described in *Gesta Francorum*, p. 84; Robert of Rheims, p. 854.

Ergo metu solo[a]1 superati deseruerunt
Menia, terga fuge nullo cogente dederunt.[2]
Ast[b] ubi sol rediit nocturnaque lumina texit
Lumine maiori,[c] nostris ignota retexit
Gaudia, quos subitum regnum,[d] non pugna uocabat   420
Expectata diu,[3] quibus urbs seruire parabat.
Parthe fugax,[e]4 ubi magna[f] magis miracula queres?
Aduena, sero tuus hostis, modo fit tuus heres!
Sufficit hec acies multis non multa ruinis,[g]
Est et ab Archois[h] tibi mors immissa pruinis.[5]   425
Vrbe uiri fortes insperata[i] potiuntur,
Hostiles portas quasi ciues ingrediuntur.
Bella Deus pro[j] gente sua secreta mouebat,[k]
Militibusque uiam[l] dux preuius expediebat
Datque suis aurum telluris ad ima retrusum: 430
Nec[m] cumularat opes nostrorum Parthus ad usum.
Dum[n] castrum tenet obsidio, proceres[o] tenuerunt
Hanc urbem portumque rates illic habuerunt.
Rex quoque Maraclee[p]6 nostris obstare nequiuit,
Collaque[q] submittens optatum fedus iniuit.   435

---

[a] solo metu *AD*   [b] at *F*   [c] maiore *D*   [d] pegnum *D*
[e] fugaux *F*   [f] magnas *D m. pr.*   [g] ruinos *D m. pr.*   [h] Athois *BC*
[i] insuperata *D*   [j] per *D*   [k] monebat *D*   [l] militibus quoque uiam *A*
[m] nunc *D*   [n] cum *F*   [o] nostri *AD*   [p] Miraclee *A; ?* Maniclee *D*
[q] tollaque *A*

So, conquered by fear alone,[1] they left their battlements and
turned their backs in flight, though no one compelled them.[2] But
when the sun returned to blot out the lights of the night with its
greater brilliance, it laid bare joys unknown to our men: [420] a
suddenly acquired kingdom summoned them, not a long-awaited
battle,[3] for the city was made ready to be at their disposal. Runa-
way Parthian,[4] where will you look for greater miracles? The
stranger, of late your enemy, has now become your heir. This
force, few in number, was enough for the downfall of many, [425]
and death was sent down to you from the frosty north.[5] The brave
men gained possession of the city they had not hoped for, and they
entered the enemy gates as though they were citizens. God was
waging secret warfare on His people's behalf, going ahead as their
captain, smoothing the way for His knights [430] and giving His
men gold hidden in the depths of the earth, even though the Par-
thians had not heaped riches up for our men's use. While the
blockade held fast the fort, the nobles held fast this city, and their
ships had a harbour there. The king of Maraqiyah[6] too was unable
to withstand our men, [435] and bowing low his neck he entered
into the treaty they desired from him.

---

[1] BCF correct the metre here with the change to *metu solo*.
[2] The crusaders occupied Tortosa on 17 Feb. 1099.
[3] Cf. Ovid, *Met.* xiii. 183; Juvenal, *Sat.* viii. 87.
[4] Cf. Ovid, *Remedia amoris*, 155.   [5] Cf. Jer. 6: 1, 10: 22.
[6] Maraqiyah was 10 miles north of Tortosa on the coast. On hearing news of the
latter's capture, its emir recognized Raymond's suzerainty. See *Gesta Francorum*, p. 84.

Iam, duce materia[1] cuius pars magna peracta est,[a]
Inspicimus propius[b] portum, finemque[c] laboris.[2]
Obscurat,[d] fateor, puerilis pagina grandem
Historiam, uersusque[e] leues onus aggrauat[f] ipsum.
Quod tamen incepi, sed non quo tramite cepi   5
Aggrediar, sensumque sequar, non uerba sonora,
Nec[g] patiar caudas[h] sibi respondere uicissim,
Pruriet et nulli modulatio carminis auri,
Quodque coartabant[i] humilis stilus et rude metrum,
Latius effundet prolixa relatio rerum:[3]   10
Sic[j] collum luctantis equi frenumque uolantis[k]
Contrahit[l] egrediens primum[m] de carcere cursor,
Ast, ubi proximus est[n] mete, mox laxat habenas;
Iamque meas[o] ego laxaui,[p] nam proxima meta est.[4]

Cum[q] Deus abiectis ducibus populique columnis   15
Pauperibus dat regna suis[5] paucisque triumphat,[r]
Ne sua que[s] Domino sunt ascribenda[t] potenti
Applaudens humana sibi natura uocaret,
Flandrensis comes atque duces uenere Liceam,[u6]
Sed Boimundus ibi consortia leta reliquit,   20
Emensumque remensus iter redit ad sua tristis.
Magnus at[v] ille ducum Godefridus liber ad arma

---

[a] est *om.* A   [b] proprius F   [c] fineque A   [d] obsurat D
[e] uerusque A   [f] aggragat D   [g] non B   [h] fines A; fines *glossed* caudas D
[i] cohortabant D   [j] si B; hic F   [k] uolentes A   [l] contrhit F
[m] primus AD   [n] est *om.* F   [o] mea A   [p] laxaui ego B *m. pr.*
[q] dum A *m. pr.*   [r] thiumphat F *m. pr.*   [s] cum D   [t] asscribendo D *m. pr.*   [u] Licheam DF   [v] ad D *m. pr.*

---

[1] It is unclear whether this reference by Gilo to his 'subject-matter' should be taken simply as meaning the tale he is in the process of recounting, or the redaction of a written account which he is following. See above, Introd., pp. lix–lx. Blatt, *Novum Glossarium Mediae Latinitatis* (Copenhagen, 1957), art. 'materia', gives two senses, one of which leans towards the former idea, 'sujet d'un ouvrage', and the other, 'exposition du livre à commenter', to the latter.

[2] For a similar image, see above, Prologue, l. 11.

Now, led on by the narrative whose greater part is done,[1] we look more closely on our haven and the end of our toil.[2] My childish writing, I confess, clouds the noble story, and its very weight is a burden to my flimsy verses. [5] I shall, however, attempt what I began, but not along the same path that I first took, and shall pursue the sense of the story, not fine-sounding words; I shall not allow the verse-endings to respond to one another by turns, and the charm of the poetry shall tickle no one's ears; the story which my humble pen and my unpolished verse hampered [10] shall now flow more broadly in a relaxed narrative of events,[3] in the same way that the horseman pulls hard at his struggling horse's neck and on its bridle as it flies onward, when he first sets off from the starting-gate, but when he reaches the finishing-post, he quickly slackens the reins; and now I have slackened my reins, for my finishing-post is hard by.[4]

[15] When God spurned the leaders and pillars of the people, and gave his kingdom to the poor,[5] triumphing through the few, lest human nature in praising itself should call its own the things which should be credited to the power of God, the count of Flanders and the leaders came to Latakia,[6] but [20] Bohemond abandoned their joyous company there, and returned in sadness to his own possessions, treading again the route he had trodden before. But Godfrey, that great man among the leaders, freely sprang forward

---

[3] As in the prologue, Gilo affects modesty with regard to his own skills, and in describing his poetic technique, he makes use of some of the technical vocabulary of the schools. See Faral, *Arts poétiques*, p. 86, for a discussion of the three levels of poetic writing distinguished by medieval writers, *humilis*, *mediocris*, and *grauis*.

[4] This use of the image of a horse- or chariot-race provides further evidence of Gilo's originality in adapting a common metaphor from classical verse. See above, Introd., pp. xxvii–xxviii, and also Vergil, *Georg..* i. 512, iii. 104; Statius, *Thebaid*, vi. 522–4; Ovid, *Met.* x. 652.

[5] Cf. Matt. 5: 3–4. This is a reference to Raymond Pilet and others involved in the capture of Tortosa.

[6] Godfrey of Bouillon, Bohemond and Robert of Flanders set out for Latakia at the end of February. Soon afterwards Bohemond turned back towards Antioch. See Robert of Rheims, pp. 854–6; *Gesta Francorum*, p. 84; Peter Tudebode, pp. 129–30; Albert of Aachen, p. 453.

Euolat et*a* patriam moto pater ense salutat.
Iam sordent terrena duci, iam concipit*b* ipsum
Ethera,*c*[1] nec meruit certus de munere fatum.   25
Heret*d* ei studioque pari*e* Flandrensis anhelat,*f*
Miratorque ducis meritum uirtutis honorat
In duce, quem merito magni precellit honoris.
Hi, licet exultent de successu*g* Raimundi,[2]
Se tamen alterius non inseruere labori,   30
Sed, dedignantes obsistere uiribus urbem,
Vrbem Gibellum[3] cinxerunt obsidione;
Huius*h* precipites cingebant menia fosse.
Nuntiat*i* interea Raimundo fama sinistros[4]
Rumores, ad bella suis occurrere Parthos.   35
Tunc et legatos et uerba precantia[5] consul
Dirigit ad proceres quos urbs obsessa tenebat,[6]
Qui, pro communi dampno commune uocantes
Concilium,*j* nec bella timent, nec ferre recusant
Auxilium,*k* pulsatque uiros spes leta triumphi.*l*   40
Nec mora, cum clausis pepigerunt fedus et empta*m*
Pax a ciue fuit, sociosque*n* suos petierunt.
Spe belli decepta cohors spem*o* uertit ad Archas,[7]
Atque tegit*p* castris fluuii*q* Castrensis harenas.*r*[8]
Neue diu, Godefride, tuus*s* frigesceret ensis,   45
Ad Tripolim ducis proceres*t* ut certior inde
Preda tibi quasi de pleno contingat ouili.[9]
Hostibus occurrunt hostes, leuibusque*u* sagittis
Stulta graues animos fuit ausa lacessere*v* turba,
Et, uelut improbitas muscarum ledere tantum   50
Nuda potest abigique solet crepitante flagello,*w*
Oppositeque rei morsus infigit inherens,*x*

---

a ad *D m. pr.*   *b* conspicit *F*   *c* etera *D m. pr.*   *d* herit *D*
e patri *D*   *f* anelat *A;* hanelat *F*   *g* suscessu *D*   *h* cuius *D;* ciuis *A*
i nuncitat *D*   *j* consilium *A m. pr.*   *k* axilium *D*   *l* thriumphi *F m. pr.*
m emta *F m. pr.*   *n* sotios *D*   *o* spe *A*   *p* tegunt *AD*   *q* fluuium
F   *r* harenis *B m. pr.*   *s* tutus *A*   *t* acies *D*   *u* leuibus *A*
v lacescere *BC*   *w* flagelle *A*   *x* herens *B*

---

[1] For the use of *aethera* to denote the heavenly realms, cf. Servius' commentary on
Vergil, *Aen.* iii. 583–6, and also below, ix. 119.

[2] Raymond of Toulouse, who was besieging 'Arqah.

[3] Jabala lay between Latakia and Tortosa, and was nominally dependent on Tripoli.

to take up arms, and, brandishing his sword, saluted his fatherland
as a father. By now, earthly things were abhorrent to the duke, for
heaven[1] had taken hold of him, [25] and, sure of his reward as he
was, he was yet unworthy of his fate. The count of Flanders stuck
by him, striving with equal vigour, and this admirer of the duke
paid honour to the duke's deserving courage, for he deserved to
surpass him through his own honoured position. Though these
two rejoiced at Raymond's[2] prosperity, [30] they did not involve
themselves in another's hard toil, but thought it beneath them to
assail the city with their forces; they encircled the city of Jabala[3]
and laid siege to it: ditches with sheer sides surrounded its fortifica-
tions. Meanwhile, reports of bad news reached Raymond,[4] [35] that
the Parthians were coming to fight for their people's sake. Then the
count sent envoys with a message of entreaty[5] to the nobles whom
the besieged city was keeping busy.[6] They called for a joint meet-
ing because of the joint danger they faced. They were not afraid of
fighting, and did not refuse to lend their aid, [40] for the joyful
hope of victory drove those men on. Without delay they struck a
treaty with the besieged, and peace was bought by the citizens; the
crusaders then headed for their allies. When hopes of fighting were
dashed, the force turned hopefully to 'Arqah,[7] and covered the
sands of the Camp River with their camp;[8] [45] and so that your
sword should not lie cold for long, Godfrey, you led the nobles to
Tripoli,[9] so that a more certain source of plunder, as though from a
full sheepfold, might fall to you. Enemy came out to meet enemy,
and the stupid host dared to provoke stout-hearted men with their
trifling arrows, [50] and, just like flies that in their irritating way
can only hurt bare flesh, and are regularly driven off by a swishing
flail, yet cling biting to whatever is set before them, just so the

[4] In early March, Raymond of Toulouse heard rumours that a large Muslim army
under the Caliph of Baghdad was assembling to relieve 'Arqah.
[5] Cf. Ovid, *Met.* ix. 159, among a number of Ovidian instances of the phrase *uerba pre-
cantia*.
[6] Envoys were sent to Godfrey and Robert at Jabala appealing for aid. See *Gesta
Francorum*, p. 84; Raymond of Aguilers, p. 111; Robert of Rheims, p. 856; Albert of
Aachen, pp. 456–7.
[7] Robert and Godfrey arrived at 'Arqah at the end of March.
[8] Only Gilo mentions this detail, which suggests that he may be drawing on an eye-
witness account. See Introd., p. lx. The river is presumably one of those flowing from
Mt. Lebanon down to the sea at 'Arqah.
[9] Godfrey led a successful raid on the outskirts of Tripoli. See *Gesta Francorum*, pp.
85–6. In the next verse Gilo's fondness for word-play (*hostibus... hostes*) makes the sense
obscure.

Taliter instantes uentis commissa sagitta
Infestans,[a] citraque necem dans uulnera, cedit
Ensibus[b] et fit ei clipei pretensio murus.   55
Sed quid[c] demoror hic ubi non est palma morata?
Armorum iam Parthus ope[d] post terga reiecta
Querit opem pedibus desperatamque[e] salutem.[f]
Instans miles equos calcaribus, ensibus hostes
Vrget et in multa uersatur cede cruentus.   60
Obtundunt acies gladiorum membra reuulsa,
Queque secare nequit[g] tepidus mucro conterit ossa.
Ciuibus[h] extinctis[i] ingressus inhorruit urbis,
Testificans cedem fluuius trahit inde ruborem,
Haurit et in fluuio perterrita turba cruorem.   65
Cede duces nimium predaque parum satiati
Vexatam petiere de Sem,[j1] predataque rursus[k]
Reliquiasque suas exquirunt[l] inrequieti.
Hanc[m] uallem[n] uelut intactam mirantur ab omni
Parte boues, asinos educere, postque rapinas   70
Raptori totiens immittere quod rapiatur.
Mox trahit in predam quicquid uidet impiger hostis,
Hostilesque manus replet indulgentia uallis:
Quippe[o] camelorum tria milia prebuit illis.[2]
Castra replet, uulgus reficit predatio, dantque[p]   75
Dampna moras,[q] animos externis obsidioni
Christicolis, et alunt inimici res inimicum.
Sed nec pugna ualet clausos nec machina[3] muros[4]
Frangere, quasque manus Persarum Corbana ductor,
Quas opus Antiochi timuit, populus premit ultor.   80
Christicole socios perdunt et tempora cara.
Poncius hic cecidit Balonensis,[r5] timpora cuius
Transabiit lapis ingenti conamine missus.
Occubuit Guillelmus ibi Picardus,[6] et una
De Petramora Guarinus,[s] at ille sagitta,   85

[a] hifestans A   [b] lusibus A   [c] cur AD   [d] Parthus ope iam BC
[e] desperata A; desperantamque F   [f] salute A   [g] nequid A   [h] quibus
A   [i] ex cunctis D   [j] desen A; densen D   [k] russus A   [l] querunt
F m. pr.   [m] hunc D   [n] uallam F   [o] quiculpe A   [p] dantque Gro-
cock; datque all MSS   [q] hostilesque manus dampna replet moras D m. pr.
[r] multus ibi populus prostratur F   [s] Garinus C; Warinus F

[1] See above, viii. 351 and n.; Gesta Francorum, p. 85.
[2] Robert of Rheims, p. 856 and Gesta Francorum, p. 85, give the same figure.

arrows entrusted to the wind troubled those who were advancing, inflicting wounds that fell short of fatality, [55] and then arrows gave way before their swords, as shields held outstretched became a wall against them. But why should I tarry here where the victory-prize did not tarry? Already the Parthian had thrown down behind him the aid his weapons afforded, and despairing of safety, ran away. The knights pressed on, driving their horses on with spurs and the enemy with swords, [60] bloody with the mass of slaughter they had made. Limbs that were ripped off blunted the sharpness of the swords, and what bones the warmed blade could not cut through, it simply crushed. The entrance to the city was cluttered with the bodies of the dead citizens; a torrent bore the red gore away from there, bearing witness to the slaughter, [65] and it was blood that the terrified crowd drew up from the river. The leaders, who had had their fill of killing but not of plunder, made for troubled De Sem,[1] and once again they relentlessly sought out what remained of its plunder. They were amazed that this valley [70] produced cattle and asses on every side as though it had never been touched, and that, even after previous raids, it could so often supply the plunderer with things he could carry off. The tireless enemy quickly took as plunder whatever he saw, and the generous provision of the valley filled the hands of its foe, for it furnished them with three thousand camels.[2] [75] Their plunder filled the camp and refreshed the common people; the enemy's loss gave rest to the Christians outside, and encouraged them in the siege, as the enemy's provisions nourished an enemy. But the fighting was not enough to break the besieged, nor could the siege-engine[3] break the walls:[4] the avenging people pent up the bands which the Persian general Kerbogha [80] and the stronghold of Antioch had feared. The Christians lost their allies, and also precious time. Here Pons of Balazun fell:[5] a stone hurled with massive force passed through his temples. William of Picardy[6] died there, and with him [85] Guarin of Petramora, the former by an arrow, the

---

[3] See above, viii. 153 and n.

[4] Cf. Claudian, *In Rufinum*, i. 219.

[5] Pons de Balazun. His death is also recorded by Robert of Rheims, p. 857; Peter Tudebode, p. 131; Raymond of Aguilers, p. 107. Indeed he seems to have been a close associate of the latter, and is referred to as co-author of his history of the First Crusade. See Raymond of Aguilers, p. 35.

[6] William's death is also recorded by Orderic Vitalis, v. 150; Robert of Rheims, p. 857; *Gesta Francorum*, p. 85; Baldric of Dol, p. 93.

Hic*a* iaculo, uenitque modis mors*b* una duobus.[1]
Inter tot luctus paschalis in obsidione
Lux celebratur[2] et in castris*c* festum fuit hospes,*d*
Temporibusque suis caruit sollempne serenum.[3]
Neue diu natura loci uirtusque uirorum   90
Illic decertent*e* et inexpugnabile castrum
Expugnare uolens labor expendatur inanis,
Mensibus obsessum tribus Archas deseruerunt,[4]
Atque petunt Tripolim,[5] ubi cum primatibus urbis
Dextras iungentes*f* dubiis sua*g* credere muris   95
Audent, seque ferunt ad celsa palatia regis;
Dant*h* pacem iam multotiens a rege petitam;*i*
Firmauere duces ut fratrum uincla resoluant.*j*
Tunc rex ter centum captiuos Christicolarum
Compedibus*k* uinclisque graues ab utroque resoluit,   100
Datque uiris uir dona, uiros dat dignius auro,*l*
Addit equos, aurum, populoque stipendia mittit,
Et se Christicolam fieri rex asserit ultro
Si sua Christicole ualeant attingere*m* uota.[6]

Iam tunc reddebant ematurata calore*n*   105
Arbor, messis, ager,*o* fructus, frumenta fabasque.*p*[7]
Fertilitas igitur rerum nouitasque recentis
Temporis*q* ad solitum*r* trahit agmina leta laborem.*s*[8]
Mensis erat Maii*t* cum fortes urbe relicta
Ad castrum Betholon*u*[9] uenere, diemque dieta*v*   110
Transcendens*w* uix nocte graui fuit*x* exuperata.
Inde maris litus uexata calore iuuentus
Radit*y* et ad Zebarim[10] ueniens, sitis immoderate
Dampna tulit, nec in urbe uidet quas hauriat undas,

a sic F   *b* mors omnibus F m. pr.   *c* castro BC   *d* facit hostis D
e decertant A   *f* ingentes F   *g* se AD   *h* et AD   *i* petita A
j BCF omit this line   *k* cum pedibus F   *l* D m. pr. puts this line after l. 102
m attinguere C, B m. alt. over an erasure   *n* cruore D m. pr.   *o* eger A m. pr.
p famasque B m. pr.   *q* temporibus A   *r* solitos D; solutos A
s labores AD   *t* Maius AD   *u* Bethelon DF   *v* dieque clieta (?) A
w transcendunt D   *x* fui B   *y* cadit F

---

[1] Cf. viii. 237; see also Robert of Rheims, p. 857.
[2] *Gesta Francorum*, p. 85, confirms the date of Easter Sunday as 10 Apr. 1099.
[3] Gilo makes no mention of Peter Bartholomew's vision on 5 Apr. announcing that an immediate assault upon ʿArqah should be made, and his ordeal by fire on 8 Apr. See Raymond of Aguilers, pp. 112–28.

latter by a spear, one death coming in two ways.[1] Among so many
grievous events, Easter Day[2] was celebrated in the siege, and the
feast was held in the alien setting of a military camp; what should
have been calm celebration was held in a time of crisis.[3] [90] So
that the nature of the location and the courage of the men within
the city might not long protract the fighting, and useless effort be
spent in the desire to storm an impregnable castle, they abandoned
the siege at 'Arqah after three months,[4] and made for Tripoli,[5]
where they joined their right hands with the chief men of the city,
[95] and dared to trust their property to walls of doubtful security,
taking themselves off to the the king's lofty palace; the leaders gave
the assurance of peace so often asked for by the king, confirming
peace in order to release the bonds of their brethren. Then the
king released three hundred Christians [100] from both the
manacles and the leg-irons that weighed them down; he handed
over gifts as man to man, and handed over men, more precious
than gold, added horses and gold, and sent supplies to our people.
Of his own free will the king even affirmed that if the Christians
were to achieve their desires, he would become a Christian
himself.[6]

[105] By this time, ripened by the warmth, the orchards were
bearing fruit, the harvest corn, the fields beans.[7] And so the
arrival of this fresh season with its accompanying fruitfulness
brought the joyous company back to their accustomed toil.[8] It
was the month of May when, leaving the city behind them, the
brave men came [110] to al-Batrūn, a fort;[9] their march there took
them more than a day, and was scarcely completed by a night of
hard effort. From there, the youthful band, afflicted by the heat,
made its way along the coast and suffered terrible pains from
thirst as it came to Jubail,[10] for it saw no water to draw in the city;

---

[4] The army left 'Arqah on 13 May, having arrived outside its walls on 14 Feb. The
Gesta Francorum says it arrived at Tripoli on this date.

[5] Note the hiatus at the caesura here, very rare in Gilo, but found above in the
Charleville Poet, ii. 140. See Introd., p. xxxi.

[6] See *Gesta Francorum*, p. 86; Raymond of Aguilers, p. 125; Robert of Rheims, pp.
857–8.

[7] The same produce is mentioned in the *Gesta Francorum*, p. 85.

[8] Parallel accounts are found in Peter Tudebode, p. 133; Albert of Aachen, pp. 457–
8; *Gesta Francorum*, p. 86.

[9] Al-Batrūn, a small town south of Tripoli.

[10] This coastal town was known as Byblos in classical times.

Sed labor alterius lucis duxit sitientes   115
Ad uada magna Braim,^{a1} populusque cucurrit ad amnes,^{b}
Quos super incumbens^c uix flatu sufficiente
Turba,^{d} parum uasi credens, auido rapit ore.

Venerat illa^e dies^2 qua^f uictor ad ethera^g Christus
Ascendens^h exempla suis se prebuit astris,^{3} 120
Sed graue nostra cohors iter emetitur^i in illa,
Et locat ante Baruch^j positam^k iuxta mare castra.
Post hec, transactis Sagitta^4 Surque^l duabus
Vrbibus, applicuit se predo beatus ad Acram.^{m5}
Hinc adeunt castrum Cayphas,^{n} castroque relicto   125
Iuxta^o Cesaream^6 figunt^p sua castra cohortes.
Illic letitie festum, si tempore leto
Occurrisset^q eis, obseruauere^r fideles,
In quo discipulis Dominus dedit omnia posse,
Vsus iure suo, mundo noua dona stupente.^{7} 130
Excepit tandem peregrinos Ramula^s ciues,^{8}
Ciue suo uacuata, nouos qui fugerat^t hostes,^{9}
Ecclesieque tibi sacrate, Sancte Georgi,
Que speciosa satis uicine presidet urbi,
Pontificem decimasque suas gens sancta reliquit.^{u10} 135

Hactenus armorum^{11} grauitate, calore repulsa,
Paupertate, siti, nocturno frigore,^{v} pugna
Excruciata cohors optatam uenit ad urbem^{12}
Quam Salomon opibus ditauit, Christus honore.^{13}
Iunius ardebat^{14} et sol ardebat in armis   140

---

^{a} Braym A; Barim B ^{b} annes DF; agnes A; fontes *glossed* amnes B ^{c} incombens A ^{d} tuba A ^{e} ille AD ^{f} quo AD ^{g} etera D
^{h} adscendens A ^{i} ementur D ^{j} Baruc A, D *m. tert.*; Brauc D *m. pr.*; Buarc D *m. sec.*; Baruhc F *m. alt. over an erasure* ^{k} posita A ^{l} Suique A
^{m} Achram F; Acra A ^{n} Caiphas AD ^{o} iusta F ^{p} fugunt (?) A
^{q} occurrisses D *m. pr.* ^{r} obseruare A ^{s} Romola CF; Ramdula D
^{t} fugera D ^{u} reliquid B; relinquit C; relinquid F ^{v} tempore AD

---

^{1} Probably the classical Lycus, and north of the Nahr al Kalb, which the crusaders called Dog River, and which was known in classical times as the Magoras. See *Gesta Francorum*, p. 86 and n.
^{2} Cf. below, ix. 271. ^{3} Ascension Day, 19 May 1099.
^{4} Sidon was reached on 20 May.
^{5} Albert of Aachen, pp. 457–60, and Peter Tudebode, p. 133, give the same route as Gilo. Fulcher of Chartres, pp. 271–5, adds a few more geographical details, such as the location of Acre, to the north of Mt. Carmel.

[115] but a further day's toil brought the thirsty ones to the great waters of the Nahr Ibrahim,[1] and the people ran to its streams; scarcely able to breathe, the crowd fell upon them and drank from them greedily with their mouths; they had little trust in cups.

The day had come[2] when Christ rose up to the heavens as conqueror,[3] [120] and revealed himself to his own stars, to be their pattern; but our troops trod a weary journey on that day, and pitched their camp before Beirut, set beside the sea. After these events, the blessed band of plunderers passed the two cities of Sidon[4] and Tyre, and pressed on to Acre.[5] [125] From here they went to the fort of Haifa, and then the troops left the fort behind them and pitched their camp beside Caesarea.[6] There those men of faith observed a feast which would have been a feast of joy, had it occurred at a time of joy for them, the feast when using his authority the Lord granted to his disciples the power to do all things, [130] that left the world amazed at the new gifts.[7] Eventually Ramle[8] took them in as citizens from overseas, as it was empty of its own citizens, who had fled from the newly-arrived enemy;[9] the holy race left a bishop and the tithes due to him for the church dedicated to you, St George, a beautiful church which overlooks the city beside it.[10]

[136] The troops who up to this point[11] had been beaten down by the heat and by the weight of their weapons, and tormented by poverty, thirst, the cold at night, and the fighting, now came to the city they had longed for,[12] which Solomon enriched with wealth, and Christ with honour.[13] [140] The June sun[14] burnt hot on their weapons

---

[6] The Crusaders remained in Caesarea from 26 to 30 May.

[7] Whitsunday, 29 May 1099.

[8] Ramle lay SE of Jaffa, on the road to Jerusalem.

[9] The Muslims had abandoned Ramle on hearing of the crusaders' advance. See *Gesta Francorum*, p. 87.

[10] The basilica of Lydda was the principal shrine of St George and had been burnt down by the departing Muslims. During their stay, the crusaders elected a Norman priest, Robert of Rouen, as Bishop of Lydda. See Hamilton, *The Latin Church*, p. 11; *Gesta Francorum*, p. 87; Raymond of Aguilers, p. 136.

[11] Cf. Vergil, *Georg.* ii. 1.

[12] For the siege of Jerusalem, see *Gesta Francorum*, p. 87; Peter Tudebode, p. 134; Raymond of Aguilers, p. 137; Robert of Rheims, pp. 863–4.

[13] Cf. Arator, *Hist. apost.* i. 1012.

[14] The Crusaders left Ramle on 6 June and encamped outside Jerusalem the following day.

Quando suis texere duces loca congrua castris.
Pars ea^a cui superest septentrio^b castra recepit
Normanni^c comitis, et ei Flandrensis adhesit.^{d}
Solis ab occasu tendit Godefridus in hostem,^{e}
Solis ab occasu terret Tancretius urbem.   145
E^f media, Raimunde, die tua classica clangunt.[1]
Postquam Iherusalem nostrorum cincta corona est,^{g} [2]
Eduxit leuitate[3] pares Piletus Raimundus:
Proxima dum lustrantur equis oculisque remota,
Bis centum casus Arabes predonibus offert,   150
Quos neque facta^h sui cultoris prodiga uirtus
Nec manus eripuit numerosior, aut^i fuga turpis:
Hos fuga, sed plures ex illis precipitatos
Nec fuga nec gladius saluauit, quos spoliauit
Vita nostra cohors, et equos ad castra reduxit.   155

Pluribus aptatis que sunt aptanda ruine
Festinant^j ad uota uiri, murumque priorem[4]
Inuadunt, magnisque uocant clamoribus hostem.[5]
Mox gentilis^k adest, Iudeus, Turcus Arabsque:
Missilibus,^{l} iaculis obsistitur, igne, ueneno,   160
At^m nostri iaculis opponunt pectora nuda,
Proque flagellato patiuntur dura^n flagella,
Perque graues aditus, per tela,^{o} per arma ruentes
Muri precipitant irritamenta prioris.
Disiecti fugiunt ad menia^p tuta manipli,   165
At^q dum quisque timens certat prior esse, priores^r
Turba sequens inimica suis in limine^s porte
Conterit, hicque suum Pilades prosternit Horestem.[6]
Maxima pars exclusa gemit, natique parentes
Orantes non excipiunt, pietate stupente.   170
Protinus ingenti conatu scala leuata

---

^{a} en A ^{b} septenbrio F ^{c} Mormanni A ^{d} adheret AD ^{e} A
and B m pr. put this line after l. 145 ^{f} a AD ^{g} est om. A ^{h} fata D
^{i} at AD ^{j} cestinant (?) F ^{k} gentiles A ^{l} missibus A ^{m} et F
^{n} dira BC ^{o} nec mora raignanimi (sic) per saxa A ^{p} meniam D
^{q} et AD ^{r} prioris D ^{s} lumine F

---

[1] For the disposition of the armies, see *Gesta Francorum*, p. 87; Albert of Aachen, pp. 463–4. The physical situation of the city, with the ravine of Kedron to the east, meant that an attack from this side was both difficult and unexpected. See below, ix. 277 and n.

when the leaders spread their tents over the area round them. That part over which the northern sky lies was host to the camp of the count of Normandy, and the duke of Flanders stuck close by him. Godfrey faced the enemy from where the sun goes down, [145] and from that same place Tancred terrified the city. Your trumpets, Raymond, blared out from the south.[1] After Jerusalem had been surrounded by our men encircling it,[2] Raymond Pilet led out some men who were all alike in mobility:[3] while they were roaming on horseback over territory near and far, [150] fate gave two hundred Arabs to the plunderers, and neither their valour which wasted those devoted to it nor their superior numbers saved them, nor cowardly flight; flight saved a few, but most of them were routed, and neither flight nor fighting saved them: [155] our forces despoiled them of life and led their horses back to the camp.

When they had made ready the many things which must be made ready for the destruction of a city, the men hurried to bring their wishes about, and attacked the curtain-wall,[4] challenging the enemy with loud cries.[5] Suddenly the heathen were there, Jews, Turks and Arabs: [160] they were assailed with missiles and spears, fire and poison, yet our men presented their chests all exposed to the missiles and spears, bearing this hard scourging as a penance, and rushing through the gates that bristled with spears and swords they overthrew the obstacle posed by the curtain-wall. [165] The scattered platoons fled to the safety of the fortress, but as each of them in his fear struggled to get in front, the crowd following on behind crushed them on the threshold of the gate, and became an enemy to its own side: here Pylades slew his dear Orestes.[6] The largest part of them were shut out, wailing, and human feeling received an affront as sons [170] did not let in their fathers who pleaded with them. A ladder swiftly raised aloft with a mighty heave

[2] Clearly an exaggeration, since there was no one in the east.

[3] The Latin phrase *leuitate pares* could also mean 'lightly armoured' or 'heedless'. *Gesta Francorum*, p. 87, states that this sortie by Raymond and others took place on the third day after their arrival outside Jerusalem.

[4] The assault on the curtain-wall is also mentioned in detail by the *Gesta Francorum*, p. 88; it began on Monday, 13 June 1099. Its timing followed a prediction of victory made by a hermit on the Mount of Olives: Raymond of Aguilers, p. 139.

[5] Cf. Vergil, *Georg.* iv. 76.

[6] These were a 'type' of perfect friends in classical mythology: cf. Ovid, *Epistulae ex Ponto*, iii. 2. 285, Claudian, *In Rufinum*, i. 107–8, and especially Sidonius Apollinaris, *Carm.* v. 288–9.

Prebet ad alta uiam, cui nostra iuuentus[a] adherens[b1]
Decertat gladiis et comminus impetit hostem.
Copia[c] scalarum si forte parata fuisset,
Innumeri labor ille mali labor ultimus esset.[2]   175
Obstitit hoc solum nostris, fortunaque belli
Iuuit[d] ad extremum ductos, alterna reuisens.[e]

Tandem castra cohors petit et respirat ab armis.
Fercula qui quondam noua fastidire[f] solebat
Atque uocare famem[g] dulcedine deliciarum   180
Irritando gulam nunc sicco pane repletur,
Et mentitur eis[h] pigmenti[i] limpha saporem,
Quam sitiens miles preciosi[j] comparat auro.[3]
Montis quippe Syon fons a radice citatus,
Fons Syloe,[k4] potu minimo[l] longeque petito   185
Innumeros reficit populos, et uenditur unda
Quam natura potens gratis concessit habendam.

Dum[m] uario premitur gens nostra labore, secute
Christicolas[n] uenere rates, quas[o] Iaphia portu
Excipit optato,[5] nunc urbs, tunc urbis imago.   190
Ergo uiri centum mittuntur ab obsidione,
Qui seruare rates Turcosque repellere possint.[p6]
Prefuit Acardus[q] Merulo de Monte[7] cohorti,
Atque Sabratensis[r] Guillelmus[8] cum Raimundo:[9]
Sed probus Acardus[s] cum triginta prior iuit,[t]   195
Impulsus leuitate sua plus quam[u] ratione.
Hic septingentos Arabes in ualle profunda

---

[a] fortis miles AD   [b] A adds the line Rambaudus Criminum castri Dunensis
alumpnus after l. 172   [c] copio D   [d] iuit D   [e] reuissens D m. pr.
[f] uastidire D   [g] fame D m. pr.   [h] ei AD   [i] picmentum D m. pr.
[j] preciosa A m. pr.   [k] Siloe A   [l] nimio D   [m] cum BCD
[n] Christicolis D   [o] quos D   [p] possunt D   [q] Achardus BC
[r] Sabratentis D   [s] Achardus C   [t] prior cum triginta iuit F m. pr.; cum pau-
cis ante cucurrit AD   [u] plusque D

---

[1] In view of the manuscript tradition and the transmission of the text to which it
points, the presence of the additional line after l. 172 in A alone suggests that it should
be regarded as an addition to Gilo's poem, placed independently by an interpolator
(who perhaps had access to local knowledge), rather than an original line lost at an early
stage of the transmission (accounting for its non-appearance in BCF) and omitted by D.
Rambaud is described elsewhere as a knight of Chartres: see Baldric of Dol, pp. 49 n. 12,
71 n. 7, 102 n. 8; Albert of Aachen, p. 410; Tudebodus Imitatus et Continuatus, pp. 210-19.
Châteaudun lies some 30 miles SW of Chartres.

provided a path to the heights, and our youth, clinging to it,[1] fought
it out with swords and charged the enemy at close quarters. If there
had happened to be a good supply of ladders there, [175] that toil
involving countless miseries would have been their final toil.[2] Only
this stood in our men's way, and the fortune of war helped those
who were at their wits' end, changing their plans.

Eventually the troops headed for camp, and rested from the fight-
ing. He who once used to pick at new recipes, [180] and who used
to work up an appetite titillating his palate with the subtle flavours
of hors d'œuvres, now filled himself up with dry bread, and plain
water counterfeited for him the bouquet of spiced wine: the thirsty
knights likened it to precious gold.[3] For indeed, there is a spring
which flows swiftly from the foot of Mount Zion, [185] the spring of
Siloam,[4] which was sought from afar and refreshed countless
people with a meagre drink, and its waters, which mighty nature
gave over to be possessed freely, were sold for money.

While our folk were harrassed by various trials, the ships which
had followed the Christians arrived, and Jaffa, [190] now a city
but then the ghost of a city, took them in, the haven they
desired.[5] On this account, a hundred men were sent from the
siege to protect the ships and drive off the Turks.[6] The force
was commanded by Achard of Montmerle,[7] William of Sabran[8]
and Raymond;[9] [195] but the noble Achard went on ahead with
thirty men, driven on more by his own heedless nature than by
reason. He came across seven hundred Arabs in a deep valley

---

[2] See also *Gesta Francorum*, p. 88; Raymond of Aguilers, p. 139.

[3] For other accounts of the shortages of food and water, see *Gesta Francorum*, p. 88;
Fulcher of Chartres, pp. 294–5.

[4] Cf. 2 Esd. (Neh.) 3: 15; John 9: 7, 11.

[5] Jaffa was the nearest port to Jerusalem. The Genoese galleys arrived on 17 June,
carrying food supplies and armaments. See Raymond of Aguilers, p. 141; Robert of
Rheims, pp. 864–5; Peter Tudebode, pp. 135–6.

[6] See *Gesta Francorum*, p. 88; Raymond of Aguilers, p. 141.

[7] Achard of Montmerle was a Burgundian lord who had pledged part of his
patrimony to Cluny to raise sufficient money to participate in the First Crusade. See
Recueil des chartres de l'abbaye de Cluny (*1091–1210*), ed. A. Bernard, rev. A. Bruel, 6 vols.
(Paris, 1894–1903), v. 51–3. He served with both Hugh of Vermandois and Raymond of
Toulouse. See *Gesta Francorum*, pp. 5, 88–9; Peter Tudebode, p. 135; Raymond of
Aguilers, p. 141; Orderic Vitalis, v. 160, 162.

[8] William, lord of Sabran, was still alive in 1123. See *Gesta Francorum*, p. 88; Orderic
Vitalis, v. 160. See also *HGL* iii. 491.   [9] Raymond Pilet.

Repperiens irrupit[a] in hos, hastaque reiecta
Fulmineo scindit gladio quem respicit hostem.
Tandem succubuit,[b] non pigritie, sed honesti   200
Funeris[c] exemplo, per quod monet ille[d] sodales,
E quibus elapsus unus crudele cohorti
Nuntiat exitium,[e] clamans[f] crudeliter 'ecce
Exequias, proceres, sociis[g] date quas[h] dare uite
Non licet, at mortem[i] licet hostis morte piare!'[j]   205
Talibus hortati Piletus Piletique sodales
Quos magis hortantur uirtus, uindicta suorum,
Vera fides, alternus[k] amor, requiesque laborum,
Interius mentes[l] armis celestibus ornant,
Exterius sua membra tegunt et uilibus[m] armant.   210
Inde[n] repentino uisu turbantur, et hostes
Digressi uidere suos spoliare necatos,
Et licet innumeros uideant hi qui numerari
Mox poterant,[o] tamen occurrunt, legitque uirum uir,[p]
Prosternitque suum congressu[q] quisque priori.   215
Protinus horribilis miscetur in agmine[r] pugna:
Amittunt galee cristas,[s] clipei[t] sua signa,
Euertunt gladii facies, hominesque[u] recisis
Naribus expauit tyro de cognitione
Iam dubius,[v] hos non[w] homines sed monstra putauit.   220
Hastis nostra cohors istos petit, ensibus illos,[x]
Impulit hos currens casuque peremit amaro,
Illos morte timor subita prosternit inertes.
Casibus afflicti[y] uariis gentilis Arabsque
Dant facili sua terga fuge, multisque[z] necatis   225
Vni uictor ouans dilata morte pepercit,
Per quem Persarum secreta dolosa paterent.[1]
Tres quoque miles equos et centum duxit ab hoste.[2]

Dum uacat in castris populus, sitis immoderata
Excruciauit eum.[aa3] Gladiis tellure cauata   230

---

[a] irrumpit D   [b] succumbit D; subcubit A   [c] muneris F   [d] ipse A
[e] exticium A   [f] clamat BC   [g] sociis proceres AD   [h] quos ADF
[i] mortes BC   [j] D m. pr. omits this verse   [k] alterius A   [l] mentis D
[m] ullibus D   [n] unde F; inque BC   [o] poterunt A   [p] uir om. A
[q] progressu F   [r] agmina D m. pr.   [s] chistas F m. pr., corr. to christas m. alt.
[t] clipeim D m. alt.   [u] hominumque D   [v] dubitans AD   [w] non om. D;
non hos BC   [x] illos petit ensibus istos A   [y] afflictus AD   [z] multis A
[aa] illum D m. pr.

and charged at them, and throwing aside his lance he slashed with
his glittering sword at any enemy he caught sight of. [200] In the
end he was overwhelmed, not through lack of effort but rather sett-
ing an example of a noble death, and in this he gave counsel to his
companions, one of whom slipped away and announced their cruel
end to the troops, cruelly shouting: 'Look, nobles, pay your now-
dead comrades a tribute you could not pay them while they lived;
[205] atone for their death by the death of the enemy!' Raymond
Pilet and his companions were urged on by such words, and cou-
rage, vengeance for their own side, the true faith, love of others and
rest from their labours urged them on more; [210] they embla-
zoned their minds inwardly with heavenly weapons, and clothed
and equipped their bodies outwardly with earthly ones. Then as
they set forth they were disturbed by the sudden sight of the enemy
despoiling their slain comrades, and though they who could swiftly
be numbered beheld a numberless host, still they ran to meet
them, man chose man to fight, [215] and each of them laid low his
choice at the first encounter. Straight away the column of men was
embroiled in foul fighting: helmets lost their crests and shields
their devices, swords mangled faces, and the new recruit was
stricken with terror at men with their noses cut off, [220] by now
wondering what he was looking at: these were monsters, he
thought, not men. Our troops attacked some with staves and others
with swords; some they ran at, driving them on, and brought them
to a bitter end, while fear made others inert and laid them low in
sudden death. Scourged by these differing fates, the heathen and
Arabs [225] were swift to turn their backs in flight, and after killing
many of them the exultant conquerors spared just one of them,
putting off his death, and through this man the treacherous secrets
of the Persians were laid bare.[1] The knights also led away a hun-
dred and three horses from the enemy.[2]

While the people were idle in the camp, thirst that knew no bounds
[230] tortured them.[3] A knight would plunge his head into holes

---

[1] See *Gesta Francorum*, pp. 88–9; Robert of Rheims, p. 865. Achard of Mortmerle's
contingent was massacred by the Turks, but they in turn fled upon the arrival of
Raymond Pilet. The Franks spared one Turk to tell others of the battle.

[2] The number is also recorded in *Gesta Francorum*, p. 89; Robert of Rheims, p. 865.

[3] See *Gesta Francorum*, pp. 89–90; Robert of Rheims, pp. 866–7; Raymond of Aguilers,
pp. 145–6; Fulcher of Chartres, pp. 294–6.

Miles in antra caput mergebat, luce relicta,
Pinguis ut humectet*a* tellus arentia labra.

Hic quod ab utre cadit resupino suscipit ore,
Marmora lambebat alius sudantia rore.

Aspiceres pestem languentem cuncta per ossa   235
Iam rabiem traxisse suam, nutare*b* subactis
Viribus incessum, lingueque*c* retundier*dl* usum.

Si mactat quandoque bouem librata*e* securis,
Carnibus abiectis, sorbetur ab agmine sanguis.

Esuriem tolerare libet, dolor ille dolorem   240
Hunc minuit. Prodesse famem*f* quis credere posset?*g2*

Clauserat occultos laticum gens seua meatus,
Inuentosque*h* lacus obseruans, insidiatur*i*
Christicolis, mortemque dabat querentibus undas.*j3*

Cum*k* gens letifero siccata calore*l* calorem   245
Vitalem perdit, nulloque liquore rigata
Intestina bonis nature destituuntur,
Construitur*m* studio Godefridi machina, formam
Castelli*n* retinens, multoque labore reperta.

Materiam dant ligna*o* fabris, urbique timorem.   250

Par*p* quoque castellum*q* Raimundi prouida cura
Erigit, et contra turres turrita parantur.*4*

Exstupuere nouas miseri consurgere moles
Gentiles, ipsique suas accrescere turres
Nocte laborabant, studio fallente laborem;   255

Nec minus ingentis*r* castelli compositores,
Quos ducis urgebat presentia sollicitantis,*s*
Nocturnam requiem uigilant,*t* uariasque per artes
Intempestiuum*u* ducunt sub nocte laborem.*v5*

Nox que Iudeis requiem transacta*w* reliquit*x*   260

---

a humecet *A*   *b* mutare *C m. pr.*   *c* langueque *A*   *d* retunder *D m.*
pr.; usum retundier *A*   *e* librota *A*   *f* famen *D*   *g* scribere posset *BC;*
crederet unquam *AD*   *h* immensosque *A*   *i* insidiabat *F*   *j* undam
AD   *k* dum *BCD*   *l* sicalore *F*   *m* construxit *D*   *n* castella *A*
o lingna *D*   *p* pars *D*   *q* castelli *F*   *r* ingenti *BC*   *s* sollicitantis
Grocock; sollicitantes *all MSS except* compositores *F m. pr.*   *t* requiem transacta
reliquit *D m. pr.*   *u* intempestium *D*   *v D m. pr. omits this line*
w trahens *D*   *x D m. pr. omits this line*

---

1 The rather recherché form *retundier* is not unknown in 12th-c. verse: see Walter of
Châtillon, *Alexandreis*, i. 218, iii. 146, iv. 123, viii. 393. It is an imitation of the archaic form of
the passive infinitive found in Vergil, and copied in Proba (*Cent. Verg.* 501 = Vergil, *Georg.*
i. 454–5) and Sidonius Apollinaris, *Carm.* xi. 104.

hacked in the ground with swords, leaving the daylight behind, so
that the damp earth might moisten his parched lips. One man
leaned his head back and drained what fell from the skin-bottle,
and another would lick marble stones sweating with dew. [235]
You might see the plague, which had lain dormant deep in a man's
bones, suddenly bring on its own madness, his walk become
unsteady as his strength was impaired, and his ability to speak was
suppressed.[1] If ever an axe was swung to slaughter an ox, the meat
was thrown away and the blood drunk by the crowds. [240] They
were happy to put up with starvation, for the pain of that lessened
the pain of this. Who could believe that hunger could be benefi-
cial?[2] The race of wild men had blocked up the hidden mouths of
the springs, and kept watch on the pools that they had found, lying
in ambush for the Christians and dealing death to those who came
looking for water.[3] [245] When the people became dehydrated by
the killing heat, and lost the natural heat of life, and, with no mois-
ture to slake their thirst, their inner parts were deprived of the
blessings of nature, a siege-engine was built, at the earnest
prompting of Godfrey; it resembled a castle in shape, and took a
great deal of effort to construct. [250] Its timbers gave raw material
to the carpenters, and fear to the city. With equally careful provision,
Raymond also raised up an equal siege-castle, and its towers were
built up to face the turrets of the city.[4] The wretched heathen were
astonished to see these massive structures suddenly rise up, and
they themselves [255] toiled by night to raise their own towers
higher, their zeal beguiling their toil; equally, the builders of the
massive siege-castle, encouraged by the duke urging them on in per-
son, stayed awake in the time of rest at night, and in their divers skills
drew out their unseasonable toil throughout the night.[5] [260] That
night which, when it passed over, left respite for the Jewish people,

[2] For a parallel, see Robert of Rheims, p. 866.

[3] Apart from the pool of Siloam, which was exposed to attacks from the city, the nearest
water supply was 6 miles away, and reaching it involved the risk of enemy ambushes. See
Gesta Francorum, p. 88. Note the chiasmic play on words *letifero calore/calorem uitalem*.

[4] Gaston of Béarn was responsible for the construction of Godfrey's castle, the Geno-
ese William Embriaco for Raymond's. See Raymond of Aguilers, pp. 145–6, and below, ix.
333 and n.

[5] See *Gesta Francorum*, p. 90. Although the Genoese fleet brought some building mate-
rials, wood was scarce in the hills around Jerusalem and had to be collected from further
afield. See also Raymond of Aguilers, pp. 146–7.

Lucida uelabat[a] tenebrosa sidera palla,[b]
Cum ducis artifices ad muros applicuerunt
Robora castelli minitantis solis ab[c] ortu[1]
(Nam leuius poterant irrumpere solis ab ortu).[d]
Multiplicando preces, lacrimas, ieiunia, uota,　　　265
Circa Iherusalem portant insignia Christi
Christicole, uexilla, cruces, altaria sancta.[2]
Dicere longa mihi mora finem prospicienti
Quotque quibusque[e] modis[3] breue tempus comparat hostis,
Cuius Parca necans iam rumpere fila parabat.[4]　　　270

Venerat illa dies[5] qua mortificare magistrum
Gens Iudea Ihesum[f] cupiens se mortificauit.
Hac in luce duces ad muros agmina ducunt.
Stans comes Eustachius[6] in castro cum Godefrido
Susceptos ictus reddit cum fenore duro.[7]　　　275
Ilia Turcorum transuerberat a duce missa
Non unum[g] contenta[h] latus transire sagitta.
Dux ducis exequitur curam fortisque laborem
Militis,[i] hortatur pugnantes, pugnat et ipse,
Pugnat pro duplici regno, quia querit utramque[j,k]　　　280
Iherusalem, decertat in hac ut uiuat in illa.[8]
Saxa super crates uenientia uimina[l] frangunt,[9]
Robora, scuta, uiros de castri culmine uoluunt.[m]
Mortis in articulo uirtus non defuit hosti,
Donec, qua Christum crux sanctificata recepit,　　　285
Adfuit hora, diem minuens ciuisque uigorem.[10]
Hac hora quidam de castro fortiter instans,[n]
Nomine Letoldus,[o][11] muro prior insilit urbis:

[a] ualebat *A*	[b] palla sidera *D*	[c] ad *A*	[d] *BC omit this line*
[e] quibus *AD*	[f] Deum *D*	[g] nuntium *A*	[h] contempta *F*
[i] multis *A*	[j] utrumque *ABCD*	[k] *D m. pr. omits this line*	[l] nimina *A*
[m] uolunt *D;* nolunt *A*	[n] infans *D*	[o] Letholdus *BC;* Letaldus *A*	

---

[1] See above, ix. 147 n. The *Gesta Francorum*, p. 90, also states that a siege-tower was positioned on the eastern side, where the inhabitants least expected an attack.

[2] This penitential procession was prompted by a vision in which the recently deceased Bishop Adhémar of Le Puy appeared to the priest Peter Desiderius. See Raymond of Aguilers, p. 151. The fullest account of the procession is given by Peter Tudebode, pp. 137–8, who claims to have taken part himself.

[3] Cf. Ovid, *Amores*, ii. 8. 28.

[4] The procession took place on Friday, 8 July, and the following day the siege-engine

was covering over the shimmering stars with a cloak of shadow,
when the duke's craftsmen brought the menacing mass of the
siege-castle up to the walls from the east[1] (for they could break in
more easily from the east). [265] Redoubling their prayers and
lamentations, fastings and petitions, the Christians carried
Christ's standards around Jerusalem, banners, crosses, and holy
altars.[2] It would delay me long as I look forward to the end of my
tale to tell the many and various ways[3] in which the foe made
preparations in a short time; [270] the death-dealing Fates were
already making ready to snap their threads.[4]

That day had come[5] on which the Jewish race, desiring to put to
death their master Jesus, put themselves to death. At dawn on this
day the leaders led their forces to the walls. Count Eustace[6] stood
firm on the siege-castle with Godfrey, [275] and paid back the
blows he received with hard interest.[7] Arrows shot by the duke
passed quivering right through the Turks' bellies, not content with
penetrating one side of them. The duke carried out the duties of a
general and the hard toil of a brave knight, encouraging those
fighting and fighting himself, [280] fighting for a twofold kingdom,
since he was looking forward to both Jerusalems: he fought in the
one so that he might have life in the other.[8] Rocks coming down on
the woven wicker coverings[9] smashed through them, and timbers,
shields, and men were tumbled from the top of the siege-castle.
Even on the point of death the enemy were not lacking in courage,
[285] until the hour came at which the blessed cross received
Christ, diminishing the light of day and the strength of the citizens.[10]
At this hour a certain man, Lethold by name,[11] charged bravely

was brought up to the walls of Jerusalem. The final assault on the city took place a full
week later, on 15 July. See *Gesta Francorum*, p. 90 and n., p. 93.

[5] Cf. Gilo, ix. 119. 'That day' was Friday.

[6] Count Eustace of Boulogne. See above, i. 182 n.

[7] See Robert of Rheims, pp. 366–7: 'et duros ictus iaculorum et lapidum suscipie-
bant, et quadruplici fenore recompensabant.'

[8] For the imagery of the two Jerusalems, the spiritual and the physical, see Augus-
tine, *De ciuitate Dei*, xvii. 13. See also Siberry, *Criticism of Crusading*, pp. 37–8.

[9] The siege-towers were covered with ox- and camel-hides, as a protection against
Greek fire, as well as with wickerwork.

[10] Again a reference to Friday, the day of Christ's crucifixion. The *Gesta Francorum*,
p. 90, also states that the crusaders entered the Holy City at the hour of Christ's suffer-
ing upon the cross; Raymond of Aguilers, p. 149, simply says it was at midday.

[11] Lethold of Tournai. See Orderic Vitalis, v. 158 n. 3; *Gesta Francorum*, p. 91; Peter
Tudebode, p. 140; Albert of Aachen, pp. 472, 477; Riley-Smith, 'The motives', p. 725.
Lethold's brother Engilbert also took part in the crusade.

Illum qui nimia secuit uirtute leonem
Guicherius[a][1] sequitur. Iam dux super alta choruscat   290
Menia, iam gladius[b] late[c] per iniqua[d] uagatur
Pectora, fulmineis[e] iam murus ab ensibus ardet.

Nescius[f] istorum Raimundus mobile castrum
Conducebat adhuc,[2] sed uoces auribus hausit[3]
Insolitas, turremque Dauid[4] celer ipse petiuit;   295
Nec mora, Turcorum princeps,[g] custodia turris
Cui commissa fuit, demissa uoce, roganti
Vultu, submissis oculis, a consule uitam
Postulat. Auferret[h] quis inertis[i] premia uicto?
Ecce pauens Turcus aperit sine munere[j] portam   300
Hostibus, a nostris totiens maioribus emptam.[5]
Turbidus[k] optatam prorumpit uictor in urbem,
Precipitesque uiros grauiter suus impetus urget.
Occurrit suprema dies gentilibus, illi
De bello fugiunt in bellum, lapsus[l] ubique[m] est,[n]   305
A nullo ferrum reuocatur, Turcus Arabsque
Iudeique cadunt, horum de funere pugna est.[o]
Sanguinea iuuat ire manu, gladiosque nitentes[p]
Ferre pudet qui non desudent[q] sanguinis haustum.
Inconsulta ruit gens[r] ad templum Salomonis[6]   310
Quam mortis timor exagitat, uelut esset ab illo
Vnica danda salus, talique tegantur[s] asilo.[t]
Implerant[u] plerique domum quam diximus: illis
Victorum manus incumbens[v] per lubrica strage
Marmora se rapuit.[w] Numerum quis scire cadentum   315
Milia uel ualeat, passim cum frusta[x] per omnes
Sint dispersa gradus? Longe ceruice[y] reuulsum[z]
Rore caput rubeo[aa] commixta strage natabat,

---

[a] Wicherius *BC*   [b] gladiis *D*   [c] late *om. D*   [d] unquam *D*
[e] fulmineiis *F*   [f] nesscius *D*   [g] priceps *D*   [h] aufferret *B;* afferret *D*
[i] inerti *AD*   [j] murmure *AD*   [k] turbibus *D*   [l] laupsus *F*   [m] ubi
F   [n] est *om. AD*   [o] est *om. A*   [p] gladiumque nitentem *AD;* gladi-
osque nitente *F*   [q] desudet *AD*   [r] fuit gens *D;* gens fuit *F*   [s] tegun-
tur *BC*   [t] absilo *D m. pr.*   [u] impleuerant *D*   [v] incohens *A*
[w] repuit *F m. pr.*   [x] frustra *AD*   [y] ceruicem *A*   [z] reuulsa *AD*
[aa] niueo *AD*

---

[1] Wicherus was a prominent member of Godfrey's contingent. See Albert of Aachen,
pp. 507, 522, 526, 531, 533; Baldric of Dol, pp. 47, 50; Robert of Rheims, pp. 867–8.

from the siege-castle and was first to leap on to the city wall; [290]
Wicherus[1] followed that lion, carving its way with great courage.
Soon that leader blazed forth on top of the ramparts, and soon his
sword slashed far and wide through wicked breasts, and soon the
walls were ablaze with flashing blades.

Unaware of all this, Raymond was still moving his mobile castle
on,[2] but he caught snatches of unusual cries as he listened,[3] [295]
and himself made swiftly for the tower of David;[4] without hesitat-
ing, the prince of the Turks to whom guarding the tower had been
entrusted begged his life from the count, his voice lowered, his face
pleading, his eyes cast down; and what man would be so idle as to
despoil a vanquished foe? [300] The terrified Turk actually opened
the gates to his enemies without a payment, a passage so often
bought by our ancestors.[5] In a frenzy they burst victorious into the
city they had longed for, and their own momentum forced them
headlong in a powerful charge. The last day had come for the
heathen, [305] and they ran from the fighting into more fighting,
men fell everywhere, the sword was held back from no man. Turk,
Arab, and Jew were slain, and there was a fight about their destruc-
tion. Our men were pleased to go about with bloody hands, and
ashamed to carry weapons that gleamed and were not dripping
with draughts of blood. [310] The people, panicked by the fear of
death, rushed on in utter disarray to Solomon's temple,[6] as though
it provided their only escape, as if they could take refuge in this
shelter. A good number of them had filled the building which I
mentioned; the band of conquerors fell on them, rushing on over
the marble, slippery with slaughter. [315] Who could know the
number of the thousands who fell, when their remains were scat-
tered everywhere you trod? Far and wide, severed heads bedewed
with blood floated about in the welter of carnage. You could see

[2] Godfrey's siege-tower was placed against the northern wall, whereas Raymond's
attacked from the south, and he and his troops were not immediately aware of Godfrey's
progress. See *Gesta Francorum*, pp. 90–1.
[3] Cf. Vergil, *Aen.* iv. 359.
[4] The citadel, situated on the western wall and commanded by the Fatimid governor
of the city, 'Iftikhār ad-Daulah. See Runciman, *Hist. Crus.* i. 279–81.
[5] Presumably the Jaffa gate, one of the main entrances to the city and where the pil-
grims paid their taxes. See *Gesta Francorum*, p. 91.
[6] The Dome of the Rock, the reputed site of Solomon's temple.

Abscisas aliena manus ad corpora iungi
Aspiceres, truncos[a] gemino[b] sine poplite ferri,　　　320
Cunctaque[c] membra loco uel cesa carere[d] priore,
Saucia uel remanere[e] suo.[1] Tantusque cauernis
Sanguis iit plenis[f] ut flumen adire putares.
In plano[g] uelut a summis cum montibus ingens
Grando cadit mixtisque simul tonat imbribus ether,　　　325
Tunc collecta petunt demissas[h] flumina ualles,[i]
Saxa trahunt siluasque ferunt totaque uagantur[j]
Agri planitie, gemitus dat rusticus imo[k]
Pectore, non aliter cesorum membra feruntur
Sanguine rapta suo, totidemque necantur[l] in urbe.[2]　　　330
Sed tamen illorum pauci fastigia templi
Ascensu superant, et eis sua signa dederunt
Tancretius Gastonque,[m][3] piis affectibus acti.
Hinc ad opes properant effrenes, tecta subintrant.
Vestes, diuitias, et quod satis esset auaro　　　335
Inueniunt,[n] si diuitiis satietur auarus.
Non perdit quod quisque rapit, nec uendicat[o] alter,
Quamuis nobilior, quod computat in sua pauper.

His ita completis,[p] mundata taliter urbe,
Ad sua felices uenerunt gaudia turbe,　　　340
Prostratique duces, aspersi[q] fletibus ora,
Pro Domino Domini uenerantur rite sepulchrum,
Hicque suum capitale Deo dat quisque fidelis.[4]
Mane dato non plenus adhuc tot cladibus ultor
Miles id exiguum quod adhuc superesse[r] sciebat　　　345
Sanguinis in paucis furatur, et ardua templi
Ascendens tacite subito turbauit inertes:

---

[a] trun *F*　　　[b] geminos *BC;* etiam *D*　　　[c] eunctaque *F*　　　[d] celsa carcere
D　　　[e] remanente *D*　　　[f] plenis iit *A*　　　[g] planum *AD*　　　[h] immensas
BC　　　[i] uallos *D*　　　[j] uagatur *AD*　　　[k] uno *A*　　　[l] uocantur *A*
[m] Guastonque *AD*　　　[n] priueniunt *F*　　　[o] uindicat *A;* uindica *F*
[p] transactis *F*　　　[q] aspersa *D*　　　[r] superesset *F*

---

[1] See also Robert of Rheims, pp. 867-8.
[2] Raymond of Aguilers, pp. 150-1, *Gesta Francorum*, pp. 91-2, and Fulcher of
Chartres, p. 301, give a graphic account of the slaughter following the capture of
Jerusalem.

cut-off hands joined to bodies to which they did not belong,
[320] torsos borne along without either leg, every part of the body
either cut off and far removed from its former location, or just
wounded and left where it belonged.[1] So much blood flowed into
the cellars, filling them, that you would have thought a river had
come there. Just as when a massive hailstorm falls from the
mountain-tops on to the plain, [325] and the sky thunders, mingled
with rain-showers, then rivers gather and head down to the low-
lying valleys, dragging rocks along and sweeping forests away, and
then flow all over the fields in the plain, and the peasant groans
from the bottom of his heart, in just the same way the limbs of the
slain were borne away, [330] carried off in their own blood, and as
many again were cut down in the city.[2] However, a few of them
managed to scale the temple roof, and Tancred and Gaston[3] gave
them their banners, prompted by feelings of mercy. From here
they rushed madly to plunder their wealth, and entered their
houses. [335] They found clothes and riches, enough to satisfy the
greedy if the greedy could be satisfied with riches. No man lost
what he snatched up, nor did another man, though he was more
noble, claim for himself what the poor man reckoned as his own.

When the city had been purified in this manner by the completion
of these actions, [340] the blessed bands came to the wellspring of
their joy, and the dukes, bending low and with cheeks wet from
weeping, gave fitting worship to the sepulchre of the Lord, for the
Lord's sake, and here each of the faithful gave his own due to God.[4]
When morning came, [345] the knights' vengeance was still not
sated by the downfall of so many, and in slaughtering a few they stole
what little amount of blood they knew still remained to be shed;
silently climbing the heights of the temple, they suddenly overthrew

---

[3] Gaston IV, viscount of Béarn, who was accompanied on the expedition by his son
Centule. See J. H. and L. L. Hill, *Raymond IV de Saint-Gilles, 1041 (ou 1042)–1105*
(Toulouse, 1959), pp. 29–30. Gaston and Tancred gave their banners as a guarantee of
protection to the Muslims sheltering on the roof of the temple in Jerusalem. Gaston
subsequently fought at Ascalon and after his return to the west he took part in expedi-
tions against the Muslims of Spain. See Orderic Vitalis, v. 30 n. 7, 178; vi. 400; *Gesta
Francorum*, pp. 92, 95; Raymond of Aguilers, p. 145.

[4] Raymond of Aguilers, p. 151; Fulcher of Chartres, p. 310. For Godfrey's pilgrimage
to the Holy Sepulchre, see above, viii. 305 n.

Illi precipites sese iaculantur ab alto,
Et que dat uitam reliquis animantibus, illos
Terra repercutiens morientes mittit ad umbras.   350
Occurrunt alii gladiis animoque uirili:
Supposita ceruice moras in morte queruntur.
Hi sese cedunt,[a] mortesque[b] suas inimicis
Eripuere suis, isti pugnando secantur.
Naufragium dum quisque facit sibi, quisque necatur,   355
Corpora cesorum caudis[c] religantur equorum,
Atque foras iuxta muros glomerantur inusta.
Plura quidem diuisa locis in frusta[d] iacebant
Perdiderantque notas humani corporis: illa
Gentiles nondum dampnati flendo legebant[e]   360
Et congesta simul ducebant montis ad instar.[f]

Queritur interea cui regni cura regendi
Conueniat, quis digne[g] sciat dare premia Christi
Militibus qui[h] marte sciunt superare tyrannos,
Melchisedech[i] exempla sequens, qui iusta[j] fideli   365
Victorique seni data porrexisse refertur.[1]
Diuino tandem nutu[k] procerumque salubri
Consilio regnum[l] sortitur dux Godefridus,[2]
Octaua qui regna die suscepit ab urbe
Capta,[3] uir regno dignus, cum rege beato[m]   370
        Vivat in octaua.[4]

Anno milleno de centeno minus uno
Iherusalem capitur Iulii, cum dicitur, Idus.[5]

---

[a] cadunt A m. pr.   [b] mortesque A m. pr., corr. to morteque m. alt.
[c] claudis D m. pr.   [d] frustra ADF   [e] legabant D m. pr.   [f] istar B; ista
A   [g] digna AD   [h] qui om. D   [i] Melchisedec DF   [j] iuxta D
[k] nutu tandem D m. pr.   [l] regimen AD   [m] beata B m. pr.

---

[1] Cf. Gen. 14: 18; Ps. 109 (110): 4; Heb. 7: 1–22. For senis referring to Abraham, cf.
Prudentius, Psychomachia, Praef. 1–2.
[2] Peter Tudebode, p. 142; Gesta Francorum, p. 92; Raymond of Aguilers, p. 143. On the
subject of Godfrey's title, see Riley-Smith, 'The title of Godfrey of Bouillon', BIHR lii
(1979), 83–6.

the people trapped there: these threw themselves down headlong from the top, and the earth, which gives life to the rest of living creatures, [350] struck them hard and sent them dying down to the shadows. With manly courage, others ran on to their comrades' swords, and with necks bowed they complained of death's delaying. Others slew themselves and snatched their deaths from their enemies, and yet others were cut down as they resisted. [355] While each of them brought about his own destruction and each was killed, the bodies of the slain were tied to horses' tails and were piled up outside, beside the walls, but not burnt. Many bodies were cut up, the pieces lying in different places, and they ceased to be recognizable as human bodies: [360] the heathen who had not yet been destroyed wept as they picked them up and collected them together, heaping them up like a mountain.

In the meantime, the question arose as to who should be responsible for ruling the kingdom, what man knew how to give proper rewards to the knights of God who knew how to overthrow tyrants in war, [365] following the example of Melchizedek, who is said to have offered fitting gifts to the faithful and victorious patriarch.[1] At last, through the prompting of God and the healthy counsel of the nobles, Duke Godfrey obtained the kingdom.[2] A man worthy of the kingdom, [370] he began to rule on the eighth day after the city was taken:[3] may he live in the eighth age with our blessed king.[4]

In the year one thousand and ninety-nine, Jerusalem was captured, as is said, on the fifteenth day of July.[5]

---

[3] The crusaders met to elect a ruler on 17 July. Like Gilo, however, the *Gesta Francorum* mentions the eighth day after the city was captured, which would be 22 July. There was, of course, not yet a *kingdom*: cf. the use of the term regimen in *AD*.

[4] This quasi-Vergilian half-line, with which Gilo's epic closes, is not only unique in this poem, but is (so far as we have been able to ascertain) unparalleled in 12th-c. Latin verse. The eighth age here refers to the concept of the Seven Ages of Man; see Ovid, *Met.* xiv. 144–5.

[5] Gilo's poem ends with the triumphant conquest for the Christians of Jerusalem, but it is significant that other sources, such as the *Gesta Francorum* and Robert of Rheims, continue the 'action' and conclude with the crusaders' victory over the Fatimids at the battle of Ascalon. See above, Introduction, pp. xiii–xiv, lvii–lviii, lxiii.

Hec ego composui,[1] Gilo nomine, Parisiensis
Incola, Tutiaci non inficiandus[a] alumnus.[b2]   375

[a] inficiendus *B m. pr.*   [b] *After this line A reads* finis historie Iherosolimitane; *D
reads* explicit liber de Hierusalem; *F reads* explicit historia Iherosololomitana (*sic*); *BC
read* explicit libellus Gilonis Parisiensis clerici postea Cluniacensis monachi (*B omits
monachi*) inde cardinalis episcopi de uia Iherosolimitana, quando expulsis et occisis
paganis deuicte sunt Nicea, Antiochia et Iherusalem a Christianis. *AD only have a verse
epilogue as follows:*

horum scriptorem laurum meruisse Gilonem | et cedro uiua (it cedro uina *A*) censemus
carmine digna | que nobis clare referunt et sub breuitate | tam uarios casus, tot prelia
totque tumultus | ictus tam ualidos, tot cedes, totque triumphos. | dum Gilo tanta refert,
dum tantis laudibus effert | Christicolas proceres, heroas (heroes *D*) ad omnia fortes |
laus antiquorum iam laudi (lauda *D m. pr.*) cedat eorum, | Argus (Arpus *AD*) Titides et
Larisseus Achilles | Aiax et Thiseus, Polinices et Capaneus (Canapeus *AD*) | Hugoni
(Hugonio *D*) Magno cedant et utrique Roberto (Ruberto *D*) | inuictoque duci Gode-
frido uel Raimundi (Raimundo *D*) | uiribus inuictis; potior Boimundus Atridis.

---

[1] Cf. Ovid, *Amores*, iii. 15. 3.
[2] See above, Introduction, pp. xviii–xix. The verses following ix. 375 onwards are dis-

I Gilo,[1] a resident of Paris and a native of Toucy (which by no means disowns me) composed this poem.[2]

cussed in the Introd. Sect. VII, and are found only in *AD*. They are clearly not the work of Gilo, as is apparent from their reference to him in the third person, and equally are not by the Charleville Poet (whose witness ceases in *G*, the *codex unicus* for this author, at vii. 471). They are included as an independent colophon to the poem, providing a balance to the Prologue found in *BCF* but lacking in the *AD* side of the transmission. The reference to cedar-oil is because of its use as a preservative on book-bindings to prevent decay, and hence it is used as a laudatory term. Cf. Horace, *Ars poetica*, 332, and Persius, *Sat.* i. 42. The Latin text, which is placed in the apparatus, may be translated as follows:

We hold that Gilo, the writer of these verses, is worthy of the prize, and that his poetry is deserving of flowing cedar-oil; it gives us a lucid account in a short space of the various adventures, the many battles and struggles, the mighty blows, the massive slaughter, and the many victories. While Gilo tells of such great events, and with such praises extols the Christian nobles, heroes brave in every situation, let the praise of the ancients now yield to their praise; Argive Diomedes and Larissaean Achilles, Ajax and Theseus, Polynices and Capaneus should yield before Hugh the Great and both the Roberts, before the unconquered Duke Godfrey and the invincible prowess of Raymond; Bohemond is greater than the sons of Atreus.

APPENDIX

References to Non-Gilo Manuscripts

In addition to the seven manuscripts listed in the Introduction, Section VI, a number of other references will be found in Max Manitius' monumental study *Geschichte der lateinischen Literatur des Mittelalters* (3 vols., Munich, 1911–31), iii. 667–70. These are as follows:

s. XII   zu St. Amand (Delisle, le cabinet des mss. 2, 458, 315; ist heute Paris 5129

s. XII   Bruxell. 629

s. XII   Bruxell. 10615

s. XII   Duacensis 838

s. XII   Paris 5129

s. XIII   Paris St. Germ. 460

          Résidu St. Germ. 97.4.12

          Valentian. 219

Of these entries, the first and fifth are obvious duplicates, but taken with the seven manuscripts mentioned by Riant, they appear to give a total of thirteen: four from Paris (5129, 12945, Saint-Germain 460, and Résidu Saint-Germain 97.4.12); four from Brussels (629, 7575, 10615, 10707); two from Douai (838, 882); and one each from the Vallicelliana in Rome, from Charleville, and from Valenciennes (if this is meant by Manitius' 'Valentian').

This list contains several doublets. Manitius' Douai 838 is now no. 882; 838 is its old number. The present Douai 838 is a thirteenth-century manuscript containing Saints' Lives. Similarly, Brussels 10707 is part of the same manuscript as 10615, whose full number is 10615–10729; 10707 is the part that contains Gilo's work. Although these all appear to be old numbers, none of them is listed in the *Tables de Concordance* in the catalogue of the Bibliothèque Royale de Bruxelles. Riant's '7575' is an abbreviated reference for 7575–7585, the part containing Gilo's poem being numbered 7576; it is now numbered 7442. The present 7576 contains the epitaphs of three nobles from Flanders. Brussels 629 is a gradual; the former 629 is now a part of 1125, which contains works by St Augustine. Moreover, 629 is the number which the present 10615–10729 bore early in the nineteenth century, before the present inventory was inaugurated.

Of the four Paris manuscripts, 5129 and 12945 do contain Gilo's poem; however, the other two listed by Manitius do not. According to

H. Omont, *Concordance des nos. anciens et des nos. actuels des MSS latins de la Bibliothèque Nationale* (Paris, 1903), ad loc., Saint-Germain 460 became St Petersburg F. 1. 11. This contains the *Tripartite History* of Cassiodorus and a life of St Lupus. It was formerly Corbie nos. 292 and 177. To find a connection with Gilo, we have to go back to an earlier Saint-Germain 460, also listed in a 1677 catalogue of the library of Saint-Germain under the number 796. The concordances of MSS from Saint-Germain (Paris, BN nouv. aqu. franç. 5799) give the later number of this as 505, and then 460. MS 505 of Saint-Germain became the present Bibliothèque Nationale ms. lat. 12607, which on fos. 197^v–224^r contains Gilo's *Vita Hugonis abbatis Cluniacensis*.

Again using Omont's *Concordance*, we can see that Résidu Saint-Germain 97.4.12 became Paris BN Lat. 13090. Like 12607, this also contains Gilo's *Vita Hugonis*. A second manuscript which bore the same number became MS Lat. 11944, and contains the book of Deuteronomy, with glosses, and a treatise on the Mass.

By 'Valentian 219', Manitius appears to have meant the Bibliothèque Municipale of Valenciennes; this does not, however, contain Gilo's poem. The old 219, now 228, is a collection of theological treatises and sermons; the present 219 (former 210) was formerly Saint-Amand, *Index Major* xxv, former S. 190, Sanderus 184, and is a thirteenth-century collection of sermons.

The final two manuscripts in the list, Biblioteca Vallicelliana B. 33 and Charleville 97, do contain the text of Gilo's poem. The latter is also the sole repository of the additions to Gilo's work written by the Charleville Poet.

In sum then, seven manuscripts alone contain Gilo's poem, and these are the seven listed by Riant. Manitius may well have been confused by manuscripts containing Gilo's other work, the *Vita Hugonis abbatis Cluniacensis*, though why he used such archaic references for the manuscripts listed is puzzling.

INDEX OF CITATIONS AND ALLUSIONS

Note: Roman and italic type is used in the indexes in the same way as in the text and translation, to distinguish between the text of Gilo himself (Roman type) and that of the Charleville Poet (printed in italic).

A. BIBLICAL ALLUSIONS

B. SOURCES AND PARALLELS IN CLASSICAL, PATRISTIC, AND MEDIEVAL TEXTS

GENERAL INDEX

Note: for the principal protagonists in the First Crusade, only the first reference and subsequent significant references are given.